*The Lives
of the Novel*

The Lives
of the Novel

A HISTORY

Thomas G. Pavel

Princeton University Press

Princeton and Oxford

First published in France as *La pensée du roman*
© Editions GALLIMARD, Paris, 2003
Translation copyright © 2013 by Thomas G. Pavel
Requests for permission to reproduce material from this work should be sent to Permissions,
    Princeton University Press
Published by Princeton University Press, 41 William Street, Princeton, New Jersey 08540
In the United Kingdom: Princeton University Press,
    6 Oxford Street, Woodstock, Oxfordshire OX20 1TW

press.princeton.edu

Library of Congress Cataloging-in-Publication Data

Pavel, Thomas G., 1941- author.
 [Pensée du Roman. English]
 The Lives of the Novel : A History / Thomas G. Pavel.
    pages cm
 Includes bibliographical references and index.
 ISBN 978-0-691-12189-5 (hardcover : acid-free paper) 1. Fiction—History and criticism. I. Title.
 PN3365.P2813 2013
 809.3—dc23
                          2012043265

British Library Cataloging-in-Publication Data is available

This book has been composed in Sabon

Printed on acid-free paper. ∞

Printed in the United States of America

10 9 8 7 6 5 4 3 2 1

To the memory of Joseph Frank

Art is not the study of
objective reality; it is a search
for the ideal truth.

—GEORGE SAND

Contents

IIIIIIIIIIIIIIIIIIIIIIIIIIIIIIIIIIIIIIIIIIIIIIIIIIIIIIII

Preface

More than twenty years ago, when I arrived at Princeton University's Department of Comparative Literature, the chair asked me to teach a two-semester graduate seminar on the history of the novel. A course on fictional worlds or on drama, I suggested, would make more sense in light of my background, but after giving my answer some thought, the chair was having none of it. So I set about drafting a syllabus. I was familiar with a number of important novels as a lover of literature rather than a specialist, and for prudence's sake, I adopted the usual approach, which took Cervantes's *Don Quixote*, a hilarious parody of chivalric romances, to be the first modern novel. Thinking, however, that the course should have a wider historical scope, I decided to squeeze in a story about knights-errant. Like everyone else, I knew that *Don Quixote*'s irony had sounded the death knell of such stories, but, curious to see for myself, I decided to read Cervantes's main target, *Amadis de Gaula*. *Amadis* idealizes human courage and loyalty in a quite implausible way, and yet, I confess, I found myself loving it. Encouraged, I thought I'd have a look at another species of half-forgotten narratives: the ancient Greek stories Cervantes admired and emulated.

This is how I got acquainted with Heliodorus's *Ethiopian Story*, an incredibly beautiful tale about a resilient, faithful couple ready to face the most difficult ordeals. It became clear to me not only why Cervantes appreciated the book, why the great seventeenth-century French playwright Jean Racine knew it by heart, why so many writers including Sir Philip Sidney and Aphra Behn imitated it, but also why ignoring this old novel made it impossible for us to fully understand the genre's history. To my great pleasure, several other scholars at that time were making the same discovery.

Prompted by the growing consensus, I realized that for a long time the genre had depicted either unbelievably perfect characters or surprisingly despicable ones. I also noticed that from the eighteenth century onward, the novels we call modern only partly avoided the penchant for idealiza-tion—in fact, they sought out new kinds of ideal, incredible behavior. At the same time, writers continued to find original ways of representing ridiculous or objectionable actions. The novel, it seemed to me, evolved out of a tension between the tendency to idealize human behavior and the desire to censure it. Realizing that this tension had not yet been fully investigated, I began writing this book.

After an introduction about existing histories of the novel, I devote the first section to the kinds of prose narrative that were available before the eighteenth century: the ancient Greek and the chivalric novels, both concerned with exemplary behavior, and the comic tale, the picaresque story, and the novella, which looked at human beings with disapprov-ing eyes. The idealist narratives portrayed strong souls who follow the highest moral norms without hesitation, while the anti-idealist varieties focused on equally unwavering villains, tricksters, and pícaros. A middle way—partly idealist, partly critical—can be found in the elegiac story, the pastoral, and some of the more edifying picaresque stories.

A chapter on Cervantes and his peculiar place in this history leads on to the second part, about the eighteenth century, which saw an important attempt to create a more unified form of prose narrative. Trying to por-tray plausible ideal characters, eighteenth-century writers placed them in familiar surroundings (the English countryside, for instance), paid par-ticular attention to their inner struggles, and showed their discovery of the moral law within their own sensitive hearts. Yet anti-idealism contin-ued to prosper in comic stories, the elegiac mode had its descendants in first-person narratives of unrequited love, and an attempt to return to the older form of idealism generated the gothic novel.

The third part concerns the nineteenth century. Continuing to look for believable ideal characters, writers now rooted human behavior in its historical and social context. They placed their protagonists in older, rougher periods, in faraway countries, or imagined them as exceptional contemporary beings rising above their social milieu. During this period, anti-idealism also flourished, in a variety of forms that emphasized irony, empathy, or contempt for human imperfection. At the end of the nine-teenth and in the early twentieth century, however, under the influence of aestheticism and the worship of art, novelists turned their attention to the mysteries of the psyche and took a new, rather pessimistic view of human solitude. But though many forms of modernism examined in the fourth and last part of the book relied on this view, other ways of representing human action survived or sprang up within the extraordinarily rich and diverse literature of the last century.

Rather than attempting an exhaustive catalog of authors and titles, I have emphasized the broad outlines of the history of the novel. At each stage, I discuss one or several influential novels in some detail, hoping to entice the reader to get acquainted or reacquainted with them. I have had to leave out many good writers and texts, but I hope attentive readers will easily find a place for their favorite authors in the history set out here.

My deep gratitude goes to Princeton University and the University of Chicago for the opportunity to teach this subject, as well as for the sabbatical leaves that allowed me to rewrite this book several times. Part of an unforgettable year spent at the Wissenschaftskolleg in Berlin (2010–2011) was devoted to the present version. A graduate seminar I taught at the Université de Paris-IV (Sorbonne) and lectures I gave in the United States, Québec, France, Italy, and Germany led to many exciting discussions that persuaded me to reformulate, develop, or abandon some of my ideas.

The colleagues and friends whose support and criticisms made this book possible are so numerous that I can only mention their names, but I want each of them to know how grateful I am for their attentive ear and wise suggestions.

This book would not have existed without the generosity of Marguerite and Joseph Frank. I am particularly indebted to A. S. Byatt, Joshua Landy, Franco Moretti, and David Quint for their generous advice and support. I found an enduring source of encouragement and inspiration in conversations with my literary colleagues. At Princeton these included Maria DiBattista, Caryl Emerson, the late Robert Fagles, Alban Forcione, Lionel Gossman, Robert Hollander, and François Rigolot; and, at the University of Chicago, Elizabeth Asmis, Bill Brown, James Chandler, Fred de Armas, Daisy Delogu, Philippe Desan, Daniel Desormeaux, Françoise Meltzer, Glenn Most, Michael Murrin, Larry Norman, Patrick O'Connor, Mark Payne, Lawrence Rothfield, Lisa Ruddick, Mario Santana, Eric Santner, Elissa Weaver, and David Wellbery. I learned a considerable amount from my philosopher friends: Vincent Descombes, Hans Joas, Leon Kass, Charles Larmore, Jonathan Lear, Alexander Nehamas, Terry Pinkard, Robert Pippin, and, last but not least, Gideon Rosen. My colleagues and friends at other universities—Jean-Marie Apostolidès, Srinivas Aravamudan, Ora Avni, Michel Beaujour, the late Matei Calinescu and Dorrit Cohn, Pierre Force, Claudio Guillen, Hans Ulrich Gumbrecht, Philip Lewis, Mark Lilla, Jean-Philippe Mathy, Claire Messud, Gary Saul Morson, Virgil Nemoianu, Gerald Prince, Philip Stewart, and James Wood—were wonderfully helpful and supportive.

In Québec and the rest of Canada, my generous interlocutors were Mathieu Belisle, Isabelle Daunais, Lubomír Doležel, Wladimir Krysinski, Gilles Marcotte, Éric Méchoulan, Michel Pierssens, and François Ricard. In France, Claude Bremond, Marc Fumaroli, and Marcel Gauchet offered invaluable advice; I also owe a great deal to Wladimir Bérélovitch,

Alain Besançon, Régine Borderie, Pierre Brunel, Emmanuel Bury, Antoine Compagnon, Jean Dagen, Gilles Declercq, Guyomar Hautcoeur, Yves Hersant, Claude Jamain, Françoise Lavocat, Georges Liébert, Marielle Macé, Pierre Manent, Michel Murat, Jacques Neefs, Roger Pouivet, Lakis Prodiguis, the late Rainer Rochlitz, Philippe Roger, Tiphaine Samoyault, Jean-Marie Schaeffer, Philippe Sellier, Didier Souiller, Jean-Yves Tadié, Sylvie Thorel-Cailleteau, Michel Zink, and Roger Zuber. Many thanks are due to my other friends and colleagues: Paolo Amalfitano, Jørn Boisen, Lina Bolzoni, Silvia Carandini, Marina Colonna, Bohumil Fořt, Udo Friedrich, Luca Giuliani, Loretta Innocenti, Julio Hans C. Jensen, Frank Kelleter, Gabriel Liiceanu, Mariella di Maio, Mihaela Mancaş, Guido Mazzoni, Volker Mertens, Reinhart Meyer-Kalkus, Nuccio Ordine, Barbara Piatti, Luca Pietromarchi, Andrei Pleşu, Frank Rexroth, Massimo Rizzante, Cesare Segre, Meir Sternberg, Karin Westerwelle, and Mihai Zamfir. At Chicago, Julia Chamard-Bergeron kindly helped me identify many relevant critical works. I am most grateful to Lidija Haas for her careful revisions, corrections, and stylistic upgrading of the manuscript.

Without the confidence and encouragement of Eric Vigne, my French editor, I doubt that the French version of this book would ever have been finished. The patience and support of Hanne Winarsky and Alison Mac-Keen at Princeton University Press played the same role for the English version. Lauren Lepow was a wonderful copyeditor.

The Lives of the Novel

Introduction

||||||||||||||||||||||||||||||||||||||||||||||||||||||||||||||||||||

The evolution of the novel is an astonishing success story. From its humble beginnings onward, it has shown an unparalleled ability to adapt, innovate, spread, and prevail. At almost every turn, it has found the most intelligent, effective ways to reassert its place in the broader culture.

Its birth and rise, however, are still subject to debate. There is a widespread view that the novel emerged relatively late in history, as a literary expression of modernity. Just as the Enlightenment swept away obsolete dogmas, the novel replaced archaic narrative modes. Whereas the older kinds of narratives—sometimes called romances—looked at life through distorting lenses and portrayed idealized, implausible characters, the novel, we are told, turned its attention to the ordinary lives of real people in the real world. Some even claim that this important change was triggered by a single author who, in a flash of genius, brought the first true (that is, modern) novel into being. As Copernicus revolutionized cosmology, so Miguel de Cervantes, Mme de Lafayette, Daniel Defoe, or Samuel Richardson—depending on who is making the claim—single-handedly began a new era in the history of narrative prose.

This would make the novel a modern genre: polemical, rebellious, realistic, and born from a single great pen. And to some extent, it is. Samuel Richardson's influential *Pamela* (1740) and *Clarissa* (1748) certainly challenged earlier narrative methods, offering moment-by-moment portrayals of lived experience. It is also true that some novelists—François Rabelais and Laurence Sterne, for instance—adopted a rebellious stance; that novels often aimed to describe social life realistically; and that, like any human endeavor, the genre's development frequently depended on exceptional individual talent.

Early Choices . . .

Yet in the last twenty years, the idea that the novel is a typically modern genre has been disputed. Margaret Doody's *The True Story of the Novel*

(1996) and Didier Souiller and Wladimir Troubetzkoy's chapter on the novel in their *Littérature comparée* (1997) showed that long prose narratives, far from being a recent European invention, have much deeper roots. Franco Moretti's comprehensive collection *Il Romanzo* (2001) and its partial English translation *The Novel* (2006–2007) demonstrated that the rise of the novel from the Renaissance to the nineteenth century was not so much the invention of a genre as a European acceleration of its growth, which then prompted a global expansion. Indeed, if we take early Japanese and Chinese fiction into consideration—*The Tale of Genji* by Murasaki Shikibu (eleventh century), *Water Margin* (fourteenth century), *Romance of the Three Kingdoms* by Luo Guanzhong (fourteenth century), *Journey to the West* by Wu Cheng'en (sixteenth century), and *The Story of the Stone* by Cao Xueqin (eighteenth century)—it becomes clear that the genre's roots are not confined to a single geographic space. Steven Moore's *The Novel: An Alternative History. Beginnings to 1600* examines the worldwide wealth of narratives that, from ancient Egypt to ancient China and Japan, made the rise of the novel possible.

Agreeing with this approach, the present book aims to show that the "European acceleration" of the novel (to use Franco Moretti's phrase) began as a long-term rivalry between various kinds—various subgenres—of prose narrative. Just as in present-day bookstores customers walk between shelves marked "literature," "Westerns," "mystery novels," or "science fiction," sixteenth- and seventeenth-century readers were used to distinguishing between ancient Greek novels, late medieval chivalric stories, pastorals, picaresque stories, and novellas. Each kind of story portrayed a different aspect of the human condition—heroically chaste love in the ancient Greek novel, individual valor in chivalric tales, gentle sentiments in the pastoral, deceit in the picaresque, and sudden, surprising action in novellas. Each type handled form and content in its own way. Most importantly, these subgenres formed two large groups, one of which promoted a celebratory, idealist view of human life and behavior, while the other developed a derogatory, anti-idealist attitude. Idealist narratives, such as the ancient Greek and chivalric novels, featured uplifting characters and deeds, while the anti-idealist ones, like picaresque stories and many novellas, deplored or satirized unusually bad people and actions.

In the eyes of the late sixteenth-century public, the most successful celebratory, idealist novels had been written long before, between the first and the fourth centuries, by Greek colonists established on the eastern shores of the Mediterranean. In the *Ethiopian Story* by Heliodorus, rediscovered at the end of the fifteenth century and translated into French, Italian, Spanish, English, and German, the two young protagonists, Chariclea and Theagenes, fall in love at Apollo's shrine at Delphi. After taking a pledge of chastity, they flee Greece and go through a multitude of ordeals, including shipwrecks, kidnapping by bandits, separation, and the lustful advances of unscrupulous rulers. Eventually, they reach the sacred realm of Ethiopia, where Chariclea turns out to be none other than the long-lost daughter of the Ethiopian king.

Ancient Greek novels, little read or discussed in late antiquity, were remembered and imitated in the Byzantine Empire, but not in medieval western Europe, where the public favored a different kind of idealist narrative, the chivalric stories in which brave knights and proud ladies struggle to keep their love alive in adversity. Unlike the perfect protagonists of ancient Greek novels, medieval characters can be absentminded or have trouble mastering their urges. They might forget their pledges, and their love—Tristan and Isolde's, for example, or Lancelot and Guinevere's—is sometimes adulterous. Still, provided the knight fights valiantly, his unreliability, carelessness, and even adultery may be forgiven in the end. Steeped in archaic, pagan beliefs (from *paganus*: "villager"), chivalric stories remain very close to old legends, sagas, and fairy tales, and, like them, are full of sorcerers, prophets, talking animals, charmed objects, and enchanted cities.

Renaissance writers, who worshipped antiquity and in principle looked down on medieval art and literature, were nonetheless partial to such flights of fancy. Fifteenth- and sixteenth-century Italian poets reworked chivalric stories into a new genre, the "fantasy epic." Luigi Pulci's *Morgante* (1483), Matteo Maria Boiardo's *Orlando Innamorato* (1495), and Ludovico Ariosto's *Orlando Furioso* (1532) are about the intricate adventures of medieval knights frolicking in a fairy-tale environment that is never supposed to seem fully real or plausible. At the same time, late chivalric narratives in prose continued to flourish as a distinct group of idealist, celebratory stories, the most successful being *Amadis of Gaul* (published in 1508, but written earlier), the tale of a perfect knight whose love, eloquence, and heroic feats stirred the imaginations of European readers until late in the eighteenth century.

In search of the best possible idealist narratives, late sixteenth-century writers felt they must choose between late chivalric stories in prose and the newly rediscovered ancient Greek novels, between *Amadis of Gaul* and the *Ethiopian Story*. Discerning people saw the latter as the true model of the genre. Cervantes, for one, agreed and emulated it in his last work, *Persiles and Sigismunda* (1617), which he considered his greatest literary achievement. He was not the only writer to take this path: imitations of the ancient Greek novel thrived in much of Europe from the end of the sixteenth through the first half of the seventeenth century, and were read fervently until the end of the eighteenth. Among them were Mary Wroth's *Urania* (1621), Gomberville's *Polexandre* (1632–1637),

Artamène ou le Grand Cyrus (1649–1653) by Madeleine de Scudéry, *Aramena* (1669–1673) by Anton Ulrich, and *Oroonoko* (1688) by Aphra Behn.

Equally important for the sixteenth-century public was another, more recent species of idealist narrative: the pastoral novels that flourished in Italy and Spain and later conquered England and France. The first Spanish pastoral, Jorge de Montemayor's *Diana* (1559), was very popular in the late sixteenth century, and was one of Shakespeare's sources. In the early 1580s, Sir Philip Sidney finished his *Old Arcadia*, though it was not published until much later. And at the beginning of the seventeenth century, Honoré d'Urfé's five-volume *Astrea* (1607–1627) became the longest, most complex specimen of the pastoral.

Ancient Greek novels, medieval chivalric stories, and pastorals all transported their readers into a realm quite different from everyday reality, and consequently required a drastic suspension of disbelief. Nicolas Boileau, a seventeenth-century French critic, marveled to see the beautiful young heroine of Madeleine de Scudéry's long-winded *Artamène* fall over and over again into the hands of evil brigands, and yet always manage to keep her chastity intact. Similar objections had been raised against *Amadis of Gaul* and the *Diana*. They didn't matter, though, since these novels were *meant* to offer a lofty, implausible view of the world.

Later writers and critics would assume that these inspiring but unbelievable narratives had been rendered obsolete in the eighteenth century by modern, realist novels. Early modern writers and readers knew better. Idealist, celebratory novels had never been the only fictional diet. The oldest satiric narratives—Petronius's *Satyricon* (first century) and the medieval *Roman de Renart* (twelfth century)—were not widely available, but there were other anti-idealist comic fictions to satisfy the public appetite for satire. Many of the Italian Renaissance novellas of Giovanni Boccaccio and Matteo Bandello were particularly sharp on human imperfection, while the then recent Spanish picaresque stories, *Lazarillo de Tormes* (1554, anonymous) and Quevedo's *El Buscón* (1626), described thieves and vagabonds devoid of any scruples or decency. Several of Cervantes's novellas and comic theatrical interludes, as well as the main character of *Don Quixote* (1605, 1615), are indebted to these "derogatory" narratives. The public also loved poignant anti-idealist stories, which presented human failings in a compassionate rather than sarcastic mode: tragic Italian novellas by Boccaccio, Bandello, and Cinzio, and Spanish novellas by Cervantes and María de Zayas all bemoaned people's inability to master their passions.

Another significant difference between early modern prose subgenres was that some portrayed the "world at large," while others aimed straight at the "heart of the matter." A good novel was not only expected to be faithful to the type it exemplified, whether celebratory (Heliodoran, chivalric, or pastoral) or derogatory (comic or picaresque), but it also had to link together a large number of episodes, all with similar causes and outcomes: thus the worldview it offered was both ample, since the characters were taken on a long ride, and somewhat monotonous, since they always encountered the same kinds of obstacles and had the same kinds of adventures. Ancient Greek novels and their imitations worked this way, as did comic and picaresque stories. Novellas, however, whether serious, tragic, or comic, cut down the number of episodes and went straight to the heart of the conflict. Since unity of action was the novella's strong point, they were often adapted by playwrights—Shakespeare used stories by Bandello and Cinzio for *Romeo and Juliet* and *Othello*.

Finally, although prose narratives were expected to show clearly whether they belonged to the idealist or the anti-idealist subgenre, a certain amount of variety was always welcome. Authors of Heliodorus-like novels never forgot to include some episodes about despicable characters, while those writing picaresque novels learned to embed loftier stories in them. As for the shorter, more focused novella, Boccaccio, Marguerite de Navarre, Bandello, and Cervantes published theirs in large collections, with comic and tragic stories side by side. In a culture that favored easily identifiable narrative species, these amalgamations provided a balance.

. . . AND WHAT HAPPENED LATER

While the early period should *not* be seen as mere preparation for a genuine rise of the novel in the eighteenth century, its achievements did play a major role in the subsequent history of the genre. Samuel Richardson, a self-taught writer, realized that the best features of the older narrative subgenres could be mixed together. The sublime heroes and multiple adventures of the ancient Greek novel, the humble social origins of picaresque characters, and the dramatic events of the novella could all be combined into a single narrative—as inspiring as an old romance, as close to everyday life as a comic story, and as striking as a novella. In Richardson's *Pamela*, the main character is a young woman whose virtue and resistance in the face of danger seem to come straight out of an ancient Greek novel. Yet she leads a modest, plausible life in provincial England. What's more, her heart-wrenching situation, as a servant pursued by an undeserving master, would fit well in a Renaissance novella. By mingling these features, Richardson could uplift his readers without carrying them off into a fully implausible realm, he could tell a story as compelling as a novella and as extended as a picaresque novel, and, most importantly for his time, he could show the moral equality of people regardless of their social position.

Richardson's new, more plausible idealism was an immediate and lasting success. His *Pamela* and *Clarissa* became required reading for novelists well into the nineteenth century. Yet his innovations did not remain unchallenged. Significantly, his best-known competitor, Henry Fielding, defended the older anti-idealist approach, particularly its comic version. *Joseph Andrews* (1742) and *Tom Jones* (1749) reject the representation of idealized behavior in favor of satire. Richardson and Fielding each thought only one kind of novel—his kind—should prevail. Under the influence of Richardson's moderate idealism and Fielding's ironic skepticism, people began to understand the novel as a long prose narrative whose well-constructed plot stays close to everyday life and whose characters have both virtues and faults.

Two generations later, Walter Scott, followed by Honoré de Balzac, assigned the novel a new task: it should represent not only moral physiognomies but also the historical and social texture of the characters' world. In the 1842 foreword to his *Human Comedy*, a vast fictional panorama of early nineteenth-century French society, Balzac asked writers to emulate natural science by studying each social species and its behavior. He expected the novel to become the most reliable instrument for understanding society and the individual's place in it. Balzac's manifesto was not just a symptom of the genre's new self-assurance; it also formulated a conqueror's project. Whereas early modern narrative subgenres had each addressed a specific facet of life, the nineteenth-century social and historical novel aspired to provide full, systematic coverage of humankind. Not unlike Napoleon Bonaparte, whose explicit aim was to conquer Europe and make Paris its capital, Balzac hoped to establish a new empire of literature, with the novel at its center.

And just as Europe did move toward unification, though much later and quite differently from the way Napoleon had planned it, so the novel gradually became the most influential literary genre, though not exactly along the lines envisaged by Balzac. With all its success, the social and historical novel had plenty of rivals and detractors. Gothic novelists, who had been around for a while, idealists such as Alessandro Manzoni and Victor Hugo, painters of intimacy such as Jane Austen and Adalbert Stifter, skeptics like Stendhal and, later, Gustave Flaubert, and satirists like William Makepeace Thackeray all challenged the imperial designs of social realism. At the same time, the great novels of George Eliot, Fyodor Dostoevsky, Leo Tolstoy, Theodor Fontane, Benito Pérez Galdós, and José Maria de Eça de Queirós imagined a variety of syntheses between the admirable and pitiful aspects of the human condition.

In an equally important development, the Romantics deemed the social novel unduly prosaic, unable to transport its readers beyond the borders of everyday reality. Some of the most important nineteenth-century philosophers, including Hegel, Schelling, and Schopenhauer, also felt that despite its success with the reading public, the novel was a pedestrian and uninspiring genre. Something was missing, something that—unlike historical and social realism—poetry, music, and some older narratives knew how to convey.

In answer to this challenge, the novel started a new adventure. At the end of the nineteenth and the beginning of the twentieth century, the growing cult of artistic beauty encouraged writers to infuse their prose with a new poetic fervor. Hoping to induce a special rapture in their readers, they switched from storytelling to exploring the innermost recesses of the human psyche. It remains an open question whether James Joyce's ever-surprising linguistic games, Thomas Mann's or Marcel Proust's masterfully convoluted sentences, and William Faulkner's lyricism really do represent the way the mind works. It is undeniable, though, that the modernist novel, with its sophisticated techniques, was able to go beyond popular success and secure the respect of cultural elites.

The Old and the New, Truth and Lies, Poetry and Prose

One reason why the novel's early development was not always properly understood is that for so long there were no written rules meant to govern prose narrative. From the Renaissance onward, epic, drama, and poetry were subject to complex sets of norms derived from Aristotle's *Poetics* and Horace's *Ars Poetica*. In the sixteenth and seventeenth centuries, Italian and French tragedy obeyed severe constraints concerning the unity of action, the setting of the play, its decorum, and its verisimilitude. A wealth of theoretical treatises debated the ways in which these rules had to be followed. By contrast, prose narratives were blissfully ignored by literary critics and theorists until well into the eighteenth century. Prefaces or afterwords, in discussing the art of the novel, never went beyond a few statements, often vague, claiming to value verisimilitude even, or especially, when there was none to be found in the novel itself.

The lack of a written statute, far from hindering the development of the genre, allowed its practitioners to focus on concrete ways to please the public. Just as English and American judges do not simply obey statutes, custom, and precedent, but must consider the peculiarities of each case when ruling, for a long time novelists took a pragmatic approach, feeling free to imitate existing forms or to innovate. Indeed, before the eighteenth century, when each narrative subgenre met a specific need for its readers, making them either dream, cry, laugh, or meditate, many writers moved freely from one kind of prose narrative to another, occasionally inventing new ways to tell their stories.

No playwright of the time would have enjoyed such freedom. Lope de Vega, Cervantes's contemporary, whose tragedies did not follow Aristotle's advice closely enough, had to justify his misdemeanors in writing. He managed to appease his Spanish critics, but, soon after, the overzealous French Academy publicly censured Pierre Corneille, who had dared to follow the Spanish model in his early plays. In one of his essays on drama, Corneille wistfully contrasts the freedom enjoyed by the novel with the constraints placed on playwrights. Every Italian, Spanish, or French playwright of the sixteenth and seventeenth centuries was well aware that Aeschylus, Sophocles, and Euripides, the first practitioners of their trade, had provided immortal models for the genre. And when the value of the ancient models began to be questioned at the end of the seventeenth century, critics on both sides of the debate unanimously emphasized the difference between the ancients and moderns. "First we had the good old masters, now the bad new ones," complained the partisans of the ancients. "First the bad old masters, now us," boasted the supporters of the moderns.

The existence of an established set of rules for drama enhanced historical awareness, whereas novelists did not have to dwell on their genre's past. Early modern prose writers did express strong judgments, but these rarely involved clear-cut distinctions between the old and the new. Novelists were practically oriented: they thought about the history of their trade in terms of their immediate objectives. Far from rejecting the old in favor of the new, Cervantes, like many of his contemporaries, championed *newly* discovered *old* novels—such as the *Ethiopian Story*, recently made available again—over late fifteenth- and early sixteenth-century chivalric stories, that is, over relatively *recent* prose narrative based on *older* medieval romances. His criterion was plausibility rather than antiquity: he loved the *Ethiopian Story* because to him it appeared *true to life*, whereas *Amadis of Gaul* and other chivalric stories seemed *packed with lies*.

By the mid-eighteenth century, most writers came to find both chivalric stories and long novels inspired by the ancient Greek model profoundly unconvincing. These narratives described unlikely situations; they overused the imagination, exaggerated the passions, and featured implausibly flawless characters. They *all* lied by idealizing life too much. Few eighteenth-century writers would accept that the earlier idealist subgenres satisfied an important human need—to escape the authority of the here and now—*precisely* because of their implausibility. Authors like Marivaux, Richardson, Fielding, Tobias Smollett, and Sterne aimed to reorient the novel toward the here and now; they presented this retreat of imagination as a triumph of common sense and a mark of artistic progress. They wanted to remind their readers that we live in this universe and not in another, more beautiful and generous one. "Truth," which for Cervantes just a century and a half before had meant the uplifting idealism of the ancient Greek novel, now came to designate conformity with empirical observation. And since older idealist subgenres were being rejected, the opposition between "truth" and "lies" was mapped onto the distinction between "new, modern" and "old, obsolete."

A third distinction—between "poetic" and "prosaic"—soon emerged as a major preoccupation. Romantics deplored the constraints the social and historical novel could put on a writer's freedom: they believed the power of art depended on individual genius rather than existing professional techniques or rules, and emphasized natural, unfettered creativity. They held Shakespeare in high regard, as well as oral poetry, folktales, ancient and medieval epic, and chivalric romances. Compared to the poetic energy released by these works, the social novel's obsession with the real seemed quite reductive. Even Hegel, who was no friend of the Romantics, declared in his *Aesthetics* that, while ancient and medieval epic dealt with heroes, the novel, as "the epic of a prosaic era," could describe the lives of commoners. Accordingly, critics assumed that the only real, "prosaic" novels had been written in the last few centuries. Both Cervantes's *Don Quixote*, with its ironic rejection of chivalric stories, and Mme de Lafayette's *Princess of Clèves* (1678), a tragic novella about human weakness, were retroactively granted the status of the "first modern novels," and the novel was deemed the modern genre par excellence.

Still, the opposition between the "old lies" of ancient Greek and chivalric stories and the newly discovered "truth" of the modern novel should not be overestimated. The difference is primarily one of scale. The *Ethiopian Story* and *Yvain* (ca. 1170) by Chrétien de Troyes may require a more drastic suspension of disbelief than the novels of Richardson and Charles Dickens, but those novels' readers must nonetheless make allowances for a considerable number of incredible characters and events. Fielding, for one, couldn't bring himself to believe the story of Pamela, as his parody, *Shamela* (1741), testifies. In Dickens's *Oliver Twist* (1838), not only does the plot rest on the most improbable series of coincidences, but Oliver's language, his impeccable grammar, sounds shockingly artificial. Readers nevertheless accept these "lies," just as they tolerate the barely credible sequence of misfortunes that destroy Tess's life in Thomas Hardy's *Tess of the d'Urbervilles* (1891).

Nor is the supposedly sharp opposition between the poetic transports of the older novel and the prosaic concerns of the modern very convincing. Chivalric stories, poetic as they are, highlight the faults of the great knights: forgetfulness in *Yvain*, absentmindedness in *Perceval* (ca. 1180), garrulousness in *Erec and Enide* (ca. 1170), dishonesty in *Tristan* (early thirteenth century). Conversely, seven centuries later, virtually all realist writers entered into a secret pact with the Romantic imagination. Balzac and Dickens in particular are masters of exaggeration. Their novels thrill their readers, and to call them prosaic is a blatant simplification.

Among the distinctions made between old and new, the only one that really makes sense is the difference between the epic and the novel. There is no question that the *Iliad* (eighth century BC) and the *Ethiopian Story* belong to different literary genres. So different, I might add, that there is no compelling reason to link them genetically or to see the novel as the epic of the modern era. The epic has not been "replaced" by the novel. Instead of asserting, as many critics have done, that the eighteenth- and nineteenth-century novel represents the modern, bourgeois, prosaic incarnation of the epic, it would be more accurate to say that the eighteenth- and nineteenth-century novel is the newer, sometimes bourgeois and prosaic incarnation of the *novel*.

HISTORIES OF THE GENRE

The present book aligns itself with the recent scholarship that studies the novel from its ancient Greek form to twentieth-century modernism. Yet it also draws on older approaches to the subject.

Some of the great nineteenth- and twentieth-century historians of the novel did trace its development back a long way. Their books, which are monuments of erudition and common sense, often assume, under the influence of Darwinian theory, that literary genres evolve and morph into one another through internal mutations, not unlike biological species. Erwin Rohde[1] was the first "natural" historian of ancient narrative prose and saw the Greek novel as the product of crossbreeding among the late epic, travel stories, and biography. His views need not be taken literally, but his insights about the competition between narrative species, and their possible fusion, converge with one of the arguments I make in this book—that early modern narrative culture emphasized the differences between subgenres, while later forms of the novel are the result of multiple attempts to blend these subgenres together.

The greatest achievements of the *natural history of the novel* were its large temporal scale and its attention to generic diversity. The wealth of material in Ernest Albert Baker's ten-volume *History of the English Novel*,[2] and the accuracy of many of its assessments of narrative subgenres and their evolution, make it an abiding source of knowledge. The same is true of the older book by Felix Bobertag, *Geschichte des Romans*

----

[1] Author of *Der griechische Roman und seine Vorläufer* (Leipzig: Breitkopf & Härtel, 1876).

[2] London: Witherby, 1924–1936.

und der ihm verwandten Dichtungsgattungen in Deutschland,[3] of Marcelino Menéndez y Pelayo's *Orígenes de la novela*,[4] and of Henri Coulet's *Le Roman jusqu'à la Révolution*.[5] The natural historians' willingness to explore long stretches of time is particularly helpful, and yet their vast empirical knowledge can itself sometimes become a burden: these histories do not always pay enough attention to literary art, or to the web of connections between literature and its social and intellectual milieu, and they tend to forgo complex conceptual frameworks.

These shortcomings were later corrected by literary historians who gave special attention to historical environment, to the evolution of formal devices, and to abstract concepts that can help make sense of the novel's evolution.

One of the most influential *social and intellectual histories* is Ian Watt's *The Rise of the Novel: Studies in Defoe, Richardson, and Fielding*.[6] Watt's book focuses on a few English novels written in the first half of the eighteenth century, yet its powerful insights make it required reading. According to Watt, the writings of Daniel Defoe and Richardson, the creators, in his view, of the modern, realist novel, cannot be understood without reference to the social and intellectual context of Britain in the early eighteenth century. This was a time when writers ceased to depend on wealthy protectors and began to make a living from the sales of their books, bought and read by an ever-larger public. It was also a time when individualism was gaining ground in everyday life, in religious beliefs, and in philosophy, and when scientific advances were lending philosophical empiricism a renewed prestige. The works of Defoe and Richardson, Watt argues, are part and parcel of a larger movement that includes the rise of the market economy, individualist ethics, and a modern theory of knowledge.

Economic themes are indeed always present in Defoe's novels, whose characters endlessly count up their material gains, whether they earned them by solitary, honest work, as in *Robinson Crusoe* (1719), or by the most squalid means, as in *Moll Flanders* (1722). These themes resonate with Protestant ethics as well as with economic individualism, and they indicate that writers who could no longer count on the generosity of aristocratic patrons were responsive to the issues that interested their new, middle-class readers. Watt also notices that Defoe's and Richardson's characters pay considerable attention to tangible details, as though their own credibility might depend on how accurate these details are. This

[3] Breslau: A. Gosohorsky, 1876.
[4] Madrid: Bailly- Ballière, 1905–1915.
[5] Paris: Armand Colin, 1967.
[6] Berkeley: University of California Press, 1957.

technique, which Watt calls "formal realism," aims to provide authentic accounts of concrete individual experiences, and thus has clear affinities with John Locke's empiricism and with modern science more generally.

Watt argues convincingly that innovations in literary technique depend on changes in the social structure, such as the rise of the market economy and the new status of writers and readers, as well as on the evolution of the religious and intellectual superstructure—in this case, Protestant ethics and empiricism. Yet he tends to overstate his thesis. He blurs, for instance, the differences between Defoe's prose and Richardson's. It is true that their works were published in the same half century, but Richardson's *Pamela*—with all its faults—can indeed be considered a major innovation, whereas Defoe's *Robinson Crusoe* and *Moll Flanders*, though extraordinarily powerful, exploit well-established narrative formulas: *Crusoe* the spiritual autobiography and *Moll Flanders* the picaresque novel.

Moreover, because the links are quite striking between Defoe's and Richardson's works and the crucial historical forces of the time, Watt presents their realism as the only productive trend in the history of the modern English novel. Fielding, who opposed formal realism and criticized Richardson's method and vision severely, makes only a minor contribution, in Watt's view, to the novel's development. This is the main danger in overplaying social and cultural explanations for artistic phenomena, especially when such explanations fit only one set of facts, such as the link between formal realism and the rise of commercial capitalist society. Since over time commercial capitalism prevailed over its older rivals, it is tempting to assume that in literature too, formal realism was the only successful trend. But in fact, the growth of the market economy, the spread of literacy, and the joint success of Protestant ethics and empiricism did *not* entail the supremacy of formal realism. Instead, it allowed more than one literary formula to compete, thus letting Fielding's satiric approach exercise its own influence on the evolution of the novel. Fielding's work, echoed in Walter Scott and Dickens, was a direct source of inspiration for many nineteenth-century writers, including Jane Austen, Stendhal, and Thackeray.

Perhaps, then, narrative techniques enjoy a certain independence from social and intellectual factors. The Russian formalists certainly thought so and viewed the novel's emergence as a matter of more or less ahistorical technical innovation. For Viktor Shklovsky, the quintessential novel was Sterne's *Tristram Shandy*, which pokes fun at everything narrative had always relied on: character, plot, motivation, love, conversation, and reflection.

Less extreme than his formalist friends, the Russian critic Mikhail Bakhtin devised a *history of narrative techniques* indebted not only to formalism but also to Hegel and to late nineteenth-century thinkers, such as Wilhelm Dilthey, who attempted to integrate the history of artistic forms within a more general history of the human spirit. Bakhtin's essay "The Forms of Time and of the Chronotope in the novel"[7] illustrates this kind of historical thinking. Familiar with Erwin Rohde's work, Bakhtin understood that the eighteenth- and nineteenth-century novel had a pre-history that encompassed not only a great deal of narrative prose written before Rabelais, whose *Gargantua* (1534) and *Pantagruel* (1532) Bakhtin considered the foundation of the modern novel, but also biographical and philosophical writings such as Plutarch's *Parallel Lives* (late first century) and Plato's *Dialogues* (fifth to fourth century BC).

Examining formal features, Bakhtin noticed that the action in ancient Greek novels takes place in an abstract space and time, that the characters never change or evolve, and that episodes do not follow one another according to the laws of causality. Convinced that these features betrayed a lack of formal skill, Bakhtin argued that they were finally outgrown only when nineteenth-century realist writers learned to represent time and space in a rich, concrete fashion, and to master the portrayal of psychological growth and the causal sequencing of episodes.

Bakhtin's formal description of ancient Greek novels is accurate. Yet while grasping the *formal features* of these novels, Bakhtin neglects the *inner logic* of their narrative universe. In representational arts, form is usually intimately related to content, an essential part of what makes it intelligible and meaningful, so it is not enough to argue that in ancient Greek novels time and space are abstract, psychology is rigid, and events occur arbitrarily. In order to deem these novels unsatisfactory, you would need to reflect on the reasons behind their formal qualities and show that those qualities do not help impart the intended message. But Bakhtin seldom addresses the issue of the meaning conveyed by the techniques he describes.

Nor does Bakhtin's history of narrative methods pay much attention to the environment—social, intellectual, and artistic—from which nineteenth-century social realism arose. He never asks why the concrete detail and psychological verisimilitude of nineteenth-century novels eventually replaced what he sees as the abstraction and implausibility of older works. By failing to address this question, he makes the history of narrative techniques into a mere inventory of formal features. Artistic *will to form* may well manifest the freedom of the human spirit, as many nineteenth-century German historians of culture argued. But it is equally true, as Ian Watt has shown, that this spirit does not concoct artistic

---

[7] In his *The Dialogic Imagination*, trans. Caryl Emerson and Michael Holquist (1937–1938; Austin: University of Texas Press, 1981), pp. 84–258.

forms in a vacuum, without any ties to the reality of social and intellectual life.

In order to explain the evolution of novelistic techniques, Bakhtin does
formulate a hypothesis linking the earlier novel with its social environment. He argues that in medieval and early modern Europe, a *feudal ideology* that neglected spatial and temporal categories clashed with an *anti-
ideological, popular creed* more sensitive to the real conditions of life.
As products of the feudal ideology, ancient Greek novels and medieval
chivalric stories treated space and time abstractly, whereas folk literature,
farce, parody, and satire embodied the popular creed and prepared the
way for works like Rabelais's *Gargantua* and *Pantagruel* and Cervantes's
Don Quixote, which expressed the comic, concrete point of view. In the
end, Bakhtin suggests, the popular creed conquered the novel, giving it a
new, anticonventional direction that encouraged the rise of modern social
realism.

While Bakhtin's speculations about ideology do capture the difference
between the idealizing and comic approaches in medieval and early modern narratives, his sociological notions do not stand scrutiny. It is hard to
believe a truly feudal ideology would have minimized spatial categories,
given that few social arrangements were more dependent on territorial
considerations: the foundation of the feudal system was local military
defense in the form of fortified castles closely surrounded by villages.
Temporal categories were equally crucial for feudalism, as most social
positions were hereditary, reinforcing a sense of tradition and respect
for chronological records. Besides, it is counterintuitive to attribute the
complexity, erudition, and rhetorical brio of *Gargantua* and *Pantagruel*
or *Don Quixote* to a popular antifeudal ideology. Although Rabelais and
Cervantes did rely on an age-old comic tradition, their books are the
products of a sophisticated humanist culture whose connections with
populism remain elusive.

A history that takes account only of formal artistic devices simply does
not have the means to describe the relation between literature and society,
let alone the reasons why the fictional worlds created by novelists fired
their readers' imaginations. A fourth type of historical analysis, the *reflective history of the novel*, takes on this task, focusing on the internal development of the genre and its links with the life of the human spirit. Georg
Lukács's early essay *The Theory of the Novel: A Historico-Philosophical
Essay on the Forms of Great Epic Literature*[8] is an influential example.

Lukács assumes that in order to understand its historical development,
one must examine the novel's *concept*—the way it portrays the world—
and its growth and maturation. In Lukács's view, narratives examine

---

[8] Trans. Anna Bostock (1916; Cambridge, MA: MIT Press, 1971).

the links between human beings *as individuals* and the society in which they live. This kind of representation, he continues, is difficult to achieve, given the tension between individual aspirations and the constraints imposed by the outside world. Like many German-trained scholars of the nineteenth and early twentieth centuries, the young Lukács romanticized the ancient Greek city-state, which he imagined as the most perfect and best integrated of all forms of civilization. The dominant narrative genre of that period, Lukács argues, was the epic poem, Homer's *Iliad*, for example, which described the actions of heroic men in a world whose greatness they fully understood and accepted.

Later, at a historical moment Lukács does not define very clearly, when the meaning of the surrounding world became doubtful and hard to capture in a single, powerful insight, the epic gave way to the novel, a genre that specializes in depicting an imperfect universe and a set of characters who do not quite fit within it. According to Lukács, these characters do not entirely accept the legitimacy of their world—they do not *inhabit* it in the full sense of the term, and their lives acquire meaning only by reference to a different, ideal world toward which they can aspire. Yet obviously, this ideal world has no reality outside the protagonist's longings. Lukács calls these yearning characters "problematic heroes." The most famous of them is Don Quixote, the hidalgo whose ideal of a knight-errant generously fighting to defend orphans, widows, and persecuted ladies exists only in his deranged mind. Later on, Lukács adds, the main characters of Friedrich Hölderlin's *Hyperion* (1797–1799) and Balzac's *Eugénie Grandet* (1833) would be of the same type.

The idea of a "problematic hero" and the tension between his ideals and reality generates a dialectical movement involving three moments. First, when the hero's ideal world is narrower, more restricted, than the real one, and when he remains blind to the gap between the two worlds, Lukács calls the resulting situation *abstract idealism*. Don Quixote is the best example. The ideal he believes in applies to only a small number of real human interactions—those involving charity, generosity, and self-sacrifice—and so his attempts to implement it cannot but fail. Conversely, when the ideal imagined by the main character is wider and more elaborate than the surrounding world, the clash between them leads to what Lukács terms *romantic disillusion*. In such cases, the character is well aware of the gap between the ideal and the real, but lacks the power and the means to bridge it. Lukács uses the protagonist of Ivan Goncharov's *Oblomov* (1859) to illustrate this second kind of situation—a Russian dreamer who lies in bed day after day and never does anything. In the third dialectical moment, the problematic hero, while remaining devoted to his ideal, manages to achieve a lasting *reconciliation* with the surrounding reality: this is what happens in Goethe's *Wilhelm Meister's*

Apprenticeship (1795–1796), and many more examples can be found in the nineteenth-century bildungsroman.

Lukács bases his theory of the novel on abstract concepts rather than masses of empirical data, which gives him the courage to propose new, capacious categories that address deep human concerns, and to choose his examples without reference to the usual chronological criteria—the three books he uses to illustrate the dialectics of the novel, *Don Quixote*, *Oblomov*, and *Wilhelm Meister*, form an unexpected sequence. Yet despite Lukács's wish to escape strict chronology, his views are actually confined within narrow temporal limits. The dialectic of the problematic hero, while highly pertinent for novels published from the end of the eighteenth to the mid-nineteenth century, cannot explain all those written earlier or later. Apart from *Don Quixote*, Lukács never considers a novel written before *Wilhelm Meister*. He also pays little attention to the role of individual talent. For instance, neither abstract idealism, nor romantic disillusion, nor a synthesis of the two can fully explain the complex relations between Leo Tolstoy's characters and their environment. Claiming that Tolstoy's novels represent a return to an older kind of epic, Lukács fails to notice the Russian novelist's innovations. By overemphasizing impersonal dialectical patterns, he neglects the unpredictable contributions of individual writers.

The Present Work: Core Assumptions and Goals

In the present work, somewhat as in natural histories of the novel though certainly in much less detail, I sketch out a comprehensive overview of the genre's development. From the history of narrative techniques, I have borrowed the habit of examining the craft of the novel and its formal methods. As do social historians of literature, I look at the evolution of literary genres from a wider cultural perspective. Most importantly, I owe a great deal to the reflective history of the novel. My book aims to understand the changing lives of the genre, their secret pact with permanence, and the dialogue engaged in by novelists over the centuries. I do not draw a definite temporal line separating a "before" from an "after," a line behind which the novel's past would be, as Constantin Fasolt puts it in *The Limits of History*,[9] *absent* and *immutable*—in other words, dead and buried. Approaching early novels as living literature rather than ossified historical evidence, this book hopes to recapture their appeal.

Following Lukács's example, I use concepts that apply directly to human experience, concepts meant to capture the resonance of literary works beyond the period in which they were written. That is why, like

[9] Chicago, IL: University of Chicago Press, 2004.

him, I look at long stretches of time and at the often surprising interaction between periods. The difference is that instead of placing the whole history of the novel under a single illuminating concept, as he did, I use a family of concepts, relating them when possible to the natural history of the genre. My speculations, in other words, will be somewhat less abstruse and closer to historical practice than the young Lukács's.

As for terminology, the distinction between *romance* and *novel* does capture something important, but I will avoid relying on it here. *Romance* comes from the French *roman*, which initially designated medieval narratives written in *roman*—that is, vernacular French, a Romance language. In French, the term was applied to the ancient Greek novels as soon as they were rediscovered in the sixteenth century, as well as to other early modern long narratives, pastoral, heroic, or allegorical. Later, the term was extended to the more recent forms that in English are called *novels*. In German, the word *Roman* has a similarly wide scope. The Italian term *romanzo* applies not only to all ancient, medieval, and modern long prose narratives, but also to the Renaissance fantasy epic poems by Pulci, Boiardo, and Ariosto. When Torquato Tasso, in his *Discourses on the Heroic Poem* (1567–1570), discusses the difference between ancient epic and the more recent *romanzo*, he does not refer to early novels but to these Renaissance epic poems. In English, the difference between *romance* and *novel* has something to do with subject matter, a *romance* being a story mainly concerned with love, but it also involves a chronological distinction, in which *novel* has usually been reserved for prose narratives written in the eighteenth century or later. Recently, however, classics scholars have extended the term *novel* to ancient Greek and Latin prose narratives. This change suggests a new awareness of the genre's long chronological continuity. To increase the confusion, the Italian, Spanish, and French cognates of the term *novel* are *novella* and *nouvelle*, designating a shorter prose narrative with a simpler plot. Since the term *short story* usually refers to very brief narratives, the Italian and Spanish term was adopted in English to describe longer *novellas*.

My use of the word "idealist" here has little to do with the philosophical sense of the term. It refers to narratives that draw an idealized picture of human existence.

||||||||||||||||||||||||||||

Four core beliefs give this book its direction.

First, *narratives are about human beings, the ideals and norms that guide their lives, the passions that drive them, and the action they take.* Since characters and their ideals form the true, living center of narrative genres, novels propose substantial hypotheses about human life and imagine fictional worlds governed by them. These hypotheses describe distinct human types, their relation to ideals, their patterns of behavior, and their links to the community in which they live. The novel ponders the meaning of life and of human interactions, just as epic and tragedy did before it. But whereas epic heroes belong completely to their cities and tragic characters are crushed by fate, most characters in novels are independent of the surrounding world and ready to fight against its pressures and uncertainties. By separating the protagonists from their environment, the novel, as the young Lukács saw, was the first genre to consider individuality one of the highest goods and to reflect on the individual's connections with the life of the community.

The novel asks whether moral ideals do or do not belong to the human world. If we assume they do, we need to understand why so many human beings fail to follow them. And, on the other hand, if moral ideals have nothing to do with our world, we must explain why their normative power seems so self-evident to virtually everybody. We need to reflect, in other words, on the difference between what human beings *ought to do* and what they *do*. The novel examines this difference with regard to *individual* compliance. It asks whether, in order to uphold ideals in a world that does not guarantee their supremacy, individuals must simply resist the world, act to change it, or concentrate on overcoming their own failings. As the young Lukács knew, the novel asks whether human beings can ever be morally reconciled with the world in which they are born, and *feel at home* in it.

Second, *novels portray individuals in different ways, as strong souls, sensitive hearts, or enigmatic psyches*. Strong souls are able to act in harmony with the moral ideal, an ideal that is very much part of their world and resonates, so to speak, outside and around them. They hear and follow it without hesitation. The characters in ancient Greek novels behave like this, and so, for the most part, do the knights-errant who populate medieval romances. Later, Richardson's Pamela and Clarissa will be examples of the *sensitive heart*: able to look inward, alert to their own tender feelings, they aspire to act in accordance with moral ideals but are not always successful. The protagonists in Renaissance and early modern novellas behave this way, as do those of eighteenth- and nineteenth-century sentimental novels. However, when characters cannot gain access to their own innermost recesses, when their understanding of themselves and of moral requirements becomes blurred, they exemplify the *enigmatic psyche*. Such characters can already be found in early modern novellas like Mme de Lafayette's, but they become prevalent only much later, in Henry James, Proust, and Faulkner.

These three types can be idealized and portrayed as exemplary, as in the instances just mentioned, or they can be modified in two respects. Some novels evoke a lesser perfection: skewed souls in several chivalric novels, hesitant hearts in the pastoral, and incautious psyches in Theodor Fontane's and Thomas Hardy's late nineteenth-century novels. Some novels go further, developing fully anti-idealist types: scoundrels instead of strong souls, cold hearts instead of sensitive ones, and wholly incomprehensible psyches rather than merely enigmatic ones.

Third, *while literary and, more generally, artistic genres are linked to the social and intellectual life of their time, they also enjoy a qualified autonomy*. They do not reflect the world in which they were made in every detail. Just as, in a given geographic area, the growth of a species of plant or flower is made possible by the ecological balance of the region as a whole rather than by a specific turn of a river or by a sudden solar eclipse, the success of a certain kind of writing is most often influenced by the general cultural climate rather than by this or that historical personality or event. The number of distinct early modern subgenres certainly has something to do with feudal society's organization: priests, friars, lords, knights, merchants, craftsmen, and peasants were each subject to specific ideals, norms, privileges, and often laws; mobility was limited—a knight could be promoted to the rank of lord of the manor, a penitent sinner could become a hermit, but usually your station in life was fixed from birth. It is not by chance, then, that from the eighteenth century onward, the gradual increase in social mobility and equality coincided with a propensity to blend the older narrative subgenres into a single, flexible genre—the modern novel. Still, while suggesting various links between the development of the novel and its historical context, this book will refrain from always attaching each subgenre to a single social group, or each work to a particular turn of social or intellectual history.

Fourth, *although individual decisions play an important role in the evolution of literature, the history of the novel does not consist in great writers relentlessly pushing the genre forward*. The great talents of the early period—Chrétien de Troyes, Wolfram von Eschenbach, Boccaccio, Chaucer, Rabelais, Sidney, Cervantes, Mme de Lafayette, Defoe—did not create or change the genre all by themselves. Chrétien de Troyes, Wolfram von Eschenbach, and Chaucer were superb tellers of preexisting stories; Boccaccio, Cervantes, and Sidney were stunning experimenters and inventors; Rabelais loved to play the eccentric outsider; Mme de Lafayette and Defoe honed and refined available narrative formulas. Geniuses do what they choose to do extremely well, but they do not always choose to create or transform a genre.

Since artistic and literary distinctions are approximate rather than sharply defined, at each step I propose a few *ideal types* and concentrate on a few examples, hoping to tempt the reader to discover or revisit them. I have tried to ensure that the works analyzed here are those widely recognized as some of the best achievements of the genre, but inevitably my choices also reflect my own taste and preferences. There are important authors whose works, unfortunately, I have not been able to discuss in detail. Rather than providing a complete inventory of authors and titles, this book aims to describe the major types of novel and the forces that have shaped their history.

PART ONE

The Highest Ideals

CHAPTER 1

Strong Souls,
Degrees of Perfection

|||||||||||||||||||||||||||||||||||||||||||||||||||||||||||

THE ANCIENT GREEK NOVEL

From its earliest incarnations, the novel attempted to understand the relationship between individuals and the ideals and norms meant to guide their lives. But rather than observing, depicting, and evaluating people's actions in real situations, the early forms of the novel took for granted a set of powerful ideals and set out to imagine the kind of behavior that would fully comply with them (in the idealist subgenres) or totally contradict them (in the anti-idealist varieties). The characters in the earliest, ancient Greek idealist novels are highly edifying: invincible lovers persecuted by a hostile world.

Only a few of these novels have been preserved in their entirety. Four of them tell implausible stories about ideal love and its victorious struggle against adversity: *Chaereas and Callirhoe* by Chariton (generally dated to the first century), *The Ephesian Story* by Xenophon of Ephesus (second or third century), *Leucippe and Clitophon* by Achilles Tatius (second century), and the *Ethiopian Story* by Heliodorus (third or fourth century). A fifth, *Daphnis and Chloe* by Longus (second century), is a more believable pastoral story, while the two surviving Latin novels, *Satyricon* by Petronius (first century) and *The Golden Ass* by Apuleius (second century), portray flawed, imperfect characters. A few other ancient narratives also had an influential role in the history of the novel: Xenophon of Athens's *Cyropaedia* (fourth century BC), a fictionalized description of the education of an ideal ruler; Ovid's *Heroides* (early first century), a set of first-person laments by unhappy women lovers; the *Romance of Alexander the Great* by Pseudo-Callisthenes (third century);

and Philostratus's *Apollonius of Tyana* (third century), the biography of
a saintly Pythagorean philosopher.

The Couple outside the World

The Roman Empire's dominion around the Mediterranean between the
first century and the fifth encouraged a new, pervasive sense that all lands
and peoples belong to the same, unified world. In turn, several philosophical and religious movements put the whole universe in the hands
of a single deity. A new form of spirituality advocated a rejection of the
material realm and emphasized the individual's independence from the
surrounding world—an independence that could generate both anxiety
and wisdom.

Yet some of these impulses toward a unified vision of the world and
a notion of the individual's separateness within it were even older. Most
extreme was the ideal of the ascetics, described by Louis Dumont as
individuals-outside-the-world,[1] who set themselves more stringent standards than those that govern social life. Leaving the community and
forsaking worldly goods—which includes not having children—ascetics
choose the path of spiritual enlightenment, putting themselves under
divine protection. Recognizing that these people are associated with a
higher, otherworldly realm, the community rewards their self-imposed
poverty and chastity by treating them with respect and fear. Ascetics can
be found in many cultures, but the most characteristic example is the
ancient Indian story of Buddha, the prince who renounced wealth and
power for a life of abstinence and contemplation.

Hellenistic philosophy envisaged a less drastic form of separation between individuals and their world. Aspiring to an ideal shared by Neo-
platonists, Stoics, and Epicurean philosophers alike, the *lovers of wisdom*
set themselves at a distance from the external world and, beyond its troubling instability, contemplate the divine order of the universe. They nevertheless continue to live among their peers without letting pain, disease,
or the fear of death distress them. In the Stoic version of this ideal, once
people understand the operation of universal reason and learn how to
live by its dictates, they can resist the reign of fortune. In Pierre Hadot's
formulation, the soul of the lover of wisdom becomes an "inner citadel," impervious to aggression or seduction from the outside.[2] Although
the wise do not need a personal, willful God to exercise power on their

---

[1] Louis Dumont, *Essays on Individualism: Modern Ideology in Anthropological Perspective* (1983; Chicago, IL: University of Chicago Press, 1992).

[2] Pierre Hadot, *The Inner Citadel: The Meditations of Marcus Aurelius*, trans. Michael
Chase (1992; Cambridge, MA: Harvard University Press, 1998).

behalf, they sense that beyond the disorienting workings of fortune, the universe is supervised from afar by a Providence they can trust to protect them.

Mystery religions and Gnosticism had their own ways of assuaging anxiety caused by the distance between the individual and the world. According to one of the basic tenets of Gnosticism, some souls trapped in the material realm can experience an inner awakening that brings them closer to their true, divine nature. Although there were Gnostic schools that encouraged asceticism, this awakening was not necessarily assumed to erase all natural desires. Sexual union played a major role in some mystery religions and Gnostic cults: the Valentinians, for instance, saw spiritual initiation as a marriage between the faithful and their personal angel, celebrated in a sacramental bridal chamber.

Ancient Greek novels developed a literary version of the worldview that affirms the unity of the visible world, the existence of a wise Providence, and the independence of individuals from their environment. The *star-crossed couple*, present in all these novels and fully developed in Heliodorus's *Ethiopian Story*, remains largely foreign in the world. United by a providentially inspired love, the two young protagonists realize how different they are from their surroundings. Love and fortitude provide them with an "inner citadel" strong enough to withstand a long series of ordeals that manifest the disorder of our inferior, sublunary world. Once they have overcome all obstacles, the lovers, not unlike followers of a mystery cult, cross the threshold of the sacred bridal chamber. These lovers resemble Dumont's individuals-outside-the-world, though they do not aspire to the spiritual isolation of the ascetics; they also share some features with the Neoplatonic and Stoic lovers of wisdom, and with Gnostic initiates. Through their pure, virtuous love, the lovers-outside-the-world combine the strength of the wise, the spiritual gift of inner awakening, and the joy of life in common.

Epic, Tragedy, the Ancient Novel

Written between the first and fourth centuries, idealist ancient Greek novels could count on a public familiar with these ideas. Yet the very small number found on papyri, and the virtual absence of references to them in ancient treatises on poetics and rhetoric, suggest that these works did not achieve the prestige enjoyed by classical Greek epic and tragedy.

For a long time, epic and tragedy kept alive an older way of looking at people, their surroundings, and the power of the gods. In Homer's *Iliad* and *Odyssey*, composed at least seven hundred years before the Greek novels, the heroes are fully immersed in the concerns of their tribes and cities. Their anger or misfortune may separate Achilles or

Ulysses from their countrymen, yet the epic poems revolve around their return to the community. It could not be otherwise: in a world divided into so many different kingdoms, the hero's life can make sense only in connection with his kin and birthplace. In the old epic, moreover, the gods are numerous, unreliable, and very close to the human beings. They side with their worshippers, offer advice and support, but they can also deceive, betray, and disappoint them. In the *Iliad*, Pallas Athene and Aphrodite attack each other through the Greek and Trojan warriors. For a while, Zeus protects Hector, who regularly sacrifices his best oxen to him, but when Athena intercedes on behalf of the Greeks, the father of the gods abandons Troy on the spur of the moment. High above both mortals and gods floats the shadow of fate, whose decisions cannot be appealed.

In Virgil's *Aeneid* (29–19 BC), written at about the same time as the earliest, lost ancient Greek novels, Aeneas still resembles an older kind of hero, deeply attached to his family and city. He runs away from the defeated Troy only because fate has decreed that he must found a new city where he and his followers can settle and take root. Migration does not cut their links with the world around them. Aeneas's road is full of obstacles—at Carthage, his love for Dido leads him astray; in Italy, his rivalry with Turnus delays the alliance between the Trojans and the Latins—and these challenges are much more than mere external attacks against an impregnable "inner citadel." All their tribulations truly absorb Aeneas and his fellow Trojans. As for the gods, they are as close to the mortals and as quick-tempered as they are in Homer. Aeneas's misfortunes, like those of Troy in the *Iliad*, stem from the old strife between Venus and Juno. It is true that in the *Aeneid*, the immortals' passions are seen as surprising: "Is there such anger in celestial minds?" ("Tantaene animis caelestibus irae?" *Aeneid* 1.11), the poet asks at the very beginning. It is also true that the gods and mortals work together, so that Venus's strength and Aeneas's, or Juno's power and that of Carthage, are almost indistinguishable. Later, when polytheism was a thing of the past, this fusion between human and godly action allowed literary critics to claim that the divinities in epic had always been purely allegorical. Yet you need only read Homer and Virgil to know that these angry, active gods were meant to be taken literally.

Greek tragedy began to push the gods offstage. Now and then they recite the prologue, as in Euripides's *Hippolytus* (428 BC), or express their will through oracles, as in Sophocles's *Oedipus Rex* (429 BC) and Euripides's *Alcestis* (438 BC). Occasionally, in Sophocles's *Ajax* (450–430 BC), for instance, and in *The Bacchae* (405 BC) by Euripides, they intervene directly, to punish those who oppose them, or to bring the tragedy's action to an end, as they do in the third part of Aeschylus's trilogy, the *Oresteia* (458 BC), or in Euripides's *Iphigenia at Aulis* (405 BC). But while in Homer and Virgil the gods intrude at every turn, in tragedy they act only in times of crisis. When they do intervene, their ways can be brutal—more and more, they resemble fate itself. In Homer and Virgil, the gods take clear sides in human conflicts and fight among themselves to protect their allies. In Euripides's *Hippolytus*, on the other hand, although the main character worships the chaste Artemis and rejects Aphrodite, goddess of love, Artemis does not make the slightest effort to defend him against Aphrodite's wrath. And since in tragedy the gods cannot always be entirely distinguished from fate, their individual physiognomy fades away. In *Iphigenia at Aulis*, significantly, the deity who saves Iphigenia from death is anonymous for a long time and remains invisible.

From the epic poem to tragedy, then, the gods' position gets loftier, their intervention less frequent, and their individuality less palpable. Slowly replacing fate, they begin to take on a new role, as an almighty force that guides human destiny from far above. The human protagonists of tragedy nevertheless remain as steeped in their surrounding world as the epic heroes. Kinship is central to tragedy, in which family feuds are entangled with city conflicts: Antigone (in Sophocles's play, written around 442 BC) must decide whether she is a citizen or a sister; Alcestis agrees to die as a devoted wife and subject; Clytemnestra kills the king, her husband, who sacrificed their daughter for political reasons. With the exception of those in *Ajax* and *The Bacchae*, tragic characters are usually less subject to the whims of the gods than are their epic ancestors. They are more directly dependent on fate, as are the heroes of Lucan's much later *Pharsalia*, written just before 65 AD, at about the same time as the oldest surviving ancient Greek novel. In this poem, the gods have been replaced by an almighty fate who shapes the order of the world, a fickle fortune who grants the characters success or failure, and a diffuse, mysterious, supernatural power expressed in dreams, oracles, and necromancy. (That said, not all writers followed this pattern: Statius, for one, filled his *Thebaid*, finished in 90 AD, with a multitude of gods as angry as Virgil's and often more loquacious.)

The idealist ancient Greek novel continued this trend and gave it a striking new turn. The highly individualized, anthropomorphic gods who had withdrawn from tragedy and vanished entirely from Lucan were by now invisible, impersonal beings, ready to merge into a single deity. The memory of their old names survived for a while, but Eros in *Chaereas and Callirhoe* or *Leucippe and Clitophon*, and Apollo in the *Ethiopian Story*, are little more than stand-ins for Providence: the old gods have been absorbed into the almighty fate that used to override them. Capricious fortune has become an unfailingly hostile force, but its power ranks far below that of Providence and can be overcome by the inner strength of the protagonists.

In Heliodorus's *Ethiopian Story*, Chariclea and Theagenes, who meet at Delphi during the festival celebrating the Sun god Apollo, fall in love at first sight. The reader soon realizes that Apollo of Delphi is only one of several incarnations of a solar divinity that rules over the entire world. Chariclea's Greek family intends to marry her to another man, but Kalasiris, one of the Sun god's Egyptian priests, helps the young lovers stay together. He persuades them to run away from home, and escorts them on their journey. The lovers suffer many misfortunes, and after being captured by pirates and shipwrecked, they find themselves in Egypt's capital, Memphis. Arsake, wife of the Persian governor of Egypt, falls in love with Theagenes and sentences Chariclea to be burned alive. But the fire spares the heroine, who has a protective talisman and also, significantly, begs the Sun and the Earth for help. The couple's final destination, fixed long before their meeting at Delphi, is the legendary kingdom of Ethiopia, whose king turns out to be Chariclea's real father. After yet another series of ordeals, the Ethiopian king decides to outlaw human sacrifice, and the lovers are allowed to marry and serve as priest and priestess of the Sun god and the Moon goddess. At the end of the text, as if to reiterate the reference to the solar god, the author identifies himself as Heliodorus, a Phoenician from Emes, descended from the Sun.

Invisible yet omnipresent, Providence presides over the plot and the characters' destinies. Chariclea's life depends at every turn on the servants of the Sun god: Sisimithres, Ethiopian priest of the Sun, saves the little girl and entrusts her to Charicles, a Greek priest of Apollo who happens to be in Egypt, improving his knowledge of sacred things; later, she is protected by Kalasiris, whose actions are explicitly inspired and directed by Heaven. Throughout the novel, the characters act according to a higher, hidden plan, whose meaning is finally revealed by the denouement: it not only allows Theagenes and Chariclea to live happily ever after, but also reforms the laws of the country they will inhabit.

The Unity of Mankind and the Rule of Fortune

There is a new unity of peoples here. Chariclea continually defies distinctions based on race, nation, or lineage. Her mother, Queen Persina, says that at the moment of conception she obeyed instructions she had received in a prophetic dream about a picture hanging on the wall. When she looked at the painting of Andromeda—the legendary Ethiopian princess, whose skin is here assumed to be white—the royal seed changed shape, and the child was born with white skin. Afraid she would be accused of adultery, the queen abandoned the baby, who was rescued and brought to Greece, where Charicles raised her as his daughter. Providence itself

has made Chariclea resemble Andromeda, as a reminder that human beings descend not just from their human ancestors, but also from a higher
spring.

We are very far from the epic heroes so deeply rooted in the soil where
they were born, whose love of the native land is usually their main spur
to action. Occasionally they may be forced into exile, as Aeneas is after
the fall of Troy, but the ties to home never weaken. A true epic hero trusts
only his country of origin and views foreign places with suspicion or even
hatred: the Greeks lay waste to Troy after their victory; Ulysses longs to
go back to Ithaca; Aeneas leaves Dido and wealthy Carthage behind to
build a new Troy with his own hands.

Tragedy does sometimes question the civil laws of the hero's native
country in order to assert the power of older religious obligations. More
frequently, however, especially when no divinities intervene, the laws of
the city have the last word: in Sophocles's *Philoctetes* (409 BC), which
sees a great Greek warrior abandoned by his comrades-in-arms on a desert island, the civic arguments with which Ulysses defends this fateful
decision are remarkably persuasive. Even when the strength of religious
arguments is overwhelming, as it is in *Antigone*, the tragedy does not
uphold the values of a world wider than the city-state, Thebes. Antigone
wants to bury her brother Polynices according to the old funeral rites, but
since Polynices died waging war against his own country, its present ruler,
Creon, forbids his burial. Against Creon's sense of public order, Antigone
invokes the gods of the hearth and the sacred duty of families to bury
their own. Rejecting the unity of the city-state, she defends the older, narrower sanctity of blood.

By contrast, the *Ethiopian Story* questions both family ties and the
loyalty due to the state. Born in Ethiopia and raised in Greece, Chariclea
acquires a new family and a new name. She believes she is a Greek native,
but since the call of love is stronger than her duty to her family and city,
she leaves them without hesitation. Among the three characters Chariclea
calls "father" in the course of the novel, she owes her existence to the
Ethiopian king Hydaspes, her education to the Greek Charicles, and her
happiness to the Egyptian Kalasiris, who leads her and Theagenes back
to Ethiopia. Theagenes, born in Thesalia from Achilles's line, leaves his
native country to follow his beloved to Africa. When Charicles and his
fellow citizens find out that the lovers have fled Greece, their anger is presented as slightly ridiculous: clearly, once Heaven decides what it wants
to do with someone, the city should not have a word to say about it.

Belief in a single deity has often gone together with a sense of human
life as an exile from the eternal homeland, or with an ascetic rejection
of the material world, and yet monotheism does not necessarily involve

contempt for earthly existence. Long before the *Ethiopian Story*, the book of Exodus (sixth to fifth century BC) described the Israelites' escape from slavery, their wandering in the Sinai desert, and the discovery of the Promised Land. Told from the viewpoint of the escapees, the biblical narrative presents Egypt—a foreign country—as the land of exile, while Canaan is seen as both an earthly and a divine homeland. The God of Israel grants his people freedom and, at the same time, the opportunity to put down roots. Chariclea and Theagenes, on the other hand, find their earthly and heavenly refuge in Ethiopia, far from the original home of Hellenistic culture. At the time the novel was written, the memory of Greece was a source of pride and nostalgia for Greek-speaking colonists like Heliodorus, living under Roman rule on the eastern shores of the Mediterranean. To understand how dramatic Chariclea and Theagenes's decision to flee Greece must have seemed to the novel's original readers, we need to imagine a story from the Jewish diaspora that describes Jerusalem as the place from which the main characters must *escape*. For the star-crossed lovers, however, neither their place of birth nor the cradle of Greek culture defines their lives.

The wide world that opens up once the protagonists leave family and country behind is governed by an astonishingly hostile fortune. Stormy seas, dark caves, Memphis with its temples, palaces, and prisons, the fortress of Syene caught in the pincers of a spectacular siege—all threaten the young lovers. Up to a point, the descriptions of these places resemble those from the epic tradition. In the *Aeneid*, for instance, the stormy sea, the peaceful creek where Aeneas lands, and the magnificence of Carthage fill the Trojans' hearts with fear and hope. Yet epic characters, whether faced with adversity or with good fortune, live and fight in a world whose diversity is irreducible: Troy is not Carthage, and Carthage is not the new Troy waiting to be built in Italy. In the ancient Greek novel, the various obstacles the protagonists encounter seem to merge into one gigantic adversiarial force that isolates and torments them relentlessly.

A POLITICAL TYPOLOGY

Although uniformly hostile to the protagonists, the imperfect human world nevertheless contains remarkable political diversity. The *Ethiopian Story* begins in medias res, when a gang of bandits haunting the Nile delta finds a wrecked ship on the opposite bank, surrounded by dead bodies. An extraordinarily beautiful young woman rests on a rock not far from the site of the disaster, looking at a wounded young man who lies at her feet. Far from any lawful community, these two—Chariclea and Theagenes—are at the mercy of the greedy, lustful bandits. The gang knows no honor and no loyalty: its regime is one of *savage freedom*. Meanwhile, Kalasiris, temporarily separated from his protégés, recounts what happened before the shipwreck. He describes the *civilized freedom* of Delphi, an idealized incarnation of the Greek city, with its sumptuous ceremonies honoring Apollo. With all its freedom and respect for laws, Delphi cannot provide a refuge for the young couple's star-crossed love. Family and civic tradition threaten them just as much as, if not more than, do the gangsters in the Nile delta.

When the lovers reach Memphis, they meet the worst form of human organization, *savage authority*. Arsake is ruling Egypt while her husband, the Persian governor, is away. Smitten with Theagenes, she uses the institutions meant to defend public order—the law, the guards, prison—to indulge her passions. In the end, caught in the web of her own schemes, she has to let the lovers go. They spend some time in the Persian governor's military camp and take part in the siege of Syene before heading for Meroe, the Ethiopian capital. The fourth and last political regime, *civilized authority*, is perfected in Ethiopia before the reader's eyes when King Hydaspes, yielding to the demands of the enlightened crowd and the clergy, abolishes the custom of sacrificing foreign intruders to the gods. It is clear that savage regimes, whether free or tyrannical, deserve only contempt, but the novel also seems to say that neither freedom nor tradition alone can guarantee happiness. For Heliodorus, order is worth more than freedom (Theagenes, who comes from a Greek republic, chooses to live in the kingdom of Ethiopia), but compassion prevails over tradition (the king finally abolishes human sacrifice). Thus the novel appears to endorse monarchy, corrected and guided by an alliance between people and clergy, as the ideal form of civic organization—a view that might, incidentally, help explain the success of Heliodorus's novel in sixteenth- and seventeenth-century Europe.

THE FLAWLESS LOVERS; THEIR ALLIANCE WITH PROVIDENCE

Political reflections, however, remain mostly in the background of the *Ethiopian Story*, whose main stage is bursting with the tribulations of the couple in love. The novel is full of incidents reminiscent of the sort of classical comedy in which young love challenges parental authority—lies and stratagems, false illnesses, the lovers' flight. But in the comedies of Menandros, Plautus, and Terence, love is born and blossoms in the family home, and in the end the lovers come back to their parents to ask for forgiveness and approval. After letting youth aspire to self-rule, the comic plot unerringly moves toward reconciliation within the tiny familial milieu. By contrast, the feelings that unite Theagenes and Chariclea are on a worldwide scale. Their passion cuts family ties, breaks through the gates of the city-state, and, letting them sense their higher calling, leads them to seek and find happiness in the heart of Africa.

Traveling together, often in the most enticing solitude, the lovers never feel the gnawing of physical desire. This remarkable self-possession is a necessary condition for their successful separation from family and country, as well as a sign of their superiority over the rest of humankind. While in comedy love is usually impulsive and capricious, in the idealist ancient Greek novel, the strength of the protagonists' love guarantees their independence and self-respect. Always chaste, the lovers also reject all external temptations. (The exception is Clitophon, who momentarily yields to the passion of another woman at the end of book 5 of *Leucippe and Clitophon*. He does so, however, only because the woman in question has helped him recover Leucippe, his lost beloved.) Endowed with supernatural beauty, a visible mark of their divine election, Chariclea and Theagenes arouse the guilty desires of those around them. Pursued by other people's passions, they remain faithful to each other, and when in the end love unites their bodies, it is only because the longing for perfection has already united their souls. There is an apparent exception to this rule of chastity in *Chaereas and Callirhoe*, when Callirhoe, separated from her husband, is forced to share another man's bed. Yet her misfortunes, which end when Aphrodite helps her find her true husband again, call to mind the notion—rare in the ancient Greek novel—of the exiled soul suffering the humiliation of bodily life before returning to its heavenly home.

Strong and faithful, the protagonists of the *Ethiopian Story* do not waver under the blows of fortune. Shipwrecks, kidnapping, separation from one another, persecution, imprisonment, and torture have not the slightest influence on these creatures purer than crystal and tougher than steel. They never give in to adversity; they never negotiate with it—they always resist. It makes no sense, therefore, to deplore the absence of psychological growth in ancient Greek novels. These characters do not grow because they are perfect from the beginning. Their constancy and calm contrast strongly with the inexhaustible energy of the epic hero. Epic characters exist only insofar as they fight, their personal qualities—Achilles's anger, Ulysses's cunning, Aeneas's piety and valor—determining the nature of their conflicts. In tragedy, the characters' hubris—Ajax's pride, Clytemnestra's rage against Agamemnon, the rigid legalism of Creon and Pentheus—drives them down the wrong path. By contrast, the protagonists of idealist ancient Greek novels rarely take the initiative. They do not act; they merely *resist the ordeals* to which they are subjected. This is undoubtedly the reason why they lack specific features, their serene expressions and shining eyes making them seem more divine than human.

The lack of specificity might call to mind the stereotypical characters in fairy tales. When examined carefully, though, the characters in ancient Greek novels have a distinctive new feature: the inner space, the soul. Always stronger than the world around them, the star-crossed lovers aim to survive and, at the same time, to be worthy of their calling. Since the world in which the action takes place is so obviously imperfect, the heroes' ordeals and adventures draw attention to their strong souls, where love, faith, and respect for the moral good reside.

Idealist ancient Greek novels thus link two forces without which their plots would make little sense: on the one hand, a silent Providence, far above the world, yet always present; and on the other hand, its human associate—the hidden, inviolate space within the protagonists' souls. Wise Providence and the strong human soul seem to have set up an alliance against all that separates them: the natural world and human society. Thanks to this alliance, the star-crossed lovers do not fully belong to the surrounding world. And because they look at that world from a providential perspective, they perceive the transience and contingency of fortune's reign.

CONTINGENCY AND INNER SPACE

The *Ethiopian Story* begins on the banks of the Nile, and the meandering of the plot may at first seem quite disorderly. The story might as well have begun in the prison at Memphis, Chariclea and Theagenes could have been captured by the bandits *after* their time at Arsake's court, and they could have had many more adventures before reaching the Ethiopian capital. The young couple's adventures might indeed seem initially like a series of interchangeable episodes that could go on forever—the kind of awkward, incompetent plot that can never reach a credible conclusion. But the overwhelming sense of contingency is by no means a result of the author's lack of skill or imagination, nor of an inability to depict a world governed by stable laws. Instead, it represents a sophisticated reflection on human destiny.

In older narrative genres—myths, fairy tales, and epic poems—events are used sparingly, and each must throw some light on the characters' motives, as well as on the overall meaning of their lives. In the *Iliad*, the conquest of Troy is a punishment for the abduction of Helen, and Achilles decides to resume fighting to avenge the death of his friend Patrocles. In the *Odyssey*, Ulysses wanders across the Mediterranean because of Juno's hatred; he tears himself away from the beautiful Calypso and heads home because he cannot find true happiness far from his ancestral soil. Oedipus kills his father Laios on a public road because he must defend his right of way; his downfall is the gods' punishment for Laios's rape of the youth Chrysippos years earlier. The fairy-tale hero kills the dragon to save the king's daughter, then marries her because his valor must be rewarded. All these plots demonstrate the *coherence* of the world. Because idealist ancient Greek novels aim to depict the reign of fortune, that is, the surrounding world's *incoherence*, they have to use long series of episodes bound together by arbitrary links.

The realization that life is full of random, incoherent events is a belated, noteworthy achievement of human thought. To understand that human action and its results are *not* fully motivated—and therefore that a successful life requires both inner strength and the help of Providence—one needs to set oneself free from the impulse to find precise, even punctilious explanations, whether local or cosmic, for every single event. The old polytheistic system is particularly rich in such explanations, which match each phenomenon or event with an ad hoc myth about the intervention of a specialized deity. Ovid's *Metamorphoses* (finished in 7 AD) offers a superb who's who of such interventions. However, when human beings grasp the idea of a universal reason superior to the perceptible chain of events, the contingent side of their lives becomes apparent. Wisdom then consists in realizing that behind the profusion of vain, ephemeral incidents lurks a higher, sometimes incomprehensible order. The star-crossed lovers' long sequence of adventures rests on these insights. A string of tenuously linked episodes illustrates the instability of fortune, warns the reader against the false coherence of myths, fairy tales, and epic poems, and suggests that only virtue, tacitly helped by Providence, can grant the protagonists a happy ending.

Yet randomness is not the last word in the idealist ancient Greek novel. A closer look reveals that the seemingly random episodes are organized, even at the level of the visible world, by a set of principles more powerful than mere chronological succession. The political regimes portrayed in the *Ethiopian Story* offer a clear example. Beyond the storms, gangs of bandits, wars, and tyrants, the reader can grasp a coherent political view that explains the behavior of the different groups of characters and the earthly meaning of the protagonists' journey. The cruelty of Arsake, or the stupidity of the bandits, senselessly fighting among themselves over their loot, may seem to lack a credible motive within the plot; nevertheless, these episodes succeed in making palpable the ideas of savage freedom and authority. Although the meaning of each isolated incident is not always fully apparent, the careful reader eventually understands the abstract forces that govern most of these events. The idealist ancient Greek novel is a speculative genre.

The contrast between the seeming randomness of the events and the abstract categories that structure them has something to do with the difference between the characters' immediate perception of their ordeals and the reader's subsequent reflection on their meaning. By stringing incidents together without attributing each to an explicit cause, idealist ancient Greek novels try to show how human beings experience the present independently of previous or subsequent events—in short, how they are *surprised by life*. As we have seen, the protagonists' resistance to the whims of the world signals the existence of an inner, inviolate space. Similarly, in order to notice and be outraged by the arbitrariness of fortune, the characters must have their own individual perspective. Much later, Samuel Richardson would suggest this individual perspective by depicting the characters' inner feelings moment by moment, but the ancient Greek novel had a different method, staging a multitude of dramatic events and reversals to make manifest the heroes' subjective experience—the surprise of life and the difficulty of predicting the future. Byzantine frescoes, instead of calculating the dimensions of a figure as the human eye would see it, often use size to stress a character's importance, so that the figure of Virgin Mary is sometimes much larger than the less illustrious saints or angels around her. In the same way, the ancient Greek novel exaggerates the randomness of events in order to emphasize the mystery of the immediate future and let the protagonists' fortitude dazzle the reader.

||||||||||||||||||||||||||||

By portraying strong souls who resist the chaos of the world, the ancient Greek novels offered an early version of narrative idealism—the art of imagining fictional worlds based on ideals rather than on actual human behavior. Remembered and imitated in the Byzantine Empire but forgotten elsewhere, these novels would be rediscovered and deeply admired in Western Europe in the sixteenth century. In the meantime, the need for an uplifting representation of human ideals would be met by other narrative genres, the most influential being the chivalric story.

CHIVALRIC NOVELS

Chivalric stories, unlike ancient Greek novels, are about professional warriors and their heroic deeds. Yet just like their predecessors, these stories examine the ways in which people, irresistibly attracted by moral ideals, are hurt by the difficulty of implementing them in real life. The strength and virtue of knights-errant verge on implausibility, but the main issues they face are immediately recognizable and very human: how can the good and its normative consequences be so obvious to each of us and yet so often fail to rule the world? Why are principles of loyalty and generosity so compelling and yet so frequently violated?

The ancient Greek novel answers these questions by separating the star-crossed lovers from the rest of the world: love, virtue, and mutual faith require them to withstand ordeals but take as little initiative as possible. Chivalric novels are also set in a terribly imperfect world, but their protagonists take on the task of making it livable and just. Without ever doubting that they are part and parcel of this world, they relentlessly exercise their outstanding powers in the cause of justice. They pursue both *inclusion* and *superiority*.

JUSTICE, FAME, ADVENTURE

The lively period from the middle of the twelfth to the end of the thirteenth century gave birth to a great many narrative works: there were long poems inspired by ancient epic (Benoît de Sainte-Maure's *Roman de Thèbes*, ca. 1155, *Roman d'Eneas*, ca. 1165, and *Roman de Troie*, ca. 1170, adapted from Statius, Virgil, and Latin versions of Homer's *Iliad*); verse narratives celebrating the military exploits of Charlemagne and his paladins (e.g., *The Song of Roland*, mid-twelfth century) or describing the conflicts between them (e.g., *Raoul de Cambrai*, twelfth to thirteenth century, *Renaud de Montauban* or *Les Quatre filz Aymon*, twelfth century); Nordic epic poems, the best known being the *Nibelungenlied* (twelfth to thirteenth century); religious stories about the hereafter (e.g., *Visio Tnugdali*, ca. 1150); legendary lives of saints (e.g., *Vie de Saint Alexis*, eleventh century); tales of adventure and love (e.g., *Floris and Blanche-flour*, mid-thirteenth century); and, in a different literary key, allegorical narratives such as *Roman de la Rose* by Guillaume de Lorris and Jean de Meun (thirteenth century). This list is by no means exhaustive: there are many other kinds of medieval narrative, including stories about the formation of royal and aristocratic dynasties (e.g., Jean d'Arras's *Roman de Mélusine*, fourteenth century), as well as the Crusade cycle (e.g., the twelfth-century *Chanson d'Antioche*, which incorporates the mesmerizing fairy-tale story of the *Swan Knight*).

But the most successful group of medieval stories, the "Matter of Britain," deals with the adventures of the legendary King Arthur and his valiant knights. Their authors are some of the best poets of the twelfth and early thirteenth centuries: Chrétien de Troyes, who wrote in French, followed by the Germans Gottfried von Strassburg and Wolfram von Eschenbach, all familiar with the work of their immediate predecessors and their rivals. Later, among the vast number of chivalric stories written in prose in the thirteenth, fourteenth, and fifteenth centuries, many of those that remained popular until the beginning of the seventeenth century, or even the eighteenth, were linked directly or indirectly to the Matter of Britain, thanks in great part to the fifteenth-century *Morte d'Arthur* by Thomas Malory.

How close Arthurian romances are to actual medieval life is an open question, but the fictional worlds of chivalric novels do to some extent appear rooted in historical reality. In the tenth to twelfth centuries, although western European kingdoms were centralizing their administrations, local lords were still in charge of the management and defense of their fiefs, which gave them considerable responsibilities, as well as irresistible temptations for abuse. Knights served as trusted vassals to their feudal lords, helping to keep watch over vast stretches of land that escaped any authority other than the local, and they often rose to prominent positions through merit or matrimony.

What is now the western part of France belonged to an Anglo-Norman kingdom that flourished on both sides of the English Channel under the Plantagenet dynasty and extended as far south as Aquitaine. Neither this kingdom nor the German federation known as the Holy Roman Empire was ruled from the center. In both realms, assertive central power, whether temporal or spiritual, was unwanted. For the emperors of the German federation, the main worry was the Roman Church's struggle for supremacy in Europe. In the eleventh century, Hildebrand, Pope Gregory VII, declared all Christian knights to be vassals of St. Peter, meaning that their loyalty to the Church should supersede fealty to their feudal lord. His ambitions were not universally welcomed, and the Anglo-Norman Christianized version of the Grail legend underscores these feelings. In it, the biblical character Joseph of Arimathea carries to Britain the lance that pierced Christ's breast and the cup that collected his blood, suggesting a direct, non-Roman link between the sacred events in the Holy Land and the kingdom of Arthur.

Though connected to the times in which they were written, chivalric novels do not describe the medieval world in its actual details but, like the ancient Greek novels, illustrate a set of ideals. Knights are expected to *win fame* by outshining all potential rivals, courageously *enforce justice* once they are recognized as true heroes, and *be loyal* to their sovereign and true to their own word. They also feel the call of a highly civilized *courtly love* and of *service to God*; and when their kings misbehave, knights have a duty to *rebel*.

The society in which chivalric novels take place lacks a well-established system for keeping order and requires its members, especially the powerful ones, to abide by the law voluntarily. Human malice, however, ceaselessly breeds abuses and violence. Knights-errant, whose mission is to defend the persecuted, the weak, the widow, and the orphan, travel from place to place seeking out abuses and restoring justice. Since offenses are local, the knight's task can be performed relatively quickly, but as redress is scattered and piecemeal, there can be no truly decisive fight leading to a lasting stability. The vulnerability of the social order is a central theme, and nothing in chivalric romance occurs more frequently or energizes the characters more effectively than fresh upsurges of betrayal and violence.

The concrete form taken by these upsurges and the efforts to repulse them is the *adventure*. Day after day, at King Arthur's Round Table, in their own castles, or on the road, knights are on watch, waiting to be called for help. As soon as they learn that brutality and injustice have flared up anew, their chivalric oath, which prevails over any other desires and obligations, requires them to leave their friends, family, and sovereign, to drag themselves from the arms of their beloved, climb on their horses, and go off to fight. Knights are not mercenaries fulfilling a contractual obligation; they are heroes giving themselves to the world, and one can often sense a mysterious bond between a knight and his adventures, such that each adventure "looks for" a certain knight, and he alone can and must take it on.

However, their sense of mission does not require the knights to forswear all rewards. They yearn for recognition, and their adventures partly serve to gain them *fame*. Knights rush to defend the poor and the persecuted, but they are also stunningly assertive whenever there is an opportunity to prove their superiority over their rivals. A knight's honor would be soiled forever by the smallest sign of cowardice or reluctance to face a challenge. Consequently, in addition to *heroic* adventures—those that right scandalous wrongs—knights-errant willingly subject themselves to *qualifying* tests meant to assert their worth.

In the Catalan story *Tirant lo Blanc* by Joanot Martorell and Martí Joan de Galba (1490), the young hero undertakes eleven mortal combats to prove himself worthy, killing the eleven distinguished knights who have challenged him. The authors probably intended these eleven pointless slaughters as a mockery of the knights' unquenchable thirst for recognition. A century later, the chivalric addiction to fame would be one of the main targets of Cervantes's satire in the first part of *Don Quixote*. *Tirant lo Blanc* and *Don Quixote* are late novels, though. Earlier chivalric stories present the effort to prove one's worth in the best possible light.

In Chrétien de Troyes's *Yvain or The Knight with the Lion* (late 1170s), which reshapes an older Celtic legend whose contours are still perceptible in the Welsh *Mabinogion* (fourteenth century), the struggle for recognition and fame plays a crucial role. Both in *Yvain* and in the Welsh *Owein or the Lady of the Fountain*, the young protagonist's first act is a qualifying feat that publicizes his valor and earns him promotion. Yvain learns that his friend Calogrenant has passed by an enchanted spring, triggered its destructive force, but failed to defeat its irate guardian. Yvain rushes straight to the magic fountain, activates its harmful powers, fights the lord who guards it, and kills him. Does this amount to a crime? Not in *Yvain*'s mixture of fairy tale and chivalry, in which the fight legitimately tests the young knight's prowess. Having proved his worth, Yvain falls in love with the widowed lady of the fountain, Laudine, and with the help of Lunete, her benevolent lady-in-waiting, ends up marrying her. Since Laudine needs a strong fighter to defend her domain and its fountain, Yvain is elevated by marriage from simple knight to the enviable rank of "lord of the manor."

In his first adventure, Yvain seeks fame for its own sake and achieves it without righting any perceptible wrong. In other cases, qualifying adventures involve a fight for justice as well. In Wolfram von Eschenbach's *Parzival* (early thirteenth century), Parzival's father, Gahmuret, defends the beautiful Belacane, queen of the North African kingdom of Zazamanc, against the army of an unsuccessful suitor. Gahmuret wins the battle and marries Belacane, with whom he has a son, Feirefiz, Parzival's beloved half brother. In Gottfried von Strassburg's *Tristan* (early thirteenth century), the hero challenges and kills his parents' enemy Morgan, as well as the fearsome Morold (Morolt), scourge of Cornwall. Most of the first book of *Amadis of Gaul* by Garci Rodríguez de Montalvo (published in 1508 and based on a lost fourteenth-century work) is devoted to Amadis's building a reputation as a defender of justice. Describing his progress from boy wonder to young hero in great detail, the book is filled with difficult qualifying tests, all underscoring his invincibility and impeccable moral vision.

THE SKEWED SOUL, THE TEST OF LOYALTY

Amadis's perfection is a feature of late chivalric novels. In the twelfth- and early thirteenth- century stories, knights are not as spotless. These wellborn, highly energetic warriors often suffer from an inexplicable weakness that temporarily robs them of their sense of duty. Whereas in ancient Greek novels the star-crossed lovers always do the right thing, the knights-errant portrayed by Chrétien de Troyes, Wolfram von Eschenbach, and Gottfried von Strassburg do not hide within their breast a strong, impregnable citadel that safeguards their ideals against any temptation. There is an elusive kind of insufficiency in these knights' souls. It might be mere weakness, due to immaturity or forgetfulness, or it might reveal a painful conflict between different chivalric ideals. In the terms used by Bernard de Clairvaux (1090–1153), the *anima magna*, or great soul, of these knights can also be, at least to some extent, an *anima curva*, a slightly skewed soul.

This deficiency affects neither their fight for justice, which defines the knights' mission on earth, nor their struggle for fame and recognition. The more personal requirement of *loyalty*, however, is not as scrupulously observed. In some of the twelfth- and early thirteenth-century Arthurian stories, the male character breaks his commitments or falls in love with his sovereign's wife. Ready to face any challenge bravely and rush to vanquish evil, these heroes nonetheless do not know how to keep their own forgetfulness, distraction, or love from interfering with their duty. They cannot always fully reconcile their eminent place in the world, their superiority, with the duty and respect they owe the lady they love or the king they serve. In a society that cannot function without individual service and devotion, personal loyalty, that most essential feature, is also the most vulnerable.

Yvain, for instance, lightheartedly transgresses the code of loyalty, but later confronts his error and overcomes it. Despite winning recognition, requited love, and promotion to lord of the manor by slaying the enchanted fountain's defender, Yvain is not yet a true, faultless knight. When his friend Gawain persuades him to return to Arthur's court to continue jousting and fighting for a while, Laudine agrees on condition that her new husband will not stay away for more than a year (three months in the *Mabinogion*), and in Chrétien de Troyes's version, she offers him a magic ring that protects true, loyal lovers. Although Yvain pledges to observe the deadline, he forgets to return. A year later (three years in the *Mabinogion*), Lunete, the lady-in-waiting, arrives at Arthur's court, publicly accuses Yvain of disloyalty, and takes back the ring in Laudine's name. What follows is one of the most moving moments in Arthurian romance. Yvain realizes not only that he has lost his beloved, but that his word and his loyalty have been discredited in front of everyone. Stricken with grief, losing his senses, he tears his clothes off and runs to hide in the forest. This is not something that would happen in an ancient Greek novel, where the infallible characters entrust themselves to divine Providence, caring little for the world's opinion. For Yvain, who both belongs to the world and aspires to be better than it, the loss of his superiority calls for a self-imposed exclusion.

A contemporary reader may wonder about Yvain's behavior. Could a man who has just married the woman he loves leave her so soon after the wedding for a frivolous reason and for such a long time? And would she agree so easily? In a novel by Flaubert, a situation of this kind would seem out of place. But Chrétien de Troyes did not write nineteenth-century novels. The legends he took as models were based not on the observation of actual behavior, but on exemplary situations with their own significance. Why should Yvain, out of the blue, cross the country seeking a magic fountain, find it, trigger its power, and kill its legitimate defender? Not because young people in the twelfth century went around looking for enchanted springs and challenging the lords guarding them, but because a legendary knight is supposed to go through a qualifying test to earn fame and promotion. Why should Yvain leave his bride and forget to return for a year? Not because such things were done in the Duchy of Champagne or in the Anglo-Norman kingdom at that time, but because in order to gauge the hero's maturity and loyalty, a symbolic test is required. Far from reasoning that no real person would behave that way, Chrétien's public admired this strikingly unusual setup.

The whole story hinges upon Yvain's broken promise. Having failed the loyalty test, the young knight must prove his worth all over again. He begins to feel human again when two damsels and a lady treat his wounds and a hermit feeds him warm food. In the forest, Yvain meets and helps a lion, whose gratitude and devotion reawaken his moral sentiments. His physical and moral energy must now be put to use. Under the name "the Knight with the Lion," with his face hidden under a helmet, Yvain saves a maiden from being defiled by an evil giant and his servants, frees a large group of young women from an abusive master, and solves a judicial dispute between two sisters about their inheritance. Earlier in the novel, his fight at the enchanted fountain had merely shown how strong and fearless he was. By helping persecuted women earn sexual dignity, fair compensation, and equal access to wealth, Yvain reveals himself as a champion of justice. Having thus proved that he is a true knight, he returns to his beloved's castle, now ready to satisfy her legitimate demands for loyalty.

Love, Chaste and Adulterous

Chrétien de Troyes's *Yvain* offers a happy resolution of the tension between chivalric pursuits and the loyalty required by marital love. This resolution is possible because Yvain's love for Laudine is of the chaste, legitimate kind. Three features define it: chaste love does not interfere with the knight's calling, in particular with his commitment to justice and his loyalty to his superiors; it is not pursued for its own sake, but leads to matrimony; and in some situations, it is asymmetric. Yvain meets and falls in love with Laudine purely because he happens to have challenged and slain her husband. Once he is in love, marriage is his only aim, but Laudine does not accept him on the spur of the moment. She needs to be wooed, courted, persuaded.

Asymmetry allows women to weigh the merits of their suitors and condescend to hear their plea only when their worth is unquestionably proven. It can also be found in stories of illicit love, such as Lancelot's passion for Queen Guinevere in Chrétien de Troyes's *Lancelot, the Knight of the Cart* (after 1177), where it emphasizes the difference in rank between the lady and her courtly lover. However, when passion unites the two lovers against society, whether in the case of chaste love against the parents' will, as in *Floris and Blancheflour*, or in the context of the beloved's intended marriage to someone else, as in Chrétien de Troyes's *Cligès* (ca. 1176)—or, as we shall see, in *Tristan*—the young man and woman fall in love at first sight, as if the urgency of the situation dispenses with the delay usually required by courtly love.

Chivalric love, though, is not always legitimate and chaste. Pursued for its own sake, it prevents the knight from accomplishing his main task, the quest for justice, and this distraction is considered beneath his dignity and therefore worthy of punishment. In Wolfram's *Parzival*, the main character's two uncles, Anfortas, the wounded king of the Grail castle, and Trevrizent, the hermit who guides Parzival back to it, have chosen love in their youth as their only battle cry. Their mistake was severely punished, in Anfortas's case by an incurable injury, and in Trevrizent's by the loss of knighthood. Openly adulterous, Lancelot's love for Arthur's wife, Guinevere, clashes with the knight's loyalty toward his king. It obviously cannot lead to marriage. But it is as asymmetric, as obsessive, as frenetic as the early stages of chaste love. This frenzy has ominous consequences. Far from undermining Lancelot's martial strength, his guilty love fortifies it: he heroically rescues Guinevere from Méléagant, her kidnapper. But lack of loyalty corrodes the knights' world, indirectly contributing to its destruction, as reported in the French *Death of King Arthur* (thirteenth century) and in Malory's *Morte d'Arthur* (1485).

In Tristan and Isolde's story, the clash between adulterous love and loyalty reaches its apex. In the versions told by Béroul and Eilhart von Oberg, as well as those found in Thomas of Britain and Gottfried von Strassburg, Tristan and Isolde are portrayed as devoted lovers and eager partners in disloyalty. Their behavior is quite unusual. True, in the German epic poem *Nibelungenlied* (late twelfth century), the two women protagonists, Kriemhild and Brunhild, harbor an inextinguishable hatred against one another and skillfully hide their evil feelings. Brunhild brings about the death of Siegfried, Kriemhild's first husband, and Kriemhild orchestrates the destruction of the Burgundians who have killed him. But these women are epic heroines and, as such, can afford to be as angry as Achilles in Homer's *Iliad* and, in addition, to conceal their anger. Arthurian romance, on the other hand, usually depicts characters whose skewed souls, *animae curvae*, may fall prey to error yet remain open to remorse.

Tristan, strikingly, is not one of them. A wild, unruly energy runs through his story, giving its characters a dangerous depth—the depth of a passionate love that, not unlike the hatred of Kriemhild and Brunhild, must remain hidden from the eyes of the world. Endowed by legend with all kinds of perfections, Tristan is not only an invincible hero, but also a charming person, a crafty strategist, a hunter well-versed in the tricks of the trade, an accomplished musician, and a fluent speaker of several languages. Yet because he falls in love with Isolde, the Irish princess meant to marry his uncle King Mark, the young hero must sustain a long battle of ruses and counterruses against the monarch and his courtiers.

Like his beauty, courage, and generosity, the hero's resourcefulness is present in every variant of the story, from Thomas's (in French, ca. 1160) to Gottfried's German version (before 1210). They all describe a character adept at disguising himself, telling fibs, and taking advantage of his opponents' credulity. Most remarkably, although Tristan and Isolde sometimes grow weary of having to lead a duplicitous life, split between illicit passion and a lawful, but unbearable, existence at court, they never feel remorse for their dishonesty. Love, their story seems to say, sweeps away all other duties. This is not always the case in chivalric novels: Lancelot ends up feeling deep remorse for his adulterous affair with Guinevere. Why then does Tristan forget loyalty so easily and so permanently?

Earlier in the novel, Tristan fights the powerful Irish duke Morolt, who comes to Cornwall each year to collect his tribute of gold, silver, and, more ominously, Cornish young men and women. Tristan kills his opponent, freeing King Mark from the humiliating levy. During the fight, Tristan is seriously wounded, and because only the Irish queen, Morolt's sister and Isolde's mother, has the ointment that can heal his wound, he sails to Ireland. When Irish sailors are sent to check his boat, he pretends to be a merchant attacked, robbed, and wounded by pirates. At the Irish court, he tells the same story, asking for help. If the queen knew he was Tristan, slayer of her brother, she would undoubtedly kill him, but being deceived, she hosts and cures him.

The episode is crucial. Tristan's victory against Morolt should normally count as a qualifying feat that elevates a young knight's status, granting him marriage and lordship. In Tristan's case, however, victory does not lead to promotion or matrimony. King Mark understands his debt to his nephew and declares him heir to the crown, but envious courtiers press the king to take a wife, and Tristan complies, forfeiting his own reward to return to Ireland and woo the beautiful Isolde for his uncle. Neither Tristan nor the poet pronounces this forfeiture unjust. Yet by renouncing compensation, Tristan seems to accept that the world of lordship and matrimony is not for him.

Another world, an enchanted world of love, opens its gates to him. Passionate and illicit, Tristan and Isolde's love remains indifferent to marriage, lordship, heirs, dynasties, and powerful alliances. It is also a symmetrical feeling: unlike the ladies who let their knights pine for a while before accepting them, Isolde falls in love with Tristan right away and with an intensity equal to his. In Gottfried's version, she has befriended him during his first visit to her mother's court. Later, when he returns to woo her on behalf of King Mark, Isolde notices a notch in his sword that matches a metal splinter found in Morolt's head, and realizes he is the man who killed her uncle. Tristan lies in a bath before her, unarmed. She holds his sword in her hand, but her sympathy for him prevents her from avenging her uncle's death, as required by the law of retaliation. The magic potion the two lovers will later drink works not only as an aphrodisiac but also, perhaps, as a way of mitigating the implausibility of a lady of high rank falling in love so quickly and yielding so willingly.

Should one conclude from Tristan and Isolde's story that courtly love is essentially incompatible with wedlock? No—in fact, in Arthurian stories chaste love that leads to marriage is as chivalrous and respectful to the lady as illicit love. *Tristan*, far from being a typical example of courtly love, is one of the most unusual chivalric love stories. Gottfried goes out of his way to emphasize its strangeness. How can we not find it extraordinary—this self-sufficient passion that creates its own environment, keeps the lovers entranced, and persuades them to forsake the shared human world? Seen from love's dizzying distance, the laws of chivalry, loyalty included, mean little, and indeed, the two lovers feel no inner conflict or compunction for their actions. Their attempt to give up the common world may well seem a source of bliss, but it brings along its share of sorrow. It offers the delight of deceiving or simply forsaking their fellow human beings who understandably condemn illicit love, but it remains deeply painful: this renunciation can never lead to a stable, undisturbed fulfillment. Much later, Richard Wagner's opera *Tristan and Isolde* developed the tragic potential of this insight, portraying two lovers engaged in a gigantic struggle against the world, who reach ecstasy only in death. Gottfried does not go so far. His poem gracefully calls attention to the couple's deft maneuvers in deceiving the enemies of their passion. Sadness in this poem is never fully extricable from playful joy; joy always borders on pain. Alluring, intoxicating as it is, unchaste love fails to realize the chivalric ideal of keeping the lovers *in* the world and lifting them *above* it.

A Knightly Brand of Piety

The stories of the Holy Grail added an explicit form of knightly *piety* to the ideals of chivalry. Like Chrétien de Troyes's earlier and unfinished *Perceval, le Conte du Graal*, Wolfram's *Parzival* portrays a strong soul with a weak spot, in this case a mixture of naïveté, shyness, and inability to gauge people and situations. And as in the other chivalric novels of this period, the hero's actions are carefully motivated. In Chrétien's *Yvain*, the young knight's fit of madness occurs when he realizes his own disloyalty; in Gottfried's *Tristan*, the hero finds refuge in love when the world fails to reward his deeds properly. Parzival's naïveté is a result of his upbringing. His mother, Herzeloyde, has lost her beloved husband Gahmuret in a joust in faraway Baldac (Baghdad). Pledging never to let their son become a knight, she raises him in a forest where he will not see men, arms, or knightly exercises. But in spite of his ignorance, the young boy's nature takes over one day, when he meets a party of knights in shining armor, who look like gods to him. He rushes to Arthur's court to be dubbed a knight.

The mounted men Parzival meets on the road may look like gods, but they are not the true God. Beyond the chivalric virtues the young man duly acquires, a genuinely holy vocation awaits him. In his simplicity, he is unable at first to hear its call. Led by a mysterious power to the castle of Munsalvaesche, Parzival meets his uncle, the wounded King Anfortas, sees the Grail—a plate of garnet hyacinth—and shares the lavish meal it miraculously provides. He has been summoned there for a reason. Had he shown compassion and asked Anfortas about his illness, the king would have been healed and the young knight crowned as his successor. But Parzival fails to speak, and the next morning he finds that the king and his court have vanished.

As the richly ornate cathedral of Freiburg-im-Breisgau (1230–1330) differs from the graceful simplicity of its Norman counterpart at Coutances (1210–1274), so Wolfram's majestic, complex narrative contrasts starkly with Chrétien de Troyes's elegant, understated *Perceval*. The German *Parzival* includes many more characters and episodes alongside the main story line, some evoking a bygone time when Christians and non-Christians faced each other as true knights bound by the laws of honor—Gahmuret's adventures in Africa and the Near East are one example. Further exploits take place in a blurred geography that blends the Iberian lands with western France, England, and Wales: Gawan's feats of arms stand out here. A model of chivalric virtue, Gawan (Gawain) crowns his career by taking over the Castle of Wonders, owned by the sorcerer Clinschor. After passing the test of the Wonder Bed—a shower of stones and arrows followed by a struggle with a bloodthirsty lion—Gawan frees a crowd of ladies held prisoner by Clinschor.

In a narrative mode scholars call "interlacing," Gawan's path often crosses Parzival's, but the two warriors never become rivals. Gawan's domain is the earthly world, with its martial and magical dangers. His conflict with Clinschor is devoid of religious meaning—not unlike Yvain's fight at the enchanted fountain, it represents one of the many challenges a fearless knight must face. When Wagner wrote his *Parsifal* libretto in the nineteenth century, he merged Gawan's purely secular struggle against

Clinschor with Parzival's spiritual quest. In Wagner's opera, Parsifal performs the feats of Wolfram's Gawan as well as his own, while Clinschor, renamed Klingsor, turns into a treacherous former knight of the Holy Grail. But in Wolfram's narrative, magic is never seen as a fraudulent flight from religion. In accordance with medieval beliefs, magic belongs entirely to the human world, and since Parzival is meant to transcend it, defeating Clinschor is not his task.

This does not mean that Wolfram's hero ever fails to prove his knightly valor. Once Parzival gets over his youthful naïveté, he emerges from every encounter a faultless warrior, perhaps more so than Gawan. His only remaining flaw is anger against God, a painful corruption of the knightly brand of piety. One snowy Good Friday, after years of wandering in vain in search of Anfortas, Parzival meets the hermit Trevrizent and pours out his affliction. The hermit scolds him and gives a long sermon about God's love and the Grail's powers. Wagner did grasp the importance of this moment, whose faint echoes are heard at the beginning of *Parsifal*'s third act. Quite remarkably, unlike Yvain, Parzival does not have to go through a long and stressful ordeal to redeem his flaw. When the time is ripe, the Grail's power takes him back to the castle of Munsalvaesche, where he finally asks Anfortas the question that can put an end to the wounded king's suffering. Parzifal then becomes the new lord of the Grail and leader of the monastic community (modeled after the Order of the Templars)—but the depth of his earlier despair is not forgotten. As though to draw attention once more to that spiritual despair and its place in the story of the Grail, Trevrizent lets Parzival know that his very defiance has caused God to take pity on him. The character's redemption does not require a full break with his flawed past: his insubordination and his devotion are one in the eyes of God.

If Wolfram's *Parzival* achieves a synthesis between the chivalric ethos and the aspiration toward piety, later on, in *The Quest for the Holy Grail*, chivalric values become largely ornamental, bringing the religious quest to the fore. Part of the long, intricate *Lancelot* written in French in the early thirteenth century, *The Quest* is a successful literary work, but not for the reasons narratives usually please their readers. Motivation has virtually no place here, suspense disappears, and the story takes the form of a long ceremony whose stages are announced well in advance and whose symbolic meaning is solemnly revealed. Five of King Arthur's knights, Lancelot, Bors, Perceval, Gawain, and Galahad, are called to embark on the wondrous quest for the Holy Grail. Their adventures are not primarily of this world but point to a higher, spiritual realm.

At every step, a saintly man explains the religious meaning of events. Perceval, for instance, alone on a mountain peak, witnesses a struggle between a lion and a magic serpent, and rushes to help, killing the serpent and befriending the lion. Falling asleep, he sees two ladies, one riding a lion, the other a serpent. When he wakes up, a man in priestly garb tells him that the lady mounted on the lion signified the New Law, while the lion itself was Christ, bringing faith and hope, belief and baptism. The knights meet other priests or monks who reveal the Legend of the Tree of Life and the Story of the Three Tables—the table of the Last Supper, that of Joseph of Arimathea, and the Round Table of King Arthur—as well as the story of the Grail's journey from the Holy Land to Britain. All those who take part in the quest are helped and enlightened, but only Galahad, the incarnation of knightly and saintly perfection, is allowed to glimpse the Holy Grail at the moment of his death. A seemingly Arthurian story thus becomes a symbolic narrative of mystical union with God.

The contrast with Heliodorus's *Ethiopian Story* could not be more striking. While in the ancient Greek novel the individual's strong soul has forged a stable, permanent alliance with Providence, the deity in *The Quest for the Holy Grail* tempts and tests the knights, setting traps along their way, letting them waver, wander, and sometimes despair. The God of this story is hidden and incomprehensible. In other chivalric stories, knights-errant strive both to prove that they are part of the world and to serve God by rising above it. The *Quest* disturbs their self-possession, undermines their links with the visible world, and wears out their sense of superiority.

Religion here remains close to the wealth of magical elements inherited from older legends and folktales. The enchanted fountain in *Yvain*, the Wonder Bed in *Parzival*, and the love philter in *Tristan* all play a central role in the plot, and in the *Grail* cycle these elements are given still more weight, creating a mixture of Christianity and folk magic. In many late chivalric novels in prose, including *Amadis of Gaul* and *Palmerin of England*, the world is hardly recognizable as Christian—full of sorcerers, witches, giants, dwarfs, talking animals, and objects with supernatural powers.

A Perfect, Rebellious Knight

The knight who has a flaw and struggles to overcome it is one of the most appealing features of the early Arthurian novels. As time went by, however, chivalric narratives focused more and more on the figure of the perfect knight. Perfect knights are mostly content to perform their usual duties as fighters and lovers, but sometimes they must serve another ideal, that of *rebellion against tyranny*. Indeed, rebellion is crucial in *Amadis of Gaul*, a major target of Cervantes's polemic against chivalric romance. Now virtually forgotten outside Spanish-speaking countries, *Amadis of Gaul* is nevertheless a remarkable work: written late, it includes many of the elements present in earlier chivalric novels as well as some innovations. Unlike the early Arthurian romances in verse—barely remembered between the fifteenth century and the eighteenth, when they were redis-covered by scholars, writers, painters, and musicians—*Amadis* continued to be read avidly from the time of its publication until the very end of the eighteenth century. Consequently, it epitomized the chivalric novel for many writers, Cervantes included, and from the middle of the sixteenth century to the beginning of the seventeenth, it became a target for those who wanted to discredit this kind of story. They did not quite manage it, though, and when Romanticism revived the enthusiasm for chivalric nov-els, *Amadis* was translated into English by Robert Southey and enjoyed a new, if short-lived success.

The novel's present lack of popularity must have something to do with its length and clumsy construction. The three textual blocks that compose it, visibly by different authors, do not fit smoothly together. The first book, about Amadis's education as a warrior, is quite different from the second, which tells of his ordeals in love, and from the rest of the novel, which is strongly influenced by Renaissance rhetoric. In the eighteenth century, neoclassicists looked down on churches with a Ro-manesque choir, a Gothic transept, and a baroque rood-loft, but with the nineteenth-century revival of interest in the medieval period, these critics came to seem narrow-minded. Likewise, *Amadis* may at first sight seem strange and unwieldy, but in the end, like a monument built slowly over centuries, it makes a strong impression.

In contrast with the heroes of early chivalric romance, Amadis is flaw-less. No weakness, no hesitation, no secret fault ever affects his strong soul during his long, winding sequence of adventures. In the first book, loyalty and the readiness to fight for justice emerge as the principal vir-tues, with terrible consequences for their violation. In chapter 13, travel-ing at night in an unknown land, Amadis reaches a castle and asks for shelter. Dardan, the lord of the castle, refuses to open the gate, scoffs at Amadis, and then, adding insult to injury, turns down his challenge to fight. It soon becomes clear that the arrogant lord, while trying to win the love of a young beauty, has been persecuting her stepmother. When Amadis finally fights and defeats Dardan in single combat, the young beauty abandons her admirer and offers herself to the knight. Dardan is thus forced to confront the effects of disloyalty, and, hurt just as much as he has hurt others, he ends his own life.

The ideal of chaste love governs the second book. But can perfect love—calm, considered, consensual—really exist? Beautiful Oriana, daughter of King Lisuarte of England, has her doubts. She suspects Ama-dis of disloyalty and forbids him ever to appear before her (bk. 2, chap. 44). The great warrior submits meekly to his beloved's arbitrary orders and withdraws into the wilderness, accompanied by the hermit Nas-cian. The perfect knight does not protest because, once he is deprived of

Oriana's quasi-miraculous protection, his energy and martial valor vanish. Oriana, who at first sight appears human, also behaves like a goddess, floating far above her knight and the surrounding world.

Here, the blend of inclusion and superiority involves not only the knight but his lady as well. They both have special powers—martial in his case, mysteriously protective in hers—and both are expected to be fully engaged in their community and their life as a couple. Each is presented as a human being, sensitive to adversity and desire, but at the same time, each moves in a celestial orbit from which they can influence other people's destiny. Purely human yet magically transcendent, they act both within and above the world.

The last two books depict the vast conflict between King Lisuarte—once a noble monarch, now a tyrant—and his disappointed knights. The chivalric ideal requires them to rebel. The uncivilized Roman prince, Patin, falls in love with Oriana and asks Lisuarte for her hand. Secretly married to Amadis, Oriana is horrified, but her father, flattered at the prospect of becoming Rome's ally, agrees to give her to Patin against her will. Under Amadis's leadership, the outraged knights rally against the king. Amadis and Lisuarte, who have become skilled politicians, send ambassadors to friendly courts to request support. Slowly, two coalitions develop, while the sorcerer Arcalaus assembles a third army and awaits the result of the war, planning to attack the victor and secure worldwide supremacy. After winning the battle, Amadis is crowned king and leaves the task of seeking further adventures to his son Esplandian.

The majestic rhythm of the last two books of *Amadis*, especially the fourth, comes not only from the plot's unhurried advance and the relative absence of episodic detours, but also from the frequent speeches that embellish the action. In the first book, the need to defend the weak and persecuted is understood without further explanation; in the second, Amadis must obey his lady, withdraw from human society, and reflect in silence; but in the last book, eloquence is required for the revolt against political corruption. The heroes transform into orators, proficient in the Renaissance rhetoric of wisdom and justice. This change was widely noticed, and in 1559 a *Treasure of Amadis* was published, with discourses for various occasions taken from the French translation of the novel. Reprinted more than twenty times, the anthology soon became available in English and German.

|||||||||||||||||||||||||||||||

Chivalric novels opened up narrative idealism to a wider variety of beliefs and values, most importantly the individual's sense of being included in society and having to demonstrate superiority over it. The knight-errant embodies a broader range of ideals than the old, warlike epic heroes or

Heliodorus's perfect souls persecuted by fortune. The search for fame, prowess in the cause of justice, loyalty, courtly love, piety, and occasional rebellion against unjust rulers form a potent mix, creating one of the most appealing human types ever devised by fiction.

While staying faithful to their idealist framework, chivalric stories were sensitive to the actual feudal organization of society. They identified the system's most vulnerable point—its reliance on personal loyalty—and used it to show the fallibility of even the best of men. Over time, however, the pressure to describe perfect souls prevailed, ushering in the flawless characters who populate the late chivalric novels in prose.

CHAPTER 2

Helpless Souls, Tricksters, and Rascals

||||||||||||||||||||||||||||||||||||||||||||||||||||||||||||||||||||||||||

Like elite runners who get ahead of the pack at the very beginning of the race, the exemplary characters in ancient Greek and chivalric novels show their superiority early on. One can only look at them in awe, acknowledging their intrinsic preeminence. The lives and adventures of these characters appeal to our instinctive Platonism, the pleasure we feel when contemplating perfection.

Although the novelists who idealize human behavior deliberately make their protagonists implausibly faultless, they also create antagonists of the opposite type. For much as readers delight in the spectacle of excellence, they know that human nature has another, less praiseworthy side. Chariclea's virtue seems even more striking when set against the villainy of Arsake, the Persian governor's wife. Idealist novels have wicked people as antagonists and minor characters in order to enhance the normative appeal of the protagonists.

By contrast, in anti-idealist narratives, the main characters are always busy acting as they *should not act*. It is difficult, though, to cast a genuinely wicked individual as the protagonist in a long narrative. Why would readers sustain interest in and sympathy for someone whose actions are relentlessly evil? Tragedy can afford to focus on such characters—Shakespeare's Richard III, for instance—perhaps because the public knows that within a couple of hours they will be punished. In the eighteenth century, it became possible for narratives to give evil people a leading part. But for a long time, anti-idealist narratives carefully avoided repelling their readers. They treated protagonists either lightly, as helpless souls; as funny tricksters, with humor as a protective barrier between their deeds and the reader; or, finally, as true rascals who nevertheless keep an ounce of moral sense and can in the end switch over to the right side.

HELPLESS SOULS

Helpless souls simply lack the strength and courage to behave well. They observe the world's deficiencies or participate in them without ever fully understanding what is going on or how to respond. As powerless *witnesses* or innocent *losers*, they have a sense of what people ought to do, but are unable to act accordingly.

One of the earliest narratives featuring a helpless protagonist is Petronius's *Satyricon* (first century AD), copied throughout the Middle Ages, but translated too late to have an impact on the early modern novel. The surviving fragments of *Satyricon* may indicate the existence of earlier idealist novels—Petronius could be offering a comic alternative to their incorruptible characters. Roaming a world haunted by magic and superstition, Encolpius, the narrator and main character, fails to remedy his sexual failures and vaguely senses that he has no control over his fate. Yet, at least in the parts of the book that have been preserved, he never experiences a deeper feeling of inadequacy.

Satyricon is about a loser, a harmless one. One influential early example of a powerless witness figure can be found in Apuleius's *Golden Ass* (second century). Lucius, changed into an ass by a magician's mistake, watches a variety of comic adventures from the sidelines, participating only minimally and by accident. After observing other people's malice extensively, he recovers his human form thanks to the intervention of a deity, to whom he henceforth devotes himself. Like the multiple ordeals suffered by the protagonists of idealist novels, the sequence of seemingly unrelated comic adventures in *The Golden Ass* suggests a coherent, hostile world governed by fortune. Like idealist characters, Lucius gets acquainted with the world's evil without being affected by it—thanks in his case to his animal incarnation rather than to some inner strength. And just as idealist novels include secondary episodes about more fallible characters, *The Golden Ass* has the story of Eros and Psyche in it, to lift the moral tone. Psyche travels all over the world to find her beloved Eros, whom she has lost because she could not resist the desire to see his face. Caught in the shape of an ass, Lucius understands that the body is a prison which separates human beings from the invisible realm of the divine. Both Psyche the true lover and Lucius the helpless witness are tested by a long ordeal before liberation arrives from above.

TRICKSTERS, ANIMAL AND HUMAN

Always comical, tricksters come in several varieties; the most popular are the *rogue*, motivated by his own base self-interest, and the *saucy devil*, whose misdeeds do not necessarily serve any particular selfish purpose but may simply be clownish maneuvers designed to disrupt other people's lives.

The trickster—the rogue in particular—is so threatening to the requirements of social life that across cultures, tales of lonely, cunning, and unscrupulous scoundrels often portray them as animals. In Apuleius, Lucius's animal form serves to isolate him temporarily from the rest of humanity but otherwise has minimal impact on his interactions with the world. In many stories about animal rogues, though, their beastly behavior is used to expose the lowest forms of human villainy, and since their reprehensible actions are only indirectly, ironically attributed to human beings, the descriptions of them can afford to be as daring as possible, while still remaining palatable.

By far the punchiest story of this kind is the anonymous *Roman de Renart* (*Reynard the Fox*), written in verse in French by one or several contemporaries of Chrétien de Troyes during the end of the twelfth century and the beginning of the thirteenth. It describes the shameless deeds of Reynard the Fox and the constantly thwarted attempts by animal society to punish him as he deserves.

In the first and best-known of the cycle's "branches" (as philologists call the story's quasi-independent episodic sequences), Isengrin the Wolf, a high-ranking member of the animal council presided over by King Noble the Lion, lodges a complaint against the Fox for the alleged rape of his wife, the beautiful Dame Hersent. Reynard is far away, hiding in his castle, and because Dame Hersent firmly denies the charge—she lies—the Wolf's complaint is set aside. Just then, a funeral procession arrives, carrying the remains of a hen Reynard has killed; it turns out that he has also devoured the Hen's five brothers. Profoundly upset, the Lion King cries, moans, and pledges revenge. Reynard's case worsens when the Hen, from beyond the grave, starts performing miracles, curing the Rabbit of a bad cold and the Wolf of an earache he conveniently develops.

Brun the Bear is dispatched to bring the villain to court. Reynard welcomes him and coaxes him into looking for a beehive in the trunk of an oak tree. The tree hides an ambush, but the Bear, trapped and beaten, manages to escape, returning badly wounded to the Lion's court. The scandalized monarch sends another emissary, Tibert the Cat, and Reynard directs him to a priest's house where, supposedly, countless mice are living. Having stolen three hens and a rooster from this priest, Reynard knows he has set a trap for him, and the Cat, looking for the nonexistent mice, duly falls into it. His efforts to get away wake the priest, his concubine, and their son, who believe they have caught Reynard, and rush to kill him. During the fight, the Cat bites off one of the priest's testicles. While his lady faints at the sight, and her son tends to her, the Cat breaks out of the snare and runs away.

The comedy continues. The next emissary, Grimbert the Badger, persuades Reynard to repent, confess his sins, and come to court. After a tempestuous debate, the royal council sentences Reynard to death and he is brought to the gallows. Grimbert the Badger, however, privately convinces the Lion to pardon the Fox, who takes a solemn oath not to misbehave anymore: to prove his remorse, he puts on a hair shirt and, with a cross on his shoulder, goes on a pilgrimage, presumably to the Holy Land. Once at a safe distance from the Lion's court, the Fox catches the Rabbit for dinner, gets rid of his cross and hair shirt, and jeers at the king in the coarsest terms. The Lion's army pursues him, but the lucky Reynard manages to arrive safely at his impregnable castle.

Reynard the Fox represents a special kind of individual-outside-the-world: the *individual-who-spits-on-society*. His independence results from his readiness to satisfy the basest personal needs and whims against all rules of morality and decency. No higher authority, no internalized ideals of virtue, no scruples, no self-respect ever trouble him. In a way, Reynard is right to despise a society that tries but never manages to discipline him. He has opted for Will and Power, and does as he likes. Society, by contrast, pretends to be ruled by Fairness and Reason, yet virtually all its members are split between a public spectacle of just, courageous behavior and the secret urge to give in to their appetites, whether gastronomic (for the Bear and the Cat) or sexual (for the Lion's wife in the second episode, or the She-Wolf throughout the cycle). The king's council is a parody of justice, the war a show of ineptitude; noblemen are quarrelsome, priests lustful. Dumb, credulous, vain, and impulsive, these animals who cannot master themselves are easy prey for Reynard. The trickster prospers in a *society of self-righteous imbeciles*.

You might expect the rogue's abuses and the society's brainlessness to inspire revulsion and revolt. Yet *Roman de Renart* makes its readers laugh. Why? The villains in a tragedy, say, Richard III in Shakespeare, or the Cardinal in Webster's *Duchess of Malfi*, look and sound scandalously different from other people, confounding the public's conventional moral expectations, almost as though they were intruders into the human world. It is difficult to feel any sympathy for them that might mitigate our disapproval of their actions. Sometimes the villain is designed to elicit a certain amount of compassion alongside the repugnance. This is true of Claudius in *Hamlet*, yet even he is perceived as foreign to generally accepted ideals and norms. When, on the other hand, fiction highlights *ordinary* imperfection, portraying rogues or fools whom readers may find more or less recognizable from their own experience, the mixture of disapproval and familiarity provokes laughter.

The laughter inspired by *Roman de Renart* is of the cynical variety—that of Diogenes, patron philosopher of cynicism, signaling both contempt and complicity. Readers laugh because, although they may well be just as corrupt as these tricksters and fools, they feel somehow superior, insofar as they can distance themselves, laughingly, from the behavior they are reading about. That distance also protects readers from the trickster's more outrageous actions—his fits of rage, his explicit hatred of the Good. The episode in which Reynard goes to confession and ends up eating the priest—the Kite—is both one of the most hilarious and the most shocking in the whole cycle. Few literary texts written before Rabelais are as jocularly shameless as the debate between Fox and Kite about Dame Hersent, who strikes Reynard as the most beautiful female on earth, while the Kite sees her as a sinister old hag. Later, Reynard openly advocates vice, praying to God to protect all thieves, traitors, and felons, all hardened sinners, and all those who live by cunning and snatch whatever they can. The individual-who-spits-on-society knows how to preach evil.

Remarkably, though, this creature does not live and prosper entirely outside the world. Reynard is a lord of the manor and a member of the royal council: he mistreats his peers and neighbors from a position of power and privilege, so the social network he despises and abuses is in fact essential to him. To be a successful outsider, this kind of rogue also needs, to some extent, to be an insider.

LAUGHTER AND VIRTUOSITY

If we skip a few centuries (during which comic literature continued to prosper, especially in the shorter form of the *fabliaux*, as well as in the theater), we can find another outsider-insider in the Rabelais character Panurge, an incarnation of the "saucy devil" who makes mischief for the sheer pleasure of causing trouble for other people, without necessarily seeking any personal advantage.

Rabelais's *Gargantua* (1534) and *Pantagruel* (1532), followed by the *Third* and *Fourth Books* (1546, 1552), emphasize the pleasure of telling as much as the story told. Always eager to make his reader laugh, the author is conspicuously present in the text and displays an unparalleled linguistic virtuosity. His humor blends a compulsive show of learning with, in the first two books, a predilection for bodily functions, digestive—eating, drinking, urinating, and defecating—and, to a lesser extent, sexual.

In *Pantagruel*, the reader learns about a young giant, Pantagruel, son of Gargantua, King of Utopia, his long list of ancestors—a mixture of mythological names and puns on sexual organs—his prodigious appetite as a child, his studies in Paris, and his later adventures. In Paris, after browsing through hundreds of ludicrously titled books, Pantagruel meets Panurge, who tries to make himself understood by talking in fourteen languages (German, Italian, Celtic, etc.), French being the very last. Panurge's calling in life is to make trouble by targeting young scholars and women, whom he persecutes to the author's great delight.

Yet learning, laughter, and lack of decorum are not Rabelais's only interests. *Gargantua*, an account of Pantagruel's father's childhood and youth, aims higher. It is a parody of books about the education of a prince, such as Xenophon's *Cyropaedia*, and at the same time a plea on behalf of humanist culture. Still interspersed with bawdy speeches and debates about why a young lady's thighs feel fresh (chap. 39) or what object makes as the best bottom-wiper (chap. 13; answer: a little bird), *Gargantua* portrays the main character's growth from a spoiled, ignorant brat into a wise, dignified leader.

As a child, Gargantua studies under tutors specializing in useless medieval grammar and logic, until a neighboring king brings over a well-trained young page, who gives an elegant speech in classical Latin. Gargantua's father hires the page's preceptor. The new teacher, a humanist, takes the young giant to Paris, where, on arrival, he urinates on the multitude, drowning 260,418 Parisians, not counting the women and children. For a while, his teacher lets him continue with his earlier routine. Gargantua sleeps late, doesn't do any exercise, eats his fill, studies very little, and plays more than two hundred different games. Soon, however, a new schedule is implemented, requiring the young prince to wake up early, listen to a reading from the Scriptures, pray, observe the sky, get washed, perfumed, and dressed (while practicing the lessons learned the day before), read for three hours, then do sports, eat lunch while discussing the properties and virtues of the food, and continue his day with a myriad of other useful, honorable activities until late at night when, after once more observing the sky, with its comets and constellations, he has to pray and glorify God the Creator before going to sleep.

Meanwhile, his father's kingdom gets involved in a war with a neighboring country. Appointed commander of the army, Gargantua wins the war and—to reward Brother Jean, a valiant monk who has helped him during the hostilities—founds a new abbey at Thélème, meant to remedy the flaws of current monastic life. The abbey accepts both men and women on condition that they are handsome and well built; its motto is: "Do as you please." The brutish bodily life of the beginning of the book—the overeating and drinking, the shameless scatology—has now been left far behind. Wild nature is tamed, and Gargantua and his friends at Thélème reconcile natural life with the rules of wisdom.

None of these books is structured around a conflict—not *Gargantua*, not *Pantagruel*, nor the books about Pantagruel's later adventures, least of all the *Third Book*, which interminably, hilariously, debates whether the troublemaker Panurge should marry or not. The books include martial episodes that parody the *chansons de geste* and late chivalric novels in prose, but war is only one aspect of the heroes' progress, relentlessly impeded by never-ending digressions and comic scenes, toward a spiritual utopia: in *Gargantua*, the abbey of Thélème; in the apocryphal *Fifth Book*, which concludes Pantagruel's story, the Ringing Island, a mystical allegory.

In spite of its energy and verve, Rabelais's prose remained marginal for a long time. Women, the most dependable reading public for fiction, were not interested in his violent misogyny, mainstream teachers and scholars ignored the author who mocked them so viciously, less learned people failed to grasp his plethora of bookish allusions, and, from the sixteenth to the eighteenth century, society as a whole—busy trying to improve manners and social niceties—tended to shy away from Rabelais's irreverent style of humor. Several excellent comic novels were written during this period, but none attempted to imitate Rabelais's verbosity, his direct approach to bodily functions, or his passion for erudite references.

He began to be appreciated later, after Laurence Sterne, in the eighteenth century, rediscovered the pleasure of delaying a narrative's progress with lengthy, funny digressions, making wit and verve a goal just as important as character and plot, or more so. Twentieth-century modernists considered Rabelais a precursor of their own stylistic dexterity and conviction that good literature must treat the world with a certain degree of sarcasm. Thus Rabelais and Sterne became patron saints of high modernism, and indeed Rabelais's style and laughter definitely reverberate in the prose of major twentieth-century writers like James Joyce and Milan Kundera.

Amoral Pícaros

To offer an effective alternative to the idealist novel, wickedness and laughter are not enough. Spanish, German, and English picaresque novels showed the disquieting, sinful face of the trickster in an increasingly serious manner.

The rise of the picaresque cannot be fully understood without reference to two major historical developments. The conquest of America and the gold rush that followed had severe social and economic consequences in Spain, destabilizing crafts and trade, and exacerbating poverty. The bitter conflict between the Reformation and the Counter-Reformation intensified the promotion of religious dogmas and values. Picaresque novels bear witness to both these trends. The earlier ones focus on the way in which poverty destroys moral incentives: their protagonists are *amoral* pícaros who, out of naïveté or cynicism, live at peace with their own wickedness. Soon, however, these characters gave way to *morally aware* pícaros, who deplore their corrupt lives in religious terms, humbly acknowledging a higher order whose strictures they are unable to follow.

The Life of Lazarillo de Tormes (anonymous, 1554) is the autobiography of an amoral trickster. The son of a miller convicted of theft and a mother of dubious morals, Lazarillo must win his bread and shelter under several masters, all of them poor, stingy, or corrupt. He learns the art of stealing from a blind beggar and perfects his skills in the house of an avaricious priest. He then serves an indigent squire who depends on Lazarillo's talents for his food, a friar who loves secular pleasures, a preacher who sells fake indulgences, a painter, a chaplain, and a sergeant. In the end, Lazarillo is given the royal office of town crier in Toledo and marries the chambermaid of the archpriest, with whom he obediently shares her favors.

The world is uniformly hostile to Lazarillo, whose masters, regardless of the order in which he serves them, are unable or unwilling to fulfill their most elementary obligation: to feed him. As in the oldest idealist novels, the sequence of episodes does not form a well-structured plot. The time Lazarillo spends serving the penniless squire has little to do with his woes while working for the grasping priest, or with the indulgence seller's frauds. Yet every time, Lazarillo is confronted with the same difficulties, as though his various masters, each in his own way, embodied a larger force that threatens the pícaro's daily survival.

Lazarillo's abject poverty forces him to think of little else but food and shelter, and, because his wretched origins preclude a return to his family, the only fate he can imagine for himself is to remain a crook. Since the bonds of trust—especially truthfulness and respect for property—do not apply, Lazarillo has not the slightest scruple about cheating and robbing even the blind beggar who taught him to steal. The only master for whom he feels a certain amount of affection is the impoverished squire, who could live comfortably if he could find a powerful lord to protect him. The squire aspires to live by a code of personal loyalty but complains that even if he could find a protector, such a lord would probably appreciate servility over true loyalty. Lazarillo treats the squire gently, sensing that this particular master is even more helpless than he is.

Amoral pícaros are too busy struggling for survival to notice how lonely they are, but the attentive reader will realize that they never fall in love or seek a stable union. Lazarillo feels no romantic desire for his wife, and her affair with the archpriest does not bother him. Similarly, for Pablos of Segovia, the main character in Quevedo's *The Swindler*

(1626), love affairs are nothing but deception and debauchery. Since love is based on *promise*, the promise of happiness inherent in it and the vows exchanged by lovers, a world in which promises are void, vows futile, and loyalty a worthless dream can neither give birth to love nor shelter it. Picaresque novels do not explicitly target and reject the cult of love, but by excluding it from the pícaro's life, they imply, in opposition to idealist novels, that individual feelings depend on the individual's bonds with society.

The genre is particularly interested in the way the social structure regulates these bonds. Pícaros live in a society of *well-defined stations in life*: noblemen, soldiers, priests, craftsmen, merchants, thieves, and beggars. In their struggle against poverty, pícaros see society from below, noting the mores of its different groups, and learning its rules and conventions in order to transgress them for profit. In episode after episode, Lazarillo and Pablos de Segovia take the reader into a world whose ugliness and amorality do not allude, even negatively, to beauty and generosity. Within this world, their stories seem to say, the sources of the good, be they divine or human, have run dry: social norms are imposed by sheer brutality, and the bonds between people have been degraded beyond all remedy.

Only one glimmer of light is visible in this dark environment: the sneer of the villains who are pleased with themselves, the sardonic laughter of drunkards and thieves, which Velázquez captured so well in his painting *The Drunkards* (El Prado, Madrid). "Go on, try and deny that you're just like us," the red-nosed man seems to spit at the viewer, leaning unsteadily on someone's shoulder. "Just try and pretend you don't envy us! Join us if you've got the guts to enjoy your own villainy!" This cynical, defiant laughter can be felt throughout *The Swindler*. It spices up the pícaro's dishonesty with a dash of insolence—the same insolence displayed, much later, by some of Dostoevsky's most repulsive characters, along with their noisy remorse.

Preaching Pícaros

Morally aware pícaros, by contrast, never fully accept their own wickedness. Their tale is always interspersed with righteous references to God, salvation, and good behavior, and the two layers of their story—their evil deeds and their high-minded sermons—are woven together by the first-person narration. Pícaros have to narrate their lives themselves. They are not exemplary, virtuous characters like those in the idealist ancient Greek and chivalric novels, nor are they eminently visible types, wrongdoers in high places, like Reynard, or slapstick princes like Gargantua. Hidden at the very bottom of the social scale, pícaros are small-time

crooks whose forays into the upper echelons, when they occur, soon
end in catastrophe. Why would anyone but they themselves care to tell
their story?

Besides, tales about such people appeal to readers only insofar as they
manage to reveal something remarkable about humanity. Many exemplary characters, whether excellent or reprehensible, act in ways that
lift them high above common mortals. I might revere the same ideals as
Chariclea or Yvain, but I clearly do not measure up to them. Similarly,
laughing at Gargantua's adventures makes me feel close to him, but his
dimensions are much larger than mine. The behavior of the pícaros, on
the other hand, places them beneath most other people. Yet, as picaresque
stories remind us, even the lowest human beings have the capacity to look
at themselves and understand the depths of their own corruption. The
pícaros and pícaras speak in the first person not only because no one else
knows or cares about all the true details of their wrongdoings, but also
because self-examination is the best way for them to come to terms with
their own wickedness.

Looked at this way, the stories of morally aware pícaros and pícaras
are linked to the individual self-scrutiny promoted by both the Reformation and the Counter-Reformation, whose model was St. Augustine's
spiritual autobiography *Confessions*. For Augustine, God is not only the
creator and ruler of the world, but also the intimate voice directing the
soul toward the good. Self-examination uncovers the truth of human corruption and, at the same time, makes it easier for the God hidden in the
soul's depths to act upon it. Similarly, the moralizing pícaros and pícaras
are involved *both* in deeds that flout the good *and* in a relentless meditation that condemns these deeds. They supplement action with reflection
and speak in two voices, the ruthless *swindler's* and the judicious *preacher's*. The wiser voice always belongs to a later stage in the character's life
when, looking back, he or she tells the story of his or her immoral youth,
wonders how such wickedness was possible, and reflects pessimistically
on human nature in general.

In Mateo Alemán's *The Life of Guzmán de Alfarache* (1599), the swindler has one adventure after another while the moralist/preacher delivers extensive sermons full of edifying anecdotes. As a result, the novel
reaches a remarkable length, about fourteen times that of the *Life of
Lazarillo* and six times that of *The Swindler*. It is a heavy, verbose, mis-
anthropic work requiring considerable patience from its readers, yet in
the end it leaves a powerful impression. Like most early novels, idealist
or not, it consists in a long, lively chain of episodes. Don Guzmán faces
various kinds of adversity with cunning, seems to prevail, but is soon
knocked back again by fortune or human wickedness. The sequence of
adventures is not entirely arbitrary, however, since to some extent the

main character grows, acquires experience, and at last becomes capable of changing his ways.

The illegitimate son of a crooked financial broker and a courtesan who married an elderly nobleman, Guzmán loses both his legal and his real father in his early teens, and runs away from his hometown, Seville, to escape poverty. Travelers and innkeepers cheat and rob him, the police pursue him by mistake, and, after working briefly in an inn, he moves to Madrid. He routinely steals and cons people, but, having acquired a taste for card games, he always loses everything again. He enlists as a soldier, travels to Italy, and joins a brotherhood of beggars. He persuades a generous cardinal to take pity on him by pretending to suffer from ringworm. The cardinal takes him on as a page, but soon realizes he is an incorrigible crook and lays him off.

One senses a change when Guzmán meets an older man, Sayavedra, who becomes his servant as well as his best and only friend. Although most moralizing pícaros are impervious to true love, they can acquire and keep one—only one—good friend. With Sayavedra, Guzmán performs a highly successful sting in Milan, then heads to Genoa, where he meets some of his relatives and robs them of a considerable sum of money. On the way back to Spain, however, Sayavedra gets seasick and, convinced in his delirium that he himself is Guzmán, jumps in the sea and drowns.

The death of Sayavedra-turned-Guzmán may symbolize the pícaro's wish to put an end to his life as a rogue. On his return to Madrid, Guzmán does indeed become an honest merchant, but unfortunately he then marries a spendthrift, who ruins him. When she dies, Guzmán, still trying to lead a decent life, turns to the study of theology, but just as he is about to take holy orders, he falls in love with a young beauty of modest origins and marries her instead. Still a swindler at heart, he makes a living by sharing his wife with other men, until one of them, a tyrannical judge, has the couple thrown out of Madrid. Back in Seville, Guzmán is soon dropped by his wife and returns to his old vocation as a thief and a crook. Caught in the act, he is imprisoned and sentenced to the galleys.

Thinking seriously about his life, the trickster finally begins to reason like a preacher, moralizing not just about the ways of the world in general, as he has done all along, but about his own failings. Converted, enlightened, Guzmán now learns of a prisoners' plot to take over the ship, informs the captain, and is pardoned in exchange. He ends the book by promising to describe his later, virtuous life in a new volume, which in fact was never written. (It should be said in passing that writing a novel about a reformed rogue poses quite a challenge, as conversion usually makes the character's life much less exciting. Nevertheless, it has been done, notably in the second part of Ponson du Terrail's *Rocambole*, a nineteenth-century page-turner.)

Although by stepping back, a reader can make out the character's progress, the novel, like all early modern episodic narratives, reads as a description of an iniquitous world rather than a well-structured story about a swindler's fate. Guzmán's actions have only short-term consequences. He cheats, but is caught and fired; he steals, but loses his ill-gotten cash at cards or at the hands of other crooks. Punishment comes quickly, and the ups and downs of the swindler's life are clearly intended to show that dishonesty leads nowhere. Yet the novel is by no means a defense of society's existing norms. Guzmán-the-swindler and Guzmán-the-preacher, each in his own way, are individuals-outside-the-world or, more precisely, individuals-against-the-world: the swindler habitually breaks behavioral norms; the preacher denounces endemic social ills—the arrogant nobility, judicial corruption, the unfair wage system, and the harmful influence of wealth in general—with acumen and contempt.

To avoid the monotony of unremitting vice—especially when vice is treated so seriously—the novel includes several novellas. The most remarkable of them is the story of Ozmín and Daraja, two Moorish lovers of princely blood, who remain faithful to each other even when separated by the fall of Granada, the last Moorish bastion in Spain. The story belongs to a specifically Spanish kind of idealist narrative, the "Moorish" novella, which paints the old adversaries of Spanish kings as generous, sensitive, and valiant. Its model is the anonymous *History of the Abencerraje and the Beautiful Jarifa* (1565), and its echoes can be heard in the Captive's story in the first part of *Don Quixote*. The moral beauty of Ozmín and Daraja provides a welcome respite from Guzmán's ugly ordeals.

Picaresque Allegory

Written seventy years later, *Simplicius Simplicissimus* (1668), by the well-read Hans Jakob Christoffel von Grimmelshausen, is not exactly a picaresque novel, but it shares many of the genre's features, mixing them with elements borrowed from allegorical novels, utopias, and spiritual autobiographies. Simplicius eventually, and even more energetically than Guzmán, rejects the corrupt world and finds consolation in religion. Yet Grimmelshausen's novel is in many ways closer to the historical reality of its time than is Alemán's *Life of Guzmán*. Few of the evils Guzmán witnesses are unique to sixteenth-century Spain or Italy, whereas Grimmelshausen's story could not have happened anywhere but seventeenth-century Germany, devastated by the Thirty Years' War between imperial Catholic forces and North German Protestants. The history of the war, its major battles, and the long-awaited Peace of Westphalia are fully embedded in the narrative, determining all the major events in the main character's life.

Like Alemán, Grimmelshausen takes his character through several well-differentiated stages, except that in Simplicius's case, roguery is only one of them. Although his religious conversion—more extreme in its consequences than Guzmán's—involves bidding the world farewell and ending up a lonely ascetic on an island in the Indian Ocean, the hope for a *better* world is also present throughout the novel, which encompasses two utopias depicting free, peaceful societies. The portrayal of Simplicius's personality reinforces this optimism: far from being just an individual-against-the-world, he is capable of generosity even in the worst periods of his life.

Simplicius's father was a nobleman enlisted in General Mansfeld's North German army. After their defeat and dispersal at the Battle of Höchst in June 1622, he fled with his pregnant wife, but she was captured by a band of imperial cavalry and died giving birth to Simplicius. Her husband, deeply distressed, withdrew into the forest to live the life of a hermit, leaving the boy in the care of the local pastor. Until these circumstances are revealed much later, the boy believes his father is a local farmer, who has adopted him at the pastor's request. The religious war soon wrecks the region, all dwellings are burned down, peasants are killed or forced to leave, and now it is the boy's turn to run to the forest, where the hermit shelters him and teaches him to read, write, and pray. Neither they nor the reader knows they are father and son. At this stage, the boy is a naïf (occasionally reminiscent of Wolfram's Parzival), which is why the hermit gives him the name Simplicius.

This happy period ends when the hermit dies and the war drives Simplicius away to the fortress of Hanau, where he finds employment as the governor's page. He now learns the hermit's true identity but still has no idea they are related. Clumsy in the exercise of his duties, Simplicius is on the verge of being fired when his naive answers and blunders convince the governor to keep him on as the house *jester*—this is his second stage. After that, he lives alone for a while as a forest thief and rides off to dance with witches—the novel is full of witchcraft, premonitions, and soothsaying—until a group of imperial soldiers catch him and take him to their colonel. The colonel keeps him, again as a jester, and gives him a music tutor whose son, Ulrich Herzbruder ("Heart-brother"), becomes Simplicius's best friend. As in Alemán, friendship is possible, but we shall soon see that true love is not.

Simplicius changes masters again and, now known as the *Hunter*—his third incarnation—becomes a soldier and leads raiding-parties. Though still a fair-minded person who shares his booty with his comrades and officers, he begins to lead a careless, epicurean life. Having perfected his musical skills and his eloquence, Simplicius now turns into a *rogue* and a pleasure-seeker. He is caught by the relatives of one of his sweethearts and forced to marry her, but soon leaves the family home for Paris, where he sings at the opera and makes love to three masked ladies. Returning to Germany with a case of smallpox that destroys his voice and his beauty, he becomes a quack doctor, selling fake medicine to ignorant people. An accident reminds him of his mortality and God's Providence, but his repentance is short-lived. Friendship, however, melts his cold heart: when Herzbruder, sick and poor, returns from the war zone, the two friends make a pilgrimage to Our Lady of Einsiedeln, in Switzerland, where Simplicius feels the first pangs of remorse. It takes still more time before at last, fully contrite, he becomes a saintly hermit.

Rarely has a single literary character embodied more aspects of individuality-outside-the-world. Simpleton, jester, soldier, crook, pilgrim, and hermit, Simplicius goes from ascetic innocence to maturity, roguery, and back to ascetic life. He spends his childhood in the forest, far from a world whose existence barely touches him, then discovers how cruel society can be and how convenient it is to remain, as a fool and jester, at its margins. A soldier, he gets involved in the world in its most cruel incarnation—war—and accordingly loses all sense of duty toward his fellow human beings. His taste for debauchery and fraud begins to fade when he meets his old friend again, and it finally disappears altogether after an unhappy marriage and a journey to faraway places. In the end, Simplicius understands that his calling is to be a true outsider, an ascetic who lives close to God.

A more sympathetic, more thoughtful main character, and a more balanced view of the world, separate Grimmelshausen's novel from the earlier picaresque stories, bringing it closer to later novels of education. Although Simplicius does not undergo a genuine inner development, but rather moves—sometimes even jumps—from one phase to the next, the novel clearly focuses on his progress, not just on the corruption of the world. To readers and critics used to nineteenth- and twentieth-century narrative prose, Simplicius's progression through life might seem abstract or insufficiently worked out. But anti-idealist novels, just like their idealist counterparts, do not aim to portray fully individualized characters: they use archetypal figures to illustrate the main categories of human activity. Readers understand what Grimmelshausen is talking about perfectly well, just as when you look at, say, Matthias Grünewald's *Crucifixion*, you recognize that its subject is suffering and despair, even though you've never witnessed in our everyday world the facial and bodily contortions you see in the painting.

Dramatic Pícaras

Compared with earlier pícaro stories, Daniel Defoe's *Moll Flanders* (1722) and *Roxana, the Fortunate Mistress* (1724) exhibit several new features. These novels make their main characters' actions more plausible by binding their various adventures together into a single, well-designed life path. They put a strong emphasis on the social dimension of the pícaras' lives, on the actual universe in which they move: here the individual-outside-the-world is, more than ever before, an individual wrestling with historically specific problems, in this case, the plight of women in a society in which their only path to social recognition is marriage. The voices of the trickster and the preacher have grown much closer to one another, so that in the end Moll Flanders is ruled by her conscience, and Roxana becomes a morally articulate, though self-indulgent character. Moreover, the pícara's destiny either borders on drama, as in *Moll Flanders*, or, like Roxana's, turns out to be tragic.

Moll Flanders's career begins with a slow initiation into dishonesty and vice. Born in prison to a woman thief but endowed by nature with uncommon beauty and intelligence, Moll hopes to improve her standing by marriage. While serving as companion to the daughters of a rich family, she is seduced by the young heir, and though she cannot snare him, she does at least manage to wed his younger brother. Soon a widow, she marries a spendthrift linen draper who wastes more than half of her savings and ends up fleeing the law. She then weds a charming man and they leave for Virginia, where he owns a plantation. But after several years of domestic bliss, Moll finds out that her mother-in-law is none other than her natural mother, and that her husband is in fact her brother. Desperate, she returns to England, where a friendly landlady helps her find a wealthy lover. After a while, however, the lover is struck by remorse for his sinful ways and casts her off.

Moll, who is not blind to her own offenses, reflects on her situation as a kept woman still legally married to the fugitive linen draper and, worst of all, with no help or moral guidance. An *individual-lost-in-the-world*, Moll knows exactly what she wants—a good, sober husband to whom she could be a good wife—but with no way to pursue this aim, she cannot resist vice. It is hard to imagine a simpler, more direct way to link moral behavior with gender and social status. Wanting a good husband and marrying one are two different things. Although Moll finds the ideal match, an honest financial adviser who falls in love with her and offers marriage (contingent on his own divorce from an unfaithful wife), she prefers a glamorous young man who, believing she is rich, pretends to be a wealthy gentleman. The two of them genuinely fall for one another—for Moll, although a pícara, is capable of love. They live happily for a short while, but the young man—the Lancashire husband, as Moll calls him throughout her memoirs—having spent the little he owned to court her, is ashamed of his poverty and abandons his wife, eventually becoming a highway robber. The financial adviser, now a widower, proposes again and Moll agrees. After five years of contentment, Moll's fifth husband is hit by a financial disaster and dies of sorrow, leaving her alone and poor once again.

Without entirely knowing why, Moll commits her first theft. She cries, she prays, but a voice within her tempts her to do it again. Trained in the art of stealing by another woman, she succeeds in accumulating enough money to live honestly but, as she acknowledges, theft has become an addiction. Moll takes more and more risks and, after a long series of daring robberies, she is caught, sent to Newgate, the prison where she was born, tried, and sentenced to death.

In prison, Moll feels no remorse. Yet when a newly arrived prisoner turns out to be her Lancashire husband, arrested for highway robbery, she realizes that she herself has caused this young man's misfortunes. Empathy for his suffering awakens Moll to her own guilt. The prison chaplain, finding her open to repentance, obtains a reprieve for her. Then, when Moll sees a group of prisoners taken to be hanged, she converts, and, with the help of the good pastor, her sentence is commuted. Moll and her beloved Lancashire husband are deported to Virginia, where they will lead a hardworking, virtuous, and happy life.

Few stories differ more deliberately from idealist novels than does *Moll Flanders*. Instead of celebrating a pair of star-crossed lovers and their victorious struggle against the blows of fortune, Defoe's novel describes the difficulty of forming a stable couple, showing how vulnerable such couples are to death, poverty, or just hostile fate. Providence, understood as the force that oversees worldly events, refrains for a long time from intervening in Moll's favor. In her bleak world, a single woman can depend only on her own intelligence and tenacity. Moreover, her soul, far from being immune to outside pressures, is home to conflicting drives. On the one hand, Moll knows how to behave properly, how to be a loving, loyal friend and wife. She is adaptable and prudent, particularly in financial matters, and she almost never shows signs of self-indulgence and excessive self-love. On the other hand, she is subject to the desires of the flesh, yielding to her first lover; to worldly ambition, choosing her supposedly rich Lancashire husband over the honest financial adviser; and later, to a terrifying impulse to steal, an impulse sown, she claims, by the devil in her heart.

Moll's religious conversion to some extent recalls earlier moralizing pícaros. But whereas Guzmán and Simplicius avoid the hostility of the surrounding world, breaking with their past lives and taking refuge in God,

Moll's conversion not only gives her life meaning, it also allows her to return to the world—the New World, where she and her Lancashire husband achieve marital bliss, social integration, and financial security. For Moll, it *pays* to have a conscience. Yet, the novel's mercantile dimension, so carefully highlighted by Defoe, does not make Moll's conversion less convincing. Her remorse, rather than teaching her the utter contempt for corrupt humankind that Guzmán and Simplicius feel, fills her with compassion for her fellow human beings and justifies her return to the world.

Defoe's emphasis on individual conscience, reliance on society, and the coherence of one's life path does not always entail a happy ending. In *Roxana*, the protagonist's career is a tragic version of Moll's. Like Moll, Roxana is at least in part a victim of women's inferior position in society. While still a teenager, she is led by her parents to marry an inept man, who loses their entire fortune and runs away to enlist as a mercenary. As lonely and poor as Moll, Roxana gives her children away and accepts her wealthy landlord's invitation to become his mistress.

Roxana's servant and friend Amy plays a perplexing part in her corruption. As we have seen, most pícaros seem immune to true love, yet they can acquire and keep a good friend. Strikingly, this best friend is often referred to by his or her proper name. In a picaresque novel virtually all characters, except the narrator, are identified only by their occupation or family origin—the baker, the knight, the ambassador, the daughter of the merchant, etc.—which creates a peculiar atmosphere of anonymity. This rule applies to the lovers, wives, or husbands of the main character (as noted earlier, even Moll's favorite man, with whom she will live happily ever after, is known only as her "Lancashire husband"), underscoring the randomness of relations between people and the fact that no one is unique, even in an area as intimate as love and marriage. In the same spirit, the pícaros or pícaras themselves quite often lack a true proper name—Simplicius, Moll Flanders, and Roxana are all nicknames, for the good reason that these characters either do not know their true identity or need to hide it. By giving the best-friend character a real name—Amy, or Sayavedra in *Don Guzmán de Alfarache*, or Herzbruder in *Simplicius*—the authors seem to imply that only the helper, the facilitator, the person the main character can always count on, deserves a personal mark of identification. In *Roxana*, Amy takes most of the dubious or openly evil moral decisions upon herself. She plays the part of the swindler—and later, the criminal—leaving the role of preacher to Roxana, who always admonishes Amy in the highest moral terms before agreeing to follow her advice, and delivers a strong self-accusing sermon each time, for the benefit of the reader.

Like all moralizing pícaros and pícaras, Roxana is fully aware of the difference between the moral good and her own behavior, but unlike most of them, once she embarks on a career of vice, she sometimes insists that those around her should also perceive this difference. The landlord who loves Roxana has been deserted by his wife at a time when neither desertion nor adultery is grounds for divorce, but when he asks Roxana to live with him, he makes it clear that he thinks of her as his wife. Yet after several nights together, Roxana insists that Amy sleep with him as well, to emphasize the illicit nature of their relationship, and make it clear that all principles and modesty have been cast off. Whereas Moll Flanders often resists temptation and tries hard to behave well, Roxana, guided by Amy, gives in willingly. She does experience bouts of remorse, but her conscience operates through silent moods and forebodings, rather than inner debates. And unlike Moll, Roxana is not dogged by poverty and solitude. When the landlord dies, she finds herself in possession of jewelry worth a substantial sum, about eight times the size of Moll's fortune at its best, and what's more, she can rely on helpful acquaintances. She comes to vice not through necessity but through inclination; her weakness lies not so much in the urges of the flesh (though she sometimes lets the reader infer that she is not immune to them) as in her vanity and worldly ambition.

Roxana becomes the mistress of a munificent German prince, and he gives her a Turkish womanservant who teaches her the dance that will make her famous. She later meets a Dutch merchant who helps her move her money to England, and offers to marry her. Amy reports that her first husband has died in the meantime, but Roxana refuses the merchant's hand, settling for quasi-marital cohabitation. When a woman of independent means enters into a marriage contract, Roxana argues, she gives up her liberty and becomes a slave. The merchant answers that a marriage based on mutual love and common interest need not resemble bondage, but he fails to convince her.

The articulate Roxana declares to the reader that as she is rich, beautiful, and not yet old, she intends to become the king's mistress. With this goal in mind, she gives a masked ball at her splendid London residence and, dressed as a Turkish princess, attracts the attention of the monarch. Delighted by her dancing, the audience nicknames her "Roxana." After more parties and more dances, the king does choose her as his mistress. Three years later, alone again, the immensely rich Roxana decides to lead an honest life, and, with Amy's help, she takes lodgings with a family of Quakers, where she befriends the lady in charge of the household. The Dutch merchant then reappears, as eager as ever to marry her. Hearing through Amy that the German prince is no longer interested in her, she weds the Dutchman, who purchases a patent for a baronetcy to satisfy her ambitions.

Roxana should by now be the most contented woman in the world—but she isn't. Unlike Moll's, Roxana's marriage and social integration do not come after remorse and conversion. She has become a respectable woman without publicly renouncing her earlier life, which she likes to remember but must keep hidden. By contrasting Moll's deliverance with Roxana's downfall, Defoe highlights the key role of self-examination and remorse in safeguarding a person's mental health. This theme, pervasive in Defoe's fiction, is crucial in *Robinson Crusoe*, whose protagonist discovers the healing power of contrition while alone on a desert island (although compared with Roxana, he has little to atone for). Repenting for the first time, Crusoe lifts his hands to heaven and begins to look back on his life in horror at his sins, seeking nothing but an escape from guilt. This is precisely what Roxana is never able to achieve.

Without contrition, the guilty past returns with a vengeance. Roxana had abandoned the children from her first marriage, but once she is financially secure, she finds and helps them without letting them know that she is their mother. She settles one of her sons as a merchant's apprentice but is less successful in her attempts, through Amy, to take charge of her daughter Susan, the only character apart from Amy to be called by her real name. Susan, it turns out, was actually a servant in Roxana's own large household during her glory days in London and has distinct memories of her mistress dancing in a Turkish dress. Susan also knows a lot about her former employer's past links with Amy, and, piecing the details together, she concludes that Roxana is probably her mother.

Wanting to distance herself from her past, Roxana persuades her husband to move to Holland. But on the ship, it turns out that the captain's cook is none other than Susan. More and more inquisitive, the young woman finds out where Roxana lives, visits the house, and talks in such detail about Lady Roxana, the king's mistress, and her Turkish dress, that the Quaker landlady figures out her tenant's true identity. In a terrifying climax, Amy, Roxana's alter ego, murders Susan, the unwanted witness. Roxana, haunted by visions of her dead daughter, will never be happy again.

Though it belongs to the genre of moralizing picaresque stories, *Roxana* goes beyond the strict limits of the picaresque. Here, even more than in *Moll Flanders*, the genre's episodic nature gives way to a more unitary vision of human destiny. A regular picaresque novel is a series of independent adventures, each highlighting the protagonist's abilities as a trickster. In both *Simplicius Simplicissimus* and *Moll Flanders*, this sequence of episodes also portrays the main character's long-term evolution, but that evolution is a linear, step-by-step process in which causality is localized, limited to the short term. In *Roxana*, by contrast, the protagonist's fate is decided by the return of the past. Roxana's abandonment of her children and Susan's presence at the Turkish dance do not influence only the events that immediately ensue, such as Roxana's meeting her landlord, or whatever Susan does next after the masked ball—they become relevant much later, when Roxana tries to conceal her past life and Susan searches for her mother.

The long-term impact of human actions is one of the traditional topics of tragedy—think of Sophocles's Oedipus, or Jason in Euripides's *Medea*. What is more, the Christian view of morality assumes that all transgressions are inscribed in God's book of reckoning, and that repentance is the only way to mitigate our culpability. By exploiting both the tragic view and the Christian (in one of its most severe versions), *Roxana* transforms the picaresque plot into a full-scale drama of pride and fall. Hiding the past is standard practice in picaresque novels, since in order to operate successfully the pícaros or pícaras need to conceal from their next victims the existence of the previous ones. Usually, however, the picaresque genre takes for granted the *rogues' invulnerability*: after each bad deed they go into hiding, run away, or adopt a new identity. If they are caught, as Guzmán and Moll are, it is for their most recent offense. Here, however, the rogue is caught in her old snares.

Roxana also lacks the pícaro/pícara's relentless persecution by the surrounding world. Lazarillo, Guzmán, and Simplicius act dishonestly—when they do—because they must fend off the blows of fortune and the world's hostility. True pícaros, they constantly take steps to defend themselves and, as such, keep the reader on their side. Roxana, though, is a fortunate mistress, as the subtitle of the novel notifies us. Most of her dishonest deeds are committed in cold blood, for the sake of vanity and ambition rather than survival. Instead of the usual disorderly struggle waged against the world by pícaros and pícaras, Roxana's actions are designed to control her own long-term destiny. Like the other pícaros and pícaras, she turns her back on the good and on convention, but while most of them use their freedom from moral standards recklessly, she knows exactly how to benefit from it.

Rejection of common norms gives the usual pícaros/pícaras a special suppleness, which helps them navigate within a dangerous world but deprives them of their dignity. Most pícaros do not mind this loss. An individual facing a world governed by fortune can either resist it in the name of a higher good, as the characters in idealist novels do, or play tricks on it the way pícaros do without caring one bit about self-respect or inner poise. Roxana is one who manages to cheat and maneuver the world, while still trying to preserve her dignity. Hers is a risky bet, since these two goals—giving up the moral good, yet maintaining the capacity to govern oneself in a dignified fashion—are not easily reconciled. What destroys her is the unexpected alliance between fortune and the moral law. Under the rule of chance, the suppressed past might never have returned: Susan might have served in someone else's house or might not have run into Roxana later. But once the past returns, it brings the moral law with it, and the abandoned child's testimony threatens to make Roxana's degradation public. The resolution of the novel—Susan's murder, Roxana's falling prey to visions and nightmares—brings about the protagonist's defeat. Her punishment is a tortured conscience, as she can neither plead guilty in the open nor keep her inner composure. The rebellious soul becomes the site of a relentless remorse that cannot be confessed.

None of the later eighteenth-century picaresque novels revisited this subject. Lesage's *Gil Blas* (1715–1735) and Fielding's *Joseph Andrews* (1742) attempted to tone down the pícaro's independence from society, giving it the most pleasing face imaginable. Tobias Smollett's *Roderick Random* (1748) and *Peregrine Pickle* (1751) returned to the cruel humor of amoral picaresque stories, though without an amoral protagonist. Not until Laclos' *Liaisons dangereuses* (1782) can one find an exploration of the link between moral turpitude and inner torment to match *Roxana*'s.

The Ideographic Method

Idealist novels project a coherent fictional world-at-large that looks quite different from the real one. This method, which could be called *ideographic*, shapes the imaginary world according to a leading idea, whose impact can be felt in every single episode. The idealist novel's credibility does not come from the details it describes, although quite often such details are abundant and believable, nor from a correspondence between the events of the story and readers' everyday experience. Instead, readers are *first* invited to grasp the leading idea—in this case the separation between human beings and the hostile world around them—and *then* to ask themselves whether this idea, however abstract and strange it may seem, might not in fact relate to the actual world in which they live. Once understood, the idea is expected to help clarify the general meaning of the actual world, rather than testify to its perceptible details.

Since the leading idea is an abstract one, novels based on it tend to be implausible. In order to hammer the idea into the reader's mind, they simplify and exaggerate the features of the characters and their environment. Idealist novels emphasize the essential attributes of the protagonists (Chariclea's virtue, Parzival's valor) and the antagonists (the cruelty of Arsake and Clinschor) to the detriment of their incidental qualities, which are deliberately ignored. This exclusive focus on the essential features creates characters who seem relatively flat, but whose main qualities reach an exceptional intensity. As the leading idea has to assert itself in time and space, the plots of these works tend to be episodic and repetitive, covering a long period and a panoramic geography. Last but not least, idealist novels are usually presented impersonally, as third-person narratives, as though to convey the main idea's objective force.

Picaresque novels use the ideographic method as well, only they depict disreputable people instead of admirable ones. Just like the idealist novels, picaresque stories use a multitude of episodes to underscore an abstract idea—again, the separation between human beings and their world, this time seen as a source of wickedness rather than an opportunity for the display of moral splendor. The adventures of Lazarillo, Guzmán, or Moll Flanders, like those of the characters in idealist ancient Greek and chivalric novels, only make sense by reference to a hostile, unpredictable surrounding world. Ancient Greek and chivalric characters resist this environment, pícaros take advantage of it and deceive its denizens, but the behavior of all these characters is shaped by an abstract view of the world. The pícaro's personality is as simplified as that of the noblest Greek lovers, the most valiant knights-errant, the most virtuous shepherds, because in picaresque as well as idealist novels the characters display only those features that illustrate the leading idea. For the same reason, picaresque plots are as episodic and repetitive as idealist ones, and similarly require a long time frame and a panoramic space.

Nevertheless, the picaresque novels differ from the idealist through the extensive use of *familiar details* from everyday life and through the *testimonial* first-person narrative. These two features evoke the world's imperfection, rather than making the story more plausible or realistic in the nineteenth-century sense of the term. When Moll Flanders tells us that, passing by an apothecary shop in Leadenhall Street, she saw on a stool in the corner a little bundle wrapped in a white cloth, we are not expected first to be impressed by the exactness of the description, and next to infer a social or moral lesson from it. By this point, the reader has fully grasped the novel's leading idea—the moral gap between Moll and her world—and so can infer that the little bundle is waiting to be *stolen*, as a mysterious voice whispers to Moll over her shoulder. Similarly, the first-person narration is not meant to make the story more credible, but rather to emphasize how worthless the character is, since no one else would want to speak about him or her. Equally, first-person narration helps to show that even the worst human beings have the capacity to look within themselves and, in some cases, to repent. Just as the abundance of exotic happenings and the objective, third-person narration invite the reader of the *Ethiopian Story* or *Yvain* to reflect on the meaning of human ideals, so the profusion of familiar objects and the confessional tone in *Lazarillo* and *Moll Flanders* are intended not so much to represent the surrounding world faithfully—since, taken as a whole, a picaresque story is as implausible as any ancient Greek or chivalric novel—as to formulate a general hypothesis about its moral inadequacy.

CHAPTER 3

The Center of Action: Elegiac Stories and Novellas

||||||||||||||||||||||||||||||||||||||||||||||||||||||||||||||||||

The long narratives we have considered up till now acquaint their readers with an image of the world-at-large. Starting with a clear program, these novels depict souls whose initial disposition determines all their actions. The virtuous characters relentlessly resist the world and the cunning ones swindle it, each doing so in a series of similar situations. A large number of episodes, unfolding over a considerable time and space, gradually build a homogeneous image of the universe. Unity of action matters little.

In a parallel tradition, there were short narratives whose action unveiled, at a single stroke, a limited but crucial aspect of the world. These stories illustrate clear, easily grasped ideas—that fate plays unsuspected tricks on mortals, that cleverness is a formidable asset, that illicit love brings unhappiness, that revenge takes monstrous forms, or that curiosity is a dangerous vice. But rather than supporting a long, episodic plot, these ideas disclose themselves in a single salient example. Sad or funny anecdotes, memorable examples of vice or virtue, these narratives focus on the main issue and on the particular place where the action happens. And instead of following a preestablished program, the characters listen to their hearts.

Broken Hearts

Two main types of story take this approach. One emphasizes conflict, the other reflection. The *novella*, whose specialty is action, was one of the most fertile narrative prose genres of the Renaissance and early modern period. The less numerous *elegiac stories* focus on love's sorrows and the ruminations they inspire.

The ancestor of the elegiac tale is Ovid's *Heroides* (between 25 and 16 BC), a cycle of poems conceived as letters from famous women to the men who have rejected them or are wandering far away: Ariadne to Theseus, Dido to Aeneas, Medea to Jason, Penelope to Ulysses. St. Augustine's *Confessions* (397–398), a deeply emotional dialogue with an absent God, might have had a rhetorical influence on Renaissance and early modern elegiac stories too. The letters (1132–1138) of Abelard and Heloise, two young French lovers separated by his clerical vows and her family, were also read avidly at the time.

New fictional treatments of the theme were few, but at least two of them attracted considerable attention: the fictional *Elegy of Lady Fiammetta* (1344–1345) by Boccaccio and, much later, *The Letters of a Portuguese Nun* (1669), written by the Count of Guilleragues but published anonymously and presented as the authentic letters of an abandoned young woman. In both cases the plot turns on the love between an unattached man and a woman who is either married, as in Boccaccio's story, or living in a convent. After leading the woman astray, the man deserts her. Lady Fiammetta and the Portuguese nun express their agitation in sentimental outpourings, but their disappointment never leads to action.

In Boccaccio, a happily married noblewoman falls in love with a young man she sees in church. She describes the nature and extent of her feelings and recounts a debate with her old wet nurse, who scolds her, as well as a vision of the goddess Aphrodite, who advises her to yield to her passion. When Fiammetta and Panfilo (as the two lovers nickname themselves) have enjoyed their clandestine pleasures for a while, Panfilo leaves the city, promising to come back soon. He never returns, and the distressed Fiammetta learns that he has married someone else. Comparing her fate with that of the ancient deserted women, she complains that her pains are greater than theirs, and concludes by asking her little book to speak forever of her anguish. While relying on widely used classical topoi— Ciceronian speeches, prophetic dreams, the appearance of the goddess of love, detailed allusions to famous mythological figures—Boccaccio unerringly establishes the features of the subgenre: the simple plot, the small number of characters, the absence of episodes, and the self-absorbed complaint in the first person.

Guilleragues's *Letters* makes use of these features, enhancing the main character's charismatic presence and detailing her inner drama. A very young Portuguese nun writes to the French officer who has seduced her and then left for France. The first letter, answering a note from her departed lover, still harbors a glimmer of hope in the midst of suffering. Written six months later, the second letter laments his silence, reluctantly considers the possibility that he is gone forever, and ends in deep sadness. But her passion is still alive, and in the third letter, despite suspecting that her lover has deliberately toyed with her feelings, and pitying him for having missed out on the higher pleasures of true love, she reasserts the violence of her attachment. In her fourth letter, she is still desperately in love, to the point that she dreams of becoming a servant to her lover's future wife, just to be close to him, but by now she has realized that she deluded herself in thinking the French officer would deal with her in good faith. Deciding he probably won't even read her letter, she finally seems to accept her fate. The fifth and last letter signals her recovery. She is now repelled by her lover's conduct: her heart, she writes, created an idol and believed in it blindly. A recent message from the officer, with its ridiculous civilities, has at last convinced her that he is unworthy of her. Without hiding her contempt, she reflects on the vanity of passion, on her own imprudence and her pain. To some extent still in love, sometimes almost asking the officer to return, she is nevertheless able to let him know that she won't think of him anymore. As in Boccaccio's story, the consequences of a private drama are described by the victim in the first person. But here the tone, less dependent on classical rhetoric and mythology, has a touch of spontaneity.

These stories highlight serious transgressions whose results, while devastating for the individual, do not affect society. Virtually invisible from the outside, the misfortunes are confined to the protagonist's heart. Elegiac stories are an unobtrusive presence among early modern narrative genres, but their attention to the fallibility of a single, isolated individual make them an important precursor of the eighteenth-century portrayals of sentimental self-examination.

The Novella—Brevity, Coherence, Induction

Compared with other narrative subgenres, the novella's most striking feature is *brevity*. Initially, it maintained close links with the oral tradition, and many of the subjects of Renaissance novellas can be found in Hans-Jörg Uther's index of folktales.[1] Like folktales, early novellas consisted of a single joke, an anecdote, a brief piece of gossip (the Aarne-Thompson-Uther types 1200–1999), or a slightly longer story (the Aarne-Thompson-Uther novella types 850–999) told at a gathering of narrators, as in Boccaccio's *Decameron*, or read aloud in one session. The shortest novellas could have been told in just a few minutes, but even later, in seventeenth-century Spain—when novellas got longer and were read aloud, like the

[1] *The Types of International Folktales: A Classification and Bibliography Based on the System of Antti Aarne and Stith Thompson*, 3 vols. (Helsinki: Academia Scientiarum Fennica, 2004).

story of *An Ill-Advised Curiosity* in the first part of *Don Quixote*—the reading would not have lasted more than a few hours.

Unlike idealist and picaresque novels, which reinforce their point with long sequences of similar episodes, novellas avoid putting undue pressure on the listener's or reader's memory, concentrating on a single incident or a set of closely related events. They focus on a facet of human strength or imperfection, seizing hold of it in the heat of the action, so that *unity of action* becomes essential. Many Boccaccio novellas consist of just a couple of narrative moves: desire and fulfillment, offense and revenge, crime and punishment, test and success. When the action involves more than two or three moves, its unity comes from the tight causal links between episodes. Desire once fulfilled, for instance, can inspire hostility or meet with a sudden challenge; it might be favored or hindered by an unexpected change in circumstances. Or it may simply require a more gradual approach. But novellas always emphasize the main goal the characters pursue and the limited number of steps they take to achieve it.

This unity of action favors an *inductive* approach to the representation of behavior. A single uncommon situation or turn of events triggers an unexpected response from the characters, inviting readers to infer a specific truth about human nature. The divide between individuals and their world is not an initial datum that shapes the course of the action—as it is in both idealist and picaresque novels—but instead *results* from a conflict between the protagonists and the social milieu to which they genuinely and permanently belong. This conflict is depicted as astounding, even scandalous, such that the ordeals of virtuous characters, as well as the transgressions of imperfect ones, are conspicuously at odds with the society's usual ways. Novellas come in various forms, from short, funny anecdotes to longer, dramatic stories, and touch on a whole range of subjects. And because characters are portrayed as intimately connected to their concrete social and family environment, what counts here is not the soul's general, abstract disposition, but the unusual impulses of the heart. Thus insights into the *moral psychology* of the characters have a better chance to develop.

Since brevity, unity of action, and the inductive approach rule out a long-term familiarity with the characters and their behavior, novellas—the early ones especially—resolve their conflicts spectacularly fast. In Boccaccio's *Decameron* 4.9 (1350–1353), Sir Guillaume de Roussillon kills his wife's lover and lets her know at dinner that the tasty morsel she has just enjoyed was the cooked heart of her beloved. The lady throws herself out of a window and dies. In the *Decameron* 4.8, the young Girolamo, deeply in love with Salvestra, learns that her family have arranged in his absence for her to marry another man; Girolamo sneaks into her house and bed and, after confessing his love, breathes his last. In the story of the

Moor and Desdemona, in Giraldi Cinzio's *Gli Hecatommithi* (1565, 3.7), an unscrupulous ensign kindles his commander's jealousy using Desdemona's lost handkerchief as one of his "proofs" and thus incites the Moor to murder his innocent wife. Concentrating on Sir Guillaume's monstrous revenge, Girolamo's extraordinary love, and the Moor's fateful gullibility, the three novellas reach their conclusions in no time at all.

To make induction easier, novellas take place in a setting assumed to be real and easily identifiable. Portrayed as common mortals, the characters act in ways much more familiar to the reader than the behavior described in ancient Greek, medieval, or picaresque novels. The novella's types (the devoted young woman, the frivolous young man, the jealous husband, the unfaithful wife, the monk in love) fit quite well into everyday psychology, at least at the beginning of the stories. Once they face a major challenge, however—adultery, cruelty, the loss of a beloved, a friend's deviousness—they might react in the *least* expected fashion: Sir Guillaume forces his wife to eat her lover's heart; Girolamo dies in his beloved's bed; the Moor strangles Desdemona. The characters in novellas are both the most plausible and the most astonishing in Renaissance and early modern narrative literature.

While long novels specialize in one kind of behavior, novellas can depict laughable, disturbing, or admirable conduct, adopting the proper tone for each—comic, serious, or high-minded. Since the genre's major features are quite stable, sometimes the same plot framework can serve for comedy or drama. In one of Matteo Bandello's *Novelle* (1554, 2.36), young Nicuola, whose beloved Lattanzio is pursuing the beautiful Catella, dresses up as a page, unwittingly kindling Catella's desire. Here, mistaken identity is a comic device, and in the end Nicuola becomes Lattanzio's wife, while Catella marries Paolo, Nicuola's almost identical brother. As we shall see later, one of the episodes in Montemayor's pastoral novel *Diana* (1559) is based on Bandello's story, but with a tragic inflection: the woman who falls for another woman disguised as a page dies of grief when her passion is rejected.

Whether comic, serious, or tragic, novellas are rarely required to be wholly plausible. In Peronella's story, for instance (*Decameron* 7.2), the believable elements are the setting (a quiet, secluded street in Naples), the characters (a poor mason, his pretty wife, and her young lover, Giannello), and the motivation—lust. Giannello regularly visits Peronella while her husband is at work. One morning, the mason unexpectedly comes home. Peronella hides her lover in a vat, claiming she has sold it to someone who is now inspecting it. The lover comes out, and the husband gets into the tank to repair it before the sale. Peronella thrusts her head into its opening to direct her husband's work, while Giannello makes love to her from behind. The farcical event—adultery committed under the credulous husband's nose—is designed to elicit in the reader a sense of complicity with the transgressors, and perhaps also some disapproval at their feat. The implausible event strikingly evokes the coarse pleasure of insubordination.

Similarly, in serious and tragic novellas, a plausible context does not necessarily yield an equally believable plot. In Boccaccio's *Decameron* 10.10, a nobleman, Gualtieri, marries Griselda, the daughter of a peasant, and then several years later, wanting to test her constancy, pretends he has killed their two children and decided to marry a woman of higher birth. Griselda humbly accepts her husband's decisions. Moved by her strength and patience, Gualtieri reassures Griselda that he loves her and that the children, still alive, will be brought back. Not only is this story implausible (and, if I may add, revolting), but it makes no perceptible effort to mitigate its implausibility. The clarity of the thesis (the perfect submission of a virtuous but lowborn woman), the improbability of the plot, and the happy ending made the story unusually popular. It appears in the Aarne-Thompson-Uther index of folktales as type 887, *Griselda*, and was rewritten by Petrarch and Chaucer, among others.

The story of Ulrico and his wife (Bandello 1.21), which has a lighter, comic tinge, and the melodrama of Dorotea and Locrino (Cinzio, 5.2), are equally implausible and promote an equally clear thesis. To some extent related to the Aarne-Thompson-Uther type 882 (and therefore to Shakespeare's *Cymbeline*), Bandello 1.21, is about a Hungarian nobleman, Ulrico, recently married, who decides to go to the king's court to gain renown. As the couple lacks the means to sustain the lady's rank at court, she stays home to administer their modest fortune. Although Ulrico has complete faith in her virtue, a Polish wizard gives him an enchanted mirror whose color will keep him informed of her behavior. At court, two noblemen, learning that Ulrico's wife is living alone her castle, make a bet that one of them can seduce her. They try, but the lady, pretending to give in, entraps them, locks them up, and forces them to spin wool for a living. The enchanted mirror lets Ulrico know that his wife is chaste, and the two noblemen become the laughingstock of the Hungarian court. The high point of the story—when the lady tricks her seducers—is meant to delight the readers: the surprise is not so much her virtue, well established from the beginning, as the ingenious way in which she takes the two men prisoner and compels them to do a job conventionally reserved for women.

In Cinzio 5.2, Locrino, an honest Byzantine merchant, is imprisoned by a powerful lord for refusing to share his wife, Dorotea, with him. Dorotea manages to free her husband and the couple runs away. During their journey, Locrino becomes convinced that his wife has died, and wants to kill himself, but—unlike Juliet in Bandello 2.9, and in Shakespeare's

Romeo and Juliet—Dorotea wakes up in time, so they return home, place themselves under the protection of the emperor Constantine, and live happily ever after. Conjugal love proves stronger than a hostile environment. Although it has the usual trappings of verisimilitude—the historical context; accurate topographical details about Constantinople—this novella is a small-scale idealist novel, praising its characters' inflexible virtue.

Novellas, then, are not part of a clear, definite drive toward plausibility, yet the unity of action and the use of real settings do grant them considerable *revelatory* power. Actions people might never take (a husband feeding his wife the heart of her lover; a woman enjoying her sweetheart's favors while sticking her head into the vat in which her husband is working) and situations that might never occur (a team of seducers rushing to a virtuous lady's castle; a brother marrying the woman who had fallen in love with his almost identical cross-dressing sister) are so skillfully placed in a believable environment, linked to natural passions and desires, and emphatically presented as unique, that they end up revealing something truthful, in a comic or painful way, about human behavior.

MOTIVATION AND COMPLEXITY

The challenge faced by the protagonists of novellas can be, in the simplest cases, *external* and *perceptible*. They meet it by opposing the forces that threaten them. Sir Guillaume (*Decameron* 4.9) takes revenge brutally and openly for his wife's betrayal. Girolamo (*Decameron* 4.8) is crushed by Salvestra's parents' decision to marry her to another man. Quite frequently, this external adversity is linked to chance, which plays a major role in many novellas. The stories told in Boccaccio's *Decameron* 4 describe loves that end unhappily, while the love stories included in *Decameron* 5 reach happy endings only after cruel and unfortunate adventures. Many of Bandello's and Cinzio's novellas deal with similar situations. Critics have long since pointed out that Shakespeare's tragedies do not conform to Aristotelian precepts, since the downfall of their main characters often comes about through trivial mix-ups—for Othello, the loss of a handkerchief, for Romeo, a mistake about a sleeping potion—rather than the majesty of fate. The reason is that in the Italian novellas from which Shakespeare borrows his plots, the protagonists, far from being "larger than life" from the very beginning, become tragic characters only when confronted with a mixture of other people's behavior and chance events.

In the Moor's story, he is forced to confront *external* yet *hidden* adversity. Influenced by an enemy posing as an ally, the Moor unwittingly becomes an instrument of his own demise. This pattern is a common one in comic novellas as well as tragic: Peronella's husband, for instance, unsuspectingly helps her to deceive him. In early novellas depicting this type of adversity, motivation nevertheless remains straightforward, since the rogue excites the most predictable impulses in his victim: jealousy, lust, greed, or vanity. As we shall soon see, seventeenth-century novellas would refine this type of plot considerably.

Innocent or guilty passions the character must struggle against are examples of *internal*, yet *perceptible* adversity. In Cinzio 8.5 (a distant source for Shakespeare's *Measure for Measure*), Iuriste does not fight his dishonorable desire for Epitia, but in the *Decameron* 10.3, Mithridanes, who envies Nathan's reputation for generosity, eventually renounces his urge to outdo him. Another type, unexplored before the eighteenth century, is the *internal*, yet *hidden* adversity. It occurs when characters, like the heroine of Abbé Prévost's *Manon Lescaut* (1731), are unable to read their own hearts. But Cervantes and Mme de Lafayette describe equally enigmatic cases in which *internal* adversity is both *perceptible* and *incomprehensible*: the protagonist feels certain passions and identifies them clearly, yet cannot understand their nature or raison d'être.

The writers of early novellas handled external, perceptible adversity and its consequences straightforwardly. Boccaccio's and many of Bandello's are not only brief, but also simple and transparent. The impulses of the heart quickly lead to action. Sir Guillaume jumps straight from offense to revenge, and his wife instantly commits suicide; Romeo secretly marries Juliet as soon as they can, and when Juliet's family finds another husband for her, the lovers run away without delay. The striking events at the core of the novella go well with this elementary psychology. Having sex with your boyfriend a few feet away from your husband, cooking the heart of your wife's lover, committing suicide next to your beloved's sleeping body: these acts are all the more memorable because they stem from the simplest kinds of motivation—lust, anger, or despair.

In some of Cinzio's novellas there are more complex psychological situations. For Iago's schemes to succeed (to use the names Shakespeare bestowed on Cinzio's characters), he must be friends with the Moor and Cassio, he needs to force his own wife, Emilia, to spy on Desdemona, and he must use the opportunities offered by chance, distorting their meaning on the spot to suit his purposes. The mixture of long-term strategy and short-term decision making complicates the links between psychological motives and action. Iago is at least as evil as Sir Guillaume, and patience and hypocrisy give him additional, unpleasant depth.

Similarly, the stories of Oronte and Orbecche or Iuriste and Epitia involve external enemies who present themselves as friendly and magnanimous. In Cinzio 2.2, Oronte, a young Armenian and the favorite courtier of the Persian king, Sulmone, courts and marries the king's daughter, Orbecche, without her father's approval. The couple flees to Armenia.

Nine years later, pretending to pardon them, Sulmone invites his daughter, her husband, Oronte, and their children to the Persian court. After secretly slaughtering Oronte and the children, Sulmone offers their mutilated bodies to Orbecche, who takes revenge by stabbing her father and then kills herself.

In Cinzio 8.5, Iuriste, the imperial judge at Innsbruck, promises beautiful Epitia that if she will consent to become his mistress, he will pardon her brother, sentenced to death for rape. She agrees, but on Iuriste's orders her brother is executed anyway. The young woman lodges a complaint with the emperor, who, after compelling Iuriste to marry her, sentences the dishonest judge to death. But Epitia, now Iuriste's legitimate wife, persuades the emperor to pardon him. Oronte and Orbecche's story piles horror on horror—Iuriste and Epitia's ends peacefully. In the former, most of the characters are assassinated by treachery. In the latter, although Iuriste's lie and betrayal are repulsive, the laws of Innsbruck condemn Epitia's brother to death, whereas Iuriste's seduction of the young woman is—according to the ideas of the time—redeemed by marriage.

Stories involving hidden adversity need more time and more examples to persuade the reader than do those built around external, perceptible conflicts. This is probably why some of Cinzio's novellas are longer than Boccaccio's. Bandello's novellas are already rather complicated: Romeo and Juliet's story involves several moves, countermoves, and interventions of chance. Yet while in Bandello the relative complexity of the action is external (the conflict between the Montagues and the Capulets, or the Capulets' decision to marry Juliet off against her will), in the examples from Cinzio, the intricacies of the plot originate in the duplicity of characters like Iago, Sulmone, and Iuriste.

In small-scale idealist novellas, in which the characters are challenged by fate or chance, the number of narrative moves also increases. We might therefore surmise that Cervantes's *Exemplary Stories* (1613) are so long in part because they were written at a time when the *Ethiopian Story* had become known and widely admired, prompting him to inject a dose of Heliodorus-inspired idealism into his novellas. In *The Little Gypsy Girl* and *The Illustrious Scullery-Maid*, the main characters are beautiful and virtuous young women who live happily in modest households, not knowing their true origins, until young men from noble families fall in love with them, and, with the help of chance, the women find their true, aristocratic parents. This story line, reminiscent of Chariclea's discovery of her royal blood, requires a certain amount of time to work itself out.

It also calls for the narrative to begin in medias res, so that the earlier events are revealed only later. Fourteenth- to sixteenth-century Italian, English, and French novellas remain close to their oral origins by virtually always telling the story from the beginning. By contrast, you will remember that the first scene of the *Ethiopian Story* introduces its main characters as two unnamed, unfortunate travelers reeling from the effects of a shipwreck, leaving the secret of the protagonist's birth and the background to the plot to emerge only much later. Cervantes sometimes adopts this formula—*The Generous Lover*, for instance, opens with the lonely complaint of a captive whose full story will become known subsequently—but on other occasions, as in *The Illustrious Scullery-Maid*, he uses the simpler kind of opening for his male characters and keeps the heroine's origins secret, revealing the truth only when the time is ripe for the resolution of the conflict.

The formal influence of ancient Greek novels is not the only factor here. Cervantes's novellas contain much longer dialogues and descriptions than do the Italian ones, and whereas the use of description may be traced back to idealist novels, the spirited dialogues come from Cervantes's experience as a playwright. *Rinconete and Cortadillo*, a funny portrait of a brotherhood of thieves, often sounds like one of his short comic plays. The same is true of *The Little Gypsy Girl*, which blends a light, witty tone, appropriate for the scenes involving the nomadic gypsies, with a more sentimental style suitable for the idyll shared by the young protagonist, Preciosa, and Andrés, her suitor. Theatrical liveliness is a general feature of Cervantes's novellas, regardless of their subject. The novellas proposing an ideal of perfection (*The Generous Lover, The English Spanish Lady, The Force of Blood, The Little Gypsy Girl, The Illustrious Scullery-Maid*), just like those that expose social vices and prejudices (*The Jealous Old Man of Extramadura, Rinconete and Cortadillo*, and to some extent *Lady Cornelia*), and those with a satiric aim (*The Glass Graduate, The Dialogue of the Dogs*), are all heavily weighted toward showing people in conversation and action.

GENDER UNDER SCRUTINY

Critics often prefer Cervantes's darker novellas, and although they cannot resist the charm of *The Little Gypsy Girl* and *The Illustrious Scullery-Maid*, they tend to find those that depict ideals of perfection (*The Generous Lover, The English Spanish Lady, The Force of Blood*) less successful. We should not forget, however, that the latter stories, as well as the secondary plot involving Lucinda, Cardenio, Dorothea, and Fernando in the first part of *Don Quixote*, develop a recurrent theme in Cervantes's prose: the struggle between erotic desire and long-term commitment. Do promises made under the spell of lust—promises that may drastically affect someone else's life—lose their binding force once desire is satisfied?

In the society Cervantes was portraying, a young woman's honor depended on her ability to resist male intemperance. Loss of virginity and subsequent pregnancy signaled the woman's failure to stand firm. But since ideal love was assumed to be an irresistible force leading to permanent union, a man inflamed by desire could commit himself, or pretend as much, to the woman he loves. What's more, since before the Council of Trent (1545–1563), marriage was defined as an exchange of pledges between two individuals rather than a sacrament celebrated publicly, an oath taken in private was assumed to be as valid as a written contract. In such a context, male inconstancy—with all its comic connotations—had extremely serious consequences for the woman. The blend between the comic and the serious is, by the way, particularly striking in works that feature the legendary character Don Juan. Tirso da Molina's *El Burlador de Sevilla* (1630), Molière's *Don Juan* (1665), and Mozart's *Don Giovanni* (1787) mix Don Juan's comic antics as a seducer with heart-rending scenes revolving around the plight of the women he has seduced.

In the novella-like story in the first part of *Don Quixote* (the source for Lewis Theobald's drama *Double Falsehood*, 1727), Don Fernando, son of a powerful duke, falls in love with Dorothea, the beautiful daughter of a wealthy farmer, and promises marriage but, after slaking his lust, abandons her. Next, he manages to separate young Lucinda from her beloved Cardenio and almost succeeds in marrying her. But Lucinda, secretly betrothed to Cardenio, runs away. In the end, chance brings the four lovers together at the same inn, where they make their peace. In *The Force of Blood*, the young, wealthy Rodolfo kidnaps and rapes the beautiful Leocadia, who secretly takes a silver cross from his room before she is brought home. Pregnant, Leocadia hides from the world and raises the child with the help of her parents. Years later, she meets Rodolfo's parents, who notice the cross, understand the young woman's secret, and arrange for Rodolfo and Leocadia to meet again and marry. In *The Two Young Women*, Teodosia lets herself be seduced by her young neighbor Marco Antonio, who runs away as soon as he has deflowered her. Dressed as a man, Teodosia travels to Naples, where her seducer now lives. On the way, she meets a young woman whom Marco Antonio had promised to marry. They find the wrongdoer and make him regret his follies; Teodosia marries him, while her traveling companion weds his brother. The damage is repaired, but in all these examples the male culprits fail to undergo any genuine moral growth. Instead they obey their instincts, forget all about their bad behavior, and when in the end they marry their victims, they do not seem to recognize the suffering they have caused. Yet these young men are not portrayed as clearly evil. When circumstances once more bring them close to the women concerned, they don't refuse marriage. Both the offense and its supposed reparation are performed in the same careless, irresponsible way.

Cervantes's stories of seduction and reconciliation portray men who neglect their obligations without fully turning their backs on society. They are by no means as immoral as the pícaros, since social pressure from parents, friends, or the victims themselves easily brings the offenders back to their duty. Nevertheless, they remain blind to the moral dimension of their actions and lack the ability to deliberate—prospectively or retrospectively—on their behavior. With no dependable insight into their own hearts, these characters believe themselves to be sincere when they promise to marry the young women they desire, but then quickly turn into frivolous knaves when they want to abandon them.

Barely sketched in the novellas about seduction and reparation, this failure of self-knowledge and self-control becomes the main target of *An Ill-Advised Curiosity* (*Don Quixote* pt. 1, chaps. 33–35). Anselmo and Lothario are best friends. Married to the beautiful, virtuous Camilla, Anselmo feels the urge to test her fidelity and asks Lothario to try to seduce her. In the name of friendship and prudence, Lothario advises him to give up such strange ideas. Anselmo himself understands how peculiar his request is: "I see . . . and acknowledge that . . . I fly the good and pursue the evil. Yet, this supposed, you must consider that I labour under the infirmity to which some women are subject, who have a longing to eat dirt, chalk, coals, and other things still worse, even such as are loathsome to the sight, and much more so to the taste."[2] Knowing that his "infirmity" is harmful and degrading, Anselmo is nevertheless aware that it does not place him among the villains who act basely out of self-interest. Unlike, say, the Moor's ensign in Cinzio's novella, Anselmo acts against his own interest. The urge that drives him to his ruin is an intimate, strange, and shameful one that has no name in the usual vocabulary of passions and vices. The author labels it "ill-advised curiosity," but Anselmo calls it "a desire so strange, and so much out of the common tract of other men" (p. 281), "an infirmity," a "frenzy" (p. 290), "a foolish and impertinent desire" (p. 320).

Anselmo is unable to foresee the consequences of his actions. At first, he asks his friend to court Camilla just for a short time. Yet he prolongs the experiment indefinitely despite, or perhaps because of, the proofs of his wife's fidelity. His foolish and impertinent desire blinds him to the course of action his wife and friend might eventually take. Counting—wrongly—on Lothario's indestructible loyalty, Anselmo fails to predict that if Camilla does succumb, it will be impossible for him to discover the truth, since the two lovers will then be united against him. When, in the end, Lothario falls in love with Camilla and she yields to his passion,

[2] Cervantes, *Don Quixote*, trans. Charles Jarvis (Oxford: Oxford World Classics, 1998), p. 290.

Anselmo finds out only when the two of them, fearing the betrayal of a corrupt servant, decide to run away together. Anselmo dies of despair, his widow goes into a nunnery, and Lothario finds death on the battle-field. The *enigmatic psyche* and the penumbra surrounding it are the sub-ject of this story. Explored further by the French novella several decades later, this penumbra would become a central issue in late nineteenth- and twentieth-century prose.

||||||||||||||||||||||||||||||||

Just as important for the novella's sexual politics was María de Zayas's exploration of violent, amoral male behavior in a society with no means of—and perhaps no interest in—prohibiting it. Never before *Novelas Amorosas y ejemplares* (1637; *Amorous and Exemplary Novels*) and *Desengaños Amorosos* (1647; *Disenchantments of Love*) had women's point of view been so fiercely defended, nor the indictment of sexual injustice expressed so persuasively. In earlier novellas, men who fail to respect the norms governing sex and marriage are scolded—and some-times punished—in the very name of these norms, whose validity no one would think of calling into question. Even in the memorable examples of jealous husbands whose cruel passion leads to murder, like Boccaccio's Sir Guillaume de Roussillon or Cinzio's Moor of Venice, the emphasis falls each time on the criminal hubris of the individual character rather than on established, accepted gender injustice. These stories never cast doubt on the institutional framework that makes possible, even endorses, male mistrust of women and violence against them. Thus, in Griselda's story, Gualtieri, who suspects his wife is unworthy of him but finally changes his mind, is never censured, since in the *Decameron*, the reestab-lishment of marital links is enough and counts as a praiseworthy return to social norms.

As for the seduction of a young woman, it is considered an offense only when it fails to lead to marriage—hence Epitia, finally wedded to her lying seducer, implores the emperor to pardon him for winning her dishonestly. Cervantes's narratives of seduction (*The Force of Blood* and the story of Fernando and Dorothea in *Don Quixote*) partly conceal this bias in favor of men by focusing on the more general issue of honoring one's promises. Male sexual inconstancy, Cervantes's novellas suggest, can be brought under control through an appeal to the transgressor's sense of loyalty and his desire for long-term happiness.

In Zayas's novellas, by contrast, the very norms that dictate gender relations are under attack. Family and society, far from helping restrain male violence, favor its outbursts. In the *Disenchantments of Love* (1647), seduction is portrayed as an unscrupulous, unpunished endeavor, jealousy reaches horrific climaxes, and the sense of personal honor, which

in Cervantes functions as a check on male inconstancy, provides justification for the most vicious acts. In Zayas's world, the excesses of *honra*
("honor," understood as concern for one's reputation), which have a
comic resonance in Cervantes's *The Jealous Old Man of Extramadura*,
acquire an unbounded power to harm.

Because Zayas's evildoers often escape punishment, some of her stories
end on a note of profound pessimism. In Italian tragic novellas, by virtue
of what is known as "poetic justice," the final catastrophe either persuades the guilty side to recognize its fault, as when, in Bandello's story,
the death of Romeo and Juliet prompts the Montagues and Capulets to
make peace, or leads to the punishment of the villains, as when Cinzio's
Moor is executed and the scheming ensign tortured to death. In Zayas's
stories, poetic justice is often absent. In "The Most Infamous Revenge"
(*Disenchantments of Love* 2), Don Carlos, a wealthy young nobleman,
seduces Octavia, who is wellborn but poor. When his father arranges for
him to marry the well-off Camilla, Don Carlos, by now grown weary of
Octavia, does not hesitate to abandon her. When Don Juan, Octavia's
brother, learns what has happened, he decides to take revenge by seducing Don Carlos's wife, Camilla. But since Camilla rejects his courtship,
Don Juan dresses up as a woman, gets into her room, puts a dagger to her
breast, and rapes her. Even though Don Carlos knows his wife cannot be
blamed for what happened, he administers a poison that makes her body
swell up monstrously and kills her after many months of suffering. Both
men run away unpunished.

Fathers can be as cruel as husbands. In "Love for the Sake of Conquest" (*Disenchantments* 6), Laurela, a beautiful fourteen-year-old, is the
victim of an elaborate seduction scheme devised by a family friend. Don
Esteban persuades her to elope with him but abandons her in the church
where he had claimed they would be married. Laurela's uncle and father,
refusing to listen to her explanations, lock her up and murder her in a
prearranged accident. Laurela's sisters take refuge in a convent, where
they find contentment, sheltered from the world of men. There is no hint
of remorse or punishment for the father or uncle to clear up the tale's
sinister atmosphere.

Blind cruelty is the prerogative of all-powerful men, but some powerless women also turn to the dark side. In "Too Late Undeceived" (*Disenchantments of Love* 4), Don Martin sleeps with an unknown lady, falls
desperately in love, and later finds and marries her. But a female slave
falsely informs him that his wife has had an affair with her cousin. Don
Martin burns the cousin alive and locks his wife in a kennel, forcing her
to drink from the dead man's skull and eat only scraps from his table.
As a reward, the slave becomes Don Martin's mistress, but two years
later, gravely ill, she admits that she lied. Don Martin stabs his mistress

to death and rushes to free his wife, who has just died of a broken heart. The man goes mad. In "The Ravages of Vice" (*Disenchantments of Love* 10), the unmarried Florentina initiates a long affair with her sister's husband, Don Dionís. Hoping to win him for herself, Florentina arranges for a servant to accuse her sister of adultery. In a fit of rage, Don Dionís kills his wife and no fewer than eleven servants. He then commits suicide—though not without first stabbing Florentina. She survives, however, and after sending her suitor Don Gaspar to inspect the house full of corpses, she tells him what happened. Don Gaspar arranges a king's pardon and advises her to retire to a convent, where Florentina finds happiness in seclusion.

In Zayas's fictional world, erotic desire can work in two equally ugly ways: it may involve a sly attempt to win the other person's sexual favors—lust can be found in both men and women, as the stories of Don Carlos, Don Esteban, and Florentina show; or it may generate the urge to master the other's person body, and this impulse seems specifically male. Fathers and husbands share a manic fear that another man might penetrate their daughter's or wife's body, forever staining the woman and making her unworthy to live, even if the woman was forced or gave her consent under the false impression it would lead to marriage. Panic-stricken, fathers and husbands cannot think in terms of innocence or guilt, but rush to dispose of the woman's defiled body as secretly and efficiently as possible.

Zayas's world is not consistently evil. Some of the *Amorous and Exemplary Novels* end well, often with the help of premonitory dreams, ghostly apparitions, and, in two cases, spectacular miracles—as in "Triumph over the Impossible," where a lover's prayer brings his beloved back to life. Ideal love can prevail over the corruption of this world, but its victory can rarely be achieved with society's support. In Zayas's novellas, the realm of ideals has little power over real human interactions. Hers is an unstable universe, governed by wild impulses and archaic phobias. Individual hubris meets no obstacle, couples are volatile, loyalty nonexistent, and marriage dooms men to insecurity and women to the murderous tyranny of their husbands.

A free narrative flow, frequently changing the narrator's point of view, mixing story lines, and appearing to have reached a conclusion only to introduce new, unexpected developments, enhances the sense of instability created by the subject matter. Zayas's technique allows her to portray a world in which individuals are neither entirely cut off from society nor linked to it by a stable set of higher ideals. In these unsteady circumstances, unable to resist their own passions and circumvent the hostility surrounding them, women can find peace only by withdrawing from the world.

A less chaotic universe, albeit no less tragic than Zayas's, is evoked in the French novellas of the late seventeenth century, particularly those by Saint-Réal and Mme de Lafayette. While further expanding the size of their novellas to the extent that some, like *The Princess of Clèves*, were later retrospectively labeled novels, these authors continued to emphasize the unity of action, the spectacular nature of the events related, and the real-life setting of the story. Like the Italian and Spanish novellas, these focus on the private lives of their characters, highlighting both the transparent impulses of the heart and the "inner opacity" of perplexing, incomprehensible passions.

Don Carlos by Saint-Réal (1672) tells a dark story of unspoken love, suspicion, and jealousy, later dramatized by Friedrich Schiller (1787) and turned into an opera by Giuseppe Verdi (1867). The action is set a century before the novella's composition, at the court of Philip II of Spain. Don Carlos, heir to the throne, is in love with Philip's young second wife, who was initially meant to marry the son rather than the father. The two young people are a model of innocence and discretion, but the apprehensive courtiers around them guess their secret. Political factors reinforce the rivalry between father and son. The prince wants to end the war against the Protestants in the Netherlands, an aim the Inquisition opposes. A search of the young prince's apartments turns up his correspondence with leaders of the Protestant rebellion, as well as a suspiciously friendly letter from the queen. The king, advised by the Inquisition, orders the execution of Don Carlos.

The striking event—a son's execution ordered by his own father—and the oppressive atmosphere of the Spanish court are in step with the tradition of the tragic novella. But none of Saint-Réal's Italian predecessors, still less their French imitators (Charles Sorel and François de Rosset), is as adept as he is at portraying the tiniest details of the characters' moral psychology. Compared with the subtle maneuvers of Don Carlos and his enemies, the actions of Bandello's Romeo and Juliet seem incredibly obvious. Saint-Réal's art consists in achieving the most dramatic conclusion from a succession of barely visible inner and outer movements.

Mme de Lafayette's *The Princess of Clèves* (1678), the most mature and complex work of the period, while occasionally alluding to idealist novels, is based on a dramatic plot typical of a novella. It continues Cervantes's reflections on enigmatic psyches and shares Saint-Réal's interest in surveillance and dissimulation. The court of Henri II as portrayed by Mme de Lafayette in detail—too much detail, according to her contemporary critics—resembles Saint-Réal's Spanish court, governed by mutual suspicion and abounding in secret alliances, capricious love affairs, false promises, and treasonous plotting. The court's depravity, however, which in Saint-Réal's *Don Carlos* forms the center of the story, here only provides its background. The foreground belongs to a few dignified characters who, unfortunately, lack reliable self-knowledge, fail to govern their passions, and tear each other apart.

At the beginning, the worthiest character is M. de Clèves, a perfect lover lost in a world that fails to appreciate him. He falls in love with the beautiful Mlle de Chartres, but because her family, though old and distinguished, does not enjoy the favor of the court, he cannot propose to her as long as his father is alive. When M. de Clèves, after his father's death, does ask for Mlle de Chartres's hand—an act considered generous, given her family's situation—he is gratefully accepted. The young wife, whose only friend and adviser is her mother, aspires to be a perfect spouse but is unable to govern her feelings. She remains indifferent to her husband and falls desperately in love with the Duke of Nemours, a lady-killer who, though usually as unreliable as the other courtiers, seems on this particular occasion to be capable of true love.

When her mother dies, the princess in love has no one else she can depend on, so she turns to her husband for advice and help. But by confessing to him her feelings for another man, she takes an extraordinary risk. Like Anselmo in Cervantes's novella, the princess fails to foresee the long-term effects of her actions. M. de Clèves becomes jealous, harboring wild suspicions and stooping so low as to ask her to name the man she loves. The princess remains silent, but Nemours has secretly witnessed the dialogue between husband and wife, and cannot refrain from talking to a friend about it; the rumor spreads, until the two spouses, unaware that Nemours has overheard their conversation, accuse each other of indiscretion. Despite his wife's profession of innocence, M. de Clèves dies, unable to bear his disappointment.

The princess, by contrast, matures and gathers strength. As a naive young woman unable to feel anything but respect and friendship for her loyal husband, she discovered the power of eros by falling in love with a man who did not quite deserve it. Later, realizing she is partly responsible for her husband's death, she rejects Nemours's marriage proposal. She could perhaps forget that her love and Nemours's indiscretion had led to M. de Clèves's death, if she were sure that Nemours would be a faithful husband. Conversely, she might be able to accept that sooner or later Nemours would go back to his old, frivolous ways, if she didn't feel she had a duty to her late husband's memory. But put together, the memory of M. de Clèves and the conviction that Nemours's love won't last persuade her to refuse him. The experience of passion, which destroyed M. de Clèves, has fortified his widow.

CHAPTER 4

An Isolated Realm,
Hesitant Lovers:
The Pastoral

IIIIIIIIIIIIIIIIIIIIIIIIIIIIIIIIIIIIIIIIIIIIIIIIIIIIIIIIIIIIIIIIIIIIII

Somewhere between, on the one hand, lengthy idealist novels about strong souls running across the wide, hostile world and, on the other hand, short novellas whose characters, confined to a narrow space, follow their heart's impulses, there was an intermediary genre. The pastoral imagines a conspicuously fictional, secluded Arcadia, in which gentle young people go back and forth between constancy and weakness, caprice and devotion, and, not unlike the narrators of elegiac stories, live only for love. Notably, in the pastoral the denouement is rarely tragic and the characters' hesitations do not prevent the light of beauty from flooding their lives.

Arcadia, a remote area whose inhabitants, not yet corrupted by civilization, live peacefully as shepherds and fruit-gatherers, was celebrated in Theocritus's short poems about life in nature's midst (third century BC) and Virgil's *Eclogues* (37 BC). The pastoral environment later reemerged in the poetry of Petrarch, Garcilaso de la Vega, Clément Marot, and John Milton, as well as in Renaissance epic, which sometimes includes an Arcadian episode, as in Tasso's *Jerusalem Delivered* (1581) and Spenser's *The Faerie Queene* (1590). The narrow confines of Arcadian realms proved particularly well suited to the theater, as evidenced by Tasso's *Aminta* (1573), Guarini's *Il Pastor Fido* (1590), and Shakespeare's *As You Like It* (ca. 1599).

As for the pastoral novel proper, the ancient Greek *Daphnis and Chloe* by Longus (ca. second century) was translated into modern languages only after 1559, probably too late to influence a genre that had been reinvented earlier and according to different principles. Boccaccio wrote a pastoral novel—his *Ameto* (*Comedia delle ninfe fiorentine*, 1341)—independently of Longus's narrative, and so did Jacopo Sannazaro, whose *Arcadia* (1504) relies heavily on Theocritus, Virgil, and their fifteenth-century Italian followers. The most successful pastoral novel of the sixteenth century, *Diana* by Jorge de Montemayor (1559), continues Sannazaro's tradition, as does Cervantes's *Galatea* (1585). Sir Philip Sidney's *Old Arcadia* (1580) and Honoré d'Urfé *Astrea* (1607–1627) attempted to give the genre a stable, harmonious form, while remaining close to the pastorals of Sannazaro, Montemayor, and Cervantes.

The Golden Age

In depicting Arcadia, these fictions convey an important anthropological insight about social hierarchy and the division of labor. They assume that human beings who live off the bounty of nature can to some extent dispense with private property, can ignore, as Cervantes's Quixote argues in his speech on the Golden Age, "these two words *meum* and *tuum*. In that age of innocence," Quixote continues, "all things were in common: no one needed to take any other pains for his ordinary sustenance, than to lift up his hand and take it from the sturdy oaks, which stood inviting him liberally to taste of their sweet and relishing fruit. . . . All then was peace, all amity, all concord" (pt. 1, chap. 11, p. 77). Shepherds belong to a relatively more advanced stage, in which pastures may still be held in common, but, since herds belong to their owners, the distinction between *meum* and *tuum* is not fully ignored. Nevertheless, a sense of equality still prevails and labor is not excessively hard. Guided, but not ruled, by a higher class of priests whose task is to observe the constellations, understand the changing seasons, and pray to the gods, Arcadians are free, serene, and pious.

By implication, the invention of agriculture—when the plow forces nature to bear fruit—brings about a dramatic change. It requires a life of toil, fosters private ownership of land, and leads to a stricter division of labor. Even more than breeding cattle, agriculture depends on astronomical knowledge, thus reinforcing the role of the priests who observe the stars and converse with the gods. As a family of laborers now produces more than it consumes, large food reserves can be stored for later use, as Joseph advised Pharaoh to do in the Bible story (Genesis 41:33–36). Stockpiles, however, invite predators, hence the need for an army to defend the provisions. Agriculture ends up permanently splitting people into three social orders: those who labor, those who fight, and those who observe the skies and pray. Having raped Mother Earth, society must now endure the harsh rule of men over men and the scourge of war. Once this stage is reached, how can one avoid dreaming of a time before this coercion and of a place where the old ways still survive?

Arcadia embodies this dream. It hosts peaceful shepherds who worship pagan gods and intermingle freely with nymphs and magic creatures. Arcadia's neighbors may well be subjected to war and violence, but their mores have no impact on this blissful realm, deliberately presented as a wishful fantasy, a figment of poetic imagination. The kingdom of Ethiopia in the *Ethiopian Story* and King Arthur's court in the Arthurian cycle exemplify norms that ought to govern all human communities. Arcadia, by contrast, is designed as an exception to the rule: "Are not these woods / More free from peril than the envious Court?" the Duke exclaims while living in the forest of Arden (Shakespeare, *As You Like It*, 2.1.3–4). He adds wisely: "Here feel we but the penalty of Adam," meaning mortality. This way of life might well suit some people but cannot provide a dependable ideal for the rest of the world—in any case, its interactions with that world are minimal. Occasionally, characters unhappy with their fate seek refuge, as does the exiled Duke in *As You Like It*, in Arcadia, or leave it to look for solace elsewhere, but most of the time, behind the cliffs and forests surrounding its borders, Arcadia remains alone and unreal.

The absence of internal strife, reinforced by a strong sense of immunity to conquest, allows the inhabitants to lead a peaceful communal life. They trust each other; they share their joys and sorrows; they worship the same gods and perform the same ceremonies together. Arcadia harbors a *trusting, empathic society*, which accepts its members with all their qualities and faults. The only authority that is sometimes difficult to abide by is that of parents over their offspring, but since the parents usually hide in the background, open clashes remain unlikely. As a *locus amœnus*, a charming, undisturbed place, Arcadia favors *otium*, leisure, and allows the shepherds to spend most of their time on contemplation, daydreaming, love, song, and poetry. Free from external adversity, Arcadians live in a world of tender feelings and calm reflection. Love, chaste love, is what these gentle hearts worry about.

Idyllic and Contemplative Pastorals

In the *idyllic* version of the pastoral, love is depicted as a naive, beneficent emotion that leads to marriage and social integration. Longus's *Daphnis and Chloe* describes the mutual attraction of two adolescent villagers, the gentle seduction of Daphnis by an older woman who teaches him how to make love, and the wedding of the young couple. In the idyll, love is simple and natural; it attains its goals without meeting any serious obstacle, internal or external. This version of the pastoral played a role in the eighteenth-century revival of the genre, giving it its happy, carefree mood, but it had only a modest impact on the Renaissance pastoral.

Sixteenth-century authors developed a different version of the genre, emphasizing the *contemplative* side of Arcadian life. In Nicolas Poussin's painting *Et in Arcadia ego* ("I too am in Arcadia"), the three young shepherds deciphering these Latin words on a funeral stone accept the reminder of their mortality with softly smiling faces. Likewise, the characters of Renaissance pastorals reflect on their love in both poetic and philosophical terms. A pastoral novel does not just tell a story. It includes convoluted conversations and lyrical passages in much larger quantities than later taste would find acceptable.

Reflections on love in these novels follow the Neoplatonic teachings of Marsilio Ficino, whose commentary on Plato's *Symposium* (ca. 1475), later filtered through Leone Ebreo's *Dialoghi d'amore* (1535) and Mario Equicola's *Libro de natura de amore* (1525), influenced all major pastoral novels of the sixteenth and early seventeenth centuries. These novels conceive of eros as a cosmic force lifting human beings toward the One, the transcendent source of beauty, goodness, and truth. The Neoplatonic bent is made explicit in Sannazaro's *Arcadia*, as well as in *Diana*, *Galatea*, *Old Arcadia*, and *Astrea*, which all include sermons or debates about the nature of love.

In Sannazaro's pastoral, the priest-shepherd Enareto teaches the other shepherds to transcend the suffering of unrequited love. In the fourth book of Montemayor's *Diana*, the sage Felicia gathers her followers at her palace, hidden in the woods and adorned with sculptures of ancient gods and heroes. The main male character, Sireno, asks Felicia to explain why love, supposed to be born of reason, never listens to it. Her long answer paraphrases section 1.3 of Leone Ebreo's dialogues, "Human Love and the World of Passions." In Cervantes's *Galatea*, a similar debate takes place in the grove where the shepherds gather around a fountain for their siesta. In answer to Lenius, who rejects love, the shepherd Tirsius, its defender, makes the distinction between the true, radiant face of love and the earthly circumstances that might obscure it. The priestly figure reappears in d'Urfé's *Astrea* in the guise of the high druid Adamas, who teaches young Celadon that love gives the world its fundamental law: it is the reason why the Creator brought the universe into being, and provides the norm that governs the multitude of creatures. In the realm of material objects, its name is sympathy, that is, alchemical affinity; in animals, love drives the desire to perpetuate their species; and finally, human beings, in principle at least, should love God in his creatures and all creatures in God.

In d'Urfé's novel, most shepherds, realizing that the soul is more perfect than the body, love according to the spirit rather than the flesh. Yet some accept the heart's desire for the passing beauty of the body. Enlightened lovers, such as Sylvander, consider sensual love impossible, for those who love want their feelings to be reciprocated, and the body alone can never return their affections, since love resides only in the soul. Besides, if the beloved died, would one still love the body? The hedonist shepherd Hylas begs to differ. If the soul had no body, Hylas would never be in love, because for him, the body is "the most beautiful and perfect work of the gods."[1] Faced with the profusion of beauty and erotic power that floods the universe, he interprets this abundance in quantitative terms. "When I decide to love a lady," Hylas declares, "I first consider her beauty . . . And suddenly I feel a mass of love in my soul, equal to the prize and valor that is in her, and when I love, I go spending this mass of love, and when I have used it all to serve the lady for whom I amassed it, I have nothing left for her" (*L'Astrée*, 3:348).

FORLORN LOVERS, POETIC TRANSPORT

As these debates show, peaceful Arcadia does not always protect its inhabitants from less commendable varieties of love. Afflicted by the frequent contrast between ideal love and conduct that falls short of it, Arcadian shepherds are often unhappy and ready to complain about their sorrows. With a few exceptions, such as Galatea and Elicio in Cervantes's unfinished *Galatea*, love brings them pain and misery. It troubles them, puts them to the test, and leads them on the winding paths of doubt, disappointment, and jealousy. The final goal of these trials is to steer the shepherds toward incorruptible love, but the way there is difficult and full of traps.

Notably, ordeals in love foster shyness, oversensitivity, and, quite often, a propensity for resignation. In chivalric novels too, love—chaste or adulterous—afflicts and disorients people, sometimes unsettling knights-errant who would otherwise be the first to confront adversity. Lancelot humbly begs Guinevere's favor; Amadis hides in the forest under the name of Beltenebros—the Dark Beau—because of Oriana's unfounded suspicions. But chivalric novels celebrate lasting feelings that make lovers proud and strong, while in pastoral stories, love is an obsessive, painful, and sometimes unstable passion. The character typical of Renaissance pastoral is the *forlorn lover*, hesitant, vulnerable, often helpless, who either has failed to inspire a strong attachment or has been rejected by his beloved. This *unstable couple* can and often does find happiness in the end. Yet because Arcadian love is frequently the result of a cosmic, impersonal force rather than an individual one, and because these characters lack the firmness of their ancient Greek or chivalric equivalents, a happy resolution is never guaranteed.

---

[1] Honoré d'Urfé, *L'Astrée*, ed. Hugues Vaganay (1619; Geneva: Slatkine Reprints, 1966), 3:51–52 (my translation).

Usually, these lovers are lost in thought. Only now and then do they open their mouths to express their grief in poetry and song, as though the Arcadian meadows and groves were a stage on which to recite their melancholy parts. In one of the most common pastoral scenes, an Arcadian walking in the woods, alone or with a friend, happens to hear the lonely eclogue of an unknown shepherd. The passersby lend the song a friendly ear, inquire about the singer's sorrows, and offer to help. The singer tells his or her story, offering a narrative to explain the background to the lyrical passages.

In Sannazaro's *Arcadia*, poetry is the most important element, to the extent that the stories of the shepherds in love seem designed only to link the beautiful eclogues to each other. In *Diana* and *Galatea*, Montemayor and Cervantes excel in most poetic genres available at the time—eclogues, sonnets, rondels—showing mastery of the different stanza forms (octaves, sextines, triplets) and verse patterns (traditional Spanish octosyllables, as well as heptasyllables and hendecasyllables). *Galatea*, at half the length of *Don Quixote*'s first part, contains eighty splendid poems, adding up to forty-five hundred lines. Although these poems can be appreciated without reference to the adventures of the characters who recite them, for Cervantes, as for Montemayor, the poetic passages naturally blend with and ennoble the narrative.

LANGUISHING ACTORS, SECONDARY PLOTS

What with philosophical conversation and poetry, the action here develops less than in other narrative genres, so that early Renaissance pastorals generally lack a clear-cut main story line. In Boccaccio's *Ameto*, set in Etruria, an Italian equivalent of Arcadia, the main character wanders through woods and glades, sings songs, and listens to the nymphs who grace the land with their beauty. One by one, the nymphs tell their love stories, delighting Ameto's eyes and mind. These stories, told in a poetic language rich in mythological references and allegorical imagery, remain as distinct from one another as the tales in Boccaccio's later *Decameron*. Without a central plot, *Ameto*'s unity derives from the artful succession of the nymphs' stories and their contribution to Ameto's development.

In Sannazaro's pastoral, the Arcadian landscape continues to encourage confession rather than action. The young characters—native shepherds and ill-fated lovers from elsewhere—sing the beauty of the land, deplore their amorous misfortunes, and seek a cure for melancholy. The narrator Sincero tells how his unrequited love led him to look for consolation in Arcadia. The lovelorn Clonico, eager to regain control of himself and bring love back within its proper limits, seeks advice from the priest-shepherd Enareto, the great expert in mysteries human and divine. Within the sacred grove of Pan, the young men reach a cave where, on either side of an altar, hang scrolls inscribed with the laws of pastoral life. Enareto advises them to leave love behind and embrace wisdom. The ultimate horizon of this realm is melancholy: in the end, the narrator, with the help of the nymphs, discovers the funeral urn of his beloved. Even more static than Boccaccio's *Ameto*, Sannazaro's *Arcadia* and its sumptuous setting seem to beg for action. But the motivation, decisiveness, and movement that could provide the Arcadian landscape with genuine human conflict are not part of Sannazaro's project.

In Montemayor's *Diana* (1559), the framing story takes place in a Spanish Arcadia on the banks of the River Ezla and features two unhappy shepherds, Sireno and Silvano, both in love with the shepherdess Diana. Silvano's feelings have never been reciprocated, but Sireno and Diana loved each other tenderly until, while he was away temporarily, Diana's parents ordered her to marry the unpleasant, compulsively jealous Delius. Disconsolate and helpless, Sireno sings of his love, accompanied by his former rival Silvano, now his best friend. As Diana is married, her virtuous suitor cannot do anything but deplore his fate and forget his love, which he does with the help of the sage Felicia. Similarly, in Cervantes's *Galatea* (1585), two exemplary shepherds, Elicio and Galatea, love and trust each other, but this wonderful situation generates no conflict, and when, at the end, Elicio learns that Galatea's parents plan to marry her off to another man, the potential clash is deferred until the novel's second part, which Cervantes never wrote.

The stagnant framing story in both *Diana* and *Galatea* creates an auspicious environment in which secondary plots can unfold. The main characters in each listen compassionately to other shepherds and nymphs who come along to tell them their troubles. Full of movement, their stories revolve around the struggles between love and a variety of obstacles, some external—the whims of fortune—some internal, including the usual fickleness and duplicity of pastoral love and the more enigmatic, never perfect match between the "I" and the body.

Two episodes in *Diana* develop these themes: Selvagia's and Felismena's. During a celebration at Minerva's temple, Selvagia, a Lusitan maid, is courted in jest by another woman, Ismenia. Taking advantage of Selvagia's naïveté, Ismenia pretends to be a man named Alanio, who, she claims, has disguised himself as a woman in order to be accepted in the temple. This Alanio does exist and is in fact Ismenia's own cousin and lover. He soon meets Selvagia and, forgetting Ismenia, falls in love with her—she reciprocates. To win Alanio back, Ismenia pretends to favor another shepherd, Montano, who has courted her for a long time. The inconstant Alanio gets jealous and switches back to Ismenia, who meanwhile has truly fallen in love with Montano. But then, Montano meets

Selvagia and transfers his affections to her. Confusion reigns, since Selvagia now loves Alanio, who is pursuing Ismenia, who is enamored of Montano, who worships Selvagia. In a celebrated passage, the beautiful shepherdess describes this circle of unrequited loves: "It was the strangest thing in the world to hear how *Alanio* sighing said, Ah, my *Ismenia*; and how *Ismenia* said, Ah my *Montano*; and how *Montano* said, Ah my *Selvagia*; and how *Selvagia* said, Ah my *Alanio*."[2] Wounded and disoriented, Selvagia seeks refuge on the banks of the Ezla.

Diana's next secondary plot is inspired by Bandello's story of Nicuola, Lattanzio, and Catella (2.36). A young woman named Felismena, a warrior who reveres the goddess Diana and is thus out of favor with Venus, responds favorably to the passionate courtship of the noble Felix. But Felix, sent by his father to a princely court, soon forgets Felismena and instead pursues a lady named Celia. Realizing that she is not his first and only love, Celia resists. Meanwhile, Felismena arrives at court, disguised as a man and calling herself Valerio. Taking Felismena-Valerio on as his page, Felix asks him (her) to deliver a letter to Celia, who instantly falls in love with him (her). Now Felismena loves Felix, who is chasing Celia, who, unwittingly closing the circle, dreams of Felismena-Valerio. Rejected by the other woman in disguise, Celia dies of grief; Felix runs away in despair. The disconsolate Felismena searches for him all over Spain.

In *A Midsummer Night's Dream*, Shakespeare presents the circle of unrequited loves with indulgent humor. Montemayor's novel, in contrast, looks very gravely at the ease with which people fall in love, how lightly they discard their loved ones to pursue a new target, and the role of vanity in such changes, as when Alanio, jealous of Montano, comes back to Ismenia. These stories depict the pleasure of conquest, and of deception—Ismenia misleading Selvagia, for instance—as well as the surprising impulses of the heart, which never can be fully ruled by reason, as is clear when Ismenia, pretending to prefer Montano, ends up truly loving him.

Diana's gender confusions—Felismena-Valerio being a woman disguised as a man; Ismenia claiming to be a man disguised as a woman—call attention to the puzzle of the union between a visible body and the indiscernible individual who is or has that body. In Selvagia's story, two seemingly identical bodies, Ismenia's and Alanio's, in fact belong to two different shepherds. The resemblance allows Ismenia to hide who she is and pretend to be Alanio. The indistinguishable bodies correspond to different persons. Conversely, two falsely distinguishable bodies can belong to the same person, as when the cross-dressing Felismena appears to be the page Valerio. Both cases emphasize the distinction between the visible,

---

[2] Jorge de Montemayor, *Diana*, trans. Bartholonew Yong, ed. Judith M. Kennedy (Oxford: Clarendon, 1968), p. 42 (slightly modified).

sometimes deceptive body and the invisible "I." "*I* am not the body you see," Ismenia seems to say; "The body you see is not *I*," Felismena-Valerio echoes. Always a danger, this noncoincidence between body and person becomes more noticeable than usual in Arcadia, where the shepherds, tried and tormented by love, tend to lack a strong, resilient "I." And as we shall soon see, in *Astrea* the game of falsely distinguishable bodies is crucial in Celadon's progress on the path to personhood.

The last secondary episode in *Diana*, about the beautiful Belisa, who is loved by two men—Arsenio and his son Arsileo—and for a while feels attracted to both, explores yet another facet of human weakness. Since, in contemplative pastorals, love's aim should be to reach the ultimate source of beauty, goodness, and truth, the transcendent One, it is expected to concentrate on a single object. To love two different men is a serious fault, and in Belisa's case it seems to lead to tragedy, for both suitors meet their deaths while courting her, the father unknowingly killing his son, and then committing suicide when he realizes what he has done.

Montemayor's great skill, often imitated by later authors of pastoral novels and plays (including Shakespeare, who, as well as using Selvagia's story for *A Midsummer Night's Dream*, drew on Felismena's in *The Two Gentlemen of Verona*), consists in devising unusual erotic imbroglios. He is less interested, however, in showing how the characters themselves might resolve these intricate situations. As though love could only tangle the threads of individual lives, but never unravel those knots, the lovers' predicaments are elucidated or solved by magic rather than human action. Selvagia's happiness is achieved thanks to the sage Felicia, who puts her to sleep alongside Sireno and Silvano, the two men in love with Diana, then touches their heads with a magic book that makes Sireno forget Diana and kindles a mutual love between Selvagia and Silvano. The wandering Felismena meets two knights fighting in the forest and saves the life of one, who turns out to be her beloved Felix; a nymph who witnesses the scene gives Felix a magic potion that makes him fall back in love with Felismena. As for Belisa, magic explains away the death of her suitors: it turns out that a famous wizard, himself in love with the young maid, had used two spirits, disguised as the father and son, to stage their fictive murder and suicide.

In Cervantes's *Galatea* the secondary plots are even more dramatic, occasionally transgressing the limits of Arcadian serenity and goodwill. The novel opens with the story of Lisandro and Leonida, who love each other and want to get married, but meet an unhappy, violent fate. Her brother, manipulated by a jealous, rejected admirer of hers, stabs Leonida, believing that he is taking revenge on a different young woman, who has refused his love. Lisandro finds out what happened from his dying beloved and rushes to kill the guilty brother. Another subplot ushers in not one but two pairs of seemingly identical siblings, the brothers Artidoro and Galercio, and the sisters Teolinda and Gelasia, who fall in and out of love with the right and the wrong people. The story of Timbrio and Silerio, narrated by the latter in the second and third books of *Galatea*, is a short Heliodoran novel of adventure, taking place far beyond Arcadia's borders, in which the characters are subjected to the inexplicable whims of fortune.

THE HEROIC PASTORAL

Because pastoral love does not depend on decisive human action, and because the main couple's final reunion usually occurs as unexpectedly as their earlier separation, pastoral novels often cannot develop a credible sequence of events or reach a neat conclusion. The need, on the one hand, to compensate for the static main plot, and, on the other, to show the variety of love's labors, creates an irresistible temptation for the writer to produce yet another forlorn lover, yet another unhappy couple, thus undermining the coherence of the work as a whole. This may be why neither Montemayor's *Diana* nor Cervantes's *Galatea*, nor even d'Urfé's *Astrea* was finished by its author. In Montemayor's case, the fate of the main characters, Diana and Sireno, is left on hold at the end of the novel and reaches a happy resolution only in Gil Polo's *Enamoured Diana* (1564), considered the most successful continuation of Montemayor's work. Cervantes never put his plans to finish *Galatea* into practice. *Astrea* has two different endings, one written by d'Urfé's secretary along the lines his master had indicated, the other by Marin le Roy de Gomberville, a successful seventeenth-century novelist.

In *Old Arcadia* (1580), Sidney answers this challenge with the most coherent Arcadian plot to date. But in order to do so, he takes the bold step of casting aside those features of the pastoral that inhibit decision and action. All traces of the Golden Age and the classless society are gone. Arcadia is reconceived as a safe haven for members of the martial caste—kings, princes, and their families—who for important reasons decide to hide temporarily among shepherds. Behind their disguises, the characters keep up their princely ways: the elegant affections and valiant behavior are theirs alone, while local shepherds act like low-class buffoons—greedy, obtuse, and sometimes mindlessly rebellious. Equality is only a pretense, skillfully circumvented when necessary. The shy, hesitant characters of Sannazaro and Montemayor have disappeared, and in their place a band of born leaders conspire to achieve their lofty goals. Melancholy gives way to burning desire, and instead of resignation, the urge to act runs through this genuinely *heroic* pastoral. Yet, as in the older, contemplative pastorals, love remains the principal motivation, rivalry and disguise sow confusion, and, at the formal level, poetry alternates with narrative prose.

Built on the model of a five-act drama, *Old Arcadia* describes the vain attempt by King Basilius of Arcadia to circumvent an oracle according to which one of his daughters will be stolen "by princely mean," the other will embrace "an uncouth love," the king will commit adultery with his own wife, and a foreign power will sit on his throne. Leaving the city, Basilius and his family hide among the shepherds. Two young princes, Musidorus and Pyrocles, turn up there after a shipwreck, fall in love with Basilius's daughters, and, to get round the father's protective measures, disguise themselves—Musidorus as a shepherd, Pyrocles as an Amazon. Musidorus wins the love of one daughter, while the supposed Amazon unwittingly captivates all the other members of the family: the king, the queen—who senses that he is really a man—and the second daughter, who feels "an uncouth love" for the disguised Pyrocles. After many tightly woven adventures, Basilius, believing he holds the beautiful Amazon in his arms, makes love to his wife, the queen; Musidorus and his beloved elope; and for a short while Euarchus, king of Macedon, replaces Basilius as ruler of Arcadia. The oracle's prediction thus fulfilled, the royal couple can return to the city, and their daughters happily marry the two princes.

Old Arcadia has not enjoyed the success it deserves. Increasingly fascinated by Heliodorus, by late chivalric novels, and by the energy of Italian Renaissance fantasy epic, Sidney reworked his novel, bringing the action closer to the wilder adventures in the *Ethiopian Story*, *Amadis of Gaul*, and Ariosto's *Orlando Furioso*. In the second version, war and violence enter the plot; there is even less sense of human weakness than in the first version, and not so much space for lyrical poetry. The first three books of *New Arcadia* are three times as long as their counterparts in the older version, but because Sidney never finished it, its publishers tacked on the much more compact ending from *Old Arcadia*. The first version was not published until the twentieth century, so only *New Arcadia* (1593) was known at the time. It reads as a hybrid, yet still excellent achievement, combining the pastoral celebration of love with the taste for martial adventures.

INNER GROWTH

In comparison with Sidney's heroic pastoral, d'Urfé's *Astrea*[3] comes across as a return to the earlier, Golden Age Arcadia. It is also an ambitious attempt to join together the idyllic, the contemplative, and the

---

[3] Vol. 1, 1607; vol. 2, 1610; vol. 3, 1619; vol. 4, 1627; vol. 5, finished by Balthazar Baro, 1628.

heroic pastoral by combining *Daphnis and Chloe*'s emphasis on the main couple with the art of conversation and the secondary plots developed in Montemayor, and the martial energy of Sidney's *Old Arcadia*. The size and structure of the novel are remarkable. More than twenty-five hundred pages of prose and verse amply develop the figure of the forlorn lover, the unstable couple, the friendly, empathic society, and the heroic fighter into a striking new vision of personal growth.

At the center of the action, d'Urfé puts the young shepherds Astrea and Celadon, who live on the bank of the River Lignon in the Forez, an Arcadian region of France. They are part of a community of young people whose goal in life is to find true love. With the exception of Hylas, the hedonist who defends ephemeral attachments, all the characters—Celadon and Astrea, Sylvander and Diana, Lindamor and Galathea, Ergastus and Leonida—aspire to fall in love with a single being whom they would never abandon. These lovers are all honorable, but not equally deserving. Galathea and Leonida, who lack clear-sightedness and self-mastery, both fall in love with Celadon before discovering, or returning to, their true companions. D'Urfé's Diana is more steadfast, but because she does not fully understand the law of universal sympathy, she resists Sylvander's love for a long time. Only Celadon and Astrea recognize from the beginning that they are made for each other and willingly confess their feelings. Do they form a perfect couple? Not quite. A misunderstanding breaks them apart.

Astrea and Celadon have exchanged vows of fidelity but must keep their relationship secret to fool their disapproving families. To cover their tracks, Astrea asks Celadon to court another shepherdess, Aminta, and he reluctantly agrees. Semirus, who is also in love with Astrea, manages to convince her that Celadon is genuinely attracted to Aminta. In an attack of jealousy that recalls Oriana's capricious banishment of her beloved in *Amadis of Gaul*, Astrea forbids Celadon ever to come near her again. The desperate young man throws himself into the river, but survives and hides in the woods. Astrea, believing him dead, bitterly deplores her fit of rage. A praiseworthy love that pursues the soul rather than the body, a love in accordance with the laws of universal sympathy, turns out to be just as capricious as the most superficial and ephemeral feelings.

Because true passion requires blind obedience to the lady's slightest wish, Celadon, like Amadis, never attempts to defend himself before the earthly Astrea. Alone in the woods, he builds a rustic temple to the heavenly Astrea, the goddess of justice. The Gallic druid Adamas discovers his hideout, brings him provisions, and, after initiating him into the mysteries of the Gallic religion, persuades Celadon to approach his beloved disguised as Alexis, a young druid woman. Astrea is struck by the beautiful Alexis's resemblance to her dead lover, but she befriends the young woman without suspecting who she really is. The two of them, innocently close, attend the thanksgiving ceremonies of the druids and vestals. A war episode adds a heroic touch to the pastoral, allowing Celadon to demonstrate his strength and courage. At the end of the novel, the two meet again at the Fountain of True Love.

The main plot is a long, elaborate account of the lovers' progress toward self-mastery and mutual trust. Following the tradition of Renaissance pastoral, d'Urfé portrays characters split between the impulse toward the ideal and the obstacles presented by youth, innocence, and gullibility. And like his Italian and Spanish predecessors, d'Urfé depicts a tormented Arcadia, in which the effects of this split are painfully felt. The novelty here is in the meticulous description of the lovers' advance toward perfection.

Celadon goes through five stages, coinciding with the five parts of the novel. First, disappointment leads him to despair and attempted suicide. Next, he seeks refuge in the forest, not unlike other forlorn lovers in earlier pastoral novels. But while virtually all of these characters soon find friends who sympathize and help, the lonely Celadon is effectively cut off from Arcadian society. No one can see him except the nymph Leonida, who catches a glimpse, and Adamas, who enjoys higher, priestly powers. Sheltered by the fog of solitude, Celadon has the leisure to give himself over to his love, without confronting the real-world anger of his beloved. Turning away from the real Astrea, Celadon now worships the celestial version, and the Twelve Tables of the Law of Love that adorn the forest temple he builds for her. At this stage, Celadon struggles to overcome his despair by clinging to his ideals in their purest form.

Next, in order to escape solitude, Celadon must learn how to go beyond himself. Disguised as Alexis, Celadon *becomes* the young woman so fast and so well that no one guesses the trickery. Whereas in the forest he had listened only to his love—as though the outside world did not exist—now, so as to live close to Astrea, he must forget himself and his love, and pretend to be another human being. To make his disguise plausible, Celadon follows an imaginary script that defines proper behavior for a young druid woman. Neither Astrea nor his own brother recognizes him, for the good reason that, as Alexis, the shepherd acts according to a pattern that cannot possibly be his own.

Yet, in a revealing scene, Astrea asks Alexis to remain close to her for the rest of her life. Struck by these words, which remind him of the day Astrea banished him from her presence forever, Celadon-Alexis has tears in his-her eyes. Astrea wants to know the reason for these tears, and Alexis, who obviously cannot mention Celadon, nonetheless tells a story based on his misfortunes. Alexis claims to have been bound by the most perfect friendship to a beautiful druid virgin who, after several happy, companionable years, chased her away without any explanation. Astrea is so moved that she promises to sacrifice her blood and life to keep Alexis's friendship (3:274).

Here, Celadon-Alexis learns to look at his personal misfortune as an instance of a general category: the wounds caused by love quarrels. Although the story he-she tells Astrea is modeled on Celadon's own torments, it acquires a hint of universality. What happened to Celadon, the invented story seems to say, could happen to anyone. Alexis's imaginary biography makes Celadon feel less unusual, less forlorn: it frees him from the burden of being an exception. Astrea's anger when she hears about Alexis's ordeal also highlights the authority of the general norm. In the fever of jealousy, Astrea mistreated Celadon, yet when she hears about an offense analogous to hers, she immediately senses its injustice. She is thus capable of realizing, in principle at least, how unfair behavior like her own can be.

Now that he has found out how to escape despair, cling to his ideals, and look at the world through someone else's eyes, Celadon is ready, not unlike a medieval knight, to prove himself in the fight for justice. During his participation in the siege of Marcilly, described in the fourth volume, the shepherd becomes a martial hero. In Baro's version, the novel's fifth volume concludes with a magic ceremony. Thanks to her friendship with Alexis, Astrea has grown to understand and regret her earlier fit of jealousy. Still believing Celadon to be dead, she calls on his spirit to appear. At Astrea's call, the young shepherd shows himself in his masculine incarnation. At the end of Shakespeare's *As You Like It*, the masks also fall during a scene with ritual undertones. And as in Montemayor's *Diana*, the solution to love's labors cannot be left entirely to the lovers themselves. Having finally evolved into a mature, generous couple, Astrea and Celadon deserve the protection of the god of love, who allows them to marry, though not before a human sacrifice is requested, prepared, and—as in the *Ethiopian Story* and in Giovanni Battista Guarini's play *Il pastor fido* (1590)—happily canceled.

The Recesses of the Human Heart

For a present-day reader, the journey to maturity depicted in *Astrea* certainly lacks the verisimilitude of a nineteenth-century bildungsroman. The same can be said of the adventures of Musidorus and Pyrocles in Sidney's *Old Arcadia*, and those of various unstable couples in *Diana* and *Galatea*. These adventures are too closely shaped by the Neoplatonic ideal of love to persuade readers used to the psychological insights of the nineteenth- and twentieth-century novel. Yet sixteenth- and seventeenth-century authors of pastorals were quite familiar with the innermost reaches of the heart. Cervantes, for instance—but similar examples could be found in Montemayor, Sidney, and d'Urfé—examines amorous behavior with an analytic power every bit the equal of that in nineteenth- and twentieth-century novels. If Cervantes does not take his narrative on the psychological path, it is because for him, as for d'Urfé and most other writers of pastorals, a concern for psychology begins to make sense only when true love is absent.

In the third book of *Galatea*, the wise Damon describes jealousy as a terrible sickness. Later, in the fourth book, Lenio, the great foe of love, speculates on the origin of jealousy. Love, he notes, should ideally fix on incorporeal beauty. Yet its birth depends too much on corporeal eyes, which look at corporeal beauty. A craving for this kind of beauty, which can never be fully possessed, brings the lover torture, fire, pain, and death. To answer Lenio, the shepherd Tirsio distinguishes between love and desire, where love is a delectable force that carries us toward the good in the form of beauty. According to Tirsio, Lenio considers love an enemy only because he has always seen her mixed with harmful, lecherous desires.

Far from being the most interesting layer of the self, as they seem to be in late nineteenth- and in twentieth-century novels, here the heart's innermost recesses primarily create obstacles on the path to true love. As Shakespeare puts it, inspired by the same Neoplatonic teachings: "Love is not love / Which alters when it alteration finds, / Or bends with the remover to remove" (Sonnet 116, lines 1–4). In Arcadia, one's enigmatic psyche is not a guide but an impediment.

Hence the multitude of stories that complement *Astrea*'s main plot all have a psychological component, but not necessarily a psychologically plausible conclusion. These stories, forming an encyclopedia of love's trials, turn on the existence, in the heart of happy Forez, of the Fountain of True Love, which magically shows those who look into it the face of their true beloved. Unhappy couples travel there from every corner of Gaul for a solution to their problems. However, since the fountain is under a temporary spell, visitors instead submit their disagreements to a tribunal of nymphs. Not unlike Fiammetta's solutions to a variety of questions about love in book 4 of Boccaccio's *Filocolo* (1338), the nymphs' decision is final, and the lovers pledge in advance to accept it.

One memorable case, at the very beginning of the second volume, is that of Celidea, Thamire, and Calidon, which, like Montemayor's story about Belisa, involves a rivalry between two men from different generations of the same family. Young Calidon and his uncle and guardian Thamire are both in love with Celidea, who reciprocates the older man's affections out of gratitude for his kindness to her. But Calidon's passion is so intense that Celidea's indifference puts his life in danger. In order to save him, Thamire tells Calidon he is willing to give her up. The young man recovers. Celidea, hurt that they have made this arrangement without consulting her, refuses to marry Calidon—and indeed, when Thamire, seeing that his nephew is now restored to health, begins to court her again, she rejects him too. Both men continue to pursue her, and the three of them go to the tribunal of the nymphs in search of justice. Once they have all spoken, the nymph Leonida pronounces the judgment.

Given the rightful hierarchy of passions and duties, Leonida states that the greater offense is Calidon's stubborn claim to Celidea's hand. Thamire, who had raised his nephew with kindness, was prepared to save Calidon's life by letting him marry Celidea, whereas the ungrateful young man refuses to repay his uncle's generosity. Almost as serious is Thamire's offense against Celidea in attempting to control her life without asking for her consent. Nevertheless, in offering her to Calidon, he acted against his own interest and out of affection for his young ward, which mitigates his fault. Leonida then assesses the relative worth of these characters' love. She condemns Calidon's feelings because, despite their intensity, they are unrequited and therefore fruitless. Thamire's come closer to perfection, for the best loves are those rooted in nature, which are reciprocated. Once the superiority of their love is established, Leonida decides that Celidea must forgive Thamire and agree to marry him, because, she reasons, there is no offense that cannot be overcome by someone who knows how to love.

The characters in the main plot—Astrea and Celadon—find out for themselves the right way to observe the laws of true love. The story of Celidea, Thamire, and Calidon—not unlike the intervention of wise Enareto in Sannazaro's *Arcadia* or of Felicia in Montemayor's *Diana*—shows how forlorn lovers and unstable couples, misled by their individual longings, fall short of the ideals that govern the emotions. Nevertheless, accepting that their vision may be distorted, these characters do not let their impulses determine their fate—they ask for guidance. Conflicts in love become subject to a complex jurisprudence that weighs the public consequences of the most intimate feelings. Arcadian lovers may not always find the ideal rule of conduct within themselves, like the characters in ancient Greek and chivalric novels, but when a higher authority guides them toward the good, they recognize it and gratefully acknowledge its power.

CHAPTER 5

Don Quixote and the History of the Novel

||||||||||||||||||||||||||||||||||||||||||||||||||||||||

In 1986 Milan Kundera asserted, paraphrasing Hermann Broch, that "a novel that does not discover a hitherto unknown segment of existence is immoral."[1] For a good part of the twentieth century, this maxim did indeed serve as a norm for high literature, requiring writers to explore uncharted areas of the human psyche. Marcel Proust, James Joyce, Alfred Döblin, and Kundera were actively looking for such unfamiliar terrain. In early modern times, however, writers were not aiming to discover and annex new territories so much as to excel in those already available within the existing framework of genres and approaches to human existence. They loved culture more than conquest.

Cervantes's literary career offers a persuasive example. Eager to tackle and succeed in a variety of literary genres, Cervantes tried his hand at theater, but although his *Siege of Numancia* (1582) may strike us now as a powerful tragedy, his contemporaries were not entirely convinced by it; indeed, it would be fair to say that his most charming theatrical pieces are the short, simple, funny *Interludes* (1615). He also strove to succeed in the highest genres of prose narrative, but there too his talent for simpler, direct storytelling prevailed. We have seen that his *Galatea* depicts the torments of the heart, successfully inserts lively subplots into the main Arcadian story line, is adorned with marvelous poems, and includes riveting debates about true versus earthly love. *Galatea* did contribute to the growth and maturation of the pastoral by emphasizing, in the tragic episode of Lisandro and Leonida, how dark and unhappy Arcadia can

---

[1] Milan Kundera, *The Art of the Novel* (1987; New York: Harper Perennial, 2000), pp. 5–6.

be. But it enjoyed only moderate success, and, in any case, it did not thoroughly reshape the genre.

Cervantes's contribution to the development of the novella was more substantial. He held to the unity of action and the unexpected denouement of the Italian novella while expanding the descriptions and dialogues. In *An Ill-Advised Curiosity* he explored the as yet untouched domain of the psyche's enigmatic impulses. And in many of the *Exemplary Stories* he did what he was best at: telling a relatively simple story in a relaxed, friendly voice.

The realization that he excelled in lighter, simpler narratives did not weaken Cervantes's desire to be remembered for works in difficult, uplifting genres. In particular, he could not remain indifferent to the ongoing debate about the future of the idealist novel. For centuries, the prototype of an ideal hero had been the medieval knight-errant, willing to confront the world's evils, seek glory, and worship a quasi-divine lady, but in the 1540s, the translation of the *Ethiopian Story* and of Achilles Tatius's *Leucippe and Clitophon* into several European languages challenged the supremacy of chivalric stories. As Jacques Amyot, the French translator of Heliodorus, explained in his influential preface to the translation published in 1547, the *Ethiopian Story* provided a welcome relief from the wild implausibility of the tales of chivalry. Amyot, whose words were later included in the Spanish translation of the *Ethiopian Story*, asserts that:

> Most of the books of this kind written long ago in our language . . . are most of the time so badly composed and so far from any plausible appearance that they seem to be the visions of a sick man dreaming under fever rather than the invention of a man of wit and judgment.[2]

Good stories, he claims, are those that,

> in addition to the pleasure they bring us, serve to file down (so to speak) and better sharpen our judgment, such that pleasure does not remain pointless. (p. 160)

(In the translation by Cervantes's contemporary Fernando de Mena, Amyot's words are: "Lo cual es al contrario en la mayor parte de los libros de esta suerte que han sido antiguamente escritos en nuestra lengua española . . . mas antes están las más veces tan disonantes y tan fuera de verdadera similitud, que paresce que sean antes sueños de algún enfermo

---

[2] Jacques Amyot, "Proesme du translateur," in *L'Histoire aethiopique*, trans. J. Amyot, ed. Laurence Plazenet (Paris: Champion, 2008), p. 159 (my translation).

que desvaría con la calentura, que invenciones de algún hombre de es-
píritu y sano juicio." And the next quotation: "allende del placer que nos
dan, sirven aun a limar (a manera de decir) y acepillar de más en más el
juicio, de suerte que el placer no sea del todo ocioso.")[3]

Why should Amyot have thought so? Why would the adventures of
the valiant Amadis of Gaul seem like "the visions of a sick man dreaming under fever," further "from any plausible appearance" than those of
Theagenes and Chariclea in the *Ethiopian Story*? Why would ancient
Greek fiction deserve to be emulated by sixteenth-century writers?

Late chivalric romances, as we know, portray invincible knights who
battle powerful warriors and magicians, and worship a magnificent lady.
The hero is an individual in and above the world, incomparably stronger
than other men, a dispenser of justice, and a guarantor of peace. In ancient Greek novels, by contrast, the virtuous young man and woman who
resist the blows of fortune on their way to salvation are individuals overwhelmed by the world, whose only hope of resisting the external pressures is their innocence and the protection of Providence. On one side,
strong knights always ready to draw their swords; on the other, secretive,
patient fugitives. In *Amadis of Gaul*—marvels and magic; in Tatius and
Heliodorus—trust in the power of Providence. In chivalric romances—an
endless search for fame; in *Leucippe and Clitophon* and in the *Ethiopian
Story*—an uncertain progress toward deliverance.

The contrast between these two ways of conceiving the human ideal
could not be sharper. Is the best possible human being a man, sword in
hand, imposing justice from *above*, or is it a man, a woman, a couple
pursued, harassed, hunted, and finding solace in an *inner* sense of justice
and in Providence's help? The choice goes to the very core of the human
condition. Can we fight ceaselessly to impose our law on the world, or
should we simply fortify ourselves against the world's relentless adversity? Does virtue consist in asserting our superiority over those around
us, or should we listen silently to the counsel of our own souls? Set off in
the late 1540s, this debate ended in a decisive victory for the latter view
and its literary embodiment, ancient Greek fiction, which served from
then until late in the seventeenth century as the model for a considerable
number of then highly successful, nowadays little read, idealist novels.

Cervantes took an active part in this debate, which involved not
only two ways of idealizing human beings, but also two ways of understanding politics and religion. As an alternative to the loosely managed medieval kingdoms of *Amadis*, the *Ethiopian Story*, as we have
seen, portrays a variety of political arrangements—anarchy, tyranny,

---

[3] *Historia etiópica de los amores de Teágenes y Cariclea*, trans. Fernando de Mena, ed.
Francisco Lopez (1587; Estrada, Madrid: Aldus, 1954), p. lxxx.

democracy—culminating in the wise kingdom of ancient Ethiopia. In opposition to the chivalric novel's medieval Christianity still steeped in primitive enchantment, the ancient Greek novel alludes to a transcendent Providence guiding the individual invisibly toward salvation. For Cervantes, living in relatively well-administered sixteenth-century Spain as the Counter-Reformation was striving to uproot the remaining beliefs in magic and superstition, the *Ethiopian Story* was clearly much closer to his time's political and religious ideals than was *Amadis*.

For the assiduous, earnest side of Cervantes, that is, for the writer determined to succeed in some of the most respected narrative genres—the pastoral and the serious novella—the new vogue for Heliodorus-like novels offered a splendid opportunity to achieve true recognition. Hence his dedication and pride in writing *Persiles and Sigismunda*, a Christianized version of the *Ethiopian Story*, published posthumously in 1617, which he thought of as his best, most enduring work.

But before (or while) Cervantes the ambitious and hardworking craftsman began writing in the manner of Heliodorus, the relaxed, funny Cervantes had a go at discrediting the rival idealist genre—the chivalric story. And how should one make fun of valiant medieval knights and their exploits, or rather, how should one make fun of them in a new way, different from the successful fantasy epics by Boiardo and Ariosto, whose half-serious, half-capricious characters are medieval knights of Charlemagne's court? Perhaps by creating a new *miles gloriosus*, a boastful knight who sings his own praises. And how to show that the stories of knights-errant have no plausibility whatsoever? By placing this *miles gloriosus* in contemporary Spain, a country administered by a strong state and watched over by a robust police force, and letting him take on the useless tasks of a private dispenser of justice. How do you make sure you hit your target—the chivalric stories? By referring to them constantly—for instance, having the *miles gloriosus* know them well and try to emulate their folly. And what narrative voice should you adopt, if not the friendly tone of a comic novella with a real setting and believable characters?

Part 1 of *Don Quixote* belonged to a project involving two complementary stages. The first stage would lead to a decisive debunking of the chivalric approach, thus preparing the way for the second stage, the creation of a Heliodorus-style idealist story, which would be Cervantes's unrivaled achievement, his eternal claim to fame. The final goal was *Persiles*. Along the way, *Don Quixote* would provide an entertaining rebuttal of knights-errant stories by showing that, just as Amyot claims in the preface Cervantes had undoubtedly read, they are so wholly implausible that they resemble the "visions of a sick man dreaming under fever"— "sueños de algún enfermo que desvaría con la calentura." This is the twist that transformed the peaceful, provincial hidalgo Don Quixana into Don

Quixote—not a mere *miles gloriosus*, a boastful knight who claims to be ready to fight yet runs away at the smallest threat, but a knight ready to come to blows for nonexistent reasons. For Quixote is a comic character less because of what he is than because of what, in his sick, feverish dream, he believes himself to be.

Not that the ideals his models embody—courage, virtue, energy—would be despicable. They are not, and *Persiles* will attempt to demonstrate it. It is just that for Amyot and Cervantes, the way in which chivalric stories handle these ideals does not make sense—or rather, not *enough* sense. In order to appreciate *Amadis* and extract its wisdom, the public needs to be aware that it includes a strong dose of fantasy and fairy tale, but, according to Cervantes and Amyot, idealist fiction should take care not to mislead its readers about the links between the fiction and the ideals it promotes. Readers of chivalric tales might either wholly dismiss the story—the fairy tales and the chivalric ideals—in which case it fails as idealist literature, or wholly accept both the ideals and the truth of the chivalric feats, resulting in a ridiculous conviction that one can implement the ideal of courage only by assuming that the world is enchanted, full of marvels and magic, and in great need of knights-errant.

This is precisely Quixote's conviction. It leads to a selective indifference to the common world, whose details are transfigured according to the rules of an enchanted one. The windmills become giants, the barber's dish a magic helmet, and a funeral procession an opportunity for acting like the much-admired knight Palmerin of England. The blindingly obvious nevertheless remains blindingly obvious, and Don Quixote, insensitive to rebuttal, is always having to invent complex fairy-tale scenarios to overcome the resistance of reality. Most strikingly, he wraps himself in an imaginary legend, a retroactive projection of his own chivalric worth. He believes he is already an invincible knight-errant, loftily surveying a world that worships and fears his valiant arm. "Happy times and happy age, in which my famous exploits shall come to light, worthy to be engraved in brass, carved in marble, and drawn in picture, for a monument to all posterity!"[4] So he declares at the very beginning of his first sally, before he has performed a single chivalric deed.

Cervantes's polemical target is clear from the destruction of Quixote's book collection in the sixth chapter of the first part. Most chivalric novels are thrown away, and although *Amadis*, *Palmerin of England* (1547–1548), and *Tirant lo Blanc* (1490) do not share this fate, they are spared rather than commended. By contrast, pastoral novels—including Cervantes's own *Galatea*—are highly praised, as is the national epic poem

---

[4] *Don Quixote*, trans. Charles Jarvis (Oxford: Oxford World Classics, 1992), pt. 1, chap. 2, p. 27.

La Araucana (1569–1589) by Ercilla. As for Heliodorus, his *Ethiopian Story* is conspicuously absent from Quixote's library, no doubt because reading it could have preserved the hidalgo's sanity.

But once he has described Quixote's folly, given a few examples of its operation, and destroyed the books that triggered it, Cervantes has, in a sense, achieved his polemical aims. On its own, the knight's first sally might have resulted in an excellent comic novella in the style of Cervantes's *Glass Graduate*, about the madness of a learned young man who suddenly becomes convinced that he is made of glass and might very easily get broken. Quixote's heroic misinterpretation of the world has richer comic potential than does the Glass Graduate's misinterpretation of his own body. Nonetheless, left as the only ingredient in a long-winded narrative, Quixote's eagerness to act as a knight-errant might soon have become tedious. Yet to keep the story a novella would have meant missing out a crucial element of the chivalric books, whose protagonists endlessly roam the world.

It is at this point—after the description and destruction of Quixote's library—that Sancho Panza makes his appearance, his presence emphasizing not only that Quixote is a "sick man dreaming under fever," but also that the chivalric ideal, exalting and nonnegotiable, contrasts with a more modest way of living based on negotiation and common sense. Now the comic register expands, allowing Cervantes to demonstrate his literary scope. All the subspecies are present: farce, with Quixote being beaten up at every turn of the road; situation comedy, as in the nighttime conflict at Maritorne's inn in chapter 16, when a small misunderstanding gradually builds to a chaotic climax; the comedy of character, featuring the knight, his squire, and the people they meet; and the comedy of manners, with a particular emphasis on conversation, as in the wonderfully entertaining dialogues between Quixote and Sancho.

But Cervantes needed more than comedy to display the whole range of his talent. He added episodes from other narrative genres, particularly those at which he had already tried his hand, the pastoral and the novella, using existing techniques and topics such as the multiple plots seen in Boiardo and Ariosto's fantasy epic, the stories of forlorn lovers used as subplots in Montemayor's *Diana* and Cervantes's own *Galatea*, and the freestanding "Moorish romance" inserted into Alemán's *The Life of Guzmán de Alfarache*. The episode of the shepherdess Marcela (chap. 14), who adamantly refuses marriage, is as elegant and farfetched as any good pastoral story, raising the tone and allowing Quixote to play a new role, that of a learned and generous elderly gentleman. In the pastoral episode Quixote steps aside, content to be a spectator and commentator rather than the protagonist. It is a move he will make more and more often.

The change of focus allows Cervantes to emphasize Quixote's humane, compassionate side. The knight-errant's arrogance, always present when he becomes the center of attention, is less conspicuous in situations where he acts as a bystander and adviser. When Quixote is not directly involved in the action, his folly transforms into a gentle, inoffensive eccentricity—as when he explains the marvels of knightly life to Sancho (chap. 10) or eulogizes the Golden Age (chap. 11). During the scaled-down interactions between Quixote and the protagonists of the interlaced stories, he is a much more appealing character than the brainless old man he was in his first sally. This new persona becomes most evident after he meets Cardenio in chapter 27, at which point the other characters take the lead, regarding not only their own affairs but also Quixote's. Everyone now attempts to catch him and take him back to his village by pandering to his mania. The risk of monotony is averted, and the novel continues according to a highly successful pattern, alternating between farcical quixotic adventures, strange but charming speeches and dialogue with Sancho, and breathtaking novella episodes narrated in the first person by their protagonists.

The novellas grafted onto the main plot of *Don Quixote* belong to various subspecies, their diversity allowing Cervantes to go through most of the available narrative genres. He moderates the sarcastic message of Quixote's story line by adding Marcela's idealistic pastoral episode, weaving in Cardenio's story with its mixture of imperfect and idealized characters, inserting Anselmo's tragic tale of inward corruption (chaps. 33–35), and letting the Captive tell his idealist "Moorish" romance, which lays emphasis on human strength, love, and faith (chaps. 39–41).

Each of these stories is embedded in the main plot in a different way. Quixote and Sancho are roaming through Sierra Morena when they stumble on the unhappy Cardenio and Dorothea, who have run away from the world. *An Ill-Advised Curiosity*, whose mood couldn't be more different from that prevailing in the main plot, is read aloud as a completely separate novella. Its links with the other subplots of *Quixote* are not clearly highlighted. But given that the resolution of the adventures of Cardenio, Lucinda, Dorothea, and Fernando (chap. 36) comes right after all the characters attend the reading of *An Ill-Advised Curiosity*, one cannot resist the impression of a deliberate contrast between a novella about the *contagion of depravity* and the danger of leading people into temptation (as Anselmo does to his wife Camilla and his friend Lotario), and the example of the *contagion of goodness*, love, and loyalty displayed when, following Lucinda and Cardenio's example of fidelity, Fernando returns to his first love, Dorothea.

Just as the wilderness of the Sierra Morena brings the lonely characters together, so the inn where so many events take place has a magnetism for everyone, including the Captive and his Moorish lady, who arrive almost immediately after Fernando and Dorothea's reconciliation and enhance the happy atmosphere by telling their story. The Captive's tale, by far the closest to the idealist mode—it portrays characters who resist the whims of fate, run away when the world does not sanction their love, and put themselves under the protection of Providence—is indicative of Cervantes's greatest ambitions, and heralds the tenor of the later *Persiles*.

||||||||||||||||||||||||||||

Don Quixote has often been labeled the first modern novel. To assess its place in the history of the genre, we must consider several questions. When Cervantes wrote the first part of *Don Quixote*, did he intend to transform the genre later called the novel? Did he write *Don Quixote* as a model for future writers? Did *Quixote* in fact become a model for novelists? And, more generally, what was its impact on the history of the genre?

The answer to the first question is a partial yes. Cervantes did intend to help transform one of the narrative subgenres of his time. He wanted to help change the way *idealist* long prose narratives were written.

The answer to the second question is no. *Quixote* was not designed as a model for later writers. Cervantes aimed to discredit existing chivalric books and increase the public's esteem for worthy idealist stories: he wrote *Don Quixote* to clear the way for the triumph of *Persiles*. A polemical, preparatory work, *Quixote* was not designed carefully in advance, as *Persiles* appears to have been. In the first part, Cervantes improvised, changing his approach as he went along. He began it as a farcical parody of chivalric stories and gradually converted it into a stylish comedy of character and manners, whose satiric mode he both enhanced and balanced by interlacing the main strand with a series of serious, tragic, and idealist novellas, each demonstrating his extraordinary range.

To the third question—whether *Don Quixote* did become a model for subsequent novelists—one can give two distinct answers. As a *character*, Don Quixote persistently haunted the literary imagination of the eighteenth, nineteenth, and twentieth centuries: there are obvious allusions, for instance, in Dostoevsky's *The Idiot* and Flaubert's *Bouvard and Pécuchet*. For *novels*, however, *Don Quixote*'s use as a model was limited. It had some impact on episodic comic novels in the seventeenth and eighteenth centuries, but even those writers who clearly emulated *Quixote*, like Charles Sorel in his *Francion* (1623) and Henry Fielding in *Joseph Andrews* (1742) and *Tom Jones* (1749), did not go so far as to choose as their main character an old maniac who nurtures imaginary love interests. Uncle Tobias in *Tristram Shandy* (1759) is of that type, but Laurence Sterne's narrative is not primarily about him. I can think of only one example of a novel built quite like *Don Quixote*—a comic, episodic story about an old, eccentric bachelor, full of embedded novellas and secondary plots—Charles Dickens's *Pickwick Papers* (1837). There might be others, but the case of *Pickwick* suggests that they probably belong to a marginal set.

As for *Don Quixote*'s more general contribution to the history of the genre, its polemical thrust against chivalric stories certainly registered, though it did not entirely prevent them, *Amadis* in particular, from being read in the seventeenth century. In France, for instance, the 1614 translation of *Don Quixote* did not stop Gilbert Saulnier du Verdier from writing the chivalric summa *Roman des Romans* in 1626–1629, nor prevent the 1629 publication of a compact version of *Amadis* that replaced the sixteenth-century translation. Cervantes's antichivalric message was heard, but not followed right away.

Interestingly, Cervantes stumbled on an essential ingredient of what later came to be the canonical form of the novel: the combination of earlier narrative subgenres. Somehow he must have felt that a successful long narrative might go beyond the strict division into types, incorporating a comic story, an idealist one, a pastoral, and a variety of novellas. Similarly, by embedding a series of other stories in *The Princess of Clèves*, Mme de Lafayette showed that the limits of a subgenre are flexible. But neither writer tried to achieve a genuine synthesis between existing narrative subgenres. To find such a synthesis, we shall have to turn to the later, eighteenth-century English novel.

PART TWO

The Enchantment of Interiority

CHAPTER 6

The New Idealism

IIIIIIIIIIIIIIIIIIIIIIIIIIIIIIIIIIIIIIIIIIIIIIIIIIIIIIIIIIIIIIIIII

Until well into the eighteenth century, narrative prose was organized as a federation of fictional subgenres, each offering its readers a different perspective on human life. Not all of these subgenres were always equally productive or important. The idealist approach, represented for so long by chivalric books, shifted when the ancient Greek novels became available again in the 1540s, inspiring a rich harvest of works that would delight readers from the end of the sixteenth century to the beginning of the eighteenth. The pastoral, very successful in the second half of the sixteenth century, declined soon after but made a comeback in the eighteenth. The picaresque, the comic novel, and the novella each had their moments of glory and decay. Yet the sense that every subgenre was responsible for a definite area of human experience helped them survive, succeed within their own borders, and interact with one another through grafting and interlacing.

The eighteenth century witnessed several major changes. First, amalgamation: a new kind of idealist novel strove to bring together the earlier subgenres' various approaches to human experience. Next, proximity and full immersion: these new novels brought their characters and action closer to the lives of their readers and devised ways to immerse them deeply in the world of the text. (As a reaction, some authors wildly exaggerated the distance between fictional and actual worlds.) Just as significant was a new sense of moral equality between people from different social classes that pervaded the novel. Finally, the contest between idealist and anti-idealist ways of portraying life continued, but instead of letting its rivals prosper, each approach claimed to be the only proper way to write novels.

Does this mean that the eighteenth-century novel moved toward a more realist representation of life? Not necessarily. What happened was that after a long period of peaceful coexistence between the subgenres, in the eighteenth century the idealist novel evolved in a new, unexpected way, prompting a readjustment of all other novelistic approaches.

THE HELIODORUS WAVE

To understand this readjustment, we must realize that implausible idealist novels, inspired directly or indirectly by Heliodorus and the ancient Greek model, prospered immensely throughout the seventeenth century. Cervantes's *Persiles and Sigismunda* (1617), Gomberville's *Polexander* (1632–1637), and La Calprenède's *Cassandra* (1642–1650) are just a few among the large number of similar works in Italian, Spanish, French, English, and German. Many of their authors were women: Mary Wroth, who wrote *Urania* (1621), Madeleine de Scudéry, whose best-known novel is the gigantic *Artamène ou le Grand Cyrus* (10 vols., 1649–1653), and Aphra Behn, author of *Oroonoko* (1688). They formed an alliance between women and the idealist novel that lasted well into the nineteenth century. Not unlike the *Ethiopian Story*, *Persiles* and other seventeenth-century specimens of the genre feature virtuous young princesses and courageous young princes whose birth is shrouded in mystery and whose love defeats all obstacles. These works, especially Madeleine de Scudéry's, are too vast and complex to be summarized here, but a subplot from Gomberville's *Polexander*, one of the most popular novels of its time, will give an idea of their tenor.

Zelmatidius, son of the glorious Inca Guina Capa and an Amazonian princess, is born in Quito during a war waged by his father. Both parents die in the conflict, and the newborn baby is found by envoys of the great Quasmez, emperor of the lands between Mexico and Quito. Quasmez has learned from a prophecy that the foundling will help him win a major war and discover a lost treasure, so Zelmatidius is raised at court, believing that the emperor is his father. Having fulfilled part of the prophecy by defeating Quasmez's enemies, Zelmatidius is sent alone to King Montezuma's court in Mexico, on a mission to recover Xaira, Quasmez's daughter, who was abducted in infancy. A second prophecy predicts that he will succeed if he can be stronger than himself. On his way to Mexico, Zelmatidius heroically releases a captive princess, liberates a province from bandits, and slays a malevolent giant.

At Montezuma's court, he falls in love with Izatida, believed to be the daughter of Montezuma and Queen Hismelita. The queen persecutes Zelmatidius despite his services to the Mexican crown, for astrologers have told her that a foreigner will one day bring down Montezuma's empire. The same astrologers predict that Mexico's salvation depends on keeping Izatida in Montezuma's kingdom. Zelmatidius has to leave.

More adventures lead him to discover the truth about his origins and find his father, who unexpectedly turns out to be alive. With his cosmopolitan confidant, Garucca—an adventurous Peruvian who has traveled to Japan, China, and Portugal and amassed a huge fortune—Zelmatidius returns to Mexico in disguise, only to find that Izatida has died. In despair, he and Garucca set out to sea, where they are taken prisoner by the Turk Bajazet, a most gallant and courteous pirate. Through Bajazet, Zelmatidius meets Polexander, a prince of French ancestry and ruler of the Canary Islands. Later, Zelmatidius is reunited with Izatida: not only is she still alive; it turns out she is none other than Xaira, the lost daughter of the emperor Quasmez, and the two lovers return to Peru as king and queen of the Incas.

A mere summary cannot capture the sumptuous setting, the charm of the adventures, or the elegance of the style. Gomberville is one of the best storytellers of his century, a precursor of Madeleine de Scudéry's immensely successful novels, but also of later transatlantic fictions including Bernardin de Saint-Pierre's *Paul and Virginia* (1788) and Chateaubriand's *Les Natchez* (written between 1797 and 1800 and published in 1826). In the Zelmatidius episode, the theme of exile is intertwined with those of origin, self-knowledge, and self-worth—the common stock of fairy tales and the ancient Greek novel. What at first appear to be Zelmatidius's family and home are in fact mere substitutes. Quasmez, who raised him, is not his real father but only a caretaker, and the land in which he grew up is merely a preparation for his true homecoming. Zelmatidius also mistakes the identity of those he loves most: Izatida is not Izatida but Xaira. Reality is concealed behind a veil through which, guided by ambiguous prophecies, the characters now and then catch a glimpse. In the end, the evil characters' machinations are thwarted, those who were thought dead come back to life, and the protagonist finds his true origin and homeland. After proving his strength *in via*, Gomberville's Zelmatidius, like Heliodorus's Chariclea, is welcomed *in patria*.

And just as in Heliodorus the Greek Theagenes is finally embraced in faraway Ethiopia, in Gomberville's novel the Inca prince befriends the Turk Bajazet and the Frenchman Polexander, admiring their courage, nobility, and solidarity. Though separated by their geographic and ethnic origins, Zelmatidius, Bajazet, and Polexander speak the same moral language and obey the same maxims. Ultimately, with all its improbabilities, *Polexander*'s fictional universe evokes a vast, hospitable canopy under which every character feels at home, greeted by friendly faces and reassured by Providence. In this serene environment, wandering is a way to discover the unity of the world.

Sensitive Hearts Here and Now—Richardson's *Pamela*

But what if the unity of the world could be evoked without an endless depiction of its various landscapes? What if, instead of placing the strongest souls far from our daily environment, writers could conceive characters who shine even brighter and impress the reader even more by living here in our own society? What if characters as exemplary as Chariclea and Theagenes were to look, speak, and to some extent act like our own neighbors? Then the idealist novel could bring them close to home, making them part of the familiar world. The landscape of the idealist novel, which once received its moral light from far above, would now plausibly resemble our own, while the moral ideals would glow within the breast of a few perfect characters.

But since virtuous characters were the specialty of idealist novels, while descriptions of actual social relations and material surroundings were developed in the novella and the picaresque, this new approach would require a mixture of genres rather than a new subdivision. To conjure up the lives of exemplary characters settled among us, a writer would have to immerse the reader in their daily experience and make their inner splendor visible. Instead of taking place in an exotic, legendary landscape supervised by a benevolent Providence, instead of portraying a star-crossed, isolated couple advancing gradually toward the threshold of the Bridal Chamber, the idealist novel would now involve a narrow, easily recognizable setting—an English country house—and a single, persecuted young woman whose inner beauty struggles to be recognized on the meandering journey toward true love.

This is the story of Richardson's Pamela, the virtuous servant who resists her lecherous master's advances until, in the end, she converts him to virtue. The novel continued the tradition of characters who valiantly resist the surrounding world, and also innovated: first, by isolating the protagonist even more drastically from her fellow human beings, and second, by placing her ordeals in a familiar, plausible environment. Literary historians who assert the deep continuity of the novel's history from the ancient Greek novel onward are correct, as are those for whom English eighteenth-century fiction represents a new departure: they have recognized the two sides of Richardson's work.

The social and cultural context in which this new departure took place is particularly significant. As Ian Watt has shown, commercial society, with its growing political freedoms, Protestantism, particularly in its pietist and Methodist incarnations, and empiricist philosophy all had an impact. The emerging political liberty and the pietist practices required human beings to be self-reliant creatures, thus making possible the *internalization of the ideal* that enjoins people, whatever their place in society, to be guided by their own hearts. Empiricist philosophy, with its attention to concrete reality, converged with the novel's new interest in the actual, everyday world.

The rise of this new approach was neither sudden nor universal. Initially, only a few writers experimented with it. The traditional federation of narrative genres survived quite well, and innovative writers were preceded, surrounded, and followed by a score of other novelists whose often admirable works did not adopt the new method. Indeed, older idealist novels were still read avidly throughout the eighteenth century. In England, a new translation of Heliodorus's *Ethiopian Story* was published in 1717. In his *Confessions*, finished in 1770, Jean-Jacques Rousseau remembers reading *Amadis* and *Astrea* as a child, and for a long time educated people were expected to be conversant with the older novels. To satisfy this need, the *Bibliothèque universelle des romans* (1775–1789) published shorter versions of virtually all the earlier narratives in European literature. The novella was very much alive, as shown by Robert Challe's collection *Les illustres Françaises* (1713, English trans. 1727) and Abbé Prévost's *Manon Lescaut* (1731). The picaresque novel continued to prosper, thanks in part to Daniel Defoe, whose *Moll Flanders* (1722) and *Roxana* (1724) we discussed earlier, but also to Lesage (*Gil Blas*, 1715–1735, English trans. 1748), Marivaux (*Le Paysan parvenu*, 1735, English trans. *The Fortunate Peasant*, 1735), and Tobias Smollett, the translator of Lesage and author of *Roderick Random* (1748) and *Peregrine Pickle* (1751). Lesage's innovation, later taken up by Smollett as well, was to portray a good-natured pícaro who slowly makes his way to success through a world full of malice and dishonesty. The amorality or sheer corruption that had been distinctive features of the Spanish pícaros and Defoe's pícaras, faded away.

In Marivaux's fiction, serenity and optimism are even more pronounced. His "fortunate peasant," Jacob, is a handsome, good-humored man who attracts women of higher birth. We do not know how Marivaux would have concluded his novel, but its anonymous continuation, in which Jacob weds a rich older woman, does make sense. Marivaux did not finish his other major novel either. *La Vie de Marianne* (1731–1741, English trans. 1736–1742), which is told in the first person, not unlike a picaresque story, also to some extent fits into the idealist tradition. The main character, a virtuous young woman, probably wellborn, lost her family as an infant and undergoes various mild ordeals, all of which she overcomes thanks to her beauty, gentleness, and good intentions.

Published a bit earlier, Montesquieu's *Lettres persanes* (1721, English trans. 1722) is an epistolary novel about a group of Persians who visit France and send their compatriots amusing descriptions of its strange customs. Naive and bumbling in their inconsequential interactions with French people, the Persian characters are nonetheless perfectly acute in their dealings with their friends and family left at home. *Persian Letters* was certainly meant as a social satire rather than a novel, but it shares with Lesage and Marivaux the serenity and elegance that made early eighteenth-century French narrative prose so successful.

Set against this background, Richardson's innovations are striking. In Marianne, Marivaux imagined an ideal character who finds in her own heart the impulse to be good, and whose adventures take place in a familiar setting, Paris. Rather than being part of a star-crossed couple, like Chariclea or Sigismunda, she is alone in the world and her lover belongs to the family of weak, inconstant males so frequently present in Cervantes's novellas. These features will reappear in Richardson's *Pamela*. Yet in Marivaux's novel, just as in the earlier idealist and picaresque stories, unity of action comes only from a sense of the world at large created by the accumulation of episodes: as he details the heroine's travails, the author gives no hint of any other underlying coherence. Moreover, because Marivaux observes the neoclassicist rules of decorum, he alternates concise narration of events with subtle moral analyses but avoids giving sensory details. In other words, he does very well what writers of his time were expected to do. The narrative energy of his *Life of Marianne*, like its contemporary *Cleveland* (1731–1739) by the Abbé Prévost, reminds us of a time when it was enough merely to mention an event for readers to grasp it fully and remember it. In these novels, as in the early Italian novellas, stating the facts was so extraordinarily important that delays, descriptions, and insistence on detail seemed superfluous. That Marivaux, one of the best theatrical plot-builders of his time, did not construct a clear plot for his novels and did not finish them might be a sign that he was not overly excited about the old-fashioned "world-at-large" method. He may have sensed that the repetitive, episodic structure, one of the main attractions of long novels, was by now becoming difficult to justify, or at least difficult to conclude as satisfactorily as a dramatic plot. But he did not attempt to change it.

In his *Pamela or Virtue Rewarded* (1740), Richardson benefits from elements found in Marivaux's prose—some argue that he borrowed them directly, others that the two writers used a common source. The features are all there: the lonely woman, not from the upper crust, her acute moral awareness, and the familiar setting. But in addition, Richardson merges his novel's episodes into a single, highly dramatic line of action, he zooms in on a myriad of details—sensory, behavioral, and psychological—and he conceives a gallery of characters, each with his or her own peculiar physiognomy. In terms of already existing subgenres, Richardson's *Pamela* thus achieved an unprecedented synthesis of the moral splendor of the idealist novel, the inner tremors described by the pastoral and the elegiac story, the picaresque's closeness to everyday life, and the unity of action perfected in the novella.

The novel's heroine, Pamela Andrews, a servant in the house of the young aristocrat Mr. B., writes letter after letter to her parents (though she never manages to send them), recounting in great detail her resistance to the master's attempts to seduce her. He relentlessly harasses Pamela, who bravely defends herself, so that in the course of their struggle the relative position of the characters slowly changes, the master's respect for the servant increasing with each display of resistance. When Mr. B. steals and reads Pamela's unsent letters to her parents—the very text of the novel—he is initially irritated by the young maid's self-righteousness and insolence. In the end, however, her inner nobility converts him: his carnal lust changes into true love and he asks for her hand. Deep down in her heart, Pamela has never been entirely indifferent to him, and she accepts.

The perfect chastity of a lowly young woman, as well as the irresponsible behavior and subsequent taming of a highborn young man, is a familiar topic from novellas. Cervantes dealt with it in his *Force of Blood* and in the *Don Quixote* subplot about Dorothea and Don Fernando. *Pamela* multiplies Mr. B.'s attempts and the heroine's innocent yet quite effective ways of resisting, stringing together a series of ordeals that— rather like those endured in older idealist novels—test and confirm her determination. The novel's unique, unprecedented intensity comes from the fact that in all these ordeals, Pamela faces the *same* man and the *same* obstacle: his intemperance, magnified by social prejudice and obtuseness. The multiple episodes of older novels and the novella's concentration on a single dramatic situation are thus skillfully blended.

Richardson's contemporary Henry Fielding made fun of this combination, and especially of the young woman's self-assurance, which he depicts in his ruthless parody *Shamela* (1741) as a mere cover for social ambition. For Fielding, who believed in the social division of literary types, a lower-class woman boasting about her own perfection could only be a hypocrite. Mr. B. himself would have agreed, at least before his conversion. Fielding's story assumes that lowborn characters tend to be dishonest, and that first-person narratives are confessions of mischief: here it is the sly Shamela who seduces and eventually marries her wealthy, confused, and undersexed master. In Fielding's view, a character like Pamela cannot belong to the actual world.

In its own way, Richardson's novel makes the same point. Pamela, not unlike the heroines of older idealist novels, is an individual-outside-the-world. To make things still more difficult, no dependable lover comforts her, as her ordeals are caused by just the man whose feelings should make him her ally. Only pícaras like Roxana or Moll Flanders are as lonely as Pamela, the difference being that unlike them, she cannot possibly count on cunning and sexual wiles. Unusually vulnerable, she sometimes resembles the forlorn shepherdess in a pastoral—Marcela, for example, in the first part of *Don Quixote*, who avoids the company of men, defending her right to live alone. Pamela's letters about her misfortune call to mind the solitary songs sung by lovers in the pastoral woods, and just as other shepherds overhear these confessions, Mr. B. learns of her distress by reading her correspondence.

The first-person narration in Pamela's letters mixes the plaintive tone proper to elegiac stories with the noble diction of spiritual autobiography and the detailed dialogue and material descriptions typical of picaresque novels. But in elegiac and picaresque stories, and even to some extent in spiritual autobiographies, use of the first person is necessary because dishonesty and evil intentions are so deeply hidden within the character's heart that no one else could discover and recount them, whereas in Richardson's novel, first-person narration acquires an entirely new function. Here, Pamela's heart is an invisible site of beauty and strength: only she can describe the treasures of sensitivity and courage it conceals. In *Shamela*, Fielding notices the novelty of this perspective and rejects it—why, he wonders, would a virtuous person need to write letters or keep a diary? And why would the author of the story show us a character's letters if not to disclose her moral wretchedness? Fielding's dismay notwithstanding, Richardson knew that the sensitive heart is the only reliable source of information about its own invisible moral splendor.

In this case, the first-person narrative enables virtue to triumph over external social factors. Reading Pamela's diary, the master realizes that the servant he assumed to be a mere target for his lust is his equal, or, in fact, his better. By radiating moral superiority, Pamela's diary domesticates him. Providence, in the older novels, had the task of freeing the characters from the shackles of earthly contingency. Here, the new power of the heart slowly but surely erodes social differences.

Pamela's moral beauty does not, however, entail full self-knowledge. Like some authors of older novellas, Richardson understands the hidden recesses of the heart. Pamela knows her duty well and follows moral norms closely, yet she does not formulate the reason why she, the most virtuous woman on earth, lingers in the house of a man who threatens her chastity. Her failed escape is symptomatic. Locked in a country house on Mr. B.'s orders, Pamela manages to get out of the garden and goes "about a bow-shot into the pasture; but there stood that horrid bull, staring me full in the face, with fiery saucer eyes, as my antipathy to the creature made me think."[1] Terrorized, the young woman hurries back into the garden. As she herself testifies, the animal is scary only insofar as her own "antipathy to the creature" *makes her think* it so. Did her panicking mind exaggerate the obstacle, persuading her to remain at her master's mercy? Or did she come back because traveling across England alone would be too dangerous? She does not give details. In Richardson's *Clarissa* (1747–1748), the heroine falls in love with an unscrupulous seducer without realizing what is happening. As in *Pamela*, the young woman's feelings are quite obvious to the reader, though not to her. In both cases

---

[1] Samuel Richardson, *Pamela*, ed. Peter Sabor (London: Penguin Books, 1987), letter 32, third Monday of Pamela's imprisonment, p. 191).

Richardson, not unlike Cervantes in *An Ill-Advised Curiosity*, portrays a character who acts without fully understanding herself: the novelty here is the artful way in which he embeds this misunderstanding in the very act of self-revelatory first-person narration.

Since all events are seen from Pamela's point of view, readers become fully immersed in her abduction and captivity. They are, so to speak, chained to Pamela's trials, as they will be to Clarissa's. Diderot, in his *In Praise of Richardson* (1762), rightly exclaims: "O Richardson, one unwillingly takes a role in your works, one gets involved in the conversation, one approves, blames, admires, gets angry and indignant. How many times did I catch myself, like a child taken to the theater for the first time, shouting: *Do not believe him, he lies to you. If you go there, you are lost.*"[2] As the first writer to use this method, Richardson confessed, through the pen of his character Lovelace: "I love to write to the *moment*." One of *Pamela's* great discoveries is the art of conveying the immediate experience of time, the intimate game of blindness, anticipation, anxiety, and hope. Through an obsessive insistence on detail, every act of aggression planned by Mr. B. is amplified by Pamela's fearful anticipation. While in older idealist novels the blows of fate take the characters by surprise, Pamela is fully aware that sooner or later her master will strike again. Her story thus includes a dilatory component, a repeated deferral of crucial events, which are always preceded by long periods of waiting, futile conversations with her evil guardian, Mrs. Jewkes, and her own growing worries.

By insisting on the immediacy of temporal experience, Richardson enhances the descriptive and psychological plausibility of his novels. Whereas Defoe's attentive depiction of objects and financial dealings and his admirable ear for spoken English offer a convincing sense of his characters' social position, in *Pamela* the never-ending details provided by the first-person narrator evoke both the concrete reality of the world and the moods of the character observing it. Descriptions in Richardson do not just fulfill a testimonial function, as though the readers were members of a jury to whom the storyteller must present all relevant facts. Immersed in Pamela's world, readers see it through her eyes, gaining indirect, but very effective access to her heart. Here is the young servant, hidden in her little cabinet, thinking of her parents, planning her escape, and at the same time going on with her writing:

> *Past Eleven o'Clock.* Mrs Jewkes is come up, and gone to bed; and bids me not stay long after her. O for a dead sleep for the treacherous brute! I never saw her so much in liquor, and that gives me hopes. I have tried again, and find I can get my head through the iron bars. I am now all prepared. I hope soon to

---

[2] Diderot, *Œuvres* (Paris: Gallimard, Bibliothèque de la Pléiade, 1951), p. 1060 (my translation).

hear her fast; and now I'll seal up these and my other papers, my last work, and to Providence commit the rest! Once more, God bless you both! and send us a happy meeting! if not here, in his heavenly kingdom! *Amen.* (letter 32, Wednesday, twenty-seventh day of Pamela's imprisonment, p. 209)

This technique is closely linked to the internalization of the ideal: it has made the character's inner life so precious, so interesting, that everything she sees, hears, or experiences deserves to be written down and considered carefully. True, the numerous details thus recorded may well sound trivial and quite useless in terms of the plot. Instead of going straight to the core of each event and emphasizing what is genuinely relevant for the story's progress, as his predecessors would have done, Richardson offers his readers what *appears* important to the characters at any given *moment*. Language, rather than describing the world in concise, abstract terms, here serves a long-winded account of the character's experience. Pamela's inner strength and vivacity give life and significance to minuscule occurrences, to everything earlier narratives, for the sake of effectiveness, left out. The sensitive heart, expressing itself in the first person, bestows worth on everything it sees. Immediate experience suddenly, irresistibly expands, to the detriment of conciseness, and perhaps even intelligibility. The seeds are sown from which the long, difficult modernist novel will later grow.

THE TRAGEDY OF INNER STRENGTH—*Clarissa*

If the sources of morality are to be found within the human heart rather than in a transcendent order, then wicked behavior must be rooted there too. But how might evil dwell in an *interesting* person rather than a mere villain or fool? The earlier examples of tricksters like Reynard or Panurge, cruel men like Sir Guillaume de Roussillon, and schemers like Cinzio's evil ensign all neglect good maxims and embrace their lower, animal side, their anger, envy, or contempt for society. They can certainly be duplicitous: tricksters like Panurge put on a serious expression while acting scandalously; Machiavellian characters like the Moor's ensign carefully hide their true intentions. But none of them has a complex inner life or cares about the intricacies of other people's. Panurge pokes fun at women's bodies, not their personalities; the ensign excites only the Moor's base instincts, his jealousy and rage. Moreover, these tricksters and villains have simple, clear-cut aims: to play pranks, to avenge an offense, to destroy someone they detest.

The internalization of the moral law makes it possible for the human heart to dismiss it deliberately and disobey its maxims proudly, even playfully. The virtuous person's negative counterpart is the sophisticated rake who pretends to act nobly while in fact pursuing reprehensible aims. English Restoration comedy boasts a variety of these characters, such as William Wycherley's Horner in *The Country Wife* (1675) or George Etherege's Sir Folping Flatter in *The Man of Mode* (1676). With the change in moral attitudes brought about by the English revolution of 1688, they became a target for righteous indignation. Losing their elegance and charm, the sophisticated rakes turned into vicious, self-indulgent men leading a life of debauchery. In William Hogarth's series of paintings *A Rake's Progress* (1732–1733), Tom Rakewell inherits his father's fortune, spends it foolishly, is pursued by his creditors and accepts the help of innocent young Sarah, neglects her to marry a rich old woman, loses his new fortune gambling, is imprisoned for debt, goes mad and ends up in Bedlam, London's mental asylum. Mr. B. in *Pamela* initially belongs to this type—a rather dull rake, lecherous yet indecisive, sly yet ineffective, brutal but bereft of natural authority.

In Richardson's second novel, *Clarissa* (1747–1748), both protagonists display an unprecedented complexity and depth: Lovelace because of his rakish ambivalence about everything good and beautiful, Clarissa because of her extraordinary strength and intelligence, which she needs in order to resist his deviousness. The contrast between the two allows *Clarissa* to go further than *Pamela* in mixing the tasks of earlier narrative subgenres. Like older idealist novels, *Clarissa* depicts the peaks of virtue; it presents a strong, well-unified conflict that would suit a novella; describes the material setting in minute detail, like a picaresque; and lingers, like pastorals and elegiac stories, on the characters' emotional states. A different kind of epistolary novel, it goes beyond the elegiac first-person narrative of Guilleragues's *The Letters of a Portuguese Nun*, still used in *Pamela*, and instead presents the various individual perspectives of Clarissa, Lovelace, and their friends. It is also the first idealist novel to use long, convoluted dialogue borrowed from drama to reveal the characters' psychology.

The close, "to-the-moment" inspection of psychological shifts gives *Clarissa* its impressive size—which almost rivals that of seventeenth-century idealist novels by La Calprenède and Madeleine de Scudéry—but its action is quite simple, lasts a bit less than a year, takes place in a narrowly circumscribed region between St. Albans and London with a short epilogue in Italy, and involves only a few main characters, though there are a good many secondary players. The plot is triggered by a conflict in the Harlowe family over inherited money and social position. As nouveaux riches, the Harlowes aspire to join the aristocracy, and when their beautiful, smart, well-behaved young daughter Clarissa receives a sizable inheritance from her grandfather, her parents consider marrying her to Robert Lovelace, heir to an earldom. But Clarissa's brother James wants a title of his own and knows that a certain Solmes can help him become a lord: sabotaging the match, he poisons the family's relations with Lovelace and convinces his parents to coerce Clarissa into marrying Solmes. She is unwilling and accepts Lovelace's insincere offer to help; though her parents forbid it, she reads his letters and occasionally answers them. Then one day, when they have arranged to meet in her parents' garden, Lovelace stages a fake emergency that forces Clarissa to run away with him.

The family's quest for social advancement at the expense of their daughter's happiness could easily be the setup for a comedy, a classic case of young people's plans thwarted by parental opposition. Or it could be the start of an older kind of idealist novel: in the *Ethiopian Story* too, Chariclea runs away from her family with Theagenes, her true love, and since her disobedience has nothing to do with impulsive erotic desires, she asks him to take a chastity pledge, which he gladly does. There are plenty of similar situations in later idealist novels. But Clarissa, like Pamela, is completely alone, with no faithful lover to support her. Deeply offended by the Harlowes' rejection of their alliance, the very man whose help she trustingly seeks is planning to use her to settle the score. Deprived of any external support, Clarissa suffers ordeals created by everyone around her. For her family, she is the means to purchase social advancement; for Lovelace, she is the instrument of his revenge.

Once he has Clarissa in his power, Lovelace keeps her in various places, including a brothel where the madam and the prostitutes are disguised as elegant ladies. Beginning to recognize Lovelace's duplicity, Clarissa refuses his marriage proposals and escapes, but is caught and brought back to the brothel. Calculating that the loss of her virginity would force her into marriage, Lovelace, with the madam's assistance, drugs and rapes her. Profoundly distressed and determined not to give in, Clarissa escapes again and hides away, gravely ill. Protected by a kind, poor family and by Belford, a friend of Lovelace's who has rejected his libertine past, Clarissa waits to die, full of remorse for having disobeyed her parents, yet proud of her virtue and trusting in a better afterlife. Soon after Clarissa's death, Lovelace is killed in a duel with Morden, one of her cousins.

The most conspicuous feature of *Clarissa*'s plot is that it doesn't end with the earthly triumph of virtue. But although the heroine's trials eventually kill her, they cannot obliterate her. On the contrary, they enhance her inner strength. Though Clarissa suffers and dies, her image shines, illuminating the prosaic, ordinary lives of those around her. That is why Richardson not only resisted his friends' suggestions that he give the story a happy ending by letting Lovelace marry the young woman, but also devoted many, many pages to her last days, her will and funeral, and the universal mourning and recognition of her superior nature. He made sure the reader couldn't miss the tragedy's cathartic power.

Clarissa takes place in a narrow social milieu in which a small number of characters cannot avoid interacting with one another; at the same time, they try to hide the strong, contradictory passions that unbalance them. Clarissa's contradictions are the easiest to resolve. She is attracted to Lovelace in spite of his bad reputation and would certainly allow herself to love him if he proved worthy of her. But she is a tough judge of people, as we see in her early fights with her siblings, and as soon as Lovelace shows his ugly side, her love turns to contempt. Lovelace, however, cannot cure his divided self. He has an amiable side and an arrogant one; he loves Clarissa, yet occasionally resents and even detests her; he would do whatever she wants in order to marry her, yet he resorts to one hoax after another. Clarissa's death shakes him deeply, yet he remains merry and foolish. Although he knows Clarissa's cousin Morden is ready to avenge her, Lovelace cannot help being haughty and provocative, until the fatal duel becomes inevitable. Critics who interpret Lovelace's behavior as a voluntary self-punishment, a near suicide, are forgetting his irrepressibly rakish side. Lovelace dies because he takes serious things lightly, including Clarissa's life and reputation—and his own.

As in *Pamela*, Richardson presents experience with a vivid immediacy, but since in *Clarissa* the letters are written by several characters, perspective is crucial. His technique of describing every detail reaches its peak here. Never before had a writer spent so much time on the words exchanged by a mother and daughter in the heat of their domestic rows, on each nasty remark two sisters make about each other, on every sentence a seducer utters, sincere or hypocritical, along with each burst of hatred or pride in his heart. There are pages and pages of dialogue with no other point than to make readers feel the pulse of the events. Describing her older sister's airs to her friend and confidante Anne Howe, Clarissa puts Arabella onstage as if in a comedy, noting her words, intonation, and gestures, every tiny variation in her expressions of arrogance and resentment. When Anne Howe sends Clarissa a letter portraying Lovelace as a dreadful seducer, he intercepts and annotates it, bringing the three characters and their feelings together before the reader: Anne's contempt for Lovelace, Clarissa's horror at discovering the truth about her "protector," and Lovelace's rage at seeing himself unmasked. Scenes, emotions, and arguments capture readers' attention, immersing them in the action.

The sublime, ideal character is brought home to our everyday world; the various subgenres blend into a new form; the narrative, able to jump from the most trivial deed to the highest tragedy, traces every nuance of speech, feeling, gesture, and mood. After Richardson, the novel would never be the same again.

Subjective ideography—*Julie, or the New Heloise* by Rousseau

Innovations, however, do not change everything right away. Rousseau wrote his *Julie, or the New Heloise* in the late 1750s, soon after reading *Clarissa*, with Richardson's technique fresh in his mind. Yet Rousseau chose to develop only one of Richardson's novelties: the depiction of an exemplary character living here and now, among us. The contemporary norms of French writing—and even Richardon's last novel, *Sir Charles Grandison* (1753–1754), in which the ideal character is a man and the conflict is milder than *Clarissa*'s—may have persuaded Rousseau to settle for a tamer approach. Psychological complexity; violence, deception, and clashes between characters; the unity of action; and the dramatic sense of total immersion—all are kept out. The extraordinary vigor of the protagonist has mellowed. Instead of a lonely, independent woman like Pamela or Clarissa, capable of resisting a lustful or treacherous male, Rousseau imagines a young woman ready to give herself to her lover, obey her family, and cooperate with those around her. Rousseau uses the epistolary technique, adds echoes of chivalric love—as in *Amadis*, passion is consummated without parental consent or an official marriage—lyrical outbursts, and endless didactic passages. He also sketches out, at least in the novel's first half, a situation typical of the novella—conflict between a young couple and the woman's family.

The beautiful Julie, daughter of the Swiss baron d'Étange, and the learned Saint-Preux, her tutor, fall in love, and Julie does not hesitate to yield to him. Their desire to marry is thwarted by external obstacles: her father refuses to accept a commoner in the family; Julie's secret pregnancy, which would have justified the union, ends prematurely; and, finally, Julie's mother dies of grief when she discovers her daughter's secret correspondence. The lovers give in: Saint-Preux leaves Switzerland to visit Paris and travel the world, while Julie follows her father's advice and weds the man he has chosen for her, M. de Wolmar, a virtuous atheist. She discovers the tranquility of marriage and writes to friends about her enlightened opinions on a huge number of domestic issues. In the novel's sixth and last part, Saint-Preux returns home and befriends Wolmar, who knows of his early involvement with Julie and, as a sign of trust, appoints him to teach the couple's children. The three characters are to be like siblings. Yet Julie's heart is troubled. When one of her children falls into a lake, she jumps into the water to rescue him; she catches a cold and dies, confessing at the last that she still loves Saint-Preux and hopes to join him in the afterlife.

The success of the novel in the eighteenth century and its influence in the nineteenth have something to do with Rousseau's acceptance of the French tradition of elegant moderation. His writing, like that of Guilleragues, Mme de Lafayette, and Marivaux, has a remote quality. Characters recount and judge emotions and events rather than experiencing them; like Arcadia's shepherds, they choose song over action. In a novel of more than seven hundred pages, only half a dozen episodes occur in the external world: Julie gives herself to her tutor, her father forbids their marriage, she miscarries, her mother finds out about her love affair, Julie marries M. de Wolmar, and she saves her son's life and dies. All other events are purely interior. After Julie confesses her love for Saint-Preux, he exclaims: "How changed is my state in just a few days! What bitterness is mixed with the sweetness of coming closer to you! What sad reflections besiege me! ... O Julie, what a fatal present from heaven is a sensible soul!"[3] He wanders in the woods, climbs rocks, dreams of Julie, and beseeches her to abandon the chimera of chastity. Seeing his inner turmoil, Julie agrees to become his lover.

Society condemns premarital love, but Julie's heart approves it, even though it requires concealment. Her worry at the beginning of the novel is not how to bring her feelings into line with social conventions, but how to persuade society to ratify her clandestine love. Gradually, however, she learns to take account of other people's feelings, to understand the private reasons behind society's prejudices. When Julie's father refuses to accept Saint-Preux, she submits—but not only out of obedience to parental authority or convention. Julie first discovers, after her mother's death, that her father is a person worthy of her respect and compassion. For the sake of his happiness, she is willing to acknowledge his convictions about class difference, and to act accordingly. Later, when M. de Wolmar serenely listens to Julie's confession and accepts Saint-Preux as a friend, the three characters form a small community: in their ideal of perfection, personal virtue converges entirely with the world's requirements. The three of them share a mutual sympathy and comprehension, showing that friendship can cross class boundaries. Here, instead of the strong individual-outside-the-world portrayed by Heliodorus and Richardson, we have calm, considerate individuals who seek to reconcile their heart's desires with their social obligations.

To represent this type, Rousseau invented a method that could be called *subjective ideography*. Few remarkable things happen outside the characters' hearts, and what takes place within them is reported only in general terms. External events happen quickly, almost without warning. Julie confesses her love to Saint-Preux at the very beginning of the novel (letter 4) and gives herself to him soon thereafter. Her mother's death is just as sudden. Without lingering on the nature and progression of her illness, Julie abruptly announces: "She is no more" (pt. 3, letter 5, p. 258). Julie describes moral qualities and feelings much more extensively, but she refers to them in abstract terms, passing over the concrete details and situations. She says of her mother:

> Pure and chaste soul, worthy spouse, and incomparable mother, now you live in the abode of glory and felicity; you live; and I, condemned to repentance

[3] Jean-Jacques Rousseau, *Julie, or the New Heloise*, trans. Philip Stewart and Jean Vaché (Hanover, NH: University Press of New England, 1997), pt. 1, letter 26, p. 73.

and despair, forever bereft of your care, your counsel, your gentle caresses, am dead to happiness, to peace, to innocence: I can feel nothing now but your loss; I can see nothing now but my shame; my life is nothing now but sorrow and suffering. (pt. 3, letter 5, p. 258)

A fluent synopsis of emotions thus replaces any description of what they actually feel like.

Richardson's moment-by-moment first-person narrative allows the reader to look at the world from the characters' own perspective, perceiving what they actually see and hear in real time. Rousseau's characters, like Marivaux's, rephrase their experiences in graceful, general terms. For instance, this is Saint-Preux's account of a boat ride on Lake Geneva:

[W]e were soon more than a league from the shore. There I explained to Julie all the parts of the superb horizon around us. I showed her in the distance the mouths of the Rhone whose rushing current suddenly stops after a quarter of a league and seems hesitant to soil with its muddy waters the azure crystal of the lake. I pointed out to her the protruding mountains, whose corresponding and parallel angles form in the space between them a bed worthy of the river that fills it. (pt. 4, letter 17, p. 422, slightly edited)

He does not let us see the landscape; he reports a speech about it ("I explained to Julie," "I showed her," "I pointed out to her") incorporating charming poetic flourishes, as when he imagines a personified current that "seems hesitant to soil . . . the azure crystal of the lake." Always alert at his rhetorical post, Saint-Preux protects his speech from any possible invasion by the untamable realness of the world.

In terms of moral psychology, Rousseau's novel represents a strategic withdrawal. It portrays inner life only insofar as the subject's own gaze can perceive it, leaving aside anything outside his or her conscious awareness. Cervantes, Mme de Lafayette, and, later, Richardson, often hint at their characters' silent thoughts and unacknowledged passions. Rousseau's characters do not lack a certain depth—how could they, given the barrage of feelings and opinions they relentlessly report?—but his moral optimism makes for a plot devoid of hidden, puzzling inner conflicts. Rousseau does not examine human imperfection; he lingers on the splendor of the heart. The abstract language he uses is no handicap, for the power of *The New Heloise* comes not from immersion in actual experience, but from the inner beauty of the characters. Rousseau's achievement is his creation of a new, seductive version of moral idealism.

Resistance to the New Idealism

PLAY AND LAUGHTER

Richardson's innovations combined an idealist notion of inner strength, a picaresque attention to the material world, the novella's unity of action, the pastoral impulse toward intimate confession, and the theater's attention to dialogue. Immersed in the protagonists' immediate experience, the reader is invited to look at reality through their eyes. A variety of characters populate these novels, some heroic, some gentle and friendly, some rakish, some wholly corrupt. Potentially comic situations occur now and then, but Richardson never resolutely crosses the border between serious, uplifting narrative and comedy.

Rousseau, who also sought a new, persuasive way to portray and recommend virtue, did not go as far as his English predecessor—he creates fewer harrowing situations, less frenzied action. He depicts sensitive hearts who listen to their inner desires and learn to reconcile them with moral duty and social obligations. As for comedy, Rousseau, whose voice seems to tremble with emotion most of the time, ignores it entirely.

Tom Jones: THE HUMAN COMEDY AND THE PROMOTION OF THE AUTHOR

Earlier we saw how Henry Fielding, shocked by *Pamela*'s implausible virtue, reacted at once. In his *Shamela*, published five months after Richardson's novel, Fielding rebuffs its main inventions: the enchantment of interiority and the moral equality of people from different social classes. For Fielding, it was obvious that a first-person confession must reveal bad behavior, and that a mere servant could not possibly be as honorable and self-assured as Pamela pretends to be. Moreover, as his own novels soon showed, he did not appreciate Richardson's detailed "to the moment" narration of the protagonist's experience or the never-ending accumulation of words, gestures, clothes, and furniture. To Fielding, overly individualized settings may have seemed inappropriate for a literary genre meant, in his view, to describe "not Men but Manners; not an Individual, but a Species."[1]

The novel's calling, Fielding argues, is not high drama, sublime souls, or riveting conflicts. Rather than striving to evoke serious but uninteresting perfection, the novel should examine the amusing truth of human shortcomings. Drawing on Aristotle, Horace, and Longinus, as well as seventeenth-century literary theorists, Fielding explained that epic, like drama, leans toward either tragedy or comedy, and that it can be written in prose or verse. The absence of meter does not disqualify a prose narrative from being a kind of epic, since it still contains all the other epic features, "such as Fable, Action, Characters, Sentiments, and Diction." Fénelon's *Adventures of Telemachus* (1699) is, like Homer's *Odyssey*, a serious epic poem—the only difference is the presence of meter in the latter. Fielding clearly prefers to call Fénelon's book a prose epic rather than a romance, because romances, whatever their noble aspirations, do not interest him. He does not hide his contempt for "those voluminous works called *Romances*, namely *Clelia*, *Cleopatra*, *Astraea*, *Cassandra*, the *Grand Cyrus*, and innumerable others which contain, as I apprehend, very little Instruction or Entertainment" (*Joseph Andrews*, preface, p. 3).

Instead, he defends the "comic Romance" which is "a comic Epic-Poem in Prose; differing from Comedy, as the serious Epic from Tragedy: its Action being more extended and comprehensive; containing a much larger Circle of Incidents, and introducing a greater Variety of Characters" (pp. 3–4). It differs from serious romances, such as pastorals and Heliodorus-like novels, in being funny rather than solemn and, significantly, "by introducing Persons of inferiour Rank, and consequently of inferior Manners, whereas the grave Romance, sets the highest before us" (p. 4). Less than two years after the publication of Richardson's *Pamela*, Fielding explicitly rejects the possibility of a "grave Romance" about someone of inferior rank, because it seems clear to him that such a character would have terrible manners. In order to be credible, stories about people of modest background, like Joseph Andrews, the brother Fielding invents for Pamela, must be comic, "ludicrous," and occasionally even

[1] Henry Fielding, *Joseph Andrews*, ed. Douglas Brooks-Davies (Oxford: Oxford World Classics, 1999), bk. 3, chap. 1, p. 164.

"burlesque" (p. 4). As far as Fielding is concerned, new idealism is simply not a viable approach to the novel as a genre.

On the title page of *The History of the Adventures of Joseph Andrews, and of his Friend Mr. Abraham Adams* (1742), Fielding specifies that his book is "Written in Imitation of The Manner of Cervantes, Author of *Don Quixote*." Where Quixote obviously, ridiculously failed in his efforts to emulate the behavior of the knights-errant in older chivalric "grave Romances," Richardson's Pamela, with the air of a virtuous lady from one of those "voluminous works," implausibly succeeds in her act. Cervantes's *Quixote*, then, can be assumed to have refuted Richardson long in advance. The true alternative to the hoary old idealist novels, Fielding seems to say, can be found in Cervantes's and his own brand of comic stories, not in Richardson's effort to bring the ideal back home and plant it in the virtuous heart of a servant woman. The legend of Cervantes as the founder of the right kind of novel originates here. Significantly, among the "voluminous works called *Romances*," Fielding did not list Cervantes's *Persiles*, first published in English in 1619, two years after its original Spanish edition, and made available again in English translation in 1741, a year before the publication of *Joseph Andrews*. Fielding did not realize that, while *Don Quixote* made fun of chivalric romance, its author did not reject all "grave Romances" but wanted to discredit the knight-errant variety in favor of the Heliodorus-inspired kind, the kind he soon proceeded to write himself.

In *Joseph Andrews*, the story of Pamela's brother, who chastely resists his mistress's attempts to seduce him, and in *Tom Jones* (1749), Fielding defies the notion of inner perfection and avoids the subjective viewpoint: both stories are told in the third person by an omniscient narrator. The plot of *Tom Jones*, famed for its intricacy, follows the adventures of a foundling raised in a Mr. Allworthy's household alongside Blifil, the legitimate son of Allworthy's sister. Tom is an often impulsive but generous young man, always successful with women. He competes with the deceitful Blifil for beautiful Sophia Western and, thanks to Blifil's maneuvers, is turned out of Allworthy's house. Sophia, whose father wants her to marry Blifil, also runs away. Tom ends up in London, where Sophia diligently searches for him. After various escapades, he is on the verge of being hanged when it is discovered that he is in fact the elder natural son of Mr. Allworthy's sister. His half brother Blifil is punished for his wrongdoing, and Tom, recognized as Allworthy's heir, marries Sophia.

The plot of a Richardson novel is organized as a simple series of actions, all leading in the same direction, and all subordinated to the individual perspective of the characters. Fielding, by contrast, complicates the plot, letting each character follow his or her own path until a more general, consistent pattern emerges, bringing all the subplots together.

Rather than the old comic or picaresque accumulation of analogous episodes, Fielding takes as his model not only *Don Quixote*, but also theatrical comedy, with its maze of incidents and its satisfying resolution. Thus
no single character can fully control or even understand what happens.
The author himself oversees the novel's action, and is therefore the only
one able to narrate it. Richardson's first-person or epistolary narrative
enhances psychological intensity, but limiting the narrative perspective to
one shared with the characters themselves does mean losing any higher
authorial vantage point from which to survey their life paths. Fielding
writes from this higher point of view, just as the then recent representatives of the idealist tradition La Calprenède and Madeleine de Scudéry
had done before him. Fielding may dislike their voluminous romances; he
nonetheless emulates the construction of their works, whose complicated
plots are unfolded and brought to resolution with impeccable mastery.

The various plotlines appear to diverge, but even though they drive
the protagonists of *Tom Jones* far from home, the characters never truly
get away from each another. The seemingly wide world they travel across
turns out to be a set of familiar places, in which the same people keep
showing up. Like *Quixote*, *Tom Jones* evokes a small, welcoming space
in which family members and friends are found everywhere—each under
a variety of names—and all congregate in the same privileged spot, as if
drawn by its magnetic power. Quixote meets his ubiquitous friends—the
barber and the priest—in different places; the masks they wear hide who
they are. Behind these masks, the knights-errant who challenge Quixote,
and the beautiful ladies in distress who ask for his help, are in fact his
neighbors and friends, plotting to bring him back home. In this way, a
few characters suffice to populate a vast fictional space. In *Tom Jones*
too, the main character interacts with a tiny group of people who belong
to Allworthy's household and play multiple roles. Partridge is in turn a
Latin teacher, barber, and Tom's road companion; Mrs. Waters, Captain
Waters's wife, who seduces Tom at Upton, is none other than Jenny Jones,
the woman presumed to be Tom's mother. Tom's slow progress from his
native village to Upton and then to London is thus an opportunity to
meet his own relatives and friends over and over again.

The magnetism of the space seems to guide the characters to the spot
where they are needed. Just as virtually everybody gathers by chance at
Maritornes's inn toward the end of *Don Quixote*'s first part, in *Tom
Jones*, the inn at Upton brings together Tom, Sophia, her father, Partridge,
Mrs. Waters, a certain Mr. Fitzpatrick who will later contribute to the
denouement, and the lawyer Dowling, who knows the secret of Tom's
birth and breathlessly crisscrosses the novel in all directions. Bumping
into each other for no apparent reason, the characters seem to turn up
only so that they can pursue, avoid, embrace, or hit each other in front

of the reader. But beyond the implausible coincidences, one senses a kind, amused Providence at work, which in the end will solve all misunderstandings, thwart the villains' plans, provide the orphans with good parents, and bring lovers together.

This Providence works hand in hand with the storyteller himself, who skillfully arranges the twists and turns of the action. He makes his presence felt in the very act of narration, examining the characters' machinations and self-deceptions with an irony both gentle and devastating. In a rightly famous scene (bk. 5, chap. 5), Tom has fallen in love with Sophia and goes to his mistress, Molly Seagrim, a young woman of easy virtue, to let her know that their relationship is ending. At first, Molly's family pretends she is not at home, but her sister, with a malicious smile, tells him that Molly is confined to her bed in the attic. Tom climbs upstairs to find the attic door locked. He and the reader will soon discover that Molly is inside with another man, but for the time being, they just see her open the door and assure Tom that she had not heard him knocking. To describe Molly's confusion without letting the cat out the bag, the storyteller pretends to meditate on the paradoxes of human nature: "The extremes of grief and joy," he tells us, "have been remarked to produce very similar effects; and when either of these rushes on us by surprise, it is apt to create such a total perturbation and confusion, that we are often thereby deprived of the use of all our faculties." Molly, disconcerted by Tom's presence, "for some minutes . . . was unable to express the great raptures with which the reader will suppose she was affected on this occasion." As for Tom, "he was so entirely possessed, and as it were enchanted, by the presence of his beloved object, that he for a while forgot Sophia, and consequently the principal purpose of his visit."[2]

Molly, caught in the act, is unable to feign joy quickly enough, while Tom, caught off guard by his desire, forgets the virtuous aim of his visit and fails to notice the signs of her deception. The storyteller/moralizer presents the situation in a deceptively serious tone, lingering on each character's momentary point of view, only to abandon it as soon as the circumstances change. A few moments later, Tom gets a grip on himself and informs Molly that he will not be seeing her anymore. Bursting into tears, she proclaims her love for him. But an old rag nailed to the rafters comes loose, revealing, against the wall, a man who turns out to be Mr. Square, Tom and Bliffil's philosophy tutor. "Square no sooner made his appearance, than Molly flung herself back in her bed, cried out she was undone, and abandoned herself to despair." The imperturbable commentator continues: "This poor girl, who was yet but a novice in her

---

[2] Henry Fielding, *The History of Tom Jones*, ed. R.P.C. Mutter (London: Penguin Books, 1966), p. 214.

business, had not arrived to that perfection of assurance which helps off a town lady in any extremity" (p. 217). Square, who has previously been presented as a pedantic preacher of Greek and Roman virtues, is treated in the same tone: "Philosophers are composed of flesh and blood as well as other human creatures. . . . They know very well how to subdue all appetites and passions, and to despise both pain and pleasure; and this knowledge affords much delightful contemplation, and is easily acquired; but the practice would be vexatious and troublesome and, therefore, the same wisdom which teaches them to know this, teaches them to avoid carrying it into execution" (p. 216). This is how human beings are made, Fielding hints: weakness, the tendency to err, and lack of self-knowledge are the hallmarks of our condition. The task of the "comic Epic-Poem in Prose" is to portray these general features with indulgent irony.

The storyteller who guides the strands of the plot to a successful conclusion, the moralizer who points out the gap between the characters' posturing and their true behavior, and the literary theorist who patiently explains what he is doing in the first chapter of each of the novel's eighteen books, are merged together into a single, powerful figure: the *author*. Different from a mere narrator, but also from the actual Mr. Fielding, the author's mission is to invent the story, keep it clear and coherent, comment on it, guarantee its moral and artistic poise, and offer it, in his own voice, to the reader. Understood this way, the author has always been more or less visible in narrative texts. What Fielding achieves is an explicit recognition of this role.

This recognition is an important event for the history of the genre. In early idealist novels, the protagonists' incredible perfection required a certain amount of discretion on the part of the author. It would sound redundant to praise or reflect on behavior that obviously follows the highest standards. In chivalric stories, the author could express a moral view now and then, especially in the early specimens of the genre, with their slightly flawed characters. Occasionally, the author might comment on the artistic structure of the work, but the storyteller, moral commentator, and craftsman never fully coincided. In later chivalric novels, perfect knights-errant like Amadis give eloquent speeches themselves, as does their later disciple Don Quixote. In the picaresque genre, the protagonists' wretchedness is such that the author prefers to let them speak rather than have to discuss such deplorable creatures. In tragic novellas, which focus on less despicable forms of human imperfection, third-person narration and moralizing remarks are appropriate. Yet the genre's brevity and its dramatic events tend to dissuade the author from making comments that might dilute the power of the story. Significantly, the best novella-writers, Boccaccio, Cervantes, and Mme de Lafayette, are careful not to speak too often in their own voice, and those who do so, the lesser-known François

de Rosset and Jean-Pierre Camus, have rightly been considered too loquacious. As for Marivaux, Richardson, and Rousseau, they endow their
characters with sufficient moral energy to speak for themselves.

When Fielding rejects the new, contemporary idealism, he does not go
back to the ignominy of the pícaros, nor does he intend to explore parody
or burlesque. Comic epic must stay close to nature, which provides it with
enough material for laughter. The characters should be neither absurdly
burlesque nor excessively admirable, but stand halfway between caricatures and icons. What is required then, especially for a novel as complex
as *Tom Jones*, is a storyteller careful not to deviate from nature, who can
highlight the characters' comic imperfections, invent a suspenseful plot,
and comment on its moral implications. What is more, the literary craft
involved in writing a comic epic deserves to be explained and defended.
These various tasks (to be coordinator of the fictional universe, moral
guide, and literary theorist) can certainly be performed tacitly—this was
Cervantes's approach in *Quixote*. In making the tasks visible, Fielding
takes on the new idealism, addressing the truth of human imperfection,
and at the same time claims mastery of narrative discourse.

PLAYFUL FICTION: *Tristram Shandy* AND *Jacques the Fatalist*

Fielding gently mocks his characters' faults yet seems to recognize their
right to make mistakes, offering individual blunders and miscalculations
a respect usually reserved for virtue. Without the example of this witty,
tolerant, morally reliable, consistent voice, it is difficult to imagine how
Laurence Sterne and Denis Diderot could have written *Tristram Shandy*
(1759–1767) and *Jacques the Fatalist and His Master* (1773–1775?).
Both writers also adopted Richardson's great discovery, the technique
of writing "to the moment," which slows the narrative flow to a virtual
standstill: Sterne and Diderot carried it to its limits.

They are also deeply indebted to genres Fielding carefully avoided, particularly those involving "learned wit," and narrative parodies of classical
texts. The mixture of humor and erudition is exemplified by Jonathan
Swift's satire *A Tale of a Tub* (1704) as well as by Rabelais's *Gargantua*
and *Pantagruel*, which Sterne knew and admired. Among seventeenth-
century Italian and French verse parodies of classical texts, the best
known were Giovanni Battista Lalli's *Eneide travestita* (1633) and Paul
Scarron's *Virgile travesti* (1648–1653)—the latter had enjoyed a tremendous success in England. In all these texts, telling a story is less important
than the pleasures of farce, digression, and accumulated nonsense.

Tristram Shandy's first-person narrator does not dwell on his own life;
the plot is virtually nonexistent, and the characters lack energy and a
sense of purpose. Announced as an autobiography, the book is filled with

interminable digressions, so that its hundreds of pages barely manage to cover the first five years of Tristram's life. In fact, the main characters are Tristram's father and uncle, Walter and Toby. Each appears to have a goal in life, but neither pursues it successfully. Walter would like to enjoy the pleasures of paternity but hates to fulfill his conjugal duties; his first son died young, and his second, the ugly Tristram, was wounded in the genitals early on. Uncle Toby dreams of marriage but does not seem fit for conjugal duty either, given the groin injury he sustained during the siege of Namur. He talks obsessively about the siege, reenacting its events with the help of his faithful subordinate, Corporal Trim, but avoids giving details about his injury to widow Wadman, his inquisitive fiancée. The story lacks all the features that make a regular eighteenth-century novel possible: most obviously young, healthy characters eager to assert themselves against adversity, whether adventurously, like Tom Jones, or virtuously, like Clarissa.

In the absence of a well-structured plot and energetic characters, the text relies on a relentlessly playful discourse. The suspense here comes not from the action, but from the turns of the narrator's talk, which draws on Richardson's dilatory technique of writing "to the moment" and on Fielding's humorous commentary, but also on the tradition of the moralizing pícaros who endlessly reflect on the meaning of the human condition. The book opens with a meditation on the very beginning of the character's existence—his conception:

> I wish either my father or my mother, or indeed both of them, as they were in duty both equally bound to it, had minded what they were about when they begot me; had they duly consider'd how much depended upon what they were then doing;—that not only the production of a rational Being was concerned in it, but that possibly the happy formation and temperature of his body, perhaps his genius and the very cast of his mind . . . —Had they duly weighed and considered all this, and proceeded accordingly,—I am verily persuaded I should have made a quite different figure in the world, from that in which the reader is likely to see me.[3]

But in fact readers are not likely to see much of Tristram, and the few childhood episodes they witness offer no hints about the character's adult life or his reasons for writing an autobiography. And the melancholy tone of the first few lines soon gives way to bawdy farce:

---

[3] Laurence Sterne, *The Life and Opinions of Tristram Shandy, Gentleman,* ed. Ian Campbell Ross (Oxford: Oxford World Classics, 2009), vol. 1, chap. 1, p. 7.

> Pray my Dear, quoth my mother, have you not forgot to wind up the clock?—
> Good G..! cried my father, making an exclamation, but taking care to moder-
> ate his voice at the same time,—Did ever woman, since the creation of the
> world, interrupt a man with such a silly question? Pray, what was your father
> saying?—Nothing. (p. 7)

Lack of sexual desire, in Tristram's parents' case, and the inability to satisfy it, in Uncle Toby's, are being used to poke fun at the most important
feature of contemporary novels: their love plots. The reader's supposed
intervention, "Pray, what was your father saying?" and the embarrassed
answer, "Nothing," mock the self-assurance of the usual narrative voice.
As the work unfolds, the pleasure of linguistic performance takes over:
jumping from English to Latin, from description to sermon, from bouts
of story (always interrupted by countless asides) to erudite digressions,
the narrator contrives to stun and hypnotize his reader. To a certain extent, the resulting sense of contingency recalls the novels in which a capricious fortune relentlessly persecutes the characters, except that here the
surprises come from discursive games rather than events.

Tristram's volubility frees language from its links with empirical evidence, so important for Richardson, which is mentioned only so as to
be discarded again. A description of Corporal Trim (vol. 2, chap. 17)
provides a good example:

> He stood before them with his body swayed, and bent forwards just so far,
> as to make an angle of 85 degrees and a half upon the plain of the horizon;
> — which sound orators, to whom I address this, know very well, to be the true
> persuasive angle of incidence; — in any other angle you may talk and preach;
> — 'tis certain, — and it is done every day; — but with what effect, — I leave
> the world to judge! (p. 97)

This passage is only the beginning of a long rhetorical flight, but you can
see its direction: starting with a concrete detail (the angle of the corporal's bow), the narrator changes his tone, as though to scoff at that detail.
A few lines later, the description, still in an objective, precise style, gives
Trim the features of a puppet:

> He stood, — for I repeat it, to take the picture of him in at one view, with
> his body sway'd, and somewhat bent forwards, — his right leg firm under
> him, sustaining seven-eighths of his whole weight, — the foot of his left
> leg, the defect of which was no disadvantage to his attitude, advanced
> a little, — not laterally, nor forwards, but in a line betwixt them; etc.
> p. 97)

As in Rabelais's prose, linguistic waves seem to burst over the substance of what is being said, reducing the story to a mere pretext for the storyteller's rhetorical virtuosity. But while Rabelais's stylistic exuberance matches his gigantic characters and their bursts of energy, *Tristram Shandy* contrasts the narrator's irrepressible loquacity with the lamentable specimens who populate his novel. Between the verbal cornucopia and the poverty of the plot, the reader senses a disturbing gap, as though the familiar split between character and world were being replaced here by a breakup between the story and the discourse that plays around it.

Some critics have argued that Sterne was the first author to convey the full freedom of human subjectivity. It is true that he captures the adventurous flexibility of human speech more convincingly than did any previous writer of prose, save Rabelais. Moreover, Sterne knows how to evoke individual inflections and idiosyncrasies of language. Yet *Tristram Shandy*'s oral vividness belongs to the *presentation* of the story rather than the characters portrayed in it. These characters, far from embodying subjective freedom, are mere caricatures. The narrator freely expresses whatever comes to mind (often half copying, half distorting other learned texts), but he does so as a commentator, not a character within the story. The representation of free human beings in the actual world is what Richardson and Rousseau's new idealism aimed to achieve—a task Sterne ridicules tirelessly.

If, nevertheless, *Tristram Shandy*'s Walter and Toby are unforgettable *as* characters, it is precisely because they fail to act or think properly, instead devoting all their time to futile hopes and pointless posturing. In a stunningly innovative polemic against heroic idealism, Sterne is perhaps the first to dedicate a long narrative to a tedious, uneventful, inconsequential way of life. Much later, and in a different context, Goncharov's *Oblomov* (1859) would take up this task, which would also have its place in the work of Anton Chekhov. But the gloomier nineteenth- and early twentieth-century versions would project a sad, compassionate wisdom about human frailty, quite different from Sterne's satiric depiction of underachievers and fools.

|||||||||||||||||||||||||||

In *Jacques the Fatalist and His Master*, written in the early to mid-1770s, Denis Diderot, though he does not achieve anything like *Tristram Shandy*'s linguistic virtuosity, surpasses Sterne in his ability to blend verbal playfulness with narrative invention. While Sterne lets the story wander in all directions, Diderot narrates his tale quite freely but also puts together a coherent, plausible story line. The story is told polyphonically by the author-inventor, Jacques, his master, and a few other characters. It brings together the multiple-plot technique from *Tom Jones*, the complex narrative interlacing found in Galland's French translation of the *Arabian Nights* (1704–1717), the picaresque world of crooks and prostitutes, the serious novella, and Richardson's trick of writing "to the moment." The tone is delightfully relaxed, reminiscent of Rabelais and Sterne (at one point the latter is even accused, in jest, of having plagiarized Diderot), and equally close to Fielding's literary-theoretical interventions and ironic commentaries. The labyrinthine plot can be fully grasped only at the very end, when each story reaches its conclusion and the adventures recounted by the master gradually come to fit with Jacques's narrative. Only then does the reader understand what has happened: the master is the victim of an appalling amorous swindle and, in revenge, kills a man in a duel; Jacques is accused of the murder, arrested, and condemned to prison; he escapes, becomes a bandit, and after various adventures is reunited with both his master and his beloved. The author, now disguised as the "publisher," pretends not to be entirely convinced by the denouement, which, he submits, sounds a bit apocryphal.

From the very beginning, it appears that the text is being invented in front of the reader:

> How had they met? By chance, like everyone else. What were their names? What does it matter to you? Whence had they come? From the nearest possible spot. Where were they going? Do we ever know where we are going?[4]

These questions receive no answer. Right away, Jacques and his master begin to converse, and the next page sketches out their most important features: the master's placidity and his valet's fatalism. As soon as Jacques starts the story of his love affairs, the author turns to his readers again and comments mockingly:

> You see, dear reader, that I am well on my way, and that it is completely up to me whether I shall make you wait one year, two years, or three years for the story of Jacques' loves, by separating him from his Master and having each go through all the vicissitudes that I please. What's to prevent my marrying off the Master and making him a cuckold? Shipping Jacques off to the islands? (p. 4)

Asserting his very real freedom of invention, the author demonstrates that he can interrupt the course of the story and emphasize his own importance as often as he likes, introduce seemingly irrelevant subplots, and let other voices tell their own stories.

---

[4] Denis Diderot, *Jacques the Fatalist and His Master*, trans. J. Robert Loy (New York: Norton, 1959), chap. 1, p. 3.

Among these voices, Jacques's is the most memorable. He narrates his love affairs without ever changing the subject or missing out any detail. The master, exasperated, implores Jacques to go faster. Pretending to obey, he jumps to the very end of the story, says he is in love, and drops hints about a pretty brunette whose hands the master has taken and held more than once on the sly. The master asks him to explain what he means. Jacques is willing to give details, on condition that the master will let him tell his story as slowly as he sees fit.

Beyond the author's banter and the funny side of Jacques's dialogues with his master, the novel contains two drastically different types of story. Along with that of the master's misfortunes, the embedded narrative about Mme de la Pommeraye and the Marquis des Arcis fits the tradition of the serious novella. Here, love involves vicious conflicts in which corrupt, resentful hypocrites deceive innocent, generous characters—virtue is equated with a gentle naïveté. These stories are couched in a familiar eighteenth-century French prose style: cõncise and highly effective. Jacques's tale, by contrast, emphasizes the immediacy of real-life experience, often sounding like a parody of Richardson's moment-by-moment approach.

The author speaks from on high, the master keeps a comfortable distance from his own unhappy experiences, but Jacques, trapped within his narrative, looks at the world through the only available porthole: his own eyes. This outlook, which in Richardson so often evokes the character's independence from the actual, concrete course of events, has a new mission here: Jacques believes in universal determinism, so for him each event, no matter how insignificant it may seem, is entirely relevant. His fatalism justifies the promotion of humble people to the rank of respectable characters, for only in a determinist world, where every event, every person is unique and indispensable, can all human beings proudly enjoy the right to recount what happens to them. Jacques's fatalism seems implicitly to question the logic of the new idealism's interest in virtuous people from modest backgrounds: equality among human beings, if it exists, is a matter of universal physics rather than morality.

In their time, like Rabelais's *Gargantua* and *Pantagruel*, Sterne's *Tristram Shandy* and Diderot's *Jacques the Fatalist* had a limited impact on the history of the novel. *Tristram Shandy* had many contemporary readers and admirers, but its real success began later, when German Romantics were celebrating individual genius and artistic nonconformism; and in the twentieth century, it was embraced with enthusiasm by formalist critics and modernist writers. A section of *Jacques the Fatalist* was translated into German by Schiller; he and Goethe admired its aesthetic freedom, so different, they thought, from the strict rules of the prevailing neoclassicism. Like *Tristram Shandy*, it began to be fully appreciated only in the twentieth century, when the rise of modernist literature helped critics and readers to accept and enjoy gratuitous linguistic play.

SUBLIME TERROR

Jacques the Fatalist's story stays closer to nature—a deterministic, blind nature—than the adventures of Richardson's exalted souls. Fielding also conceives his characters as faithful to nature—that is, to human imperfection and fallibility. Richardson's new idealism may have claimed to have discovered true inner greatness in eighteenth-century England; on closer inspection, Pamela and Clarissa are as implausible as the awe-inspiring princesses of old Greek and heroic novels. Moreover, while these princesses live and act in an imaginary milieu that fits their superhuman virtues, Pamela and Clarissa's perfection might seem out of place in Richardson's obsessively plausible scenery. Fielding declared the new idealism too far from nature. Conversely, since its aim was to adapt the ancient novel's characters to contemporary everyday life, other writers accused it of spending too much time on reality, thus neglecting the powers of the imagination.

The Gothic Novel

The gothic novel, invented in the second half of the eighteenth century, stands up for the imagination, turning away from empirical reality to celebrate the pleasures of total implausibility. It brings back the chivalric setting, with its castles, dungeons, and legendary monsters, and in order to make a strong impression on its readers, it discards believability and invents *atmosphere*. The sad, oppressive, frightening atmosphere is meant to mesmerize the reader and cast doubt on the supposedly objective descriptions of the material and social environment found both in the picaresque stories and in Richardson's prose.

Since plausibility is not an issue, a new type of protagonist emerges—wild, malevolent, demonic characters, who never seem to run out of energy. In earlier eighteenth-century fiction, constancy and energy seemed mutually exclusive: the virtuous women, with their inflexible morals, are often rather passive; the only characters bursting with energy are crooks, skirt-chasers, and villains, people like Fielding's Tom Jones, Richardson's Lovelace, and Smollett's Roderick Random. The gothic novel puts virtue at an even greater disadvantage, emphasizing the noble heart's defenselessness. Once vulnerability becomes the mark of virtue, evil forces naturally feel invincible. While it is true that gothic novels end with a providential restoration of order and justice, it is usually the villain's self-destructive bent that makes this possible, rather than any effective resistance by the virtuous characters.

These features—the appeal to the imagination, the shocking implausibility of the historical context, the medieval setting in which all the world's a prison, and the contrast between the energy of the evil characters and the weakness of the virtuous ones—are all present in the first specimen of the subgenre, Horace Walpole's *The Castle of Otranto* (1764). Walpole sets out his intentions in his preface to the second edition. The book attempts, he writes, "to blend the two kinds of romance, the ancient and the modern. In the former, all was imagination and improbability: in the latter, nature is always intended to be, and sometimes has been, copied with success." But in recent romances, he continues, "Nature has cramped imagination."[5] As he explains, Walpole uses fantasy for the actions of the main characters, calling attention to the extraordinary situations in which they find themselves; their servants, on the other hand, he aims to draw from life, expecting these more naturalistic portraits "to incite smiles" (p. 44). Thus Walpole returns to a hierarchical view of society: the ideal of greatness is suited to the higher echelons, and comic inadequacy to the lower. The egalitarian message of the new idealism makes no sense in the archaic, wildly implausible world depicted here.

The Castle of Otranto is about the fall of the tyrant Manfred, whose ancestors usurped the throne of Otranto. Before dying, Alfonso, the principality's last legitimate sovereign, secretly begot a line of heirs, his grandson being a young man named Theodore. The tyrant's only son, Conrad, is crushed to death when a gigantic helmet miraculously falls on him in front of the castle. Desperate for a male heir, Manfred deserts his wife Hippolita in order to marry Isabella, his dead son's fiancée, but his plans are foiled by Hippolita, Isabella, Theodore, and Manfred's own daughter, Matilda. Isabella seeks refuge in the castle's vast underground passages and escapes with Theodore's help. In attempting to kill Isabella, Manfred stabs his own daughter, Matilda, by mistake. The truth about the usurpation is finally made public, and Manfred abdicates; Theodore succeeds him and marries Isabella.

Nothing in this plot is credible because nothing attempts to be so. The theme of the legitimate sovereign may have had some resonance for the contemporary public, but the idea of supernatural intervention in such matters would have seemed far-fetched. Similarly, readers could not miss the fact that in Manfred's case a monarch's natural desire for male heirs reaches a monstrous, artificial height. The fate of Conrad and Matilda,

---

[5] Horace Walpole, *The Castle of Otranto*, in *Three Gothic Novels*, ed. Peter Fairclough (London: Penguin Books, 1968), p. 43.

who die so that Manfred can be punished, must have appeared equally incongruous in a period when fictional characters were chastised or rewarded in person rather than through their children. Far from bringing back the exquisite radiance of ancient Greek novels and their sixteenth- and seventeenth-century imitations, the kinds of imagination and improbability embraced here signal a new way in which art was expected to affect its audience.

The Castle of Otranto's gloom recalls Edmund Burke's views on the sublime—which involves awe and horror in the face of what is vast, dark, uncertain—as recently published in his *A Philosophical Enquiry into the Origin of Our Ideas of the Sublime and Beautiful* (1757). According to Burke, since the idea of pain is much more powerful than that of pleasure, the sublime, pain, and danger, in their interconnections, inspire the most powerful emotion a human being can feel. Following this recipe, Walpole turned his back on the weak emotions aroused by literary works that stayed too close to nature, instead piling on the frightening figures, situations, and speeches. A certain narrative simplicity enhances this approach. *The Castle of Otranto* leaves out precise description, reflections on the characters' states of mind, and authorial comments and digressions. Like many earlier works of fiction—chivalric novels, Italian novellas, eighteenth-century French novels—the story never lingers on ineffectual details. Its only aim is to incite dread.

Gothic novels induce fear in two ways: by designing an oppressive setting and by granting diabolical characters an inordinate amount of power. *The Castle of Otranto* develops the first method. Its plot and style are mediocre, its characters insipid, yet the atmosphere is unforgettable. At the novel's center lies the castle. Easily accessible to outsiders but difficult to escape for those inside, it acts as a trap and a prison. The tyrannical Manfred controls everything above the ground—the rooms, the corridors, the courtyard, and the prison cells—but has no power over the labyrinth hidden in the cellar. In a quite remarkable inversion of familiar symbolism, open, well-lit spaces, like the castle's yard or the great halls, are associated with servitude and death, whereas dark, suffocating areas, such as the castle vaults or a cave on the seashore, promise a fragile, vulnerable freedom. Readers do not need to sympathize with the characters—as they do with Pamela, for instance—in order to fall under this novel's spell: the scenery alone bewitches them.

The Mysteries of Udolpho (1794) by Ann Radcliffe offers a new version of such surroundings, this time explicitly linked to the characters' inner feelings. In a graceful, melancholy style, Radcliffe describes the captivity of Emily St Aubert, a young orphan from a good family who accompanies her aunt, Mme Cheron, to the castle of her husband, the evil Montoni. Here is the first description of the castle (pt. 2, chap. 5):

Towards the close of day, the road wound into a deep valley. Mountains, whose shaggy steeps appeared to be inaccessible, almost surrounded it. To the east, a vista opened, that exhibited the Apennines in their darkest horrors; and the long perspective of retiring summits, rising over each other, their ridges clothed with pines, exhibited a stronger image of grandeur, than any that Emily had yet seen. The sun had just sunk below the top of the mountains . . . , but his sloping rays, shooting through an opening of the cliffs, touched with a yellow gleam the summits of the forest, that hung upon the opposite steeps, and streamed in full splendor upon the towers and battlements of a castle, that spread its extensive ramparts along the brow of a precipice above. The splendor of these illumined objects was heightened by the contrasted shade, which involved the valley below. 'There,' said Montoni, speaking for the first time in several hours, 'is Udolpho.'[6]

Emily contemplates this spectacular scene with apprehension. The fortress she catches sight of is not so much a building as a state of mind.

The same dreamlike drive sustains *The Monk* by Matthew Lewis (1796), but this time the terror comes from demonic intervention. Convents, haunted castles, and underground prisons abound, but the center of interest here is the protagonist, not the scenery. The monk Ambrosio, a preacher renowned for his zeal, cannot resist the charms of the beautiful Matilda, who has worked her way into the monastery disguised as a novice. Enslaved by sensual passion, Ambrosio then gets obsessed with Antonia, one of his flock. With Matilda's assistance, he kidnaps the young woman and hides her in a cellar, where he rapes and kills her. Arrested and put in prison, Ambrosio receives a visit from Satan himself, who reveals that Antonia was Ambrosio's own sister and that Matilda was sent from hell to destroy him. To escape capital punishment, Ambrosio signs a pact with the devil, but his new master, after freeing him from prison, takes his life.

Poorly written, awkwardly constructed, Lewis's novel nevertheless fascinates its readers. Its main character is an individual-outside-the-world, but in this case a depraved, malignant man rather than the angelic young woman of the new idealist novel. The sensitive heart capable of resisting the world has been replaced by a cold heart, unable to resist the basest impulses and ready to form an alliance with the devil in order to satisfy them. In earlier novellas, violent conflict has psychological roots; here, the violence lacks motivation. In *The Monk*, terrifying acts, just like the

---

[6] Ann Radcliffe, *The Mysteries of Udolpho*, ed. Bonamy Dobrée (Oxford: Oxford World Classics), 1966, p. 226.

dread-inducing scenery in Walpole and Radcliffe, are a primordial element needing no explanation.

Once moral authority is placed within the individual heart, a genuine return to earlier forms of idealism becomes impossible. Providence's role has been replaced by human self-mastery, and the effort to find a moral force that transcends it summons demonic figures. Beyond the gothic novel, this discovery made possible works such as *Les Liaisons dangereuses* (1782) by Choderlos de Laclos, and the novels of the Marquis de Sade.

CHAPTER 8

Love: Romantic
and Impossible

‖‖

From Sentiments to Solitude

Both comic, playful novels and gothic fiction, then, represented a strong rejection of the new idealism. Yet the innovations of Richardson and Rousseau continued to reverberate through the second half of the eighteenth century. Sentimental novels followed the examples set by *Pamela*, *Clarissa*, and *Julie, or the New Heloise*, while novels of manners owed a great deal to the debate between the new idealism and its opponents.

Evelina (1778) by Frances Burney, which looks at London society through the eyes of a naive, kind, provincial young woman, navigates between satire on contemporary manners and a moderate version of idealism. From a good family struck by misfortune, Evelina is as innocent as Marivaux's Marianne and as perceptive as Matthew Bramble, writer of most of the letters in Tobias Smollett's last work, *The Expedition of Humphry Clinker* (1771). She sends her letters about London's high life and her various suitors to her tutor, but the real addressees are young female readers who need to learn how to choose a good husband. The generous Lord Orville, after entertaining some doubts about Evelina's social position, grows to appreciate her dignity and asks for her hand. By contrast, Sir Clement Willoughby, a self-important bore, earns the contempt of Evelina and her friends. Willoughby is a kind of heir to Mr. B., and though Evelina probably does not have the fortitude that might allow her to convert someone like him to virtue, she radiates enough charm to please a higher-ranked young man.

The sentimental novel heads in the same direction. It depicts credible surroundings, good but not exactly awe-inspiring people, and dreadful situations that never lead to genuine catastrophe. Goldsmith's *Vicar of Wakefield* (1766) tries to tone down the implausibility of the new idealism. The narrator, a benevolent pastor and father, reflects on the unexpected twists and turns of fate. The complex action—recalling the same kinds of theatrical plots as *Tom Jones*—includes a financial disaster that later turns out not to have happened, a rake's fake wedding that is in fact valid, a mysterious suitor who emerges as a generous benefactor, and several other mild dramas, all ending well. The obvious question is whether, in the ordinary environment depicted by Goldsmith, sensitive hearts can plausibly overcome human wickedness and the world's hostility.

This issue, raised by Richardson's *Clarissa*, resurfaces in Goethe's *Sufferings of Young Werther* (1774). This short novel provides the sensitive heart with psychological credibility, thus solving the new idealism's most notable difficulty. To achieve this feat, however, Goethe's story refrains from endowing the main character with genuine strength. The lyrical tone, the absence of decisive action, and the denouement based on resignation recall elegiac stories, while the novel's confined milieu, small number of characters, and stark conflict between love and marriage are reminiscent of an early novella. Werther's first-person confession, not unlike those found in early picaresque tales, is presented as credible simply because few people would invent a story as pitiful as his about themselves. The premise is well known: young Werther falls in love with the beautiful and virtuous Charlotte, who is engaged to another man. Werther tries to accept his misfortune, but since he can neither challenge his rival nor abandon his dreams of love to pursue a career—for high society humiliates and rejects him—he kills himself.

The themes—inner beauty, weakness, the break between character and world, the impossibility of satisfying the noblest desires, suicide—all show how carefully the author considered Richardson's approach, and most especially Rousseau's. Like them, Goethe creates his character by breathing new life into older narrative elements. Werther descends, via the eighteenth-century pastoral, from Boccaccio's Fiammetta and d'Urfé's Celadon, the passionate lady and the shepherd whose lives are poisoned by the cruelty of their beloveds. But whereas in the pastoral, the world itself is full of wonders, coincidences, and disguises, in Goethe's story, the enchantment of the world originates in Werther's heart. Like a magic lantern, it fills the world with eerie light and passing shadows:

> Wilhelm, what is the world to our hearts without love? What is a magic-lantern without light? You have but to kindle the flame within, and the brightest figures shine on the white wall; and, if love only show us fleeting shadows,

we are yet happy, when, like mere children, we behold them, and are transported with the splendid phantoms.[1]

But his hopes are not destined to be realized. Reading the adventures
of Chariclea, Amadis, or Celadon, the reader knows (and the characters
sense) that their desires are out of the ordinary, that the emergence and
fulfillment of their longings have something providential about them.
Since the very moment of their birth, these desires seem already, like invisible javelins, to have hit their target. When the new idealism places
moral strength *within* the human heart, Pamela and Julie play the role of
Providence and, when they see fit, fulfill their lovers' wishes. In Werther's
story, the object of desire vanishes; the dreamer grasps only shadows.
It is certainly not by chance that, one stormy evening, Charlotte looks
through the window and utters the name of a poet:

> [H]er eyes wandered over the scene; she raised them to the sky, and then
> turned them upon me; they were moistened with tears; she placed her hand
> on mine and said, "Klopstock!" at once I remembered the magnificent ode
> which was in her thoughts: I felt oppressed with the weight of my sensations,
> and sank under them. It was more than I could bear. I bent over her hand,
> kissed it in a stream of delicious tears, and again looked up to her eyes. Divine
> Klopstock! why didst thou not see thy apotheosis in those eyes? (bk. 1, June
> 16, pp. 17–18)

Unable to hope for a real union with the beloved, passion turns toward
the realm of imagination. The two characters, in their admiration for a
poet they find divine, share a moment of communion, deeply moving
and hopeless. In earlier idealist novels, virtuous passion was remarkably
effective; here, nostalgia and poetic sadness prevail. Werther's reverence
is stronger than desire: "She is sacred to me. All desire is silent in her
presence" (bk. 1, July 16, p. 27). He dreams without hoping, and since he
cannot act, he has no choice but to withdraw from the world. In the end,
poetic elation leads to solitude and death.

   In the dispute about the plausibility of the noble heart, *The Sufferings
of Young Werther* supports neither Richardson and Rousseau's solution—
magnificent but implausible inner strength—nor Fielding's moral skepticism. With Charlotte and Werther, Goethe aptly differentiates between
two kinds of sensitive heart, between her way of finding peace in an imperfect world and his inability to accept that world.

---

[1] Johann Wolfgang von Goethe, *The Sufferings of Young Werther*, trans. Harry Stein-
hauer (New York: Norton, 1970), bk. 1, July 18, p. 27.

Refinement and Implausibility

Flaring up within his heart, Werther's poetic love fails to evaluate its chances of success, and it damages, even destroys the lover's links with his surroundings. To understand fully the narrative links between poetic elation and solitude, one has to consider, alongside the debate on inner strength and plausibility, a different narrative tradition. This alternative tradition—highly successful in the eighteenth century but less productive in the nineteenth—avoids involvement with empirical reality; instead, it keeps alive the elegance of the older high genres, epic or lyric. Openly ideographic, these narratives depict human beings as incarnations of ideals and situate them far away from their readers. Whether *ancient* or *foreign*, their worlds are rarely plausible but always conform to a higher, more refined taste.

The "ancient" option, directly inspired by Greek poetry and philosophy, includes the immensely popular *Adventures of Telemachus* (1699) by Fénelon, *The Temple of Gnidus* (1725) by Montesquieu, Wieland's influential *Story of Agathon* (1766–1794), and the return of the pastoral promoted by Gessner (*Daphnis*, 1754) and Florian (*Estelle*, 1788). *Letters from a Peruvian Woman* (1747) by Mme de Graffigny, Marmontel's *The Incas* (1777), and *Paul and Virginia* (1788) by Bernardin de Saint-Pierre belong to the "foreign" strand, whose predecessors were the seventeenth-century heroic novels that seductively described non-European civilizations: *Polexandre* by Gomberville, *Zaïde* by Mme de Lafayette, and *Oroonoko* by Aphra Behn.

The works belonging to this tradition are openly devoted to the moral education of their readers. *The Adventures of Telemachus*, like Xenophon's *Cyropaedia* (fourth century BC), describes the education of a prince—in this case, one who lives in a mythological past and learns the principles of good government from the goddess Athena, disguised as Mentor, an old adviser. Marmontel's *Belisarius* (1767) celebrates a Roman general who, after losing favor with Emperor Justinian, lives humbly as a blind beggar. Wieland's *Story of Agathon* is a philosophical bildungsroman set in Athens at the time of Plato. Narratives with foreign themes, and a rejuvenated pastoral, praised the Golden Age and the civilizations still close to it. A parallel set of comic narratives underscored the strength of this new ideographic line: Jonathan Swift's *Gulliver's Travels* (1726), Voltaire's philosophical stories *Zadig* (1747), *Micromegas* (1752), and *Candide* (1759), Samuel Johnson's *Rasselas* (1759), and *Die Abderiten* (1774–1780) by Wieland.

Since didacticism naturally tends toward either hope, as in Fénelon, or irony, as in Swift, this tradition for a long time stayed away from more

pessimistic reflections on the clash between noble characters and the outside world. Not until the last third of the eighteenth century did these
works begin to represent heroes crushed by the maleficent forces of fate
or history. In Marmontel's *The Incas*—a tragic epic in prose, a kind of
Iliad told from the point of view of the Trojans—the generous Incas are
wiped out by the cruelty and fanaticism of their conquerors; in Bernardin
de Saint-Pierre's *Paul and Virginia*, the young protagonists' happiness is
destroyed by unpredictable tropical storms.

In the most memorable instance of this approach, Hölderlin's *Hyperion*
(1797–1799)—set in an imaginary modern Greece that, despite its decay,
inherits the classical beauty celebrated by Fénelon and Wieland—fate and
history forge an alliance against the hero's inner greatness. This short
epistolary novel describes the fate of a character who believes he has been
chosen by the gods, until events gradually disprove the divine nature of
his mission. The story, like *Werther*, is plausible precisely because its main
character, a man with a sensitive heart and grand aspirations, ends up
being defeated. It is as though these two novels were aiming to prove that
the new idealism's weak point was not so much the *existence* of a character who entertains high ideals, as the worldly *success* of such a character.
And just as in Goethe's story, the unity of action does not derive from the
convergence of all the plot's strands toward a single conflict—as is the
case in Italian and Spanish novellas—but from the *conceptual* unity of
the character's fate, following a formula laid out in *Telemachus* and *Story
of Agathon*. As for the prosaic nature of the surrounding world, it is never
evoked through detailed empirical description, as in Richardson's prose,
but suggested allusively by the protagonist's disappointments and pain.

Hyperion is a young man on a deliberate quest for inner growth,
which he pursues by searching for friendship, love, and meaningful action. Growth, however, involves separation. None of the three significant
connections in his life will last. His mentor, Adamas, leaves him once his
education is finished. Later, Hyperion breaks with his best friend, Ala-
banda, and decides to move away from his beloved Diotima, whose love
he fears might make him forget his own great calling. He aims higher than
Werther, whose only dream is a quiet life beside his Charlotte. Despising
private happiness, Hyperion dedicates himself to Greece's freedom.

During the struggle for Greek liberation, however, he finds that the
human world is hopelessly fallen. The beautiful and righteous community for which he is ready to give his life turns out to be beyond reach.
During the siege of Mistra, Hyperion's soldiers massacre not only enemy
fighters but also their own compatriots, trapped inside the city. Before
this battle, Hyperion was convinced that human beings had evolved from
an earlier "rude" age to their present-day "polite" stage. Now, however,
he sadly realizes that people are essentially savage, and he gives up hope

of their salvation. The defeat of the naval fleet he joins, his captivity, and Diotima's demise—caused by her belief that Hyperion is dead—all deepen the moral wound received at Mistra. Alone, the young man wanders around, deploring the world's inhumanity. Not long ago, he had believed that the source of eternal beauty had not yet run dry; now he is struck by what he sees as the ugliness of his contemporaries. Avoiding people and their corruption, he finds his only comfort in nature. Hyperion's retreat is, in a way, more depressing than Werther's suicide. Goethe portrayed his character as a weak man, but not even Hyperion, whose inner strength is matchless, can enforce exalted ideals in a world that has no place for them.

EXALTED LOVE AND ITS CRITICS

Hyperion's pessimism throws doubt on every single human concern: friendship, love, the fight for freedom. However, for pessimistic novels written at the end of the eighteenth century and the beginning of the nineteenth, the most frequent target is exalted love. Yet while *Werther* and *Hyperion* depict the *world's* insensitivity to the protagonist's sensitive heart, other novels emphasize the moral incompetence of human beings themselves. These novels do not condemn the universe's inability to acknowledge human splendor, but pass judgment on the heart itself, which, whatever its poetic aspirations, fails to identify the right moral solutions. It was in fact Goethe who would eventually formulate the clearest objection to the eighteenth-century belief that human beings can find the moral law in their own hearts: this doctrine ignores the existence of the passions, which determine our behavior in ways that resist comprehension and bear little relation to morals. Their power is the subject of *Elective Affinities* (1809), in which, half a century after Rousseau's *Julie, or the New Heloise*, Goethe rejects its views on love and morality.

Rousseau himself was aware that the search for the moral law in one's own heart is made difficult by the unpredictability of the passions and by the influence of social norms. Part of his solution to this is to play down the conflict between love and morality by suggesting that Julie discovers her moral autonomy precisely because of her feelings for Saint-Preux. The other part is to imagine a charitable reconciliation between personal morality and social norms, as when Julie, who cannot make her father accept her union with Saint-Preux, nobly resigns herself to filial obedience and marries Wolmar. Yet this solution, which distinguishes between passion and marriage, between impulsive desires and the reasonable decision to abide by social norms, is not fully supported by the novel's plot. Julie hopes to get pregnant by Saint-Preux to gain her father's consent, knowing for sure that he would prefer her to marry beneath her station than to be dishonored; because her hopes fail to materialize, she has to break up with her lover. What Julie takes to be a reconciliation between her moral autonomy and social norms is, at the factual level, merely a mixture of bad luck and society's bias against unwed mothers. As for the pure, unadulterated friendship that later unites Saint-Preux, Julie, and Wolmar, it is meant to give the impression that human beings can free themselves permanently from their passions. Marriage puts an end to the protagonists' torments, as it does in most eighteenth-century novels, but here—presumably because the marriage is loveless—it fails to conclude the novel itself. After marriage, life goes on, Rousseau says. Passions go on as well, Goethe will add later.

The founders of the new idealism realized that the governing power of the heart must entail full mastery over one's passions. This is the reason why Richardson's Pamela does not confess her true feelings for her master, even to herself, and never acts on them directly. Similarly, Clarissa controls her affection for Lovelace perfectly. As for Rousseau's Julie, she does not seem to marry Wolmar *in spite* of the absence of love, but *because* of it. In the ancient Greek novels and their sixteenth- and seventeenth-century imitations, the good characters are authorized to fall in love only if they profess the deepest commitment to chastity and to the moral ideal in general. Likewise, eighteenth-century new idealism allows lovers to disobey the laws of society, provided they act according to an even higher norm. Only Rousseau, in the first part of *The New Heloise*, allows love to follow no rules but its own, and consequently to bypass the norms of chastity; but, as though realizing the gravity of this transgression, he does not have the nerve to grant Julie and Saint-Preux the palm of marriage.

German Romantics were the first to include passionate love explicitly in the sphere of human self-government. In their view, far from obstructing self-mastery, passion gives it a deeper meaning, even a cosmic one. Passion, they believed, embodies the heart's instinctive search for plenitude and beauty, palpably manifesting the infinite concealed in each of us. The stories that support this view, Novalis's *Heinrich von Ofterdingen* (written in 1798–1800 and published posthumously in 1802) on a theoretical level, and Friedrich Schlegel's *Lucinde* (1799) more directly, define love as a poetic force whose origin, according to Novalis, is the revelation within the world of what lies beyond it—a revelation that fulfills a fundamental impulse of our being. Poetry and love disclose the transcendence involved in the very act of living and allow cosmic powers to radiate through the veil of daily life. And just as poetry relentlessly resists greed, insensitivity, and inertia, passionate love is authorized to go beyond obtuse social conventions. Novalis, for whom the essence of the soul is luminosity, sees the relationship between spirit and world as a form of lighting up, something that brings human beings to an extraordinary state of radiance. Poetry illuminates people's singular beauty and brushes conflicts aside, the way light seems to dissipate the clouds. In the same way, all obstacles, including death, vanish in the presence of true love. In *Heinrich von Ofterdingen*, love is not the central topic, but when it occurs, it takes the form of a sudden, infinite illumination.

It is Schlegel's *Lucinde* that shows in detail how this kind of sentiment is meant to operate. Love as illumination can be accessed only after a long journey riddled with errors and disappointments. Like *Werther*, Schlegel's novel continues the tradition of the elegiac story, whose purpose is less to build a convincing plot than to convey the main character's moods. Therefore the reader has to trace the development of the protagonist, Julius, indirectly, through a variety of contemplative passages. However, once one gets used to the half-light of the poetic eloquence, it is possible to follow his progress on the road to the highest passion. First, Julius falls in love with an adolescent girl who is willing to give herself to him; but he is reluctant to take advantage of her. Tortured by desire, he then devotes himself to a beautiful courtesan whose wit and intelligence he admires. But they have a fight, and she commits suicide. Julius, deeply dejected after her death, is cured only when he meets the first woman to move him profoundly. Alas, this exceptional being is married to a friend of his. Under her celestial influence, the young man devotes himself to art, hoping to create an eternal masterpiece. A few inconsequential love affairs keep him busy until, finally, he meets Lucinde, a young Romantic artist who has deliberately broken with society's rules and routines. This time, sensual pleasure precedes true love, which will soon come to enhance and ennoble it. With Lucinde by his side, Julius's life acquires the perfection of a work of art: the enigma of his existence now has a solution.

Lucinde thus supports Novalis's idea that love resembles poetry, but stops short of considering it a form of unique, final illumination. Comparing the human spirit with Proteus, a sea god who can take a variety of forms, Julius reflects on its mobility and realizes that love, as a revelation of the soul to itself, partakes in its perpetual self-reassessment. Love, then, does not necessarily and immediately involve both spirit and body, since it is quite possible to begin by sharing only sensual pleasures, before great love emerges. But although this schema integrates passionate love into the realm of the flesh and subordinates it to human plasticity, its role in the individual life remains fundamental. Even though Julius's heart responded to several other women before Lucinde, and even though it took him two years of happiness in her arms to experience absolute love, once he does come to understand this love, which mixes passion, sensuality, and friendship, it puts its stamp on his destiny. Thus the discovery of the one person who deserves to be loved—or better, the only one who holds in her being the secret of existence—is a product both of necessity, since without this person you can never fully become yourself, and of contingency, because the discovery depends on a chance encounter. To avoid missing this encounter, the sensitive heart must be constantly on the watch.

But because the person seeking love must be ready for the most unlikely changes in life, his or her relation to social norms becomes quite complicated. Significantly, Lucinde has freed herself from society even before meeting Julius. Neither social duties nor family life can trouble their paradise: in the end only a group of free people, a spiritual family whose members constantly change, will revolve around the happy couple. However, since most human beings live in society, *Lucinde*'s reader cannot help asking what would have happened if, at the time of his decisive encounter with Lucinde, Julius, rather than being free, had been married to another woman. And what would happen if one day, while living with Lucinde, this true Proteus, perpetually ready to change, were to find another muse, whose charms might promise him a new, even better solution to the mystery of his existence? How can one be certain to love exactly the being who embodies one's destiny, rather than some sketchy foreshadowing of an even more sublime person who has not yet arrived? And, when that person does arrive, how should one handle the new, even more passionate love?

This possibility of a revelatory love that comes late brings us back to Goethe's *Elective Affinities*. The book ponders *Lucinde*'s dilemma: if love is an answer to the enigma of existence, how can one know that a particular love brings the *final* answer? Borrowing and modifying the theme and scenery of *The New Heloise*, Goethe's novel describes the happy life of a couple living in the country, sharing their time with a few friends. The idyllic scene resembles the life of Julie, Wolmar, and Saint-Preux in the second half of Rousseau's novel. But while Rousseau's characters float serenely above the passions, Goethe's are wholly subjected to their violence.

Baron Eduard and his wife Charlotte are both on their second marriage—having acquired, like Julie, Julius, and Lucinde, a certain amount of life experience—and they love each other tenderly. To add a bit of zest to their peaceful life, Eduard invites his best friend, a captain, to join them at their castle. (An echo: Cervantes's Anselmo constantly asks his friend Lotario to visit his home.) Charlotte, in turn, invites her niece Ottilie, a calm and attractive young woman. There is an inexplicable mutual attraction between Charlotte and the Captain on the one hand, and Eduard and Ottilie on the other: Goethe compares it to the elective affinities in chemistry that ensure compatibility between substances. The feeling between Charlotte and the Captain remains innocent, but Eduard and Ottilie's fascination for each other gradually becomes irresistible. Goethe's tone is more balanced, less exalted than Schlegel's, but the reader realizes that in his belated love for Ottilie, the baron has found the answer to his own enigma. He prefers death to a life without her and so, to end his torment, he goes to war, returning just as deeply in love as before he left. When Ottilie dies soon after, Eduard cannot survive.

Rousseau's characters are stronger; and they learn from experience. In her youth, Julie lets herself be carried away by passion, but she ends up appreciating the wisdom of the moral constraints imposed by society, and adopts them with remarkable dignity. Saint-Preux willingly follows her example. In Schlegel's *Lucinde*, passionate love plays a crucial role in the growth of the individual, but nothing suggests that it can help set up stable links between individuals and society. For Rousseau, romantic experience leads to social integration; for Schlegel, it justifies seclusion. Few of the characters in *Elective Affinities*, though, learn from their pasts. The passing of time, the accumulation of experience, do not affect the basic features of a person; fate can strike at any age, and the memory of earlier ordeals does not cushion its blows.

This is particularly true when the lover becomes convinced that the beloved is the only true answer to the riddle of existence. In idealist novels, old and new, this conviction can be reached only once in a lifetime: passionate love—brought about by Providence or born in the depths of a heart that knows how to govern itself—flares up early in life and leads to wedlock. However, once Romanticism conceives of individuals as perpetually searching for their own essence, and offers them the latitude to act according to their passions, no societal norm will be able to prevent or limit the gradual discovery of the true self through a succession of ever more spectacular love affairs. Nothing protects today's lovers against a new love tomorrow, a new idol to guide them further into their own depths.

Goethe is careful not to present romantic love as an illusion, as nineteenth-century writers will so often do; he shows a deep respect for Eduard and Ottilie's conviction that they are made for each other. He does emphasize, however, how relative this conviction is. Before leaving home to go to war, Eduard spends the night with his wife, who gets pregnant. For Eduard, this is just a whim of fate, but Charlotte interprets it as a sign that Heaven wanted to prevent their separation and build a new link between them. Eduard thinks only of his love for Ottilie; Charlotte invokes Heaven, the past, the existence of a new being. For Goethe, far from being mere routine, mere chains, the links established in the past and approved by society have a value at least equal to that of a new, powerful set of feelings. Later, Charlotte's child will die in an accident unwittingly caused by Ottilie, his death symbolizing the pain and destruction a late passion brings into a balanced, settled world.

By casting doubt on the way individuals handle their passions, and by rejecting love's claim to rule our lives, *Elective Affinities* supports Rousseau's verdict in favor of social norms. Yet it also criticizes one of this verdict's major premises: the idea that human beings are fully capable of governing themselves and their feelings. In a more skeptical vein, Goethe highlights the incomprehensible, untamable side of the passions, calling it *das Dämonische*, that is, the rebellious spirit hidden in each of us. While recognizing the existence and the strength of this spirit, Goethe does not necessarily approve its effects. His novel does pay tribute to the Romantic view of life—the perpetual changing of the personality in search of the absolute; the importance of fortuitous encounters—but at the same time it censures Romantic love for encouraging contempt for society and excessive faith in each individual's ability to discern his or her life path.

||||||||||||||||||||||||||||

Although reluctant, then, to accept the Romantic exaltation of love, Goethe never questions its reality, its depth, and its sincerity. He just objects to the idea that once passion makes its claims, all other considerations should disappear. The stages in our lives and the place we occupy in society involve certain duties: we should be wary of fervent, intoxicating feelings that may endanger our fragile links with our past and with others.

Benjamin Constant's *Adolphe* (written in 1806, revised in 1810, and published in 1816) takes up the tradition of the French novella and short novel, with its suspicion of passions and virtues. Mme de Lafayette's *Princess of Clèves* and Prévost's *Manon Lescaut* are among Constant's models, as is seventeenth-century moralist reflection on the role of self-love (*amour-propre*) in moral life. According to La Rochefoucauld's *Maxims* (1665–1678) vanity hides behind magnanimity and moderation, fear behind fidelity, self-love behind love. Seen from this perspective, the Romantic rhetoric of inner greatness, the search for the absolute, and the striking but nebulous moral ideas all serve to cajole the self and stifle its vigilance: only a severe moral language can set us on the path to self-knowledge. A partisan of this approach, Constant portrays Romantic love in a devastating light, showing that passion, far from solving the enigma of existence, is often an illusion, or worse, a pretext used by the self to disguise its addiction to vanity, sensuality, inaction, and cowardice.

Adolphe is a German from a good family, educated at the University of Göttingen, who quite early in life rejects the unpleasant pressures of common sense. The young rebel earns a reputation, which his actions later confirm, for being immoral and unreliable. He ignores the maxims that guide relations between men and women in his milieu—liaisons are permitted, but only marriage is respectable; nothing could be worse for a young man than a long-term relationship with someone whose wealth, birth, and social position do not exactly match his own—and decides to win the heart of Ellénore, the mistress of a Polish count, a passionate woman whom society accepts but does not respect. Torn between shyness and vanity, Adolphe experiences an agitation that resembles love quite closely. The irritation caused by Ellénore's resistance sharpens his desire, and he diligently writes her letters in the language of passionate love, of elective affinities and late, decisive encounters. Ellénore, whose great fear is to be despised for the irregularities in her past life, is not used to being treated, in the Romantic fashion, as a heavenly creature. Moved by the young man's devotion, she ends up yielding to him. The two of them feel very close to what Schlegel called the solution to one's life's enigma.

Ellénore, alas, was not designed by nature to make Adolphe happy. Anxious, jealous, she soon begins to weary her younger lover. The age difference, the social gap, the Polish count's jealousy, and the requirements of Adolphe's career threaten their liaison. Adversity frustrates Adolphe, but it increases Ellénore's passion and determination. She breaks up with the count and defies public opinion. Her sacrifices force Adolphe to stay with her, but by now he feels only pity rather than love. He champs at the bit, since Ellénore has become the main obstacle to his success in society. Their life together is poisoned by discontent. Sensing that a split is inevitable, the heroine falls sick and dies.

The tragic ending is caused by the ghost of Romantic love, which has taken over Adolphe's life and, by contagion, Ellénore's. Propelled by egotism and sensuality, the young seducer borrowed the language of infinite love. Its impact is so strong, and the ideas it conjures up so attractive—mutual predestination; resolution of life's mystery; giving oneself freely; contempt for society and its well-established principles—that the hunter is caught in his own trap. With the thrill of victory gone, Adolphe discovers that the arguments he used to seduce Ellénore bind him to her more effectively than any social principle. His love, Adolphe now realizes, certainly has nothing to do with the infinite passion he proclaimed earlier, but how can one possibly retract the Absolute? Frozen in his sublime posture, Adolphe is too weak to admit that in deceiving Ellénore, he also deluded himself.

As for Ellénore, once she accepts this game, it is clearly in her interest to redeem the errors of her youth by showing the world that she can nurture a true, generous passion. All her grand gestures seem to be symptoms of the noblest, least self-interested love. By breaking with the Polish count, she sacrifices her status as the mistress of an aristocrat, certainly a role less enviable than that of spouse, but still one society fully accepts. In doing this for Adolphe, she shows him that where Romantic love is concerned, she follows the letter of the law and therefore has the right to expect the same from him. She defies his father, apparently applying the rule that says true love should transcend social conventions. Yet her motivation is not entirely beyond suspicion: since her earlier transgressions have made it impossible for her to marry, how can one be sure that her contempt for family ties is purely a mark of true love and has nothing to do with resentment?

In the hell that engulfs the two characters, they never explicitly deliberate on the choice between Romantic love and social conformity, as those in *The New Heloise* and in *Elective Affinities* do. As a result, their motivations remain unclear. Does Ellénore cut her links to society in the name of love, or because of her dubious past? Does Adolphe feel impatient to regain his place in the world because of a sense of duty, or because his infatuation with Ellénore is over? In *Adolphe*, Romantic love is never more than an uncertain norm, a lofty but unreal frame of reference. The lovers subscribe to this norm and seem to abide by its strictest maxims, but on closer inspection their behavior appears duplicitous and reckless. Their grandiose ideas about passion, and the powers and rights it bestows, serve to hide their egotism and insensitivity. In the end, the cult of Romantic love, far from solving the problem of human imperfection, highlights its perennial significance.

By the End of the Eighteenth Century . . .

. . . the idealist novel had completely given up the old ideographic approach and its favorite subject, two chaste lovers who embody the highest virtues, live in a faraway, imaginary landscape, and undergo a long series of ordeals that lead at last, thanks to Providence's protection, to a happy union. A new version of idealism, invented by Richardson, portrayed sensitive hearts who live, struggle, and radiate moral beauty in the real world. This is how Diderot, in his *In Praise of Richardson* (1762), describes the transformation:

> Until now by "novel" one understood a web of chimerical and frivolous events whose reading was dangerous for taste and morals. It would be highly desirable to find another name for Richardson's works, which uplift the spirit, touch the soul, constantly breathe the love of goodness, and are also called novels.[2]

In England, the name did change, from *romance* to *novel*, both rendered in French as "roman," but beyond the name, Diderot's argument captures

---

[2] Denis Diderot, *Oeuvres*, ed. André Billy (Paris: Gallimard, Bibliothèque de la Pléiade, 1951), p. 1059 (my translation).

the substance of the change. A novel, he argues, vividly evokes a set of moral maxims, where a maxim is "an abstract general rule of behavior." When reading Richardson's novels, you rediscover these maxims by observing the characters, imagining yourself in their place, taking sides, identifying with their virtue, and rejecting their vices. Reading fiction, one would say today, involves moral inference. But moral inference also occurs when one reads the older romances Diderot rejected, so Richardson's achievement needs to be defined more precisely. In Diderot's view, Richardson does two things better than anyone else. He knows how to immerse his readers in the story—"in spite of oneself one takes a role, one gets involved in the conversation, one approves, one blames, one admires, one gets angry or indignant" (p. 1060)—and how to convince them of the proximity of the world he represents to their own:

> This author does not take you to faraway countries . . . ; he never gets lost in fairy-tale territory. The action takes place in the world in which we live; its dramatic core is true; the characters are as real as could be; they are taken from the midst of society . . . ; the passions he portrays are such as I experience them . . . ; he shows me the general course of things that surround me. (pp. 1060–1061)

Richardson's fictional world is, moreover, egalitarian, insofar as it seeks and finds moral beauty at all social levels. Finally, it benefits from generic amalgamation by blending the moral idealism of the old romances, the first-person voice of the elegiac story, the novella's unity of action, and the picaresque interest in actual, material details.

Nevertheless, full immersion, proximity, the egalitarian drive, and generic amalgamation were by no means adopted right away by all eighteenth-century novelists. Rousseau's *Julie, or the New Heloise* does achieve proximity: the action happens (to use Diderot's terms) "in the world in which we live"; the characters are "taken from the midst of society." It has egalitarian resonances, portraying inner beauty independently of social class. To a certain extent it also accomplishes generic amalgamation, by borrowing from the old romances, the pastoral novels, and the elegiac stories. But it leaves out the dramatic intensity of the novella and the picaresque involvement with the material world. Full sensory and temporal immersion, therefore, fails to take place: Rousseau does not write "to the moment," relying instead on the elegant, abstract style of French neoclassicist literature.

Few writers went even as far as Rousseau. Some, remaining true to the ideographic manner—great souls, multiple uplifting episodes, and clear moral inferences—devised a new kind of story, describing the inner growth of a young character, like Wieland's *Story of Agathon*. Equally faithful to the older system, the picaresque continued to thrive in rougher, spicier forms in England, and in a more well-mannered, blander one in France. The novella stayed alive thanks to Abbé Prévost and Marmontel, the pastoral did so in the works of Florian and Gessner, and the elegiac story survived in Goethe's *Werther*.

Fielding openly opposed Richardson's method, arguing that the novel should stick to the tradition that regards moral perfection with skepticism; it should avoid the egalitarian drive and use proximity and immersion to make readers laugh. Sterne and Diderot playfully continued with this approach. The gothic novelists rediscovered the power of the imagination, emphasizing its primitive, brutal force; these writers, with little interest in plausibility or moral inferences, tried to achieve immersion in other ways and stumbled on an important discovery—atmosphere for its own sake. The sentimental novel and the novel of manners tamed Richardson's innovations to some extent and flavored them with a dose of Fielding-like comedy.

Fielding laughed at the myth of the self-governing heart and its uncompromising moral beauty. Yet toward the end of the century, these doubts were being expressed in a new, melancholy way: sensitive hearts are too weak to survive life's realities (*Werther*); they are torn apart by uncontrollable passions (*Elective Affinities*); they are defeated when they try to impose their ideals on the world (*Hyperion*); their obedience to the laws of the heart is in reality just self-indulgent (*Lucinde*), or worse, terribly egocentric (*Adolphe*).

So, by the beginning of the nineteenth century, readers were still quite often expected to pay attention to a novel's moral discourse, rather than be immersed in its moment-by-moment psychological drama and its material details. Nonetheless, the effect of proximity was widely implemented, as most novels invited their readers to enter familiar worlds—the exception, of course, was the gothic novel. Writers continued to combine different genre elements, but not as thoroughly as Richardson had done.

Through full sensory and psychological immersion, Richardson aimed to persuade the reader that moral perfection can indeed be found in our own world. But can it? Isn't the actual world the site of fallibility and imperfection? Richardson's Pamela and Clarissa do live in a milieu that resembles the actual one, they do go through convincing psychological ordeals, but their invincible morals border on implausibility. Yet the temptation to depict ideal creatures in a world resembling ours remained strong, since only such creatures could fully illustrate the possibility of excellence and make moral inferences crystal clear. And so later writers inherited Richardson's challenge: how to portray plausible moral perfection in a world that remains as close as possible to the real one.

PART THREE

||||||||||||||||||||||||||||||||||||||||||||||||||||||||||||||||

The Roots of Greatness

CHAPTER 9

Novels and Society

|||||||||||||||||||||||||||||||||||||||||||||||||||||||||||||||||||

Throughout its history, the novel had responded to broad historical and cultural changes. The unity of the Mediterranean under the Roman Empire was partly reflected in the plot and setting of the ancient Greek novel. Spain's transatlantic adventures and the debates between the Reformation and the Counter-Reformation played their part in the emergence of the picaresque. The eighteenth-century English novel was marked by the rise of commerce, empiricism, and Methodism. But before the nineteenth century, it remains difficult to identify direct links between the novel and specific political events. Only in the early 1800s can we begin to detect immediate, palpable connections. Between 1789 and 1815 the French Revolution, followed by a long series of wars, changed Europe's political and cultural landscape, showing how radical and irreversible such historical transformations can be. The past became the object of a vivid curiosity often tinged with nostalgia. It began to seem obvious that each society and historical period is organized in specific ways that may be questioned, understood, and modified. National consciousness and pride grew considerably all over Europe. Ideas of history, society, and nation gained a new cultural centrality.

Eighteenth-century philosophers had already prepared the ground for this change: Montesquieu's *Spirit of Laws* (1748), Adam Ferguson's *Essay on the History of Civil Society* (1767), and John Millar's *The Origin of the Distinction of Ranks* (first edition 1771) reflected on the links between historical conditions and different types of society; David Hume's essay "Of the Rise and Progress of the Arts and Sciences" (1742) and, later, his *History of England* (1754–1762), as well as Rousseau's *Discourse on the Origin of Inequality* (1755) and Condorcet's *Sketch for a Historical Picture of the Progress of the Human Mind* (1795) presented historical development as an advance toward civilization; and Johann

Gottfried Herder's *This Too a Philosophy of History for the Formation of Humanity* (1774) defended the diversity of national historical experience.

Society, according to all these authors, had taken a variety of forms, depending in each case on the concrete conditions governing subsistence, authority, justice, and knowledge. It evolved from "rude" or savage stages toward an increasing degree of civilization. Each stage developed social types, ranks, customs, and cultures appropriate to its needs. "Rude" nations, fully engaged in the struggle for survival, emphasized hierarchy and worshipped a set of virtues that included courage, honor, and personal loyalty. As humankind moved on from the hunting stage to pastoral, then agricultural, and finally commercial societies, authority was gradually limited by individual rights, manners improved, and women gained recognition and respect. Still, not all of these thinkers saw historical evolution as positive, or even as having a single, universal direction. Hume welcomed the progress from the rule of men to the rule of law, but for Rousseau "rude," simple societies that remained closer to nature had a clear advantage over civilized, corrupt humanity. Condorcet was convinced that all nations were advancing toward the same happy future, whereas Herder had argued that there were many forms of happiness, and each nation would know how to design its own.

The French Revolution and the subsequent wars, however, proved that history's advance could be bloody, and that "rude," warlike virtues had by no means been left in the past. The belief that all humanity was moving in the same direction lost its appeal as a fierce national pride arose in the countries that had been temporarily subjected to Napoleon's imperial rule. Progress itself became a matter for debate. Conservatism, as formulated by Edmund Burke, promoted reverence for the past and a prudent approach to the future; the classical liberalism advocated by Wilhelm von Humboldt in Germany and Benjamin Constant in France inherited from Hume and Adam Smith a belief in the value of personal freedom; and socialism, in the early versions elaborated by Charles Fourier and Saint-Simon, hoped to establish a rational, egalitarian political system. Yet one thing was by now generally accepted: human personality and its codes of conduct very much depend on the historical and social environment.

In this context, readers and writers of novels began to find characters like Pamela, Clarissa, and Julie less plausible. Why would these women behave the way they did? What historical, national, or social forces could explain their decisions? Virtue as well as villainy ceased to obey universal criteria. Both were now assumed to originate in the particular customs in force at a certain time, in a certain place, among people of a certain social class. To make sense of a given character's qualities or actions, one had to understand them as being *deeply rooted* in a historical, social, and national soil. In Walter Scott's *The Heart of Midlothian* (1818), for instance, Jeanie Deans is as strong and virtuous as any earlier idealist heroine, but her strength is defined in specific historical and cultural terms: she is the product of her eighteenth-century Scottish Presbyterian background.

As for plausible masculine strength, writers looked for it in long-gone "rude" societies or among more recent warriors: "rudeness" and military valor had become respectable once more. Heinrich von Kleist wrote *Michael Kohlhaas* (1808–1810) in the midst of the European wars, and Walter Scott published *Waverley* (1814) just before the return of a lasting peace. Both works take history seriously—social and military history in particular. Both excel in doing what ancient epic did so well: bringing out the political stakes of a conflict, the warriors' exploits, and the course of the battles. Impressed by this similarity, Hegel argued that the novel as a genre was a recent, bourgeois incarnation of the old epic. Be it said in passing, the English version of Hegel's *Aesthetics*[1] uses "romance" for the German *Roman*; it also translates *bürgerlich*, not entirely incorrectly, as "popular," thus rendering Hegel's famous sentence "Ganz anders verhält es sich dagegen mit dem Roman, der modernen bürgerlichen Epopöe" as "But it is quite different with romance, the modern popular epic" (vol. 2, chap. 3, C.1.2.c, p. 1092), and erasing the reference to the bourgeoisie, which was so important for Marxist critics, including Lukács. In fact, at the beginning of the nineteenth century, the old, resilient genre of the novel *turned to the epic* for the first time as a guide to portraying strong characters, especially warriors. This turn was only momentary: the nineteenth-century novel would soon move beyond epic themes and techniques to focus, as Lukács persuasively argued, on the individual's efforts to understand society and come to terms with its requirements.

Ancient and eighteenth-century idealist novels showed virtuous characters acting in accordance with *extrasocial* norms. Against a hostile environment, Chariclea and Clarissa could uphold a set of ideals that came either from above or from within their own sensitive hearts. But once it is assumed that moral norms are created by society according to its needs, how can an individual resist them? One answer is that they can resist only if they live under historical or social conditions that *require* lonely defiance: nineteenth-century novels abound in exemplary figures who belong to "rude" or faraway societies (*Michael Kohlhaas*; Bela in Lermontov's *A Hero of Our Time*, 1839–1841), to disinherited social classes (Jean Valjean in Hugo's *Les Misérables*, 1862), or to professions society condemns (Fleur-de-Marie in Eugène Sue's *The Mysteries of Paris*, 1842–1843*)*. In other cases, though conditions do not require resistance, they do *allow* it. Dandies and artists in Balzac's novels and nihilists in

---

[1] Trans. T. M. Knox (Oxford: Clarendon, 1975).

Dostoevsky's reject the world and assert their individual strength without appealing to a higher moral norm. And since in "polite" (modern or democratic) societies, individuals are expected to discover for themselves how best to coexist with others, novels increasingly portrayed good people who, rather than claiming full independence, grow, mature, and gradually earn society's acceptance. The education and development of such characters—from Goethe's Wilhelm Meister, a sensitive German art lover (*Wilhelm Meister's Apprenticeship*, 1795–1796), to Dickens's David Copperfield (1849–1850), a brave, hardworking English orphan— became one of the genre's essential themes.

On their way to maturity, these individuals face a previously unknown contradiction: the norms and ideals they must follow are customary products of a human community, rather than eternal laws ruling the universe or the depths of the heart. As such, these norms and ideals have a historically and socially circumscribed value, and yet, being generated by the human collectivity, they are legitimate and obligatory. Those who happen to sense that these norms are inadequate, incongruous, oppressive—as Frédéric does in Gustave Flaubert's *Sentimental Education* (1869), followed later by a score of twentieth-century maladjusted characters— have no justification for disobeying them except their own discontent. The "unhappy conscience," as Hegel called it, would become a favorite subject for the novel, as would some individuals' conviction that another norm, much higher than social custom, should guide their personal path.

Love remained a central theme, but its treatment changed considerably. Once the community is assumed to be the source of norms and ideals, romantic love that challenges society cannot be sure of success. And in this new system, love—romantic love fit for novels—is one of the few cases in which choice depends on the individual rather than on custom or law, so a clash between love and society's authority can have serious consequences. Novels would therefore portray two different species of romantic love and their ways of handling this clash. Some lovers gradually discover their true feelings and hesitantly reach the conviction that these feelings not only originate in the deepest, unique part of their personality but also guarantee a lasting agreement with the outside world. In Jane Austen, Dickens, and George Eliot, this kind of love is portrayed as part and parcel of one's inner growth. It is sketched out in Walter Scott, and occasionally appears in Honoré de Balzac, William Makepeace Thackeray, Leo Tolstoy, and Theodor Fontane, but not in Lermontov, Stendhal, or Flaubert. The second kind, blind, passionate, irresistible—but protected neither by Providence nor by the inner moral law—transgresses the normative will of the community. This love claims to provide the highest individual bliss, but in the end society (and sometimes the individuals themselves) cannot tolerate it. It most frequently takes the form of adultery—a favorite topic of the late nineteenth-century novel—but it sometimes ensnares individuals separated by an insurmountable social or ethnic gap, as in Emily Brontë's *Wuthering Heights* (1847) or Tolstoy's *The Cossacks* (1863).

Since human action must now be understood in relation to its historical and social context, the novelist has a new, essential task: to draw meticulous portraits of the society in which the story takes place. Scott and Balzac proudly took on this responsibility, scattering erudite passages through their novels, on the historical context in Scott's case, and the social background in Balzac's. Later in the century, writers like Flaubert and Fontane would refrain from lecturing their readers on historical and social causation, but they never questioned its importance. Throughout the nineteenth century (and beyond), novels would immerse readers in a historical and social milieu through punctilious descriptions of scenery, costumes, motives, and customs. Appropriately called *realism*, this approach was not simply a stylistic method: it aimed to give the novel a new plausibility by highlighting the links between moral ideals and social truths.

Realism also intended to establish literature's credentials as a source of genuine knowledge, comparable to history and, later, to sociology and clinical psychology. No longer simply offering examples of human passions and follies for the public's entertainment and edification, novels became serious, dependable inventories of political systems, social types, professions, family arrangements, and sexual habits—a literary equivalent, as Balzac put it, of the Registry Office. In the early nineteenth century, the knowledge dispensed was historical and social; later, the novel's ambitions would expand, reaching a climax in Émile Zola's claim that literature can attain the status of an experimental science. And since reliable knowledge has normative authority, novelists felt empowered to teach political and social lessons. Kleist's *Michael Kohlhaas* defends the federal structure of the old Holy Roman Empire; Walter Scott's *Old Mortality* (1816) condemns religious fanaticism; Balzac's *Human Comedy* bursts with social and political advice. Flaubert, who made it a point of honor to avoid expressing explicit political opinions in his fiction, was nonetheless convinced that France lost the war with Prussia in 1870 because it had failed to take in the lessons of his novels. Toward the end of the nineteenth century, Paul Bourget's *romans à thèse* overtly claimed the authority to show the world how to think.

As a result, the author's importance and visibility increased. Walter Scott uses a confident authorial tone—the same self-assured voice Fielding had introduced to combine the inventor of the story, the guarantor of its moral exactitude, and the ironic commentator—to explain the background and origin of his story, guarantee its historical relevance, and add long, erudite endnotes. Similarly, Balzac often interrupts his narratives with the exclamation "And here is why" ("Voici pourquoi"), followed by detailed explanations of the action's social and political context. When Flaubert, Fontane, Eça de Queirós, Henry James, and Benito Pérez Galdós gave up direct authorial intervention later in the century, they were by no means abandoning authorial power. Historical and social knowledge was by then perfectly integrated into the novel's fabric; not unlike the moral maxims embedded in earlier fiction, this knowledge was there for readers to find, and writers assumed there was no longer any need to overemphasize it. The author remained silently omnipresent.

The Epic Turn of the Novel

Romantic pessimism excels in portraying the irreconcilable conflict between outstanding, atypical characters (Werther, Hyperion) and the world in which they are compelled to live. Inevitably, the conflict leads to their defeat. Persuaded by such examples, some nineteenth-century novelists concluded that ideal characters cannot possibly live in the mediocre, prosaic contemporary world. Yet far from assuming that such characters must always be defeated, these writers looked for social and historical milieus that might foster and recognize their greatness. History was the right place to look—authentic, well-documented history, quite different from both the imaginary landscapes of the ancient Greek and seventeenth-century Heliodorus-like novels and the fantastical Middle Ages of the gothic.

Kleist's *Michael Kohlhaas* (begun in 1805; first section published in 1808, the year of Goethe's first *Faust* and Johann Gottlieb Fichte's *Addresses to the German Nation*; full publication in 1810) is a long novella depicting a violent response to injustice in a specific historical context: the sixteenth-century social and religious conflicts within the Holy Roman Empire. The link between historical crises and dramatic moral dilemmas had already been explored in novellas such as Saint-Réal's *Don Carlos* (1672), which was read widely throughout the eighteenth century and remade by Friedrich Schiller as a political tragedy that passionately defends the Enlightenment ideal of tolerance (1787). Both works emphasize the *perennial* nature of the conflict—pure love stifled by a suspicious, envious court and also, in Schiller's play, religious and political tolerance rejected by an aging tyrant—rather than its historical specificity. Kleist's novella, by contrast, emphasizes both the universality of human passions and the social and political predicaments of a particular historical period.

Michael Kohlhaas, an honest, highly respected horse-dealer, is wronged by the young Junker (feudal lord) von Tronka, who has illegally established a new tollgate on his domain, and forces Kohlhaas to leave his stable boy and two young, beautiful horses at the castle as a guarantee of future payment. The horse-dealer seeks justice, but Tronka's family, well placed at various levels of the Saxon judicial system, prevents him from winning. In the meantime, Tronka's men misuse and damage the horses, and severely beat up the stable boy. Worse, the guards at the Saxon court accidentally hurt Kohlhaas's wife, and she dies. Having exhausted all available legal means in Saxony, Kohlhaas turns violent. Helped by a handful of adventurers, he devastates the Junker's castle and sets fire to the city of Wittenberg, where Tronka has taken refuge. Supported by an increasing number of rebels, Kohlhaas defeats the Saxon army, led by Prince Friedrich of Meissen, and declares himself the emissary of the Archangel Michael and Provisional Governor of the World. Martin Luther intervenes as mediator, convincing the rebel to lay down arms and, provided with a safe-conduct, appear in court at Dresden for a new hearing. Kohlhaas's partisans, however, continue the civil war, and after various other incidents (including the uncanny intervention of an elderly Gypsy woman who entrusts Kohlhaas with a secret prophecy concerning the future of the Saxon dynasty), the rebellious horse-dealer wins against Tronka in a Brandenburg court (for Kohlhaas is a subject of Brandenburg), while at the same time he is sentenced to death by the Imperial Court in Vienna for violation of His Majesty's peace. Kohlhaas gets his horses back, fed by the Junker himself under court order, and, having received satisfaction, calmly mounts the scaffold.

Narrated breathlessly, the novella depicts the conflicts between merchants and feudal lords, the nobility's stranglehold on governmental power, the popular impatience encouraged by the Reformation, and the federal system of justice. In this milieu, the protagonist, an honest merchant, is not destined by birth for heroism, since in principle the protection of public order and justice is the nobility's task. But Tronka fails to fulfill that task, and Kohlhaas is denied justice at every level of authority. He concludes that what has happened is not a local problem, an inevitable malfunction in a complicated system, but rather a full collapse of the institutional structure. In such cases, Kohlhaas believes, the responsibility for reestablishing public order falls on each and every individual, whatever his or her previous social condition; the war he wages on society in the name of justice is therefore a legitimate one.

One of the themes of Kleist's novella is the rise of great individuals in a decaying community. When the fabric of society is torn apart and the usual roles lose their meaning, strong people are called to action. Yet the story does not simply celebrate individual heroism and rebellion. While it is relatively easy for Kohlhaas to take up arms against the corrupt establishment and rally an army of supporters, calming the rebellion turns out to be more difficult. Persuaded by Luther, Kohlhaas agrees to surrender in exchange for a promise of justice. But once started, the war of all against all cannot be stopped; Kohlhaas's allies continue to fight. Slowly, clumsily, the federal order nevertheless manages to redress both Tronka's violation of justice and Kohlhaas's violation of the peace. Written during the period when, after the Battle of Austerlitz and the Peace of Pressburg, the Holy Roman Empire ceased to exist (1806), Kleist's story can be read, like Fichte's *Addresses*, as a protest against the destruction of a long-established political and judicial system. But unlike Fichte's pamphlet (and unlike Kleist's own political writings and drama *Hermannsschlacht*, 1808) the novella does not fall prey to nationalist pathos.

Faced with the endless wars and unstable peace treaties of the early 1800s, German Romantics could not resist idealizing older political arrangements. Novalis, Friedrich Schlegel, and Kleist's friend Adam Müller imagined a miraculously harmonious Roman Catholic Middle Ages. More sensitive to the real historical conditions, Kleist's story depicts the conflicted time of the Reformation, when the old, sturdy federal empire managed to overcome the challenge of religious civil war. In the early nineteenth century, Kleist saw a return to a flexible, multilayered German federation as the best riposte to Napoleon's dream of supremacy in Europe. Stable without being overwhelming, it could offer the long-term resilience Kleist considered the true mark of political success. While Kohlhaas does end up on the scaffold, the narrator concludes the story by noting that in Mecklenburg, in the eighteenth century, some of Kohlhaas's descendants were still living.

||||||||||||||||||||||||||||||

Kleist's novella places an exceptional figure in a plausible historical context, in which the hero's greatness is awakened by the decay of the social order. Kleist focuses on such greatness as an answer to a social crisis, rather than a result of the social and historical environment.

Walter Scott's heroes, by contrast, act generously because of their historical background rather than in spite of it. Eighteenth-century historians taught Scott that certain kinds of human greatness can be found only in archaic warrior cultures. The descriptive precision he adopted from Defoe and Richardson helped him capture the historical milieu in detail. From Smollett, Fanny Burney, and his contemporary Maria Edgeworth, he learned how to handle the diversity of customs and manners. From Fielding, he borrowed the intrusive, humorous, voice of an author fully in charge of his story.

The huge success of *Waverley* (1814) certainly had something to do with this new synthesis of heroism, a highly articulated vision of history, a wealth of local color, and a friendly narrative tone. Edward Waverley is a young English aristocrat who travels to Scotland in 1745, at the time of the last legitimist attempt to return the Stuart family to the British throne they lost as a result of the Glorious Revolution of 1688. Scott's choice of this period is significant. In 1814 the events of 1745 would still have felt relatively recent to his readers, preventing them from taking *Waverley* as a misty, gothic tale. Yet even in the mid-1740s the Scottish Highlands harbored a much older stage of civilization, whose survival made the persistence of legitimist dreams possible. The Scottish clan system preserved a network of communities whose chiefs enjoyed their subjects' unconditional loyalty. Scott describes it with affection and a dash of irony, as a system that blended the martial tradition celebrated in medieval chivalric stories with a propensity for robbery and disorder. It was a time when mountain people still obeyed the old rules of chivalry, courtesy, and rebellion; they practiced hospitality, kept their promises (up to a point), and had a strong sense of adventure. This stage of historical development, much as it may have moved Scott's readers, was by now obsolete.

As the author explains in the "Postscript, which should have been a Preface": "There is no European nation which, within the course of half a century, or little more, has undergone so complete a change as this kingdom of Scotland." The "folks of the old leaven" have disappeared, and although their hopeless attachment to the house of Stuart was founded on "absurd political prejudice," one cannot forget their many examples "of singular and disinterested attachment to the principles of loyalty which they received from their fathers, and of old Scottish faith, hospitality, worth, and honor." Destroyed by historical progress, these qualities really existed, and "the most romantic parts of this narrative are precisely those which have a foundation in fact."[2] Young Waverley discovers courage and greatness at all levels of the social hierarchy: in brigands like Donald Bean Lean, in Jacobite rebels like Fergus Mac-Ivor and his sister Flora, and in the young pretender Charles Stuart. The brave protagonist joins the rebels himself, but despite this epic detour, he resists excessive heroism and ends up appreciating Scotland in light of the progress achieved, in his view, by the Union with England.

Old Mortality (1816) shows warrior society in a darker light. Henry Morton is a witness to and participant in the seventeenth-century conflict between the partisans of the Scottish Covenant, supported by the population, and the Episcopalian Church, imposed by the English Crown with the assent of Scottish nobility. Morton tries to prevent the clash between the two camps, equally blinded by devotion to their cause. In *Waverley*, the moderate main character is surrounded by a crowd of generous, reckless Jacobites; here, only the magnanimous Lord Evandale, who saves

---

[2] Sir Walter Scott, *Waverley*, ed. Claire Lamont (Oxford: Oxford World Classics, 1986), p. 340.

Morton's life, embodies greatness. *Old Mortality*'s emphasis falls on the violence, injustice, and religious fanaticism of bygone times.

But the pessimism of *Old Mortality* is not Scott's final verdict on individual greatness. In *The Heart of Midlothian* (1818), he reflects on religious dissidence and its possibilities for a plausible kind of inner strength. The action takes place in Edinburgh in 1737. David Deans, a poor farmer and a fervent Presbyterian—therefore hostile to the official Episcopalian Church—raises his daughters Jeanie and Effie in accordance with the most rigorous principles. Nonetheless, Effie lets herself be seduced by George Staunton, a young English aristocrat who lives among brigands in Scotland under a different name. After giving birth to a child who mysteriously disappears, Effie is accused of infanticide. The tribunal does not have the corpus delicti at its disposal, but the judge concludes that the defendant's decision to keep her pregnancy secret shows she had made up her mind early on to get rid of the child. Thus Effie's sentence could be avoided if Jeanie were willing to testify that she knew about her sister's pregnancy. But Jeanie didn't know—no one did—and she is a true Presbyterian who cannot lie. As a result, the court condemns Effie to death. Having satisfied the demands of her conscience, Jeanie sets out on a journey to London; with help from the Duke of Argyle, the protector of the Scots, she is granted an audience by Queen Caroline, who pardons Effie. Back in Scotland, Jeanie marries the humble pastor Reuben Butler, and Effie weds her seducer, the wealthy Staunton, now reformed. They now discover that their son is alive: he had been kidnapped by a deranged young woman, Madge Wildfire, and given up to a band of robbers. Staunton tracks him down and tries to persuade him to become an honest man again, but the stubborn young man murders his father.

This eventful plot blends reliable historical knowledge with exuberant invention. As Scott himself testified in the "General Preface" to the 1829 edition of the Waverley novels, "Familiar acquaintance with the specious miracles of fiction brought with it some degree of satiety, and I began, by degrees, to seek in histories, memoirs, voyages and travels, and the like, events nearly as wonderful as those which were the work of imagination, with the additional advantage that they were at least in a great measure true" (*Waverley*, p. 350). In Scott's stories, a generous, improvident character—Fergus Mac-Ivor in *Waverley*; Staunton here— is involved in a variety of adventures that recall the sordid brutality of picaresque, as well as the old idealist disguises, lost children, and highborn heirs hidden among bandits. These escapades are designed to please a readership eager for extraordinary events that still retain a claim to historical plausibility. Nineteenth-century adventure novels, melodramas, and operas would later take full advantage of this desire. For instance, ending the plot with a murder whose victim turns out to be one of the killer's parents is a surefire way to astound the public—Victor Hugo, in *Lucrezia Borgia* (1833), and Verdi, in *Il Trovatore* (1853), used it to great effect. Likewise, madness, especially female madness, was a theme vigorously exploited by Scott, the operas he inspired, and later, Charlotte Brontë. Utterly confused, yet somehow knowing how to strike, the mad-woman takes it upon herself to avenge an outrageous act of injustice—as Lucy does in Scott's *The Bride of Lammermoor* (1819) and in Donizetti's opera *Lucia di Lammermoor* (1835)—or unwittingly punishes a moral transgression, as Madge Wildfire does in *The Heart of Midlothian*. In Charlotte Brontë's *Jane Eyre* (1847), the madwoman is contrasted with the virtuous one: the former virtually destroys the man who has kept her prisoner, while the latter protects the blind invalid he becomes.

In *Waverley* and *Old Mortality* the plot is propelled by the opposition between courageous but imprudent characters and a reasonable, hesitant one. In *Midlothian*, Scott ventures to portray a truly perfect character, Jeanie Deans, whose word is the measure of her righteousness. Inner strength here is not just part of an uplifting, sentimental story, but repre-sents the plausible behavior of a young woman brought up according to Presbyterian moral principles and encouraged to believe in a direct link between each human being and the Creator.

As Balzac wrote admiringly, Scott's historical realism portrays char-acters as "conceived in their century's womb, thus raising the novel to the level of the philosophy of history." He "brought together drama, dia-logue, portrait, landscape, description; he infused them with marvels and truth, these elements of the epic, he made poetry rub shoulders with the humblest forms of speech."[3] After Richardson, few writers had more of an impact than did Scott on how fiction portrays human greatness.

HISTORICAL PROGRESS

The new understanding of history linked moral behavior closely to the society that requires it. Writers who wanted to depict a truly *universal* greatness therefore had to show how certain kinds of moral choice might transcend societal rules. Alessandro Manzoni's *The Betrothed* (1827), which can be read as a remake of the *Ethiopian Story* by way of Scott's realism, tries to do precisely this. It describes the adventures of a young couple in love, whose mutual devotion defies any ordeal. The two lovers, Lucia and Renzo, are innocent villagers living in the Duchy of Milan, ruled by Spain in the seventeenth century. Their plans to marry are ob-structed by Don Rodrigo, a local potentate who unsuccessfully attempts

---

[3] Honoré de Balzac, "Avant-propos" to *La Comédie Humaine*, vol. 1, ed. Pierre-Georges Castex (1842; Paris: Gallimard, Bibliothèque de la Pléiade, 1986), p. 10 (my translation).

to seduce the young woman. To thwart him, the lovers split up for a while. Renzo goes to Milan, while Lucia hides at Como under the protection of a powerful lady. In Milan, Renzo takes part in a popular rebellion caused by a severe food shortage, and, fearing arrest, seeks refuge in the lands of the Venetian Republic. Lucia is kidnapped—on behalf of Don Rodrigo—by the ferocious Unnamed Knight, and, having lost hope of ever being reunited with Renzo, she offers herself to the Holy Virgin and makes a vow of chastity. Her prayers are heard. The Unnamed Knight miraculously feels remorse for his innumerable crimes, and, instead of keeping his word to Don Rodrigo, he takes the young woman under his protection. In the meantime, the famine devastating the duchy forces everyone to converge on Milan in search of food. What is more, foreign troops passing through Milan on their way to Modena spread the plague, and its impact is aggravated by overpopulation and inadequate hygiene in the city. Renzo and Lucia find each other among the sick and the dying in a Milan hospital, where Father Cristoforo, their old protector, absolves Lucia from her vow to the Virgin. Free to start a family, the two young people leave the country that persecuted them, and settle in the Venetian village where Renzo had found shelter.

Like Scott in *Midlothian*, Manzoni places his protagonists in a modest social milieu, conveying an egalitarian message: noble feelings, virtues, and loyalties exist independently of social origin and, indeed, can more often be found in simple people, free from the corrupting influence of wealth and power. To enhance the social plausibility of his novel, Manzoni portrays the two lovers as quite stubborn, playing to the common notion that simple people are naturally obstinate. Nevertheless, the characters' greatness, their resistance to the world's adversity, and their secret alliance with Providence remain evident.

Even more than Scott, Manzoni clearly feels that historical novels must reflect the march of human progress. Like his contemporary the French liberal thinker François Guizot, Manzoni sees class conflict as a determining factor in history: in *The Betrothed*, the nobility recklessly harms the people it governs. The novel also shows the price paid by earlier societies for ignoring basic rules of political economy, public administration, and hygiene. In his commentaries, dotted throughout the novel, Manzoni counts on the enlightened reader's interest in debates about free markets, rational government, and public health. In contrast with Scott, who wrote admiringly of the virtues of warriors in earlier times, Manzoni portrays morality as the distinctive feature of simple people, who succeeded in practicing it in spite rather than because of social inequality. In agreement with the tenets of classical liberalism, Manzoni represents the world's adversity as a combination of social oppression—perpetrated here by Don Rodrigo and, initially, the Unnamed Knight—and ignorance, exemplified by the government's inept handling of the food shortages and epidemics in Milan.

Like other liberals, Alexis de Tocqueville included, Manzoni believed that increasing equality is the result of a long-term providential project already perceptible in the teachings of Christianity. But in the interests of historical and social realism, he is careful not to depict a clergy uniformly devoted to the cause of the oppressed. The ignorant and cowardly lower clergy is contrasted with the generous Father Cristoforo and with Cardinal Borromeo, a charismatic prince of the Church. Without their charitable intervention—and moreover, without the direct involvement of the Holy Virgin, who miraculously converts the Unnamed Knight— the couple could not have escaped Don Rodrigo's sinister ploys. If the tension between the parasitic foreign nobility and the local, productive third estate does not degenerate into open tyranny, it is thanks only to the prestige of the Church and its efforts to remind everyone that true justice cannot be reduced to the workings of worldly power. As in Heliodorus's *Ethiopian Story*, the divinity and its representatives on earth are on the young lovers' side.

A generation later, in his *Confessions of an Italian* (posthumously published in 1867 and translated into English as *The Castle of Fratta*), Ippolito Nievo depicts not only the need for historical progress, but also the actual process by which it occurs—although whether the reality of such progress can meet people's expectations remains very much in doubt. The main character, Carlo, an illegitimate child staying with his aunt in the old castle of Fratta, on territory belonging to the Republic of Venice, witnesses the complicated family life of the local nobility during the last decades of Venetian independence. Carlo's life story parallels that of the fall of Venice at the hands of the French revolutionary army. Nievo is in two minds about virtually everything that happens in the novel, at both the historical and the personal level. He portrays the decay of old Venice as heartbreaking but inevitable. The French invasion brings high hopes for a freer, nobler future, for an Italian nation unified at last, but the reality of the occupation is harsh. Carlo's lifelong love, Pisana, is a headstrong young woman, noble yet unpredictable, tender yet capricious.

Carlo has kind words for the energy and beauty of the past. At Fratta, he admires the count's elderly mother, who lived in France at Louis XIV's court for a while in her youth, and still maintains the grace, rectitude, nobility, and moderation she learned at Versailles. But Carlo understands the promise and requirements of the present as well. Venice, his beloved city, is fated to lose its place in the world precisely because it is a mere city, and in modern history only nations thrive. He praises the contradictory faces of the past and present, just as he admires the two different women who coexist in Pisana: an ardent republican who thinks like a Greek philosopher, but also a carefree, provocative coquette. Unable, unwilling to make up his mind, Carlo is in love with both.

FOREIGN EXPLORATIONS

The "specious" fictions Walter Scott despised set their action in an earlier time: the imaginary antiquity of Gomberville and Madeleine de Scudéry, or the more recent, equally implausible period evoked by the gothic novel. The works of Kleist, Scott, and Manzoni were certainly better tuned to the truth of the bygone eras, but both "specious" and historically realist literature placed memorable actions in the past rather than here and now. Although Nievo is generous in his praise for the present, he entertains his own doubts about its glory, which is less spectacular than old Venice's. But if such glory was gone in Venice, it might still survive elsewhere, in regions not yet transformed by history. Nineteenth-century novelists and their public agreed that several European capital cities—London, Paris, St. Petersburg, Vienna, and Berlin—represented, along with the American Northeast, the pinnacle of a new commercial civilization. Outside these places, customs were assumed to grow more and more archaic as the distance from the center increased. The Neapolitans, the Corsicans, the Spanish, the Greeks, the Turks, the Egyptians, the Native Americans, the Cossacks, and the Chechens were all more or less thought to have preserved a "rude," nobler way of life. Foreign settings, then, were just as likely as historical ones to reveal fascinating forms of greatness.

As we have seen, seventeenth-century idealist novels assumed that the whole world was governed by the same universal ideals and norms. Courage, generosity, and faithful love—as well as treachery, cruelty, and imprudence—can be found among Madeleine de Scudéry's ancient Romans or Persians, Gomberville's Incas, and Aphra Behn's Africans. By contrast, when nineteenth-century novelists describe past times and far-away places, they focus on the features that separate these times and places from their own. And because the protagonists of these novels, rather than embodying a universal aspiration toward perfection, act according to the rules of "rude" societies, they are expected to arouse not only admiration but also a dash of mistrust.

It is possible to draw a distinction here between "analytical" and "sentimental" foreignness. The first kind extends Walter Scott's historical method to contemporary non-Western societies, caught in a global conflict with the European countries. *The Last of the Mohicans: A Narrative of 1757* by James Fenimore Cooper (1826) looks at the Native American tribes involved in the French and Indian War with the same mixture of admiration and reserve with which Scott describes the mid-eighteenth-century Jacobite Highlanders and the late seventeenth-century Scottish Presbyterians. Just as Scott brings both his characters' magnanimity and their "rudeness" to the reader's attention, Cooper divides the indigenous tribes into several categories, portraying the Mohicans as true heroes, the Hurons as unreliable, and the Delawares as still admirable despite having lost some of their former strength. In Cooper's view, North American natives in their greatness, embodied by the Mohican Uncas, and in their misery, represented by the Huron Magua, are equally ill-prepared to face the arrival of the British settlers. Some of these settlers admire the Mohicans' courage and loyalty, but for the foreseeable future the natives will not be able to keep the newcomers away. The great Manitou has hidden his face, the sage Tamenund predicts, but not forever. For now, he thinks, the pale-faces are masters of the earth, but the red men's time will inevitably come again.

The "sentimental" treatment of foreignness is not so concerned with the fate of older societies; it pays more attention to the surprise of a modern European who discovers, in a dazzling love encounter, the moral and emotional blessings of a foreign country. This approach is better served by a quick, allusive narrative than by laborious plot developments or exhaustive description: the old technique of the Italian and Spanish novellas reappears in Stendhal's *Italian Chronicles* (1837–1839). The intimate nature of these foreign encounters also encourages a direct expression of feelings that may recall the first-person elegiac story, as is the case in Alphonse de Lamartine's partly autobiographical *Graziella* (1849).

The action takes place in 1808, more than forty years before the story's publication, in an Italian fishing village, far from civilization and close to the purity of nature. Stranded on the island of Procida after a storm, a young Frenchman meets the beautiful Graziella, an innocent teenager. He reads aloud to her—the sentimental novel *Paul and Virginia*—and her heart awakens. Love rules supreme under sunny Neapolitan skies: Graziella refuses to marry Cecco, a good-natured local suitor, and seeks refuge in a convent. The Frenchman finds her hiding place and, after spending a chaste night next to her, brings her back to her family. Soon he returns to France, where he later learns that Graziella has died of love for him. The sea and its storms, the perfect love, the intervention of divinities (for Graziella is sure that the Virgin Mary has led her lover to her hideaway)—the story has all these devices, familiar from the old idealist novels. What is missing here, however, is reciprocal love. The "civilized" young man is unable to love a creature as beautiful and pure as Graziella.

Lamartine refrains from analyzing the male character, who clearly suffers from what was known around 1830 as the *mal du siècle*, a condition that rendered upper-class young men indifferent to everything that might normally bring them happiness, especially love—although this condition strangely enhanced the sick man's ability to arouse love in the women around him. Particularly vulnerable were young heiresses, like Tatiana Larina in Pushkin's *Eugene Onegin* (1833) and Princess Mary in the fifth part of *A Hero of Our Time* (1839–1841) by Mikhail Lermontov. The men suffering from the *mal du siècle* belonged to a generation too young to have fought in the wars of 1792–1815. They nostalgically imagined these wars as a thrilling epic adventure, so that the subsequent peace seemed, by contrast, a pedestrian time, bereft of heroism and nobility. Unlike Walter Scott and James Fenimore Cooper, whose praise of earlier and foreign heroic virtues was tempered by respect for the peaceful present, the next generation overidealized faraway societies and deeply despised their own. The dandies suffering from the *mal du siècle* looked down on the young women around them as products of a dull society, whose only aspiration was the contemptible state of marriage. Foreign beauties seemed much more promising.

"Bela," the first story in Lermontov's book, tells of a liaison between the young Russian dandy Pechorin and a Circassian princess from the occupied Caucasus. Strong and passionate, she could be a character in a novel by Aphra Behn. Initially excited by Bela's foreignness, Pechorin thinks for a moment that he could love her, but his devouring spleen gets the better of him. When she dies, stabbed by a young Circassian who hoped to marry her, Pechorin is shaken, but it is hard to tell whether he genuinely regrets her. Unable to resist the exotic dream, his cold heart lacks the strength to pursue it to the end.

Tolstoy, in his *Cossacks*, a long novella written between 1852 and 1862 and published in 1863, looks carefully at the moral consequences of this kind of culture shock. In France, writers seeking alien settings could choose, before reaching the eastern shores of the Mediterranean, to explore Italy and Spain, where (it was assumed) old passions and customs were kept alive. Prosper Mérimée did so in his novellas *Colomba* (1840) and *Carmen* (1845). In Russia, the search for foreignness led writers to the czar's imperial dominions in the Caucasus and central Asia, where they could encounter either the nomadic, Islamic Chechen tribal culture, a mental world profoundly different from that of Moscow and St. Petersburg, or the Cossack warriors, Russia's Christian allies, who lived in traditional farming communities. In any case, the cultural self-satisfaction of Russia's elite had its limits, as the Russian Empire had just begun to imitate the institutional structure of the western European powers. This is probably why Tolstoy's protagonist, rather than trusting the polite customs of the metropolis and viewing earlier stages of civilization with a mixture of sympathy and reserve, as a Walter Scott character might have done, is on the contrary profoundly repelled by his urban milieu and seeks a purer, truer life at the borders of the empire.

Olenin, a young man who has squandered half his fortune, decides to abandon the meaningless life he is leading in Moscow and join the Russian army in the Caucasus. Once at Novomlinsk, a Cossack village adjacent to the territory of the valiant Chechens, Olenin adopts the Cossack way of life. He makes friends with old Yeroshka, a hunter, and young Lukashka who fights the native Chechens, and he falls in love with the village beauty, Marianka. Deeply rooted in her village, surrounded by family and friends, and leading a peaceful life governed by ancestral customs, Marianka has no interest in Olenin's Russian world. For a short while, she and Olenin become closer, and he wants to marry her, but when Lukashka is seriously injured in a skirmish between Cossacks and Chechens, and is brought back half dead to Novomlinsk, Marianka realizes her true place is among her fellow villagers. Considering his education among the Cossacks complete, Olenin returns to Moscow.

The Cossacks belongs to a group of narratives that could be called stories of *regression and purification*. They describe the temporary integration of a man from "civilized" society into a community closer to nature. He is seduced by the serenity of his hosts' lives, but in the end he cannot quite adapt. Rejuvenated, wiser, the protagonist returns home. Having experienced a communitarian ideal as practiced by *other* people, he brings a dash of primitive poetry to life in the capital. Contact with the healthier foreign culture fortifies him, helping him face the adversity of his own world.

The Greatness of Small People

Meanwhile, writers continued to search for moral splendor closer to home. The quest had two mutually exclusive results: the *egalitarian* one, in which novelists tended to endow all human beings, even the humblest, with moral worth, and the *differential* one, in which they discovered or invented truly exceptional creatures.

The egalitarian authors scoured the lowest social echelons for possible heroes: orphans, poor farmers and workers, penniless seafarers, but also people marginalized or excluded from society for their offenses (criminals, prostitutes) or their infirmities (a hunchback, mental illness). Charles Dickens was one of the strongest defenders of egalitarian idealism: the humble person with a kind heart was his specialty.

In *Oliver Twist* (1837–1838), the kind heart belongs to a foundling with a spontaneous, unreflective love for the good. Born in the workhouse to a mother who dies without revealing her name, Oliver begins his life under the sign of death and hunger. He is raised in an orphanage, becomes an undertaker's apprentice, and is later adopted by the old crook Fagin, whose acolytes unsuccessfully try to teach him to pick pockets. The good-natured Mr. Brownlow, whose handkerchief is stolen by two of Fagin's partners, catches poor Oliver, but takes pity on him and gives him shelter in his house. Then Oliver is kidnapped by Fagin's gang and forced to take part in a robbery. He is wounded, but the kindly Mrs. Maylie and her protégée Rose look after him, trusting him despite the suspicious circumstances. Meanwhile, Oliver's corrupt half brother Edward conspires to deprive him of his share of the family inheritance. An intricate sequence of adventures leads to the discovery of his true ancestry. Mr. Brownlow turns out to be a friend of Oliver and Edward's father, while Rose Maylie is none other than the sister of Oliver's unhappy mother. Finally taking possession of his deceased father's fortune (he generously gives Edward half of it), Oliver settles happily in Mr. Brownlow's house; Edward moves across the ocean, leads a life of crime, and dies in prison.

There is a stark contrast between Oliver and his persecutors. On one side, a vulnerable child relying on his instinctive virtue; on the other, a sinister gang of criminals who haunt London's gutters. The urban world is not uniformly hostile but consists of separate, mutually exclusive regions: not far from the hell whose circles include the orphanage, the undertaker's workshop, and Fagin's den, Oliver finds a haven of peace inhabited by his benefactors, Mr. Brownlow and the Maylies. In the poor neighborhoods, there is misfortune and moral decay; in other areas, kindness and generosity. Evil and salvation are just a few streets apart.

As well as the spatial dimension, the clash between good and evil has a temporal one, often invisible to the characters themselves: the conflicts of the previous generation. In *Oliver Twist*, the object of the fight is an inheritance, in both senses of the term. At one level, Oliver's friends are seeking the money left by Oliver and Edward's father, Mr. Leeford, while Edward is hoarding it, but in another sense, the dead father's moral legacy is also at stake—Mr. Leeford's torment, his inability to provide a happy life for Oliver's mother, the woman he really loved, continues to haunt his children.

Fortunately, Oliver does not know what happened before he was born. Innocence, his only weapon, compels all good people to side with him. Here the vulnerability and candor that marked out virgin women in eighteenth-century novels are transferred to the orphaned boy. The sad story of his origins is revealed in the end, but not before he has triumphed over all obstacles and gathered enough strength to accept the truth.

It is not by chance, then, that the main character in *Little Dorrit* (1855–1857) is described as both a child and a woman, a mere girl who must take care of her entire family. The epitome of physical frailty, little Amy Dorrit, even more than Oliver Twist, possesses a stunning moral strength. Born in prison, she understands that her father, jailed for debt, is unable to provide for the family: always respectful and affectionate toward him, she quietly takes over the task. Amy earns the little money they need for survival by working as a seamstress for Mrs. Clennam, a tough, austere woman whose son Arthur inspires Amy's silent and initially unrequited love. After a stroke of financial luck, the Dorrits resume a comfortable life; Mr. Dorrit grows unbearably haughty, but his daughter, whose heart is unaffected by the whims of fortune, does not change at all.

While the Dorrit family lives under the spell of money and its debilitating moral influence, the Clennams are troubled by a dark story of adultery and misappropriated inheritance. On his deathbed, Arthur's father whispered to him, "Your mother," and expressed the wish that a watch containing a piece of paper inscribed with the mysterious initials DNF (Do Not Forget) be given to Mrs. Clennam. Arthur assumes that she is his mother, but it turns out that her coldness toward him is due not only to her fierce religious convictions. As Arthur will discover at the end of the novel, he is the son of a young woman Mr. Clennam seduced. Mrs. Clennam took the love child away from his real mother, who spent her life asking for a forgiveness that never came.

As in *Oliver Twist*, these characters must confront a secretly warped moral environment. Hidden in the family's past, a terrible offense weighs on the next generation. The possibility of transcending one's surroundings thus acquires a new meaning, at once more modest and more moving: by virtue of their innocence, Oliver, Arthur Clennam, and little Dorrit rid their world of its inherited flaws.

Feminist Idealism

Charlotte Brontë in England and George Sand in France reaffirmed the old alliance—in a world that subordinates women—between the idealist novel and feminist pride. Ancient Greek novels, aware of the subaltern position allotted to women in public life, depicted them as unquestionably morally superior to men. The female protagonist takes the lead, more virtuous and loyal than the best of men. To be sure, women are not praised unconditionally: one of the worst characters in *The Ethiopian Story* is Arsake, wife of the Persian governor of Egypt, who terrorizes the city of Memphis in his absence. The women who surpass men in ancient idealist novels are those who embody a purer ideal, further from the brutality of the world, closer to the gods' serenity. Chivalric stories sometimes openly identify women with a divine force. In *Amadis*, Oriana presides like a star over Amadis's destiny, giving him the strength to fight his adversaries. The rich harvest of seventeenth-century idealist novels, many written by women, revived the ancient Greek worship of virtuous female protagonists, and so did the new idealism of the eighteenth century, which placed characters like Pamela, Clarissa, and Julie high above their milieu. The beginning of Fielding's *Joseph Andrews*, where Pamela's brother, another chaste servant, heroically resists his mistress's attempts to seduce him, makes the reader laugh precisely because it seems so incongruous to attribute to a man the kind of virtuous self-mastery idealist novels have always ascribed to women.

In nineteenth-century literature, female superiority became the explicit theme of novels by women who wanted to question their own real, concrete social situation. The similarities and differences between *Pamela* (1741) and Charlotte Brontë's *Jane Eyre* (1847) are symptomatic. Like Pamela, Brontë's protagonist is a woman of modest birth who holds a subordinate position—governess—in the household of a rather unscrupulous man, Mr. Rochester. As in Richardson's novel, the master and his employee fall in love, but serious obstacles seem to make the match impossible—social difference in *Pamela*, a previous marriage in *Jane Eyre*. In both novels, the denouement confirms the woman's moral superiority, which in *Jane Eyre* is truly overwhelming. While Richardson's Mr. B. is a scatterbrained young man who gradually grows wiser through his love for a beautiful, chaste young woman, in Charlotte Brontë's story, Rochester's failings are more dramatic. Married to a woman who lost her reason years ago, he keeps her locked in the attic and hides her existence from his beloved Jane. This would make their marriage a bigamous one, and Jane is saved from dishonor only because the truth comes out during the wedding ceremony.

There are some mitigating circumstances, in that Rochester's family arranged his first marriage without his full consent. Subsequent events will nevertheless punish him with terrifying severity. The madwoman in the attic sets the house on fire, and, in trying to save her life, Rochester is crushed by a crumbling staircase: he loses his sight and the use of one arm. Jane, who has become financially independent in the meantime, marries him despite his infirmities. When Mr. B. marries Pamela, he raises his former servant to his own social level. Here it is Jane, a virtuous, loyal, healthy, and even wealthy woman, who agrees to devote her life to a handicapped, ruined Rochester, demonstrating her absolute superiority over the man she still loves.

In George Sand's novels about country life, *La Mare au diable* (*The Devil's Pool*, 1846), *La Petite Fadette* (1849), and *François le Champi* (1850), women's moral superiority seems less daunting, more congenial. They are vivacious, intelligent, and charming, while the men are inexperienced and clumsy. In her earlier *Indiana* (1832) and *Mauprat* (1837),

George Sand had painted a very dark picture of the condition of women in nineteenth-century French high society. In the novels of the late 1840s, she focuses on virtuous hearts hidden in the countryside, far from the contemporary urban scene. Sand clearly, deliberately idealizes her characters: for her, art is not the study of objective reality; it is a search for the ideal truth. She considers *The Vicar of Wakefield* a healthier, more useful book than the notorious libertine novels *Le Paysan perverti* by Restif de la Bretonne (1775) and the *Liaisons dangereuses* by Choderlos de Laclos. In George Sand's eyes, the countryside of her own time, not unlike that evoked by Virgil two thousand years earlier, was a place where poverty and servitude could not prevent people from being more beautiful and happier than the high-class city-dwellers.

Eternal childhood and beauty make her characters—Marie and Germain in *The Devil's Pool*, the little Fadette and Landry, Madeleine and François le Champi—unusually attractive. These couples bring the pastoral genre back to life; they are simpler and purer than the shepherds in Sannazaro and Montemayor, freed from the whims and hesitations that afflict them. Sand's plots are always the same: a kind, naive man meets a girl or a woman who, at first sight, belongs to a different world from his, either because she is poor, like Marie, a bit older, like Madeleine, or excluded from the village, like Fadette. Slowly, he realizes that she is the only one who can give meaning to his life. In all these stories, the woman is superior to the man because she is livelier, quicker, better adapted to life's hardships; yet she never sets great store by her abilities but generously makes herself useful. She finds happiness in love and honest cooperation.

While the feminism espoused by Charlotte Brontë—and by George Sand in her novels about the rich and powerful—emphasizes the moral splendor of strong, sometimes rebellious women, Sand's pastoral stories evoke the dream of a community in which women help men find simple ways to be happy.

But the most powerful feminist novel of the period is Anne Brontë's *The Tenant of Wildfell Hall* (1848). It offers a strong indictment of husbands' tyrannical powers, a haunting description of male alcoholism—a major issue for nineteenth-century feminism—and a reflection on the clash between infatuation and prudence in choosing a life partner. In the preface to the second edition, Anne Brontë warns us: "My object in writing the following pages was not simply to amuse the Reader . . . : I wished to tell the truth, for truth always conveys its own moral."[4] Telling the truth, in this context, means describing situations that, whether they are

---

[4] *The Tenant of Wildfell Hall*, ed. Herbert Rosengarten (Oxford: Oxford World Classics, 2008), p. 3.

entirely plausible or not, reveal what is essentially wrong with the prevailing laws and customs. To be effective, these descriptions must amplify the horror of such situations and emphasize how likely they are to occur. Here, then, is a form of ideography that does not reject vivid testimonial narration and realist representation of settings and feelings, but relies on them. A young woman rashly marries a fashionable but disreputable man and finds that not only is she unable to reform him, but his corruption reaches an unbearable scale; she leaves him and takes their child with her—an illegal act at the time; she lives under a false name and earns her keep as a painter; then, when her husband's alcoholism threatens his life, she returns to take care of him and again tries to reform him, without success; throughout all this the woman keeps her spirits up and eventually manages to start a new life. Clearly, such a woman illustrates an ideal truth—but a truth nonetheless. Her marriage is a war, her husband is the enemy, yet since morally she is his superior, she owes him something: she must try to save him from himself. The novel is complicated—two narrators, several plotlines, many characters, sharply introspective and lyrical passages, psychologically revealing dialogue, comedy and drama—but the thesis that emerges is both shocking and persuasive.

EXCEPTIONAL BEINGS, FALLEN ANGELS, DEMONS

The *differential* approach, intent on discovering or creating truly uncommon characters, was a French specialty, clearly visible in the works of Balzac, Alexandre Dumas-père, Victor Hugo, and, in a more modest fashion, Eugène Sue.

Balzac understood the importance of Walter Scott's historical realism. He adapted it to contemporary society by dividing France into distinct social and geographical regions, each endowed with a specific physiognomy whose features he strove to identify and represent. In particular, his novels capture the social dynamics that gave the bourgeoisie and its favorite instrument, money, enough power to replace the ebbing influence of the aristocracy. Balzac takes very seriously the idea that people are products of their milieu, although he still grants his characters a certain freedom of choice. Like Scott, he learned useful lessons from all the novelistic subgenres, combining the verve of the picaresque, the social insights of the novel of manners, the psychological acumen of the novella, and the idealist predilection for extraordinary characters. And just as Scott did in *Waverley*, Balzac takes on the role of the omniscient author, ready to converse with readers about the story's social and moral meaning. Thus although his characters occasionally offer first-person confessions, as in *The Lily of the Valley* (1836), for the most part it is not their responsibility to convince the reader—plausibility is guaranteed by the author's encyclopedic knowledge, loquaciousness, and wit.

Balzac's *Human Comedy* offers such a vast catalog of social types and conflicts that it would be unfair to reduce it to only one among the various strands of the nineteenth-century novel. All I want to suggest in what follows is that Balzac's realist depiction of bourgeois society enhances the vividness of his exemplary characters: here, social realism forcefully assists the idealist tradition. Balzac never ignores the egalitarian approach, searching insistently for strength and virtue in the most hidden corners of society (*Le Curé de Tours*, 1832; *Eugénie Grandet*, 1833). But the differential tendency in his work is very striking—he is particularly drawn to individuals whose merits, whether or not they are recognized, raise them high above the rest of society.

Balzac believed that the new bourgeois society could not accommodate exceptionally capable people. Dazzled, like many of his contemporaries, by the memory of Napoleon, Balzac thought that in a world overrun by mediocrity, truly extraordinary literary characters should serve as an example. As a result, *The Human Comedy* teems with people whose inexhaustible energy seems to come directly from ancient and seventeenth-century romances. But Balzac was a man of his time, and he also provides his characters with two new features. One is the professional career: greatness here is not primarily a matter of martial prowess or chastity; it must be demonstrated in the context of a specific vocation. In Balzac's novels, each trade has its genius: Bianchon among doctors, Derville among notaries, Bridau as a painter, Nucingen as a banker, d'Arthez in philosophy.

The other new feature is the possibility of failure. When the protagonists of old romances defy adversity, they can always count on the support of Providence, or at least on its approval. In Balzac's novels, Providence—or nature—endows the chosen ones with talent and energy, but in order to succeed, they cannot rely on anyone but themselves. Born in a society deeply suspicious of strength and originality, either these characters can devote themselves wholeheartedly to a great enterprise, never allowing the world's temptations to distract them, or they can put all their energies into satisfying those worldly desires, and thus waste the treasure of their talent. Balzac's characters must find within themselves the requisite constancy of purpose; they are free to choose—well or badly—what use to make of their providential (natural) gifts.

In addition to those in various trades and professions, three kinds of character can achieve a truly uncommon greatness: dispensers of justice, such as Armand de Montriveau in *The Duchess of Langeais* (1834), artists of genius like Joseph Bridau in *La Rabouilleuse* (*The Black Sheep*,

1842), and benefactors who devote themselves to the happiness of their fellow human beings, like Dr. Benassis in *The Country Doctor* (1833).

Balzac loves his dispensers of justice—perhaps too much. Montriveau, a fighter in Napoleon's Egyptian army, captured and enslaved in the desert, escapes and returns to make his appearance in the best Parisian circles. Antoinette de Langeais, a fashionable woman, decides to seduce the dark, taciturn hero, but when he falls madly in love, she makes a fool of him. In revenge, Montriveau kidnaps Antoinette with the help of the Thirteen—a secret society devoted to the rebirth of greatness—and, to show his contempt, lets her go without taking advantage of her. His behavior shatters the proud woman, who now falls in love with her tormentor. He has disappeared without a trace, and, deeply hurt, Antoinette takes refuge in a Spanish Carmelite convent.

In their own way, the incredibly complex revenge of the main character in Alexandre Dumas's *Count of Monte Cristo* (1844–1845) and the protagonist's fight against, and later for, justice in Pierre Alexis Ponson du Terrail's serial novel *Rocambole* (1857–1884) are both more convincing than Montriveau's misogynistic rage, pointlessly assuaged. The former military hero is ill at ease in the elegant salons of the Restoration, which fail to offer the proper setting for his genius. How does Montriveau prove his superiority? By persecuting a capricious woman.

Much more effective in his good deeds is the village doctor Benassis, a loner who wants to redeem the sins of his youth. Long ago, he seduced and abandoned a destitute woman who truly loved him; only when he receives news of her death does he realize how noble and disinterested she was, raising their son alone, and never asking for any financial help. Benassis understands his mistake, undergoes a moral and religious conversion, and devotes himself to his son. When the boy dies, Benassis finds his true vocation, the best outlet for his remorse: charity. In a peaceful society, charity is the only heroic action that knows no limits.

Like charity, art and reflection require ascetic renunciation. In order to succeed, great artists and philosophers must cultivate their gifts in solitude. For them, falling in love is a genuine disaster, as it directs their energies toward a single human being, and puts an end to the seclusion so essential for reaching artistic and philosophical maturity. In *The Black Sheep*, Joseph Bridau makes the right choice. A youngest son, neglected by his mother, who prefers her elder son, Philippe, Joseph grows up alone, reading and painting. While the adventurous Philippe ascends and descends the social ladder and spends all the family money, Joseph has no material or erotic needs. He gives everything he earns to his mother and his brother, and happily creates a new, successful style of painting.

The character endowed with genius can, of course, make the opposite choice. In *Lost Illusions* (1837–1843), Lucien de Rubempré is a handsome young man with a remarkable talent for poetry. His mother was born into one of the best aristocratic families, but he has to overcome his poverty, the obscurity of his father's name, and his own lack of public recognition, which his residence in the provincial city of Angoulême does nothing to counter. Fate, which has already given him beauty, intelligence, and talent, helps him on the way to success: a beautiful woman takes him to Paris, his sister and brother-in-law assist him financially, and he is welcomed with open arms by a group of young Parisian geniuses. But in the *Human Comedy*, such beginnings guarantee nothing without hard work and self-denial: Lucien must write and publish in order to make himself known. In this elitist society, he is also handicapped by his father's bourgeois surname, Chardon. What's more, the woman who gave him the courage to move to Paris is married, the money from his family that seemed a vast sum in Angoulême is worth very little in the capital, and the young geniuses who take him under their wing give him good advice but not the strength to follow it. Lucien must find this strength for himself.

To help the reader understand Lucien's failure, Balzac explains it on two levels. On the one hand, the personality is shaped by physical factors, social origins, and education. Not only is Lucien the product of a mésalliance—his parents married after his lower-middle-class father saved his aristocratic mother from the guillotine during the Terror—but since his mother raised him alone, he never benefited from the example or influence of an energetic father. Besides, his body bears the marks of androgyny. Lucien's vulnerability is thus rooted in his birth, his past, and his physical constitution.

On the other hand, whatever the role of individual temperament and education, Balzac emphasizes the character's freedom to make the right decision. When Lucien is offered a lucrative job as a journalist, his friends warn him against the dangers of the profession. Lucien's brilliance and quick thinking would make him an excellent journalist, they argue, but that is precisely why he should avoid an occupation that would take up all his time and energy. Lucien ignores their advice and becomes a successful journalist; he wins the heart of the beautiful actress and courtesan Coralie, and tastes the pleasures of elegant life. Now Lucien needs more money and resorts to unscrupulous tactics; in the end, he rashly switches his political allegiance, provoking widespread hostility and destroying his career and Coralie's. On the verge of suicide, Lucien is saved by the reprobate priest Herrera, who is in fact Vautrin, alias Jacques Collin, the great ogre of the *Human Comedy*. The two men sign a pact agreeing to devote themselves to one another's desires—Herrera's sensuality and Lucien's thirst for worldly promotion. So Lucien's careless immorality develops into a lucid, deliberate corruption.

In creating Vautrin—probably the *Human Comedy*'s most fascinating character: an unassailable felon and a leader of the criminal underworld, a gay lover capable of the most passionate devotion—Balzac continues the meditation on immorality initiated by the gothic novel and by eighteenth-century anti-idealist fiction. They had imagined a new kind of villain: initially still quite human, over time these characters acquired a frightening pallor and rigidity. The difference between Defoe's Moll Flanders and Mme de Merteuil in Laclos's *Liaisons dangereuses* is that the former, as a true *pícara*, breaks all moral and institutional laws to fight her hunger, poverty, and loneliness, whereas Laclos's character enjoys the very act of evildoing, regardless of practical considerations. In the Marquis de Sade's *Juliette or the Prosperity of Vice* (1797), the main character's aim in life is the triumph of vice. As we shall soon see, evil championed and pursued for its own sake would become the villains' specialty in nineteenth-century popular novels.

To be genuinely interesting, however, immorality must have causes and limits. The novel that offers the subtlest analysis of its causes is Mary Shelley's *Frankenstein* (1818). The scientist Frankenstein's humanoid creation hides away, fearing that his ugliness will repel human beings. He discovers a suitcase containing clothes and a few books—Milton's *Paradise Lost*, Plutarch's *Parallel Lives*, and Goethe's *Sufferings of Young Werther*—which are a genuine revelation to him. Werther's fate teaches him about despondency and makes him weep copiously, Plutarch helps him rise above his own sad life and admire the great warriors and legislators of the past, yet only Milton's poem, with its biblical drama of creation and fall, allows him to realize how unusual, how singular he is. Like Adam, the monster is the first of his lineage, and like Satan, he is full of bitterness and envy. This combination of solitude and resentment feeds the monster's rage against the universe. The only one of his kind, with no fellow creatures, incapable of love and therefore hostile to those who can feel it, the monster avenges himself by killing his creator, Frankenstein, and his fiancée. Singularity and solitude, superhuman force, bitterness toward the world: *Frankenstein*'s protagonist exhibits the features that would enduringly define the demonic hero in nineteenth-century novels.

Vautrin's grandeur, like that of Frankenstein's humanoid creature, comes from his singularity, his solitude, and his profoundly pessimistic outlook on life. Uncontested king of the Parisian underworld, endowed with unmatched intelligence and physical strength, bursting with energy and talent, he is excluded from the mainstream because of his homosexuality and his past as a convict. In this society, whose rules he knows and despises, he can succeed only through a protégé who belongs entirely to him. Unlike Frankenstein's humanoid, however, Vautrin never loses his ambition to thrive among his fellow men, nor his ability to love. When

Lucien dies (in *Splendors and Miseries of Courtesans*, 1838–1847), Vautrin, realizing that his life of crime has not helped him save the man he loves, finally converts to law and order, and joins the police force.

THE SUMMIT OF IDEALISM

In Balzac's novels, whose primary aim is to portray the boundless diversity of human activities and types, the prodigious force of characters like Montriveau, Benassis, and Vautrin remains an exception. Popular novels, by contrast, bank on precisely this kind of character. In these books, the dispensers of justice—Rodolphe in *The Mysteries of Paris* (1842–1843), Dantès in *The Count of Monte Cristo*, and Rocambole, turned virtuous in *The Resurrection of Rocambole* (1866)—are blessed with boundless drive, intelligence, and sometimes wealth. They change their identities as often as they like, and adapt with stunning ease to the most diverse milieus. They are also deeply sensitive, vulnerable, distressed, and melancholy, either because of the world's unjust treatment—the innocent Dantès's imprisonment in *The Count of Monte Cristo*—or because of the memory of some terrible wrongdoing they need to redeem, such as Rodolphe's past rebellion against his father in *The Mysteries of Paris*. Since in an egalitarian age great souls can come from all parts of society, in popular novels they belong either to the highest nobility—Rodolphe is reigning prince of Gerolstein—or to the common people: Dantès in Dumas and Largardère in Paul Féval's *The Hunchback* (1858).

Their enemies, also drawn larger than life, are cruel, unscrupulous, and involved in the most diabolical intrigues; they act out of sheer meanness, and in the case of the notary Jacques Ferrand and old Chouette in *The Mysteries of Paris*, among others, they take pleasure in evil for its own sake. Between the main protagonist and these repulsive monsters, the popular novel will sometime place a tragic mediator. She is a lost woman, but one who has kept her essential purity intact. For various reasons, the diabolical characters have her in their power, and the protagonist longs to free her.

The sublime character blighted by a stain or flaw is meant to remind readers that those struck by misfortune can have a special moral worth. Angel-prostitutes blossom in these novels: for if inner beauty has its own independent existence, if it belies appearances (Pamela's low birth) and prejudice (Julie's loss of virginity), why wouldn't the prostitution of the body leave the soul intact?

Fleur-de-Marie's life, in *The Mysteries of Paris*, is a case in point. The child of a secret marriage between Prince Rodolphe of Gerolstein and the ambitious Lady Sarah MacGregor, Marie stays with her mother when circumstances force the couple to separate. To get rid of her daughter,

Lady Sarah sets up an annuity for her and entrusts her to the notary Jacques Ferrand; he soon takes over the capital of the annuity and convinces Lady Sarah that Marie has fallen sick and died. Meanwhile, Ferrand's accomplice, Mme Séraphin, gives the little girl to a beggar, Chouette. Eventually, Marie falls prey to the Ogress, a tavern manager and procuress who forces her to sell her body. Rodolphe rescues her, not knowing she is his daughter, and Marie becomes the focus of a struggle between good and evil.

Despite her experiences, Fleur-de-Marie still has an open heart, and she radiates innocence. No bitterness, no desire for vengeance troubles her: those who meet her are instantly seduced by her kindness, piety, and generosity. Alas, if the young woman's purity is ineradicable, her fall is equally so. When her true lineage is discovered, Fleur-de-Marie's adoring father and stepmother welcome her at the court of Gerolstein. A young nobleman named Henry is secretly in love with her and asks for her hand. Rodolphe would be delighted to secure his daughter's happiness, but the princess, unable to forget her past, deems herself unworthy to be a wife and mother. She withdraws to a convent and dies soon after taking her vows.

As in Balzac, the setting in which these melodramatic events take place is described with a remarkable concern for sociological accuracy. The author seems rightly proud of the abundance of detail he provides about the life of Parisian workers and clerks, their daily worries, their budgets, their joys, and their sorrows; through attentive descriptions of places, dresses, and manners, he shows how much social diversity can be found in the modern metropolis. Sue also informs the reader of the deficiencies of contemporary legal procedures and prisons, denouncing them in his own name and adding a variety of concrete proposals for social improvement.

But readers are more likely to be entranced by the moral stakes of the story, which employs a popular version of the ideographic method. Rodolphe embodies justice and strength; Jacques Ferrand, iniquity; and Fleur-de-Marie, persecuted innocence. Because these figures are exemplary, the dangers that threaten Rodolphe and Marie move readers much more than they otherwise would, and the defeat of the abominable Ferrand means a great deal more than that of an ordinary criminal. At this level of moral intensity, implausibility does not risk making readers uncomfortable: instead, it highlights the grandeur of the principles and feelings involved.

||||||||||||||||||||||||||||

Victor Hugo's *Les Misérables* (1862), published five years after Flaubert's *Madame Bovary*, but written much earlier, has some things in common with the popular novel. *Les Misérables* undoubtedly represents the last attempt by a great writer in the realm of "high" culture to defend idealism, at a time when it faced a growing hostility from those drawn to pessimism, moral skepticism, and the worship of art for art's sake.

Like Walter Scott, Hugo believed in the greatness of the past, in progress, and in the strong connections between human beings and their historical and social environment. But, in line with progressive Christians like Manzoni and the French preacher Lamennais, he was equally convinced that people have the strength to withdraw from the outside world and put themselves under the direct protection of the Creator. These convictions shape his historical novel *Notre-Dame de Paris* (1831): its careful evocation of the Parisian atmosphere and institutions of the Middle Ages; its attempt to imagine a medieval mentality and make the characters think and act accordingly; and at the same time, the extraordinary moral beauty of the main characters, Esmeralda and Quasimodo, and the disquieting corruption of the priest Claude Frollo.

This dual belief, in the social nature of human beings and in their alliance with Providence, is equally effective in *Les Misérables*. This time, however, a huge gulf opens up between Hugo's professed historicism and the atemporal greatness of his characters. The righteous ones, Mgr. Myriel, Jean Valjean, Fantine, Marius, and Cosette, as well as their persecutors, the policeman Javert and the Thénardier family, resemble giants crossing vast landscapes, striding over the streets and buildings, looking for and calling out to each other high above the multitudes. These exceptional beings, who perform amazing physical and moral feats, are constantly drawn toward each other, as though a kind of interpersonal magnetism were keeping them close together despite changes of residence, name, and occupation. No matter where or under what name Jean Valjean manages to hide, Javert and the Thénardiers are never far away. Every time the hero appears, the rest of humanity, not unlike the choir at the opera, steps back to allow his enemies, always already lurking there, to show themselves.

Choosing his characters from nowhere near the center of bourgeois life, Hugo plants a sublime heart in a fallen woman, Fantine, and in Jean Valjean, the former convict converted to virtue, whose efforts to redeem his past are continually hindered by society. The novel emphasises Valjean's desire to reintegrate, and denounces the rigidity of legal institutions. In addition, *Les Misérables* develops two themes that resonate with the oldest idealist tradition: the providential call, and fatherhood of the spirit rather than the flesh.

At the very beginning of the novel, returning from the penal colony, Jean Valjean meets Mgr. Myriel, a bishop and friend to the poor, whose otherworldly generosity changes the former convict's outlook on life. Later, rejected by society and struggling more and more with loneliness,

Valjean is bolstered in his efforts to do good by the memory of the sub-lime bishop. He is also energized by his fatherly devotion to Fantine's daughter Cosette, whom he raises after her mother's death although they are not related by blood. Hunted by the manic policeman Javert, Valjean slips from one hiding place to the next, clasping his adopted daughter to his chest. After a great deal of effort, he manages to ensure her happi-ness. When Cosette finally marries the man she loves, Jean Valjean has no reason left to live.

The tension between these two views—one asserting people's histori-cal and social roots, the other emphasizing human loneliness and its links with the beyond—is visible in Hugo's alternation between ordinary nar-rative, full of detailed historical references, and passages of soaring, pur-ple prose. The operatic style livens up the characters' long monologues. These monologues affirm the link between unhappy loners and the divine majesty of the universe; they lodge a strong challenge against those who see human beings as mere subjects of history and society.

CHAPTER 10

From Sensitive
Hearts to
Enigmatic Psyches

|||||||||||||||||||||||||||||||||||||||||||||||||||||||||||||||||||

Providing a much-needed counterpart to the narratives that espoused moral idealism, other novelists continued to concentrate on human inadequacy. Some, notably Stendhal in France and Thackeray in Britain, were part of the *school of irony*, which took full advantage of the new interest in history and society promoted by Walter Scott and Balzac, but emphasized the thoughtless, frivolous, capricious nature of human behavior and its motives. The *school of bitterness*, represented by Gustave Flaubert, the Goncourt brothers, and Émile Zola, took social and biological determinism seriously, and drew a profoundly pessimistic picture of the human condition. Most significantly, a *school of empathy*, pioneered by Jane Austen and brought to its peak by Henry James, reflected on people's erratic self-knowledge and on the interactions between them, glimpsed from the characters' own, often unreliable point of view.

THE SCHOOL OF IRONY: STENDHAL AND THACKERAY

Stendhal's anti-idealism is deeply indebted to Walter Scott's and Balzac's concern for historical and social accuracy, which he blends with a Fielding-like witty, relaxed skepticism about moral conduct. Born in 1783 (twelve years after Scott and sixteen before Balzac), Stendhal was old enough to have read the traditional idealist novels in his youth, to have appreciated the psychological insights of Benjamin Constant's *Adolphe* (1816) as well as Walter Scott's innovations in the mid-1810s, defended the rise of French romanticism in his *Racine and Shakespeare* (1823–1825), and, in the early 1830s, recognized the power of Balzac's social analyses. Stendhal began to write narrative prose late in life: he published his *Armance* in 1827, when he was forty-four. By that time, the techniques for evoking social reality in fiction were fully developed. Historical accuracy and a careful coordination between the characters' psychology and their place in society were taken for granted. It would have been difficult, by then, to write a novel like Goethe's *Elective Affinities* or Constant's *Adolphe*, whose ideas were expressed in purely moral terms, without detailed reference to material reality or to historical and social factors. Stendhal adopted the new approach but nevertheless rejected some of the beliefs of its earlier supporters, particularly the notion, exemplified by Scott's *Waverley*, of heroism as the product of a bygone social order.

Stendhal was convinced that though social customs may change, human nature does not. An admirer of Napoleon's military achievements, Stendhal considered him the modern equivalent of the great ancient conquerors Alexander and Caesar. Martial heroism, therefore, far from being consigned to the distant past, might return at any point as the crucial virtue. In its absence, people find other ways to promote themselves, overcome adversity, and occasionally achieve social success. Their actions, though, are not driven by some deep thirst for virtue, but stem from egotistical impulses and sudden bursts of rage or desire. Different countries and periods display a great variety of customs and manners, as Stendhal, a great lover of Italy, knew well. But, striking as these differences may be, they cannot affect the deepest layers of the human heart.

The Red and the Black (1830) examines social prejudice, religious hypocrisy, and the mechanisms of individual promotion in France after the restoration of the Bourbon dynasty (1815–1830). Yet the passions and ambitions of Julien Sorel, the main character, are not merely the result of the social system that encourages and directs them. The novel's title alludes to the contrast between the prestige of a military career at the time of the (now defunct) empire and the high standing of the Church during the Restoration—the officers' uniform was red; priests wear black. From Julien Sorel's point of view, however, as a young, charming social climber, the difference between the Red and the Black is only circumstantial: under the empire, he would have served in the army; under the Bourbon monarchy, he pursues an ecclesiastical career. For him, the two paths are equivalent ways to satisfy a fundamental urge for wealth and influence. Is this urge caused by the model of Napoleon, the little man from Corsica whose individual talents raised him to the throne of France, and who, for a short while, ruled over half of Europe? Or do Julien Sorel's adventures simply resemble those of the older pícaros and pícaras who, like him, devoted their inexhaustible energies to succeeding in life, taking advantage of all available means?

Though refusing to subject his characters to strict social and historical determinism, Stendhal does show a vivid interest in foreign cultures and ethnographic specificity. He loves Italy, and *The Charterhouse of Parma*

(1839) is full of references to Italian sincerity, spontaneity, and passionate love, so different, in his view, from French attitudes. But these references recall sixteenth- and seventeenth-century commonplaces about the moral physiognomy of nations (the French are conceited, the Spanish obsessed with their honor, etc.) rather than the eighteenth- and nineteenth-century deterministic theories of history. In fact, all stereotypes about the Italian character notwithstanding, the people of Parma under the reign of Ernest-Ranuce IV seem just as vain, hypocritical, capricious, and empty-headed as the French in *The Red and the Black*. With all the obvious differences between the coldhearted, ambitious Julien Sorel and Fabrice del Dongo, the generous young aristocrat in *The Charterhouse of Parma*, the two characters choose their paths in life in the same offhand way. Just as Julien's political beliefs do not prevent him from seeking his fortune in a royalist family, Fabrice del Dongo takes up an ecclesiastical career simply because his protectors think it will lead him to a higher station in life.

In a world where personal convictions count for little, people calculate their attitudes and gestures according to the advantages they might bring. Quite often, however, they lose control. Thus, during his theological studies, Julien happens to praise the emperor for no obvious reason, in the middle of a dinner with priests. Worse, Fabrice del Dongo, who has just been appointed bishop despite his youth, gets caught up in a fight with an actor, Giletti, the lover of an actress he is courting. The fight slows down and seems about to end, when suddenly Fabrice, enraged by the thought that Giletti may have disfigured him, stabs his adversary with a hunting knife. Giletti falls dead. Fabrice runs away, but he will not be able to avoid prison and, later, expatriation. An instant of rage, an impulsive gesture disrupts his whole life. In the same way, Julien Sorel, who has managed to switch from the cloth to the uniform, has been named hussar lieutenant and granted a significant sum of money, seethes with anger when he finds out that Mme de Rênal, his former mistress, has written a letter to his protector M. de la Mole, revealing several unpleasant truths about his past. He buys a pair of pistols and shoots Mme de Rênal—though he does not manage to kill her. He is arrested, tried, and sentenced to death. Both Fabrice and Julien fail to obey the norms of their society—despite their ambitions, they cannot do what it takes to reach the top. They are, in a sense, independent beings, but it is clear that their independence, instead of serving either a higher ideal or self-interest, encourages capricious, ultimately futile impulses.

Even love, which according to the idealist dogma comes down from heaven or up from the depths of the heart—thus epitomizing the individual's freedom from the surrounding world—here becomes a strange mixture of vanity, lust, and calculation. Before Julien's first night with Mme de Rênal, a married woman he has decided to seduce to improve his chances of advancement, "He tired his brain out inventing clever stratagems—a moment afterwards finding them ridiculous."[1] Once in her room, he "forgot his empty schemes and returned to playing the part natural to him: not to please so charming a woman seemed to him the greatest of misfortunes" (p. 96). Sincerity does not prevail, though, as Julien's character is such that "he still aspired, even in the tenderest of moments, to play the role of a man used to subduing women; he made tremendous efforts to spoil what was most lovable in himself" (p. 96). Back in his room, he wonders: "My God! To be happy, to be loved, is that all there is to it?" (p. 97).

This carelessness, this inner absence, this inability to appreciate the true meaning of one's actions can be found in earlier literature, as a comic feature in Don Quixote's case, or as a serious flaw, caused by vanity, thoughtlessness, or—in the case of Anselmo in Cervantes's *An Ill-Advised Curiosity*—a distorted sense of honor. Running serious risks for no good reason, assuming inappropriate roles, and wasting energy were seen as either ridiculous mistakes or deplorable flaws—but always as departures from the general rule. Classical moral thought and older fiction understood human caprice, and realized how unpredictable the effects of anger, self-delusion, and inexplicable desires could be, but they considered them accidents rather than essential features of our condition. Stendhal is probably the first novelist to present the most serious actions people take as essentially governed by fantasy, absentmindedness, and momentary impulses. According to him, unclearly motivated, counterproductive behavior is the hallmark of human nature. The *psyche*, difficult to gauge and explain, was now on its way to becoming a central concern for the novel.

Stendhal's works are not quite there yet, and, as a consequence, one of their most seductive aspects—one his contemporaries failed to appreciate—is the absence of pessimism and bitterness. His characters are neither excessively self-assured nor fully defined by their epoch and society, making them refreshingly different from the protagonists of both earlier idealist fiction and nineteenth-century realist novels. And because they do not entirely know—or care too much—what goes on within them, they radiate a striking, fleeting charm that Baudelaire would soon define as one of the marks of modern beauty.

||||||||||||||||||||||||||||||||

Like Stendhal, Thackeray began his writing career relatively late in life, which might account for both writers' skepticism about moral posturing. He was thirty-three when he published *The Memoirs of Barry Lyndon, Esq.* (1844), a picaresque story deliberately couched in the

---

[1] Stendhal, *The Red and the Black*, trans. Roger Gard (London: Penguin Books, 2002), chap. 15, p. 95.

eighteenth-century style—language and manners included—and initially titled *The Luck of Barry Lyndon: A Romance of the Last Century*. Its first sentence heralds the novel's tone, which emulates Fielding's timeless wisdom; the fictional author of the memoirs declares, "Since the days of Adam, there has been hardly a mischief done in this world but a woman has been at the bottom of it." [2] But in fact, this sentence does not return to a tone characteristic of the previous century. Thackeray's irony thwarts this possibility: the main character's statement is nothing but the dubious self-justification of a soldier-gambler who seeks adventure all over the world. His most audacious coup consists in persuading a wealthy widow, Countess Lyndon, to marry him. Woman is by no means the cause of all mischief, when man so often tricks her and leads her astray. From his own time—the early 1840s—Thackeray looked back at a distant period, reconstituting its habits and idiom with the help of Casanova's libertine memoirs, Fielding's *Jonathan Wild* (1743), and the true story of an adventurer named Andrew Robinson Stoney-Bowes. The book is a triumph of historicist refinement. Setting aside Walter Scott's long explanations, Thackeray evokes the past from inside, as it were, through the eyes of the natives. Yet the historical distance and the irony of the enterprise are always perceptible.

In *Vanity Fair* (1847–1848), Thackeray paints a broad picture of life and manners in England in the early nineteenth century. Narrated in the third person by an authorial voice as full of tenderness and irony as Fielding's, the novel contrasts the life of the young social climber Becky Sharp with that of the naive Amelia Sedley. Becky, governess in the dissolute Sir Pitt Crawley's household, seduces the old man and then secretly marries his son, arousing the family's anger. Amelia, whose father has gone bankrupt, marries the frivolous George Osborne. He dies at the battle of Waterloo—but not before making plans to run off with the omnipresent Becky. After worshipping her husband's memory for a long time, Amelia finds out the truth about him. Deeply disappointed, she finally learns to appreciate George's friend, the generous William Dobbin, who has always been in love with her. Their marriage concludes the novel.

The nastier characters seem to come directly from *Tom Jones* and Fanny Burney's novels of manners: Sir Pitt, a barely more nuanced reincarnation of Sophia Western's father; Becky Sharp, who sometimes calls Blifil to mind; and George Osborne, who has some of Tom Jones's faults but none of his attractive qualities. The conceit and hypocrisy of these characters, and their dependence on worldly pleasures, place them in the midst of the "vanity fair." By contrast, innocent Amelia fails to

[2] *The Memoirs of Barry Lyndon, Esq.*, ed. Andrew Sanders (Oxford: Oxford World Classics, 1984), p. 3.

understand the world's corruption and misreads the characters of those around her, trusting people who do not deserve it and failing to value those who do. By showing how her naïveté is the very source of her errors, Thackeray rejects the unwavering optimism of Fielding, whose characters, with all their imperfection and frivolity, still manage to fall instantly in love with the partner chosen for them by Providence. Amelia's blindness rather resembles that of the unhappy heroines in so many eighteenth- and nineteenth-century novels: Clarissa, unable to perceive her seducer's wickedness; the women unhappily married or abandoned by their unworthy lovers in Balzac's *Human Comedy*; and George Sand's Indiana, whom no man truly deserves. In *Vanity Fair*, however, the misfortune caused by the heroine's innocence is not beyond remedy. Learning is possible: Amelia's eyes are opened, and her second marriage, less romantic than the first, is much happier. This fusion between inner beauty and the slow discovery of reality would soon become the main subject of George Eliot's novels.

The School of Empathy, I

The pastoral, the elegiac story, and the tragic novella had detected early on the presence of recesses within the human heart—depths to which the individual has very limited access. But it was only in the early nineteenth century that narratives began to examine closely people's unstable, unreliable understanding of themselves. The *school of empathy*, founded by Jane Austen (1775–1817), whose novels were published between 1811 and 1818, can be seen as an alternative to the rise of the historical and social novels. Whereas throughout the nineteenth century most novelists were interested in capturing the specificity of historical periods, national milieus, and social classes, Jane Austen's stories take place on a narrow stage, involving only characters from provincial English society, and have a limited range of interests, usually related to the kind of marriage that might make young people happy. Historical and social novels depict the world at large, or at least explicitly take it for granted; Austen focuses on a single spot that becomes the center of the action. Moreover, while most writers of historical and social novels display their awareness that the society they depict is not the only possible one, in Austen nothing suggests that a different kind of social arrangement might be conceivable.

By narrowing the space of the action, reducing the number of characters, and simplifying the plot, Austen rediscovers, perhaps instinctively, the old methods of the Italian and Spanish novella, which privileged well-focused conflicts concerning just a few individuals. With its limited space and simple plot, the novella was free to examine the consequences of various passions in everyday life, and to scrutinize its characters' secrets and their ignorance of themselves. But while a novella would concentrate on a highly memorable event, Austen's novels deal with the most ordinary happenings. Just as eighteenth-century idealism conferred a new dignity on people living in the actual world, the art of *commonplace morality*, discovered by Austen, examines the characters' smallest debates and hesitations, their least noticeable errors of interpretation, with the meticulous respect once reserved for grand moral dilemmas and momentous choices.

When Austen presents these inner debates, she pays particular attention to the viewpoint of the characters themselves. In the earlier picaresque and elegiac traditions, introspection relentlessly exposes a character's inadequacy. In eighteenth-century new idealism, by contrast, protagonists like Pamela and Clarissa never tire of contemplating their own inner splendor. As for Fielding, he amusingly debunked his characters' self-satisfaction: Tom Jones looks at himself with a certain amount of admiration and believes his actions are always justified, yet the author lets us know how mistaken he is. Austen learned from Fielding the method of the *double look*—the character's and the author's—but replaced his dismissive irony with an affectionate sense of humor, imbued with a genuine esteem for her characters.

For while Fielding could not trust the opinions people entertain about themselves, Austen was convinced that the moral norm and the right way to implement it must be (and is) discovered through inner deliberation. Far from being ridiculous fools who imagine themselves better than they are, Austen's characters are *barely* touched by imperfection. Her heroines' faults include a bit of youthful smugness, occasional deafness to other people's points in conversation, and a tendency to take others' malleability for granted. But despite the inadequate self-knowledge of Emma Woodhouse (in *Emma*, 1815) and Elizabeth Bennet (in *Pride and Prejudice*, 1813), and their errors in judging other people's needs and desires, the intrinsic value of their inner debates, particularly those concerning love and persuasion, is never called into question.

In *Emma*, for instance, the protagonist wrongly believes she can read the hearts of those around her, and therefore that she should interfere in their lives. Her friend Harriet Smith, a young woman of modest birth, is not exactly bright and has no ambition. Yet Emma, who misreads her, decides to supervise and direct her existence: she persuades Harriet to refuse the honest farmer Robert Martin, and unsuccessfully attempts to marry her to Mr. Elton, the pastor, without realizing how low his opinion of the young woman is. Harriet, meanwhile, decides she would like to marry George Knightley, the novel's wisest character, whom Emma herself loves without realizing it. The misunderstandings come to an end when Emma abandons her pretensions to rule other people's lives and accepts Knightley's hand, while Harriet listens to her heart and marries the good-natured Robert Martin.

In terms of style, Austen's mixture of empathy and critical distance takes the form of *free indirect discourse*, which relates a character's intimate thoughts in the third person. At the beginning of the novel, Emma has received Harriet at Hartfield, the Woodhouse residence, and finds her

> so pleasantly grateful . . . and so artlessly impressed by the appearance of everything in so superior a style to what she had been used to, that she must have good sense, and deserve encouragement. Encouragement should be given.[3]

Who thinks that encouragement "should be given"? The text does not say: "Emma told herself that she should encourage Harriet," or "Thinking of Harriet's good behavior, Emma told herself, 'Encouragement should be given.'" "Encouragement should be given" is attributed to Emma through empathy, but not without a slight emphasis on the distance between author and character. By saying "Encouragement should be given" without mentioning Emma's name, Austen implies, "This is what this conceited young woman thought, believe it or not!" Blending the voice of the narrator with that of the character suggests that Emma's thoughts, worthy of attention as they are, should still be considered with a dash of mistrust. Free indirect discourse is precisely meant to illustrate the human psyche's mixture of lucidity and incomprehension. Unable to grasp its own or others' motivations fully and unconditionally, it might nevertheless manage—slowly, gradually—to reach the right conclusions.

In *Persuasion* (published posthumously in 1818), Anne Elliot learns to understand herself and resist the influence of those around her. Anne was persuaded by a friend to reject the young officer she loved, who had no independent fortune; eight years later, she ignores the same friend's bad advice and listens to her own heart when the officer, now successful and wealthy, renews his proposal. Caught in her social and familial web, Anne nevertheless realizes that she can, she must, resist persuasion. Her center of gravity lies within herself; her decisions are entirely her own.

The character who initially lacks full access to her own psyche, yet gradually learns to know herself, understand her role in the world, and act accordingly, would be developed further by Dickens, George Eliot, and Thomas Hardy, whose novels emphasize both life's social dimension and the autonomy of the individual. More generally, the depiction of characters who move beyond inadequacy and hesitation toward a full

---

[3] Jane Austen, *Emma*, ed. Stephen M. Parrish (New York: Norton, 1972), vol. 1, chap. 3, p. 14.

knowledge and acceptance of themselves is a major achievement of the nineteenth-century English novel.

Although it was Jane Austen who first created such characters, the importance of her oeuvre was not understood until late in the nineteenth century, when—once the strong, explicit emphasis on social and historical factors had lost some of its appeal—small, internalized conflicts, ordinary milieus, the interplay of empathy and critical distance, and questions of self-knowledge, persuasion, and attention to others became central issues for the novel. It is all the more astonishing, given the importance of her contribution, that even those who praised Austen often expressed vague reservations. Henry James, for instance, who belongs to the same artistic family, thought the general regard for her art somewhat exceeded its real value. James was comparing Austen to other great nineteenth-century writers, like Balzac, and regretted that she did not choose a vaster stage and more dramatic conflicts. Needless to say, such regret signaled a failure to understand some of Austen's most important artistic ends.

EQUANIMITY AND CONTEMPT: FLAUBERT

Since Fielding, the adversaries of idealist novels had faced a major challenge: to avoid overidealizing characters, they had to emphasize their flaws, but in order not to draw mere caricatures, they had to make them at least partly attractive. While the dosage of irony and sympathy could certainly vary from one writer to the next (more sympathy in Stendhal's novels, more irony in Thackeray's), the simultaneous presence of both attitudes was felt to be necessary. What is more, in order to make them both clearly perceptible, anti-idealist writers for a long time adopted Fielding's method of keeping characters at a distance from which their behavior could be measured and judged. The characters' monologues in Stendhal, for instance, relentlessly remind the reader that their point of view is not entirely reliable. Only the author knows all the facts and everyone's true worth; only the author, through subtle allusions, lets the reader guess whether the character's weaknesses should be deplored or excused, and whether the sight of human imperfection calls for tears or laughter. Understated as they are, the author's interventions are nevertheless indispensable. They give the story its moral equilibrium.

In the first half of the nineteenth century, these basic requirements of anti-idealism—the need to view characters with a mixture of sympathy and suspicion, and the importance given to the author—were affected by two changes made by its rival, the idealist approach. First, for the sake of plausibility, idealist authors toned down their characters' perfection either by alluding to their painful mistakes in the past (Benassis in Balzac's *The Country Doctor*) and the present (Jean Valjean in Hugo's *Les*

Misérables), or by portraying them as too timid (Oliver Twist), too impulsive (Montriveau in *The Duchess of Langeais*), too imprudent (Dantès in Dumas's *Count of Monte Cristo*), or too indecisive (Arthur Clennam in *Little Dorrit*). Readers were thus invited to moderate their instinctive enthusiasm for these fallible characters and adopt a point of view both critical and sympathetic. As a result, none of these figures inspires the unconditional awe the reader is expected to feel for Richardson's Clarissa. Second, given that idealism, thanks to Walter Scott, had begun to rely on clear theories of history and society, Scott's disciples felt obliged to take the floor and lecture the reader about the period and social system that had shaped their characters. Authorial digressions became part and parcel of idealist novels, and Scott, Balzac, Dickens, and Hugo all indulged in them.

A double temptation thus arose for the opponents of nineteenth-century moral idealism. Since idealism now specialized in characters with a mixture of virtues and faults, the anti-idealists began to overemphasize people's imperfect, contemptible side. The kind, indulgent irony of Fielding and his followers gradually turned to coldness, then repugnance. And since authorial digressions were now entrenched in idealist novels, anti-idealism minimized the presence of the author, focusing on the characters' own perceptions. Just as Richardson, a century earlier, had found greatness in the humblest people, and attentively described their surroundings and their most intimate thoughts and feelings, in the second half of the nineteenth century the challengers of narrative idealism devoted their talents to portraying the least glamorous members of society and their immediate life experience. The difference is that instead of exalting the inner beauty of humble characters, these novels directed the reader's attention toward their weakness and mediocrity.

Flaubert's approach was the most effective. In his novels, instead of the laughable but sometimes lovable characters Fielding and Stendhal described with such verve, Flaubert examined dull, pedestrian types. His contempt for them, never explicitly formulated, is barely perceptible in the calm, steady narration, which presents the action through a multiplicity of material and psychological details. Reading Flaubert's novels requires patience and a kind of moral equanimity, a readiness to suspend all judgment for a while, but the final effect is powerful: out of the imperturbable seriousness of the presentation, a condescending irony emerges, meant to debunk all illusions about public and private life.

Three aspects of Flaubert's art have been particularly influential: the strong opposition to idealism, the blatant moral weakness of the characters, and the technique of sensory and cognitive immersion in the novel's world. Flaubert's contemporaries were struck by this immersive technique, his meticulous description of the surroundings and his use of dialogue to portray characters rather than move the action forward. "The details are counted one by one, with the same warmth. Each street, each house, each rivulet, each blade of grass is fully described! Each character, arriving on stage, first speaks about a multitude of useless, uninteresting things that only serve to reveal his degree of intelligence," wrote Louis-Edmond Duranty, the leader of the realist school in France, exasperated to find in *Madame Bovary* "the masterpiece of obstinate description, but without emotion, feeling, or life."[4] Others claimed that Flaubert's method consisted in imitating the objectivity of science, turning the pen into a scalpel, invention into dissection. In fact Flaubert was less interested in emulating the impersonality of science (as Zola would later do) than in establishing as many links as possible between his characters and their social and historical environment. His originality lies in the unprecedented accuracy of his portrayal of milieus and customs, drawn from the point of view of the characters and aptly suggesting their feelings. Thus the inner life Flaubert evokes does not comprise simply hopes, projects, and deliberations: it includes a mass of impressions, sometimes placed at the center of the character's consciousness, but often barely touching its fringes.

Here is how Flaubert describes Emma Bovary's state of mind after she gives herself to Rodolphe, the local seducer, in a forest near the town where she lives:

> All was silent; a mellow sweetness seemed to be coming from the trees; she could feel her heart beginning to beat again and the blood flowing through her body like a river of milk. Then she heard, in the distance, from the other side of the wood, on those other hills, a vague, long-drawn-out cry, a voice that seemed to linger in the air, and she listened to it in silence, as it blended like a melody with the last vibrations of her tingling nerves.[5]

The lyrical tone is the narrator's, since obviously Emma is not telling herself, "My blood flows through my body like a river of milk." It is the stylist who conjures up the silent torpor that numbs Emma, and who gives voice to her nonlinguistic experience. Incorporating the silent life of the psyche, the passage goes beyond a mere evocation of Emma's inner deliberations.

---

[4] René Dumesnil quotes this passage in his introduction to *Madame Bovary*, in Gustave Flaubert, *Oeuvres*, ed. Albert Thibaudet and R. Dumesnil (Paris: Gallimard, Bibliothèque de la Pléiade, 1951), pp. 281–282 (my translation).

[5] Gustave Flaubert, *Madame Bovary*, trans. Margaret Mauldon (Oxford: Oxford World Classics, 2004), pt. 2, chap. 9, p. 143.

This approach is usually indifferent to the fate of the characters, but one can occasionally detect a sense of concern in Flaubert's novels, either because the author feels genuine compassion or because his pity is a form of condescension. Besides, since his characters' behavior is far from exemplary, Flaubert needs to minimize the distance between them and the reader, not unlike the picaresque authors who framed their stories as first-person confessions to make the protagonists' wickedness palatable. This is why Flaubert devotes so much energy to the description of dreamlike states and inner sensations. Back home after sleeping with Rodolphe, Emma revels in the thought that she now has a lover:

> She was entering a magical realm where life would be all passion, ecstasy, rapture. A bluish immensity surrounded her, lofty heights of emotion glittered brightly in her imagination, while ordinary existence still continued only far, far away, down below, in the shadowy emptiness between those peaks. (p. 144)

This second sentence, which at first sight seems to represent the character's thoughts, is in fact couched in the narrator's language. As in the previous passage, it is not Emma Bovary who tells herself, "A bluish immensity surrounds me, etc." (which makes the sentence very different from Austen's use of free indirect discourse to reproduce her characters' articulate thoughts); it is the narrator who formulates the *silent* rapture and joy that sets Emma's psyche aglow. The poetic description of Emma's inner landscape thaws the cold relations between reader and character, as though daydreaming were the only thing that could redeem this lonely woman.

Considered more carefully, however, Emma's daydreaming, far from speaking in her favor, indicts her. Rather like other nineteenth-century writers interested in the historical past, faraway cultures, and the virtues of the lower classes, Flaubert adheres to what could be called the "law of distance": modern bourgeois society constitutes the epicenter of moral mediocrity, and both grandeur and innocence blossom in direct proportion to the characters' distance (social, geographical, historical) from it. Neither the provincial milieu in which Emma Bovary vegetates nor Frédéric Moreau's Paris in *Sentimental Education* could possibly accommodate the moral strength of a character like Flaubert's protagonist in *Salammbô* (1862)—an ancient Carthaginian warrior princess straight out of a late nineteenth-century opera—or the naive generosity of Félicité, the humble servant in *A Simple Heart* (1877).

But while other writers sensitive to the world's historical and social differentiation believed in some form of progress (Scott) that would allow noble hearts to triumph even in the modern world (Balzac, Dickens) while respectfully learning from the wisdom of older, faraway societies (Fenimore Cooper, Tolstoy), Flaubert is utterly convinced that his contemporaries cannot escape the curse of modern, bourgeois France. There is no exit from its mediocrity. As a result, its inhabitants, controlled by a system whose operation they do not understand, pursue exhausting, senseless aims. Emma's daydreaming, the reader gradually realizes, is nothing but a hopeless effort to imagine happiness.

The rejection of imaginary happiness is crucial to Flaubert's struggle against idealism. *Madame Bovary* targets love as portrayed in sentimental literature. At the convent school where Emma spends her adolescence, an old maid from an aristocratic family ruined by the Revolution lends the girls novels about

> love affairs, lovers and their beloveds, damsels in distress swooning in secluded summerhouses, postilions slain at every posting-house, horses ridden to death on every page, gloomy forests, wounded hearts, vows, sobs, tears, and kisses, gondolas by moonlight, nightingales in woods, and 'gentlemen' brave as lions, meek as lambs, unbelievably virtuous, always immaculately turned out, who weep buckets of tears. Emma spent six months breathing the dust of old lending libraries. (pt. 1, chap. 6, p. 34)

Walter Scott also gets a mention—hardly more respectful—for having filled young Emma's head with futile nostalgia:

> Later, with Walter Scott, she became enthralled by things historical and would dream of oaken chests, guardrooms, and minstrels. She would have liked to live in some old manor house, like those ladies in long-waisted gowns who, leaning chin in hand on the stone ledge of a window, spent their days gazing from beneath its trefoil arch at a white-plumed cavalier, mounted on a black steed, riding towards them from the distant horizon. (p. 34)

Later in life, Emma attends a performance of *Lucia di Lammermoor*, Donizetti's operatic adaptation of Scott's novel, and, remembering the books she used to read in her youth, she laments her fate and smugly imagines herself in a different, novel-like life:

> Ah! If only, in the full bloom of her loveliness, before the defilement of marriage and the disillusion of adultery, she had been able to root her life in the firmness of some noble heart, then virtue, tenderness, sensual pleasure, and wifely duty would have all fused into one, and never would she have fallen from so lofty a pinnacle of happiness. (pt. 2, chap. 15, p. 199)

By now she has enough experience to understand that this "happiness must surely be a fraud, devised for the despair of all desire. Now she knew how paltry were those passions that art portrays with such hyperbole" (pp. 199–200). Yet she will play this comedy for her new lover, the young Léon, who sees in her "the beloved of every novel, the heroine of every drama, the vague *she* of every volume of poetry" (pt. 3, chap. 5, p. 235).

Sentimental Education also dismisses the idea of love as revelation. When Frédéric Moreau sees Mme Arnoux for the first time, she seems to come from a romantic novel. In the grip of a powerful emotion, Frédéric senses that the closed doors of the world are opening up:

> His world had suddenly grown bigger. She was the point of light on which all things converged; and lulled by the movement of the carriage, his eyelids half closed, his gaze wandering among the clouds, he drifted into infinite, dreamy joy.[6]

In reality, only the tender, lighthearted Rosanette, whom he despises, will offer Frédéric any happiness.

Illusions are just as harmful in public life, whether those of a zealous state or, in revolutionary times, an overexcited citizenry. Political stupidity, even more ridiculous than the erotic kind, makes use of the same vague dreams, commonplaces, and empty images. Here is Frédéric asking himself, after the revolution of 1848, whether he should run in the next elections:

> The great figures of the Convention [of 1792] passed before his eyes. It seemed to him that a magnificent dawn was about to break. Rome, Vienna, and Berlin were in revolt; the Austrians had been driven out of Venice; the whole of Europe was in a ferment. Now was the time for him to throw himself into the movement, perhaps to help it forward; and then he was attracted by the uniform which people said the deputies were going to wear. He already saw himself in a waistcoat with lapels and a tricolour sash. (pt. 3, chap. 1, p. 322)

Like Emma Bovary fantasizing about personal happiness, Frédéric imagines himself as a handsome actor on the scene of history, an evening-dressed participant in the redemption of Europe.

While in Fielding and Austen flawed characters usually grow to understand their faults and find the right path, in Flaubert they become more

---

[6] Flaubert, *Sentimental Education*, trans. Robert Baldick, rev. Geoffrey Wall (London: Penguin Books, 2004), pt. 1, chap. 1, p. 13.

and more deficient. Life here is not a true *Bildung*, a process of education that brings together individual aspirations and society's requirements: instead of forming individuals, it *deforms* them. Discovering the vacuity of moral ideals, Flaubert's characters accept their own inadequacy. Emma Bovary believes for a while that she might escape the conjugal prison and experience sublime love. She soon understands that true love is nowhere to be found, and adultery—with its lies, compromises, and financial irregularities—is the only consolation she can hope for. In *Sentimental Education*, Frédéric Moreau, having made a mess of his life, painfully comforts himself with memories of his youth. In the unfinished novel that bears their names, Bouvard and Pécuchet try to master a number of domains of knowledge, but fail and abandon their quest.

Nevertheless, the characters' decay is not always complete: sometimes these moral invalids are allowed a moment of strength and dignity. In *Sentimental Education,* Mme Arnoux, repulsed by her husband's corruption, is at last ready to respond to Frédéric Moreau's long-standing, passionate love. Her son, however, falls seriously ill, and, taking this as a providential warning, she decides to fulfill her marital duty. Righteousness wins out. Deeply hurt, Frédéric Moreau becomes the lover of Mme Dambreuse, the wife of a fabulously wealthy businessman. When M. Dambreuse dies, she offers Frédéric her hand, and he accepts, seduced by the prospect of a luxurious life. It soon becomes apparent that M. Dambreuse has disinherited his widow, though she does have her own fortune, less spectacular but quite sufficient. Disappointed, Frédéric still does not change his mind. In the meantime, the Arnoux family is ruined and all their goods are put up for auction. Mme Dambreuse, who attends the sale with Frédéric, wants to buy a little jewel box that belonged to Mme Arnoux and reminds him of her. Although he warns Mme Dambreuse to leave the box alone, she keeps raising the bidding and wins the precious object. "Frédéric felt his heart turn cold" (pt. 3, chap. 5, p. 447); on the spur of the moment, he breaks off their engagement. "His first reaction was one of joy at having regained his independence. He was proud of having avenged Mme Arnoux, by sacrificing a fortune to her, then he was astonished at what he had done and an infinite weariness overwhelmed him" (p. 448). Frédéric's action is prompted by a noble impulse, but does it count as a sign of moral energy? The young man does not really love Mme Dambreuse, and the disappointment of her husband's will may also have contributed, imperceptibly, to his decision. Yet he has acted generously; his moral instinct has prevailed. True love and dignity, untouched by romantic pathos, do flicker for a moment now and then in the psyche.

Many of Flaubert's contemporaries understandably thought his message immoral. Yet, as Barbey d'Aurevilly, one of the best early critics to discuss *Madame Bovary*, wrote, "Monsieur Flaubert is too intelligent not to have within himself a firm notion of good and evil; but he refers to them so little that one is tempted to believe that he lacks them, and this is why, at the first reading of his book, he was so loudly accused of immorality—really, a calumny" (quoted by R. Dumesnil, introduction, p. 287, my translation). Mᵉ Sénard's speech for the defense in Flaubert's trial—the charge was *Madame Bovary*'s offense against public decency—made the same assertion: "Monsieur Flaubert is the author of a good book, a book that stimulates virtue by the horror of vice" (Flaubert, *Oeuvres*, 1, p. 668, my translation). The lawyer's statement may sound bombastic, but his point is valid. Flaubert's novels belong to the skeptical, anti-idealist tradition: one perceives in them the sad irony of an author who rejects the idealist illusion while nonetheless quietly defending the small yet real possibility of human decency.

The Philosophy of the Future and the Misery of the Present

Presumably owing to the influence of historical circumstances, the most pessimistic version of narrative anti-idealism was born in France under the Second Empire and bloomed after the Franco-Prussian War of 1870, the fall of the empire, and the repression of the Commune of Paris. The period of relative prosperity under the Second Empire and the gradual success of the Third Republic founded in 1871 witnessed a rich production of new novels that painted contemporary society in the darkest colors. Social and political factors—uneven, painful economic growth, the shock of the French defeat in 1870, the political difficulties of the early Third Republic—played a role, but we cannot fully understand the prevailing narrative pessimism without taking into account the interaction between the novel as a genre and the various views of history proposed during the nineteenth century.

Earlier we saw that writers who believed in strong links between human action and its social and historical context initially supported a *gently progressive* view of history. Walter Scott believed in an evolution that called for peaceful virtues as it gradually made violence and war obsolete. His martial characters embody the values of older times; the wiser, nonviolent ones herald the future. Writers who subscribed to this optimistic view, however, needed to come to terms with something eighteenth-century philosophers of history had failed to foresee: the French Revolution, followed by more than twenty years of European wars. By 1815 it was perhaps still possible for Scott, born in 1771, to consider the preceding decades no more than an accident, a passing return to archaic ways. Benjamin Constant, born in 1767, thought along the same lines, at least in his political philosophy.

For others, including Hegel (born in 1770), the French Revolution, far from being an exception, represented a necessary violent explosion, which had the providential task of establishing peace forever by bringing about the end of history. Balzac's *Human Comedy* (but not his explicit political commentaries) and Stendhal's novels to some extent converged with Hegel's view. They portray a dynamic world in which heroism plays a major part and the desire for social promotion is entirely legitimate. Progress, both writers imply, has been costly, painful, but worth the effort.

Yet soon after Hegel assumed that the recent bloody conflicts in Europe led to the triumph of the World Spirit, his disciple Karl Marx argued that the French Revolution and its sequels, far from establishing an everlasting peace, had only secured the power of the bourgeoisie and its own version of injustice and conflict. The final struggle, still to be waged, destined to bring a stable happiness, would be a worldwide *proletarian revolution*. In Marx's view, Balzac was a lucid critic of bourgeois society, discerning its flaws and contradictions, and Hugo and Dickens somehow sensed the revolutionary future.

Auguste Comte developed an alternative view, predicting the inevitable victory of positive science, which would replace religion and philosophy as the leading human endeavor. According to Comte, humanity was moving inexorably toward an enlightened, *scientific future*. Hume and his eighteenth-century friends were gentle optimists, and one can detect a dose of excitement in Hegel's views, but Marx and Comte were unabashed enthusiasts.

Pessimism had its own great defender in Arthur Schopenhauer, whose philosophy describes human life as ruled by the Will, a cosmic force that generates endless conflict and suffering. All human actions throughout history are embodiments of the Will, and as such cannot but perpetuate discord and anguish. The only possible escape from the reign of the Will is to keep one's distance from the world's folly and feel concern for its victims. *Withdrawal and compassion* offer an answer to the challenge of history. Published in 1818–1819, when Schopenhauer was thirty years old, his *The World as Will and Representation* would become influential only much later, after the publication of *Parerga und Paralipomena* (1851), a collection of his reader-friendly essays and aphorisms.

In the second half of the nineteenth century, anti-idealist writers could justify their low opinion of contemporary society in two ways. Those who shared Marx's and Comte's faith in a brighter future condemned the present severely. For those reluctant to believe in historical redemption, Schopenhauer's views offered a seductive way of saying no to the world. In France, Flaubert, who discovered him only after writing his major novels, was deeply impressed by the convergence between the German philosopher's thought and his own; Schopenhauer was admired and followed by Guy de Maupassant, and would later have a decisive influence on Marcel Proust. Schopenhauer's pessimism and compassion also reverberate in Thomas Hardy's novels in England, and Theodor Fontane's in Germany.

The Goncourt brothers (Edmond de Goncourt and Jules de Goncourt) and Émile Zola followed in Comte's footsteps: the world's ugliness, they thought, had scientific explanations, and its future salvation, at least in Zola's view, would come from scientific progress. The Goncourt brothers examined the sway physical drives hold over moral action (*Germinie Lacerteux*, 1865), and the mind's inability to keep up a fight against the flesh (*Madame Gervaisais*, 1869). Zola drew his inspiration from Darwinian theory and from the laws of heredity formulated in France by the doctor Prosper Lucas. Social and historical determinism was now coupled with a much more restrictive biological kind; Zola claimed that his novels' object of study was human *nature* in the scientific sense of the term. Chosen by Zola and his friends to advertise their program, the label "naturalism" was a sign of their remarkable self-confidence.

Naturalists were certain that while individuals have little access to their own psyche and its true motivations, human behavior, governed by heredity and society, can be fully explained in social and biological terms. If the novel would adopt a scientific methodology, Zola claimed, it could become experimental. By selecting a set of initial data for purely scientific reasons, and by following the laws of biology and society, a writer could develop an infallibly true plot and, if the topic were well chosen, throw new light on less familiar aspects of the human condition. Bypassing moral psychology, this method targeted nature alone and aimed to study "temperament not character," as Zola explained in the preface to the second edition of his *Thérèse Raquin* (1867):

> Thérèse and Laurent are human animals, nothing more. In these animals, I have tried to follow step by step the silent operation of desires, the urgings of instinct and the cerebral disorders consequent on a nervous crisis. . . . The reader will have started, I hope, to understand that my aim has been above all scientific.[7]

Like any science, the naturalist novel aimed to be exhaustive, and examined all kinds of human behavior, including those considered vulgar, repulsive, or obscene. In the name of scientific objectivity and

---

[7] Émile Zola, *Thérèse Raquin*, trans. Robin Buss (London: Penguin Books, 2004), p. 4.

comprehensiveness, it paid serious attention to the lower depths of the individual and of society, and especially to topics earlier narrative prose had touched on only in passing or in a comic tone.

Naturalist writers' interest in misery, degradation, and bodily functions cannot be traced back to Rabelais's scatological humor, to picaresque cynicism, to the saucy tone of some eighteenth-century comic novels, or to de Sade's frenzied obscenity. These texts defy the moral perspective, thus recognizing its existence. Zola, by contrast, advocates pure objectivity and "the serious pleasures of the search for truth." The author of the *Rougon-Macquart* (1871–1893)—a sweeping panorama of contemporary French society—is surprised to see himself accused of "having no other end than that of describing obscene pictures" (p. 4). In fact, his goal was to devote himself entirely to making a meticulous copy of life, even if it meant neglecting the humanity of his models. If he got too involved in depicting human rot, he did so the way a doctor can get too involved in a dissection. The accusation of obscenity, Zola argues, is especially unfair because it targets novels whose subject is poverty and vice—no one ever objected to the Goncourt brothers for depicting the defeat of a pure soul in *Renée Mauperin* (1864), nor to Zola's own portrayal of a faultless scientist in *Le Docteur Pascal* (1893).

Zola may have a point, but what really upset his adversaries and thrilled his admirers was not his scientific ambitions but his new way of describing the most disadvantaged sections of the population. By rejecting narrative idealism and its search for an innate human nobility, naturalism scrapped both the idea that moral worth can be found in people of any class—as Richardson and other eighteenth-century idealist writers believed—and the nineteenth-century "law of distance," which placed innocence and greatness either in the poorest social milieus or in faraway countries. Richardson's formula, and Hugo's and Sue's later treatment of social misfortune, held that the underprivileged, bursting with moral splendor, are immediately eligible for social promotion: Pamela becomes her master's wife, Jean Valjean acquires a vast fortune after his conversion to goodness, and Fleur-de-Marie moves in a flash from the urban underworld to a princely court. Works like *Germinie Lacerteux* and *L'Assommoir* (1877) refute this view. They focus on the essential ugliness of the contemporary world, showing that victims of social exclusion are just as corrupt as the privileged classes. For the Goncourt brothers and Zola, the poor deserve compassion not just because of their destitution, as Hugo and Sue believed, but also and especially because of the psychic destruction wrought by poverty. A society that creates and tolerates this state of affairs seems all the more culpable in that it not only impoverishes people, materially and morally, but also deprives them of the means to escape their degradation.

In *Germinie Lacerteux*, the protagonist is a servant who left her village as a poor orphan to seek a position in Paris. She is deeply devoted to her employer, Mlle de Varandeuil, an old spinster born before the Revolution. The memory of her unhappy days during the Terror makes Mlle de Varandeuil treat Germinie kindly. Germinie in turn feels the need to protect someone else, and pampers young Jupillon, the son of a dairy worker who lives in the same building. By indulging his caprices and later becoming his mistress, Germinie believes she is asserting her independence. But in fact she must now serve two masters: Mlle de Varandeuil, to whom she remains loyal, and Jupillon, who shamelessly exploits her. To satisfy his greed, Germinie not only gives him all her savings, but also borrows money in the neighborhood and even steals a small amount from her mistress. As though her moral difficulties were not enough, Germinie's body, roused by Jupillon, now has its own sensual needs: when he abandons her, she ends up offering herself to strange men in the street. She still loves Jupillon, and, one cold night, keeping a close watch on his comings and goings, she falls ill and dies. After Germinie's death, Mlle de Varandeuil finds out about her secret life but, remembering her devotion, forgives her.

In *Shamela*, Fielding argued that a servant could not possibly be sincere and virtuous; similarly, the Goncourt brothers show that by its very nature the servile condition encourages corruption and duplicity. But unlike Shamela, Germinie is a tragic figure. Her tragedy, moreover, is depressingly modern, since, as the authors emphasize, her despair is not redeemed by any sense of dignity. Germinie's desolation resembles the feeling that leads Emma Bovary to suicide: it springs from the character's conviction that her world is unjust, and utterly resistant to hope or the desire for happiness. In such a world, people are not simply defeated; they are subjected to a humiliation that has no cure. This tragedy not only lacks a redemptive horizon, it takes place at an inframoral level: Germinie's love for an undeserving man turns into nymphomania. Degrading love—a theme already treated by Prévost in *Manon Lescaut* and revisited many times in the nineteenth century—is here linked with Germinie's social position. Confined in her mistress's home, she cannot look around carefully for someone worthy of her affection; accustomed to obeying, she cannot free herself from a demeaning relationship and uncontrollable sexual impulses. The power of these urges shows how servitude can prevent people from taking charge of their own lives. If someone is kept at society's lowest level, and never has an opportunity to influence others, then nothing prepares her to rule over herself.

These complex, defenseless beings, pitiful victims of social and biological forces, proliferate in Zola's novels. The work that made him famous, *L'Assommoir* (*The Grog Shop*, 1877), is about the lives of Parisian proletarians and their failed attempts to escape their condition. The main character, Gervaise, is a laundress, whose energy, tenderness, and inability to do well gradually emerge as we follow her business deals, her marriages, her successes, and her mistakes. Three men move around her: her first husband, Lantier, a skirt-chaser; her second, Coupeau, a plumber who becomes a lazy alcoholic after a work accident leaves him an invalid; and finally the honest Goujet, a blacksmith who loves and respects her. Gervaise follows the rules for a long time, remaining honorable and diligent. Yet fate has placed her in the heart of the urban jungle, in the working-class neighborhoods of northern Paris, full of hungry, hardened people. Gervaise has plenty of enemies irked by her vitality, including Virginie, Lantier's mistress and later his second wife, and a variety of mean, envious neighbors. Gervaise seems on her way to social success when she opens her own laundry shop, but things go wrong when, to assert her new status in the neighborhood, she and Coupeau start giving frequent, expensive dinners at home. Coupeau slowly becomes stupefied with drink; Gervaise's first husband, Lantier, reappears and seduces her; she neglects her shop and loses her customers. Decay is inevitable: Gervaise's daughter Nana turns out badly, Coupeau is put in a mental hospital, and Gervaise, reduced to selling her body, dies in utter destitution. The young woman who was once so different from her milieu ends up completely corrupted by it.

Individual feelings, reflections, and behavior depend heavily on the environment. After Coupeau's accident, Gervaise dedicates herself to her wounded, depressed husband not so much because she *decides* to do so as because her psyche, in silent contact with the world, compels her:

> Her hubby had broken his right leg; everyone knew that; it would be put right, that was all there was to it. As for the rest, the broken heart-strings, that was nothing. She'd mend his heart for him. She knew all about mending hearts, with care, and cleanliness, and unvarying devotion.[8]

Unthinking solidarity, however, turns out to hide a terrible trap. Coupeau begins to drink, influenced by friends he has no idea how to resist, and Gervaise, unusually weak, lets him do whatever he wants. Later, when Lantier comes back, the ménage à trois works out effortlessly, as the characters' interests and instincts seem to converge. Gervaise has an inkling of her true position: "Yes, Coupeau and Lantier were using her up, that's the right word, burning her at both ends like a candle" (p. 286). Yet she puts up with it because the others' desires run through her, become her

---

[8] Émile Zola, *L'Assommoir*, trans. Margaret Mauldon (Oxford: Oxford World Classics, 1995), chap. 4, p. 117.

own: "Then she'd reflect that things might have turned out even worse. For example, it was better to have two men than to lose your two arms. And, feeling her situation to be natural and not at all unusual, she did her best to find a modest measure of happiness in it" (p. 287). Her devotion to the two men continues, and when Coupeau, suffering from delirium tremens, is confined to the mental hospital, Gervaise, far from being repelled, wants to guess what is going on in her husband's body: "Seeing the doctors put their hands on her old man's torso, Gervaise wanted to touch him herself. She went quietly up to him and put her hand on his shoulder. She left it there for a minute. Lord! Whatever was going on inside there?" (p. 437).

In Zola's world, characters who refuse to participate in this interpenetration of desires and instincts are denounced as nasty and mean, like Gervaise's neighbors. Those who let themselves be carried along by it, however, are eventually destroyed by the prevailing corruption. People who obsessively protect themselves are deemed evil, but those who open themselves up to their fellow human beings go down with them. Protected only by egoism, avarice, and cruelty—the bourgeois vices—people break down if they practice the opposite virtues. Zola sees the individual as, in the worst case, the site of resistance to the good and, in the best case, that of nonresistance to evil. Mere cells in the tissue of society, individuals cannot pursue their own ideals, not because of some metaphysical imperfection, but simply because their role is to join in community life, to mix with their fellow human beings in a deep, intimate fusion. For Zola it is not enough to reject narrative idealism and defend a more balanced view of the links between individuals and moral norms; he also rejects individualism, and sees society as the only meeting point between moral norms and reality. As his later novel *Germinal* (1885) would attempt to show, the collectivity is the true, the only carrier of ideals.

Pushed to its limits, this interest in human imperfection combined with social and historical determinism leads to an unusually dark view of life. Yet the hope of a better society is always present—a society that, guided by science (as in *Le Docteur Pascal*, 1893), might reconcile labor with collective solidarity.

THE SCHOOL OF EMPATHY, II

It was quite late in the nineteenth century when Jane Austen's discoveries—the plot based on everyday interactions in small communities, the careful notation of the smallest changes in the characters' opinions about themselves and others—started being put to use by other novelists, particularly Henry James.

The difficulty of reading one's own and other people's impulses, desires, and motivations had been treated in a serious, even a tragic manner in the past as well. But for a long time, this sort of fundamental incomprehension was presented as a sad, sometimes terrifying *exception* to the rule. Once novels granted a new dignity to everyday life and its most common, humble concerns, the difficulty of understanding oneself and one's fellow human beings in *ordinary* situations began to be taken quite seriously; the most trivial secrets of the people who surround us thus acquired an alarming dimension.

An additional factor exacerbates the dangers of misreading oneself or others. In a world in which moral norms and ideals are assumed to be generally shared (as is the case in Fielding's novels), or in a milieu narrow enough to ensure homogeneity of values (like that portrayed by Jane Austen), an inability to understand other people usually betrays immaturity, ill will, or the kind of blindness caused by vanity. But if the characters who populate a novel's world belong to different social milieus or nations and consequently observe dissimilar norms, a difficulty in grasping someone else's thoughts and reasons for acting ceases to be an individual fault and takes, so to speak, an objective form. In an unfamiliar situation, the most open, modest, and benevolent person risks making mistakes, simply by failing to master others' rules of behavior.

But how does one learn these rules? In earlier literature, the maxims that govern the life of a social or ethnic community were assumed to be easy to access, both for members of the community and for those observing it from outside. One knew that bad people did not hesitate to lie, cheat, or steal, and that each nation had its own features—the Spanish were proud, the Italians unfathomable, and the French capricious. This rudimentary anthropology was supposed to explain the diversity of moral behavior: if one could identify an individual's origin and profession, one could account for his or her actions.

Going one step further, Walter Scott's method emphasized how difficult it is for a foreigner to grasp the way a given community functions. When unexpected circumstances place Edward Waverley among the Highlanders, rather than learn a list of explicit rules, he silently assimilates a set of routines that at first seem mysterious. Similarly, Olenin in Tolstoy's *The Cossacks* attempts to get to grips with the villagers' mores, but each of his hypotheses is refuted by facts: the Cossack way of life cannot be easily captured.

Foreign customs, though, are by no means the most difficult case. As unusual as they seem to Waverley and Olenin, the rules observed by the Highlanders and the Cossacks apply to all members of the community. The situation becomes much more complex when the differences between two communities are less evident, and still more so when not all members of a community follow the general rule. It is this kind of situation that interests Henry James.

His novels, like Austen's, focus on a narrow social milieu, emphasizing the moral weight of everyday concerns. Like many nineteenth-century writers, James reflects on the diversity of cultural customs, but in his novels the cultures at odds are *near* one another. Moreover, James insists on something that earlier writers, for some reason, never portrayed: the tacit, inexpressible character of moral norms. He uses empathy and free indirect discourse to evoke the complexities of the psyche *directly*, as it were, without the mediation of moral vocabulary. Is this the choice of a late nineteenth-century author who wanted to display his originality, or is it a sign that around that time something new and unexpected happened to the way people understood and explained their behavior? The question goes beyond the scope of this book, but it deserves to be raised: in his *Henry James and Modern Moral Life*[9] Robert Pippin argues for the second possibility.

Like Austen's plots, James's lack adventure and suspense. His novels progress at a very slow pace: his characters waver and postpone action interminably, and their conversations revolve awkwardly around unclear goals without ever seeming to reach them. Gradually, however, the reader understands that this universe made of infinitesimal moves and barely visible reactions is vibrating with anxieties. The protagonist of James's early novella *Daisy Miller* (1878) is a young American woman who visits Europe. Coming from a family of nouveaux riches, Daisy has only contempt for the conventions of good society, and so the American community in Rome rejects her. Only Frederick Winterbourne, half in love with her, hopes she will turn out to be a respectable person despite her imprudence. The decisive moments in the story seem quite inconsequential: Daisy agrees to visit the castle of Chillon with Frederick, whom she has just met; in Rome, she and the young Italian Giovanelli are seen together in the Pincio Park; and finally she spends a long evening alone at the Colosseum with Giovanelli. These faux pas scandalize the Americans in Rome, and even Frederick scolds her severely for the incident at the Colosseum. It is a lover's severity, however, and neither Winterbourne nor the reader knows whether they should agree with the expatriates who condemn Daisy, or accept her nonconformism.

Usually, love stories side with lively young people against the prudish older generation, but in this case the community's disapproval is vindicated. Giovanelli turns out to be a fortune hunter, who was seriously offended when Daisy made it clear, after they were seen together in the

---

[9] Cambridge: Cambridge University Press, 2001.

Pincio garden, that she had no intention of marrying him. He is immune to malaria, and takes revenge on Daisy by failing to warn her that she is at risk of catching it during their night at the Colosseum. The young woman falls sick and dies a few days later. The reasons for Giovanelli's behavior are not entirely clear, but it is obvious that Daisy pays no attention to the feelings of those around her and is punished accordingly. Although initially the issue involved seems minor—should one respect social proprieties, or not?—and although Daisy's transgressions have little to do with the immorality people attribute to her, the story reveals a profound truth: if we abandon conventional, impersonal morality, we must replace it with a keen attention and sensitivity to everybody around us.

Yet this heightened awareness of other people's actions and intentions, a feature James's Americans generally lack, is not always something he presents in approving terms. Usually the refined and corrupt residents of Old Europe—Italian, French, and a few expatriate Americans—are the ones who master the art of deciphering people's psyches, identifying their vulnerable spots. Like Daisy Miller, Isabel Archer, in *The Portrait of a Lady* (1880–1881), is unable to fathom the nature and motivations of those she encounters. (Nor are we, the readers, I should add, allowed to fathom hers.) Though courted by two successful young men, a wealthy American and an English lord, Isabel prefers the much older Gilbert Osmond—an expatriate widower with a young daughter—whom she meets in Italy through Mme Merle, a French friend. Seduced by Osmond's elegance and detachment, Isabel realizes only after the wedding that he is a failure who has married her for her money, and worse, that it was planned by Mme Merle, who turns out to be the mother of his teenage daughter. More emphatically than in *Daisy Miller*, James associates American sincerity with a lack of insight, and portrays Mme Merle's and Osmond's intelligence as a form of cynicism. Yet Isabel Archer's final decision not to break up with Osmond remains enigmatic: is it pride, compassion for him, concern for the teenager who is now her stepdaughter? Difficult to know. James's characters have their center of gravity within themselves, and it moves silently.

In the culture clash James describes, it is hard for Americans living in Europe to avoid the traps of a civilization older than theirs, precisely because, in theory, Americans and Continentals value the same qualities, uprightness, intelligence, manners, and good taste; the differences—more uprightness among the Americans, a bit more taste among Europeans—seem mere nuances that would cause minimal conflict. Notably, the conflict that does ensue has a different orientation from the one experienced by Edward in *Waverley* and Olenin in *The Cossacks*. While Walter Scott's and Tolstoy's characters try to adapt to archaic customs, going through a "regressive" culture shock, James's Americans, in whose eyes the Old

Continent harbors a civilization more mature than theirs, experience a
"progressive" one. And since in Europe they are trying to adapt to more
civilized customs than their own, these Americans cannot simply pack
their bags and leave. They cannot tell themselves, as Edward Waverley
and Olenin do, that their life at home, with all its imperfections, nevertheless represents a more advanced civilization. For them, returning
home would mean accepting a cultural defeat. Moreover, the difference
between American and Continental customs—the latter resembling a set
of infinitesimal progressions from the former—is so difficult to capture
and couch in precise terms that the culture shock is felt as both an irresistible attraction and a hazy, strange discomfort.

These are Lambert Strether's feelings. In *The Ambassadors* (1903),
written in James's late, ever more allusive style, Mrs. Newsome, a wealthy,
domineering American widow, sends her friend and suitor Strether to
Paris with instructions to bring her son Chadwick back to Massachu-
setts. Once in Paris, Strether discovers the unexpected pleasures of French
life and notices that Chad has evolved into a distinguished, self-assured
person who has no interest in returning home. Strether also meets the
elegant Mme de Vionnet, who has decisively influenced Chad's manners
and tastes. Gradually realizing how refined Chad's new life is—and how
morally corrupt, for Mme de Vionnet turns out to be his lover—Strether
gives up his attempts to bring the young man back to his mother and, at
the same time, renounces the project of marrying her.

There is virtually no action in the novel, which, rather than a sequence
of adventures, traces a moral discovery. But even this discovery remains
elusive, barely discernible. The reader never learns what Strether or
Chad thinks or how they arrive at their certainties and perplexities. The
characters not only lack a well-defined moral vocabulary but seem not
to need one. After a series of incredibly vague exchanges during which
they watch each other closely (and also watch themselves as though they
barely knew who they were), the characters reach a few instinctive conclusions. These conclusions are never formulated explicitly, and yet their
force and accuracy is astounding.

At the beginning of book 4, for instance, Strether hastily declares to
Chad that he wants to persuade him to return to the United States as
soon as possible. His words have

> an effect at first positively disconcerting to himself alone. For Chad's receptive
> attitude was that of a person who had been gracefully quiet while the messen-
> ger at last reaching him has run a mile through the dust. During some seconds
> after he had spoken Strether felt as if *he* had made some such exertion; he was
> not even certain that the perspiration wasn't on his brow. It was the kind of
> consciousness for which he had to thank the look that, while the strain lasted,

the young man's eyes gave him. They reflected—and the deuce of the thing was that they reflected really with a sort of shyness of kindness—his momentarily disordered state; which fact brought on in its turn for our friend the dawn of a fear that Chad might simply "take it out"—take everything out—in being sorry for him. Such a fear, any fear, was unpleasant. But everything was unpleasant; it was odd how everything had suddenly turned so.[10]

The passage describes Strether's discomfort after delivering his message, his fear that perhaps his intervention is entirely out of place given the distance—suddenly obvious—that separates him from the young man. James evokes these feelings without naming them and concentrates instead on the interlocutors' silent face-to-face. The passage is narrated from Strether's point of view, yet without the use of free indirect discourse: empathy here consists not just in guessing and reproducing the character's articulate thoughts, or in evoking silent, solitary emotions, as Flaubert does, but in going one step further, catching a glimpse of the character's perceptions, feelings, and states of mind during his interaction with another human being. When, for instance, the narrator notices that Chad's eyes "reflected—and the deuce of the thing was that they reflected really with a sort of shyness of kindness—his momentarily disordered state," he is describing not the eyes but rather the impression they make on Strether, and the faint shock he feels at their expression.

This respectful interest in the characters' smallest shifts in feeling during their exchanges, along with the rather unexciting nature of the underlying conflicts—a bad marriage (*The Portrait of a Lady*); an expatriate unlikely to return (*The Ambassadors*); a married man who briefly relives a youthful love (*The Golden Bowl*, 1904)—highlight the moral complications involved in some of the least noteworthy human concerns. In the passage above, Strether's shyness with Chad is that of an American freshly arrived in Europe, meeting a compatriot already familiar with French manners. Strether is so afraid of Chad's pity and contempt because he suspects he may well deserve them. In judging himself, others, and their interactions, he relies on momentary perceptions rather than clear ideas. For the heroines of eighteenth-century idealist novels, the moral law resonates audibly within the heart. In James's novels, the psyche is not expected to fully articulate its fleeting insights. This peculiar kind of *moral inarticulacy* (to use Charles Taylor's term) was to guarantee these novels' later success.

---

[10] Henry James, *The Ambassadors*, ed. Harry Levin (London: Penguin Books, 1986), p. 163.

Syntheses, High Points

||||||||||||||||||||||||||||||||||||||||||||||||||||||||||||||||||||||||

Between the partisans of idealism and their adversaries, a middle way had opened up: all through the nineteenth century, many writers continued to hear the call of the ideal but tried to keep it within the limits of plausibility. Instead of impeccable virtue, their characters display a spontaneous goodwill; rather than always conforming fully to an ideal, they slowly seek and find the right path. Innate perfection is replaced by a difficult apprenticeship, and irreproachable strength by innocence and hesitation. In the process, some noble hearts come close to mystic inspiration—even to madness.

As Franco Moretti's *Atlas of the European Novel: 1800–1900*[1] has shown, the production of new novels in the second half of the nineteenth century was almost entirely concentrated in France and England. Nevertheless, with the exception of George Eliot's and Thomas Hardy's novels, the syntheses I examine in this chapter were achieved in other cultural landscapes, where, thanks to their distance from narrative fiction's centers of production, original stands were easier to take.

The Apprenticeship of Wisdom

Earlier we saw that the ancestors of the bildungsroman can be found both in pastoral novels like Honoré d'Urfé's *Astrea* and in stories about the education of young princes or distinguished souls: Xenophon's *Cyropaedia*, Fénelon's *Adventures of Telemachus*, and Wieland's *Story of Agathon*. Wieland's novel—the first version was published in 1766–1767, the last

[1] London: Verso, 1998.

in 1794, and an epilogue was added in 1800—describes the life and travels of young Agathon, a Greek poet mentioned in Plato's dialogues, who discovers the value of various philosophical systems and their links with his own existential and intellectual experiences. On publication, *History of Agathon* was considered one of the greatest achievements of its time in German prose, and its example was followed by Karl Philipp Moritz's gripping *Anton Reiser* (1785–1790) and by Goethe's *Wilhelm Meister's Apprenticeship* (1795–1796), two stories about young men's progress toward maturity. German-speaking literary critics and historians, from Friedrich Schlegel to Georg Lukács, considered Goethe's novel in particular the founding model of the modern bildungsroman. This viewpoint is undoubtedly valid, as is Lukács's assertion that *Wilhelm Meister* resolves the dialectical clash between individual and world. Nonetheless, the fact remains that certain aspects of the book, especially its diffuse, episodic plot and neoclassicist style, are closer to the late eighteenth-century ideographic wave than to nineteenth-century novels of inner growth.

These nineteenth-century works did take advantage of Wieland's, Moritz's, and Goethe's reflections on young people's journeys to maturity, on the contrast between social appearances and reality, and on the discovery of one's individuality. Gottfried Keller's *The Green Henry* (1854–1855, final version 1879–1880) and Adalbert Stifter's *Indian Summer* (1857) continue this tradition. But many nineteenth-century novels of apprenticeship are also permeated by more recent thought on the ways in which history and society shape individual destiny. In the novels of Balzac, Dickens, and George Eliot the issue is not only the protagonists' inner development, but also their proper, satisfactory integration into their world—a world finely differentiated in historical, social, and ethnographic terms. Individual growth allows the characters to discover and accept the specific conditions that orient their life. The key word here is "specific," since in these novels the aim of apprenticeship is, on the one hand, to teach the characters how to identify their own gifts and use them in the service of a particular society—in other words, how to succeed in life—and, on the other hand, to help them understand and evaluate the other members of this society.

These aims are both important and difficult to achieve, and as a result nineteenth-century novels of apprenticeship usually convey a sense of dramatic urgency. Wieland's and Goethe's characters leisurely accumulate knowledge and experience as though they had an eternity ahead of them. In the later novels, inner growth involves encountering a small number of critical obstacles: the characters make a few decisions that commit them to a certain path in life, which is then virtually impossible to change. Wilhelm Meister's progress, like a pícaro's, takes place during a multitude of episodes, loosely linked to one another. In Dickens's *David*

Copperfield (1849–1850), however, each stage in the protagonist's life is determined by the previous ones, and each decision he makes, under pressure from society and from his own past, limits the scope of his future choices. Wilhelm Meister's *journey* is very different from David Copperfield's *destiny*.

The nineteenth-century bildungsroman imagines a new solution to the problem of narrative idealism: beautiful, strong individuals do exist, these novels tell us; we need only look around to find them. Yet their ability to adjust to their social milieu and to understand others does not come directly from Providence or from their own noble hearts, but is the result of a long process of trial and error. Mistakes help them learn, at their own cost, how to lead a good life and earn their society's respect. The right choice of career is important in reaching maturity, as David Copperfield's example shows; in addition, most nineteenth-century novels associate achieving happiness and wisdom with a strenuous search for the right romantic partner.

The difficulty of finding a soul mate to share one's life is emphasized in both *Telemachus* and *Story of Agathon*, whose male protagonists initially fall in love with women who do not quite deserve their attentions. *The New Heloise* and *Clarissa* also allude to this problem, but errors never get as far as the altar: marriage, if and when it takes place, is successful and unique. In many nineteenth-century novels of apprenticeship, however, the protagonist has an unsatisfactory first marriage, thus acquiring the wisdom that makes for a happier union the second time round. Marital bliss is still the final criterion of success, but for these nineteenth-century characters it cannot necessarily be achieved at the first attempt. David in *David Copperfield*, Dorothea in George Eliot's *Middlemarch* (1871–1872), and Pierre in Tolstoy's *War and Peace* (1869) follow this pattern, which allows the heart to be mistaken *once*, the better to seek and appreciate true happiness thereafter.

Middlemarch portrays individuals within an often demanding but never truly destructive community. The action takes place at a very specific moment: the English countryside on the eve of the Great Reform Act of 1832, which extended the franchise and redesigned electoral districts. This reform, and local efforts to improve life conditions—such as the modernization of hospital services—require a particular set of moral virtues: courage, independence, and probity. The protagonist, Dorothea Brooke, a woman at a time when women did not have the right to vote, has a mission to inspire a man with the right kind of love, a love that will motivate him to win fame by making a significant contribution to society's moral progress. She learns the importance of this role by first making an unhappy marriage and later discovering true love.

Young Dorothea marries Mr. Casaubon, a much older man, in the belief that she can help him complete an important philological work. Casaubon has spent his life gathering materials for a book intended to provide the key to the mythologies of all nations, but since he knows nothing of the recent German advances in history and philology, his research, based on obsolete methods, is actually worthless. Gradually, Dorothea realizes that her husband's book will never be finished or published, and that he is a mean, jealous authoritarian.

Dorothea and Casaubon also have a serious disagreement about his young cousin, Will Ladislaw. Long ago, Casaubon's family disinherited Will's grandmother to punish her for marrying an impoverished young Polish man. Consequently, Casaubon's share of the family inheritance increased considerably, and, to compensate for the injustice, the old scholar pays part of Will's educational expenses. Dorothea wants to do more to help the young man, and suggests to her husband that he modify his will and, instead of leaving his whole fortune to her, give half of it to Ladislaw. Casaubon refuses. Suspecting his wife of being in love with the young man, he secretly adds a codicil to cut her out if she should marry him.

Neither the old pedant's jealous refusal nor the offensive provision in his will affects Dorothea's moral fortitude. Both are misguided: although Ladislaw is indeed secretly in love with Dorothea, she is incapable of feelings that conflict with her duty; and later, after Casaubon's death, when she does begin to return the younger man's affection, the threat of the codicil cannot prevent their marriage. As Will's wife, Dorothea will no longer be merely the modest helper she was in her first marriage. Instead, she will actively inspire her new husband, who has long postponed choosing a career despite his gifts, to get involved in public life as a supporter of the Reform Act; its success will guarantee him an important place in society.

The story's feminist implications are emphasized by a secondary plot about a talented young doctor, Lydgate. He founds a new hospital at Middlemarch with the aim of reforming medical practices. Yet, believing that a wife is good only for decoration, to adorn a man's house, a bit like flowers or music, he marries Rosamond Vincy, an attractive young woman who runs up debts without his knowledge and affects to be deeply hurt in the face of any criticism. Because the debts threaten the doctor's reputation, he borrows money from a banker, Bulstrode. A few days later, when a tramp named Raffles dies in Bulstrode's house, he calls Lydgate, who signs the death certificate. It turns out, however, that Raffles has been extorting large sums from Bulstrode for a long time: the people of Middlemarch naturally conclude that Bulstrode killed Raffles and that, since Lydgate owes the banker money, he must have been his accomplice. The community shuns the doctor and Rosamond abandons him. Lydgate has paid a high price for seeing women as ornaments rather than full human beings.

What Dorothea and Lydgate understand by the end of their trials is that marriage can succeed only if it acknowledges the woman's moral role. The model George Eliot offers her female readers is not that of a great heroine, a St. Theresa of Avila, whose innate passion drove her to live a life so very different from women's marital and maternal calling. Theresa of Avila was an exception, Eliot notes, but many women who possess her qualities

> have been born who found for themselves no epic life wherein there was a constant unfolding of far-resonant action; perhaps only a life of mistakes, the offspring of a certain spiritual grandeur ill-matched with the meanness of opportunity; perhaps a tragic failure which found no sacred poet and sank unwept into oblivion.[2]

Eliot wrote her novel thinking of these unhappy Theresas "whose loving heart-beats and sobs after an unattained goodness tremble off and are dispersed among hindrances, instead of centering in some long-recognizable deed" (p. 4). Married to Ladislaw, Dorothea blossoms, but her full nature "spent itself in channels which had no great name on the earth." And yet, as the author says in the novel's last sentence, her anonymity should not be lamented:

> the effect of her being on those around her was incalculably diffusive: for the growing good of the world is partly dependent on unhistoric acts; and that things are not so ill with you and me as they might have been, is half owing to the number who lived faithfully a hidden life, and rest in unvisited tombs. (p. 822)

Few writers have better recognized the moral beauty of little-known beings, or affirmed the equivalence between public heroism and private splendor: Eliot gave novels the task of celebrating the unknown bearers of the ideal.

In Praise of Naïveté

The world Eliot imagines is populated by individuals who painfully learn to govern themselves and bolster their loved ones' moral strength and

---

[2] George Eliot, *Middlemarch*, ed. David Carroll (Oxford: Oxford World Classics, 1986), prelude, p. 3.

ambition. Born in a specific historical context, they find the freedom to act and influence the world's course. To a striking extent, Eliot's characters still display the impeccable conscience and the self-assurance of the older idealist heroines: Dorothea Brooke is probably the last great example of the type embodied by Chariclea, Pamela, Clarissa, and Julie.

At about the same time, other authors, blending the idealist view with a degree of moral uncertainty, chose to portray characters afflicted by a sort of shyness or modesty, as though confused or even shamed by their differences from other people. This is often the case in the works of Tolstoy—an author who deeply mistrusts the main tenets of narrative idealism, including the apotheosis of the individual as moral legislator, and the idea that duty is indelibly inscribed in our hearts. Particularly sensitive to the artificiality of social roles, Tolstoy believes that the place people occupy in society compels them to change their perception of reality and their behavior. This change, however, lacks the normative clarity that makes Dorothea Brooke's task such a pleasant one. Tolstoy's men and women struggle naively, awkwardly with society's impositions and with their own confusing, messy moral insights.

We have already met Olenin, protagonist of *The Cossacks*, who despises Moscow's superficial life and tries to adapt to the Cossack way of living but, failing to do so, goes back home. Yet he is not defeated: among the Cossacks, far removed from his own milieu, he learns how to lead a good life on his return. Tolstoy would develop this anthropology of distance and moral self-discovery, barely sketched in *The Cossacks*, in his later novels. In *War and Peace*, Pierre Bezukhov gradually realizes that his slowness to understand what is in his own interest is not a flaw. On the contrary, his hesitancy, by placing him at one remove from selfish considerations, creates a space of sincerity, justice, and, later, happiness around him.

Speaking of *War and Peace*, one should note, as Tolstoy himself did, that it is not exactly a novel (perhaps still less a typical nineteenth-century novel): it does not primarily focus, like most other fictional works written since the mid-eighteenth century, on the life path of a single character or group of characters; nor does it develop a coherent conflict. *War and Peace* forgoes one of the major innovations of eighteenth- and nineteenth-century novels, which blend the episodic wealth of old romances with the concentration of the novella. Lacking unity of action, *War and Peace* resembles older works, particularly those whose slow progress reflects the main character's journey to maturity (*Astrea*, *Telemachus*). It is in one sense a bildungsroman, about the trials of two characters destined for each other, Natasha Rostova and Pierre Bezukhov, whose prior entanglements prevent their marriage. They both get acquainted with several social milieus and have time to contemplate their own place in the world.

War serves as background to the action and offers Pierre an opportunity to prove his courage. Occasionally, particularly in the second half of the novel, the War of 1812 becomes the center of attention, so that *War and Peace*, like Kleist's *Michael Kohlhaas* and Walter Scott's *Waverley*, to some extent participates in the genre's nineteenth-century epic turn.

Having expended a vast amount of energy on this unusual work, Tolstoy returned to common practice and wrote *Anna Karenina* (1877), a novel that combines episodic wealth with unity of action. The main story line is organized, just like a classical novella, around a striking event: the death of an adulterous woman who throws herself under a train. But like George Eliot in *Middlemarch*, Tolstoy does not limit himself to a single plot. A second strand, about the love of Levin and Kitty, takes up the bildungsroman (and pastoral) theme of mutual discovery previously explored in Natasha and Pierre's story. And rather like Scott and Balzac, Tolstoy builds his novel around a theory of Russia's modernization.

In his view, the scourge of Russian history had been the gulf between the upper classes and the commoners. Although in the past, aristocrats had often joined the people and made considerable sacrifices to guarantee the nation's survival, they remained in thrall to western European models of civilization too remote from the ordinary Russian way of life. This does not mean that Tolstoy had revolutionary ideas; on the contrary, the solutions he favors in the novel rely on individual initiatives within the established order. His portrait of Levin's brother, an anarchist embittered by his rejection of the world, is an indictment of the professional revolutionary who, in Tolstoy's view, is as indifferent as the upper classes to the genuine needs of the poor. As for Levin himself, while aware of the existing system's imperfection and injustice, he is careful neither to draw fixed conclusions nor to propose dogmatic solutions. The young landowner's incurable perplexity, just like Pierre Bezukhov's awkwardness, is an essential aspect of the human ideal Tolstoy proposes.

Cut off from the people, the upper class is busy governing the country using methods imported from elsewhere, and showing commendable self-control in the process. Karenin, Anna's husband, is a well-mannered, worthy, dutiful man—he radiates all the qualities essential to a responsible elite. In many ways, Karenin is a true hero: he spends his life serving the public good and knows no satisfactions other than those inherent in the proper fulfillment of duty. A true modernizer, he devotes all his energies to improving the life standards of the Russian Empire's indigenous populations, though he entrusts the plan's implementation to the imperial bureaucracy, thus (Tolstoy implies) dooming it to failure. When Karenin discovers his wife's affair with an officer, Vronsky, this personal misfortune enhances his nobility and sense of duty. In particular, the birth of Anna and Vronsky's daughter awakens his generosity: he forgives his wife, makes peace with her lover, and is the only one who takes proper care of the newborn. Yet social conventions continue to hold sway over the estimable civil servant, and end up getting the better of him, especially after he is converted to a fashionable version of spiritualism.

The equally artificial role society has assigned Anna seems at first to satisfy her, but the elegant Vronsky's courtship turns her head. Does she give in merely out of caprice, or is she expressing deeper feelings? Whatever the reason, once involved, Anna is convinced that her remorse ties her indissolubly to Vronsky:

> She felt herself so criminal and guilty that the only thing left for her was to humble herself and beg forgiveness; but as she had no one else in her life now except him, it was also to him that she addressed her plea for forgiveness.[3]

And a few lines later: "'Everything is finished,' she said. 'I have nothing but you. Remember that'" (p. 150). Here, with a fervor akin to Ellénore's in *Adolphe*, she makes it clear that any atonement for adultery is bound up inextricably with a ferocious attachment to the lover. Anna's words also seem to echo the thoughts of Rousseau's Julie when, without hesitation, she gives herself to Saint-Preux. Nevertheless, the difference is striking: Julie chooses Saint-Preux as a free woman, whereas Anna is a wife and mother; Julie is in full control of herself, whereas Anna totters at every step. Tolstoy, like Benjamin Constant, coldly exposes the illusion that passionate love can free people from their social obligations.

Karenin refuses to grant Anna a divorce; she devotes herself entirely to Vronsky and leaves Russia with him. Once abroad, however, she suffers bouts of torpor and of jealousy, while Vronsky finds that "the realization of his desire had given him only a grain of the mountain of happiness he had expected" (pt. 5, chap. 8, p. 465). Overwhelmed by boredom, the lovers finally understand that the beau monde's polite artificiality is preferable to the sad truth of their love in isolation. The handsome officer and his mistress come back to Russia, where Anna incurs the contempt of high society through a series of faux pas. Vronsky, whose only desire is to regularize their situation and lead a normal life, cannot hide his disappointment. At no point, however, does he consider abandoning Anna: the final tragedy is triggered by her anxieties alone. She demands not only his absolute devotion—something Vronsky offers willingly—but also a perfect, continuous, adoring attention.

---

[3] Leo Tolstoy, *Anna Karenina*, trans. Richard Pevear and Larissa Volkhonsky (London: Penguin Books, 2003), pt. 1, chap. 11, p. 149.

This requirement, the novel seems to say, is impossible to satisfy: human beings cannot live with their gaze fixed exclusively on one person, and no one has the right to expect that kind of adulation. Anna gradually sinks into depression when she sees that Vronsky, while accepting the drop in status their life in Moscow entails, still needs a modicum of independence. She becomes obsessed with the idea that he will leave her: when she sends for him to meet her at home and he, owing to a minor hindrance, is not quick enough to comply, she commits suicide.

Levin, who will marry Kitty, distantly related to Anna, discovers a different kind of romantic love. Like Olenin and Bezukhov, he belongs to the family of awkward characters who do not know themselves well, are overcome by doubts, cannot express their feelings, yet take life seriously and examine every event from all conceivable points of view. These characters do not draw attention to themselves (Tolstoy portrays lack of reserve as a terrible flaw); they modestly try to work out how to live a good life. They end up sensing the moral law within themselves, but not as a truth they can grasp right away. In Tolstoy's novels, a silent warning tells the good people whether their actions are just. They clumsily discover their path, not so much by following explicit rules and interdictions—as characters did in Richardson, Rousseau, Balzac, and Dickens—but through brief moments of inner illumination. They foreshadow Henry James's characters, whose moral insights are always silent and difficult to reach, yet impeccable. At every step, Levin works hard to understand the needs of those around him—the farmers who work for him, the society of local landowners, and his beloved Kitty. And each time he has the satisfaction of learning how to make himself useful, and how to help others do the same. Slowly but surely, Levin wins Kitty's respect and affection, and in the end he finds an unclouded happiness with her. He even discovers within himself the evidence of God's existence: his own altruism.

Tolstoy agrees in part with the anti-idealist critique of romantic love: Anna's fate debunks the imaginary rights of the heart. Like Austen (whom he most certainly never read) and Thackeray, he mocks the cruel prejudice of the society that excludes Anna and Vronsky, and the human capacity for self-deception. Vronsky and Karenin, as well as several other characters who move in high circles, are the targets of an irony as biting as Stendhal's. On the other hand, perhaps following Dickens's example, Tolstoy designs his own version of a plausible narrative idealism. Inelegantly, hesitantly, his good characters discover and embrace altruism. Naive and generous, they eventually find success and happiness. Their clumsy kindness, far from attracting the whole world's notice, creates around them a small haven of peace and well-being.

The author's own observations often suggest a similar naive generosity. Critics long ago noted Tolstoy's tendency to describe familiar objects in a wholly unexpected way, thus "defamiliarizing" them. Viktor Shklovsky[4] argued that in order to make death or war unforgettable, Tolstoy focused not on the subject in general, but on the death of a flesh-and-blood warrior. In *War and Peace*, for instance, the young Rostov, in a hand-to-hand fight with a French officer, notices that his adversary, whose pale face is covered with mud, is "young, with a dimple on his chin and light blue eyes." It was "not an enemy face . . . but rather a quite ordinary and pleasant one." The dimple on the chin, Shklovsky comments, individualizes the French soldier, making him worthy of compassion. Like all formal devices, defamiliarization (which in this example might just as well be called "individualization") is linked to the author's view of human life. Choosing a detail for its *insignificance* is like letting one's gaze glide along things without grasping their features until it suddenly stops, drawn to a momentarily striking element. This way of looking conveys a fresh, almost childish surprise, like that of a naive perception dazzled by trifles. Richardson, in *Pamela*, used meticulous descriptions of the heroine's environment to enhance the sense of her perfect self-mastery. In Tolstoy's novel, an unsophisticated, generous character catches a few surprising glimpses of the world and lets them fill him with wonder.

INFINITESIMAL GRACE

All through the nineteenth century, German novellas by Joseph von Eichendorff, Adalbert Stifter, Gottfried Keller, and Conrad Ferdinand Meyer described a set of isolated, modest individuals who radiate all the kindness their milieu can absorb.

Like a lamp in a dark room, Adalbert Stifter's characters illuminate their environment, making it habitable. In *The Bachelors* (1844; the original title *Der Hagestolz* means "the confirmed bachelor"), the teenage orphan Victor, ready to leave his native village and look for work in the city, is invited to visit his elderly uncle. The old man lives in a deconsecrated convent, on an island in the middle of a lake surrounded by forests; in this strange and peaceful setting, the two of them silently size each other up. The action is barely perceptible in a narrative almost entirely devoted to Victor's journey and the long days he spends alone in his uncle's enigmatic home. Only at the very end of the novella does the reader understand what has happened. In his youth, this uncle was deeply in love with Ludmilla, who married his brother, Hippolytus. Hippolytus abandoned her for another woman, who gave birth to a boy. And kindhearted Ludmilla raised her former husband's son, Victor: she was

---

[4] *Material i stil v romane L. Tolstogo "Voina i mir* (1928; The Hague: Mouton, 1970), pp. 86–108.

his foster mother. The uncle, a confirmed bachelor who, in a world more receptive to sincere feelings, could have had his own children, now wants to leave Victor his fortune. But first he must make sure that the teenage boy will not take after his father, and so he has invited him to the remote island. Victor's innocent dignity wins his uncle's trust.

Stifter shares the nineteenth-century interest in social context but refrains from suggesting that human beings are mere products of their world. He excels in descriptions of landscapes, journeys, calm routines, giving them an unforgettable depth. By combining precise detail with a lighting technique borrowed from Romantic painting—Stifter was himself a landscape painter—he evokes a reality on the verge of turning into a dream. He conveys the peaceful grandeur of the scenery, as well as the quiver of anxiety that can emanate from a profusion of beauty.

The world's peace, in Stifter's work, is never genuinely troubled by human agitation. Now and then the characters experience disorderly passions, which plunge them into misfortune, as in *Brigitta* (1844), or destroy the happiness of others, as in *Tourmaline* (1853), but the reader hears about these passions only indirectly, in brief allusions, as though modesty prevented the author from dwelling on such regrettable, embarrassing matters. His long novel *Indian Summer* (*Der Nachsommer*, 1857) is almost entirely devoted to minute descriptions of landscapes, homes, art objects, and journeys across Austria, to the extent that the key anecdote, the sentimental disappointment that has cast a shadow over Baron von Risach's life, emerges only toward the end, during a conversation between von Risach and the narrator. Similarly, in both *Brigitta* and *Tourmaline*, the adultery at the core of the action is reported very late, in the briefest and most vague of terms, as though it might be better for readers to avert their gaze.

This avoidance of moral disorder goes together with a patient presentation of good behavior and its advantages. Stifter's model characters actively contribute to the happiness of their community, through business (*The Bachelors*), the introduction of modern agricultural methods (*Brigitta*), private charity (*Kalkstein, Limestone*, 1853), the cult of art and good manners (*Indian Summer*). These various improvements do not directly reward the people responsible for them, but benefit their relatives, friends, neighbors, and the natural world. Like Benassis in Balzac's *Country Doctor*, the protagonists of these stories, hurt by bad luck, do not give way to despair: they find peace in devoting themselves to useful activities.

In *Brigitta*, we cross the Hungarian steppe with the young witness-narrator and reach the property of someone he met in Italy, a handsome, enigmatic officer. We visit the beautiful house, the estate, and the gardens; we watch the farmers work, properly organized and supervised by the officer. His land, he explains, is ready to blossom if well cultivated, and his men need a guide. He and four of his neighbors, including the admirable Brigitta Maroshely, have started an association of model landowners devoted to the progress of agriculture. To make the earth bear fruit, along with deserving the farmers' respect, is what, rather late in life, makes the officer happy.

The narrator senses, however, that this man's past hides a secret; little by little, after several visits to the fields and tours of prosperous estates, he learns the story of Brigitta. In her youth, her lack of beauty repelled her family and the other members of her small circle. Nevertheless, Stephan Murai, a handsome young man, fell in love with her and proposed. She accepted on condition that he offer her a truly great love. "I know that I am ugly," she told him, "and so I demand to be loved more than the most beautiful woman on earth."[5] The married couple lived happily, and Brigitta soon gave birth to a boy. But after a while, her husband had an affair with a pretty young woman in the neighborhood, and Brigitta, profoundly hurt, asked for a divorce. Left alone, she took care of her son's education and administered her estate energetically, winning her neighbors' esteem. About fifteen years after the divorce, Murai moved to an estate near hers and strove to follow her example. A chaste friendship developed between them, entirely devoted to the cultivation of the fields. At the very end of the story, an unexpected event lets us know that Brigitta's ex-husband is none other than the narrator's friend, the officer. He returned to live close to the wife he had never ceased to love. Now, an accident that threatens their son's health opens the floodgates of tenderness, and the former spouses decide to restart their life together. "O, how holy," the narrator-witness admonishes himself, "how holy must conjugal love be, and how poor are you who, having never understood it until now, have let your heart be consumed by the dark flames of passion" (p. 136).

The story's moral framework does not simply recommend a rejection of the passions, though, since it is clear that the young Brigitta was also flawed: too proud, too possessive, unable to forgive. What interests Stifter is not the ability to make good decisions early on or to avoid any mistakes—although in both *Indian Summer* and *The Bachelors* older characters regret their faults and help the young not to repeat them—but the capacity, once struck by misfortune, to take hold of oneself and give one's life new meaning. One profoundly satisfying way to live is to build up a beautiful, prosperous environment, like Victor's uncle's retreat or Brigitta's flourishing estate. *Tourmaline* reinforces these examples by examining the opposite case, that of a character who cannot master his pain and sinks into a state of depression close to madness.

---

[5] Adalbert Stifter, *Brigitta and Other Tales*, trans. Helen Watanabe-O'Kelly (London: Penguin Books, 1994), p. 127.

Stifter reverses the doctrine that divides the world into regions with their own historical, ethnic, and social specificity, each determining the qualities and fate of those who live in it. For him, the external environment is rooted in the human heart; from there it grows, blossoms, and bears fruit. "No world-spirit, no demon governs the world," Stifter writes, asserting his faith in human agency. "Whatever good or bad happens to human beings, they themselves did it." In these simple words the author expresses his conviction that people hold their fate in their own hands and can imprint their own image on the world they inhabit.

This form of idealism carries an implicit invitation: whenever people suffer misfortune, they can regain their inner balance by working to make others happy. Domestic heroism can be practiced by prominent people (Baron von Risach, Brigitta Maroshely) or by the very poorest (the village priest in *Limestone*, who saves all his earnings to provide for the local elementary school), and while in many of Stifter's stories these heroes are Austrian, *Brigitta*'s are Hungarian, the adventurous protagonist of *Abdias* is a North African Jew, and the historical novel *Witiko* depicts a period of close comradeship between Germans and Slavs. Stifter's calm version of narrative idealism examines well-cultivated lands, tastefully furnished homes, and peaceful, friendly manners, expecting them to accommodate a gentle, understated kind of human dignity.

||||||||||||||||||||||||||||||

Whereas in Stifter's fiction the sensitive heart—source of an active mutual care—unites people, other authors see in it the origin of their separation. Keller and Meyer, for instance, who are equally open to narrative idealism and the critique of it, assume that the ideals cherished by the human heart are both perfectly self-evident and impossible to achieve in reality. The novels of Theodor Fontane also explore the difficult reconciliation between the sensitive heart and the world, though without opposing good and evil in a clear-cut fashion. One of the novelties in Fontane's fiction is the disappearance of malice. Stifter avoids confronting wickedness, alluding to it only indirectly, but Fontane goes further: he doubts its very existence.

Fontane looks at the world through the eyes of each of his characters; the gaze is kind and calm, even though these characters seldom make the effort to understand the worries of those around them. Von Stechlin senior, in the novel named after him (*The Stechlin*, 1899), is a good judge of people, presumably because of his age and bonhomie. Among Fontane's other characters, only those who do not face serious challenges in life— the parents and friends of the main unhappy couple, or sometimes their doctor, like the admirable Rummschüttel in *Effi Briest* (1896)—take an interest, and usually quite a moderate one, in the others' problems. As for the protagonists themselves, they virtually never manage to understand or trust each other. What Renate von Vitzewitz says about the Ladalinski family in *Before the Storm* (1878) applies to many of Fontane's male characters: "It is a dark family and what they don't themselves own they cannot give to others: light and happiness. Their fate has always been to awaken love, but not trust."[6] This kind of person, perhaps best represented by Baron von Innstetten in *Effi Briest*, willingly obeys social norms, but cannot bridge the gap between these precepts and the vagaries of individual fate. Because these types are unshakable in their social and moral beliefs, they fail to notice the obscure needs of others, their unexplained moments of melancholy or joy.

Von Innstetten, who in his youth had hoped in vain to marry Effi Briest's mother, asks for the daughter's hand when she turns seventeen. Effi does not know her own heart very well, but, dreaming of a comfortable life, she agrees to marry this forty-year-old man, whom everyone agrees has a great future. They settle in a country town in East Prussia, where Effi gives birth to a girl. Innstetten is polite and affectionate with his wife, but often refuses her requests. He will not agree, for instance, to renovate the half-abandoned upper floor of their house, although the old curtains flapping in the night scare her and make her think the place is haunted. Life in a strange house, in a dull, provincial town far away from her parents, makes Effi anxious and sad. Without quite knowing why, she gives in to the local seducer, Major Crampas. The liaison ends when Innstetten is appointed undersecretary in a Berlin ministry and the family moves to the capital, where Effi can finally enjoy the society life she has always wanted.

Several years later, however, the baron comes across a package of old letters exchanged by Crampas and Effi. He breaks up with her, forbids her to see their daughter, challenges Crampas to a duel, and mortally wounds him. Effi is disgraced, and rejected by her parents. Only her Catholic servant Roswitha and her doctor Rummschüttel stand by her. After a while, at a friend's suggestion, Innstetten allows his former wife to see her daughter, who no longer feels much affection for her. Seeing Effi waste away, the good-natured Rummschüttel persuades her parents to take her home with them; she soon dies there, after forgiving Innstetten in her heart.

If Zola or the Goncourt brothers had written it, the novel would undoubtedly have emphasized the heartrending experience of the adulterous woman—her regrets, her bitterness, the fever of sensuous pleasures, the stupidity of her lover, the cruelty of her husband. None of this can be

---

[6] Theodor Fontane, *Vor dem Sturm* (Munich: Nymphenburger Verlagshandlung, 1957), end of chap. 61, p. 487 (my translation).

found in Fontane's book, which is about peaceful, well-meaning characters, willing to do their duty, eager to contribute as best they can to the success of communal life. None of them is led astray by romantic illusions: the only person subject to fits of romanticism is the kindly pharmacist Gieshübler, a minor character. These pillars of society are not troubled by rebellious impulses or resentment against their fellow creatures.

Fontane's world is governed by social and historical determinism, and its inhabitants sense that they are strictly confined within it. Yet far from wanting to escape their milieu, as the heroes of idealist novels do and as Flaubert's characters aspire to, Fontane's protagonists remain faithful to it. Their goodwill toward their surroundings tones down the familiar contrast between good, "positive" characters and dangerous, noxious ones. Moreover, in Fontane as in Stifter, although idealism always lurks in the background, its presence is barely perceptible. In Stifter, characters who look quite ordinary, and often suffer bad luck, are full of energy and kindness. They are exemplary beings, and their example is effective precisely because of its banality. Going further in the same direction, Fontane captures the spark of beauty hidden within insignificant people—Effi Briest, Innstetten, Cécile, and Colonel St Arnaud (in *Cécile*)—prosaic creatures who meekly submit to the conventions of their milieu.

To emphasize their wish to conform and savor the peace of a world tailored to them, Fontane, at the beginning of the action, softens any conflict between the characters. As a result of this softening—and the serene atmosphere it creates—the crisis, when it occurs, is profoundly disturbing. Effi Briest's misfortune is especially heartbreaking in that it could easily not have occurred. After all, the differences between her personality and Innstetten's are quite minimal, as their contented life in Berlin suggests. Effi does not throw herself into Crampas's arms with the passion of a disappointed wife, desperately seeking true love. The reasons for her adultery are left unclear, and the author, not unlike Stifter, is careful not to give details of the episode. Was it a whim, a moment of weakness? Hard to say, and although the letters Innstetten later finds from Crampas seem to suggest that the liaison had moments of intensity, Effi is visibly relieved when it ends.

Innstetten's revenge is equally devoid of passion. When, in Berlin, he discovers the compromising letters, his first impulse is to forgive his wife, whom he loves. Effi's infidelity is an old one, in any case, buried and forgotten six to seven years before. But as Innstetten explains to his friend Wüllersdorf:

> We're not just individuals, we're part of a larger whole and we must constantly have regard for that larger whole, we're dependent on it, beyond a doubt. . . . Wherever men live together, something has been established that's just there,

and it's a code we've become accustomed to judging everything by, ourselves as well as others. And going against it is unacceptable; society despises you for it, and in the end you despise yourself, you can't bear it any longer and put a gun to your head.[7]

A rather successful marriage, a love affair devoid of love, and a revenge without hatred: disaster need not have struck. The fact that it nonetheless strikes makes it all the more poignant.

But why does this avoidable disaster take place? By initially minimizing the divergence between characters, Fontane grants considerable weight to the imponderable differences that later separate them. Effi and Innstetten are both well-behaved, surrounded by friends, and happy to live in their country at their time; they do not have financial worries, and they feel affection and respect for one another. The only possibility for discord lies in their slightly different perspectives on life. Fontane's genius consists in relating these slightly different perspectives to the same source, the charm and rectitude that can be found in good people. For the heroines of idealist novels, their strong sense of duty and their natural charm go together: Pamela is charming because she is virtuous and Julie because she asserts her values. In Fontane's novel, charm and respect for duty split up: Effi is charming; Innstetten has strong principles. (Fontane does not always assign these features along the same gender lines: in Irretrievable—Unwiederbringlich, 1891—the charming character is the husband, Helmut Holk, and his wife, Christine Arne, is the one with the strict principles.) As for Effi, she is not a frivolous person, but simply someone whose allure and high spirits can occasionally lead her astray. Her husband is not a cold, rigid man, but in an emergency his principles do not allow for forgiveness. Without clashing directly, Effi's spontaneity, insufficiently tempered by reflection, and Innstetten's sense of duty, inadequately mitigated by generosity, do not quite work together: the combination makes disaster possible. But is this enough of a reason for the crisis that ensues? Not necessarily, and indeed in *Effi Briest* the catastrophe is actually triggered by an unusual event—Instetten's finding his wife's correspondence—similar to the striking incidents that had long been so essential to novellas. It is in *Cécile* (1887), an earlier, shorter novel, that Fontane's moral vision emerges more clearly.

In *Cécile*, as in Stifter's works, a long sequence of travel descriptions and scenes without much apparent narrative relevance imperceptibly leads to a profoundly moving revelation. During a vacation in the Harz, the young civil engineer von Leslie-Gordon meets Cécile von St Arnaud

---

[7] Theodor Fontane, *Effi Briest*, trans. Hugh Rorrison and Helen Chambers (London: Penguin Books, 1995), p. 173.

and her husband, Colonel St Arnaud. The colonel's dignified restraint contrasts with his beautiful wife's sensitivity and agitation. Bewitched by Cécile, Gordon courts her assiduously. Back in Berlin, he learns the couple's story. Descended from a family of ruined aristocrats, Cécile received no education, as her mother was convinced that "a beautiful young lady only existed to please, and to this end it was better to know little rather than much."[8] At the age of seventeen, with her mother's consent, Cécile became the reading companion and concubine of the old prince of Welfen-Echingen, who set her up in the castle of Cyrillenort. After the prince's death, she continued to fulfill the same functions for his son, who soon passed away. With the substantial inheritance the old prince had left her, she returned to her mother in Upper Silesia, where she met the colonel and accepted his hand. Learning of Cécile's past, the officer corps expressed its disapproval in a letter signed by the lieutenant colonel. St Arnaud challenged him to a duel and killed him.

Gordon is now convinced he has found the reason for Cécile's sensitivity: she must be haunted by the memories of her wild past. Emboldened by this new knowledge, the young man intensifies his courtship, but Cécile asks him to stop bothering her. "I am oppressed by many things," she writes:

> You have seen how we live: there is so much mockery around me, mockery I dislike and often I don't even understand. For the great issues do not interest me and I take life, even now, as a picture-book with pages to turn. . . . Don't probe any further. There is more tragedy in this house than you know. (p. 149)

Taking life as a picture book is the sign of a poetic resignation. But it is equally obvious that Cécile, who, through her marriage, has won the right to be respected, does not want to lose it: "This I have vowed, do not ask when and on what occasion, and I wish to keep that vow, even if I were to die for it" (p. 149).

Cécile's confession is a mark of trust, yet Gordon, instead of withdrawing, visits her at home at an inappropriate hour, putting her reputation at risk. Inevitably, the colonel issues a challenge and, after offering him a chance to make peace, which Gordon refuses, kills him with a bullet to the chest. To avoid prison, St Arnaud takes refuge on the Côte d'Azur and invites his wife to join him. "Don't take the whole affair more tragically than necessary," he writes to her, "the world is no greenhouse for over-tender feelings" (p. 171). But he then learns that his wife has committed suicide, several days after reading about the duel in the paper.

[8] Theodor Fontane, *Cécile*, trans. Stanley Radcliffe (London: Angel Books, 1992), p. 141.

Her reasons—like Effi Briest's for having an affair—are not explained. Was Cécile in love with Gordon? Certainly not to the point of dying for him. Did she want to escape her difficult position in society? Nothing proves it.

Her last wish is to be buried at Cyrillenort—the castle where she spent her youth as a kept woman—close to the princely family's funeral chapel. "I wish at least to be close to the resting place of those who gave me in rich measure what the world denied me; love and friendship, and, in addition, respect based on love," she writes (p. 172). The reader realizes with emotion that Cécile's fragility and melancholy were not at all caused by the *remorse* a lost woman restored to respectability is supposed to feel about her past; on the contrary, what she felt was a deep *nostalgia* for the life she had led at her seducer's castle. "Nobility and goodness of heart," she concludes, "are not everything, but they count for *much*" (p. 172). This short statement, which by omission privileges generosity and kindness over duty or honor, is a thinly veiled allusion to the rules St Arnaud lives by, a terrible set of principles that spread death around him and Cécile.

We know that "the great issues" do not interest her, and that she likes to take life lightly, like a beautiful story, a "picture-book." It is perhaps this sense of lightness, of grace, that Gordon's courtship brought her, as long as it didn't turn into a full-blown attempt at conquest. This is also the feeling she must have had years before at the prince's court, although the details are missing and we can only infer them from Cécile's last request. The stern moral code of duty and honor may offer its partisans the esteem of society and a source of self-respect, yet for some people, nobility and goodness of heart, even if they transgress social norms, give life its meaning.

The gap between the world and the lonely individual has grown both narrower and deeper. Society's highest precepts cannot satisfy the intimate longing for love and trust. Even the fortunate beings who seem to have achieved perfect social success may still daydream. Barely noticeable, these dreams are nevertheless powerful enough to kill the dreamer.

THE REVOLT AGAINST AUTONOMY

Nineteenth-century German novels feature characters who gladly participate in the world around them, yet deep in their hearts preserve a glimmer of something outside it. This glimmer can be a source of redemption, as it is in Stifter's stories, or it may endanger the character, as it does in Keller and Fontane, but it is always there and always carefully hidden. It may be that the need to emphasize how difficult it is to grasp inner beauty is what makes these authors interminably describe landscapes

(Stifter) or inconsequential conversations (Fontane), while devoting just a few pages to the characters' drama, usually at the very end of the text. The never-ending chatter that floods Fontane's novels contrasts sharply with the rare testimonies that come from the depths of a character's soul. These testimonies—Cécile's letter to Gordon, her last wish, the fragments of Effi and Crampas's correspondence—are always incomplete, allusive, as though these people were afraid that in expressing their feelings clearly, they might irreversibly damage something very important within themselves.

This discretion is strikingly different from the propensity of characters in Dickens, Sue, and Hugo to speak about themselves, often in an elevated tone meant to lend plausibility to the most extraordinary assertions. Equally long-winded monologues can be found in Dostoevsky, whose works borrow from the popular novel, particularly from Hugo and Sue, the whole range of effects proper to idealism: improbable plots, the contrast between sublime and profoundly despicable characters, the background of urban misery, and the moral splendor of fallen angels. But the author of *Crime and Punishment* uses this narrative style in an unexpected way: idealism's characteristic volubility here becomes the tool for a violent polemic against it.

Dostoevsky reacts against the conviction that human beings can in any way, socially or individually, govern their own lives. In Russia in the second half of the nineteenth century, the hope that humanity could take charge of its fate was defended by liberal writers like Ivan Turgenev, whose novel *Fathers and Sons* (1862) presents a sympathetic portrait of a young anarchist, and by Nikolai Chernyshevsky, whose *What Is to Be Done?* (1863) promotes radical revolutionary ideas. To challenge these stances, Dostoevsky asks a simple question: once people declare themselves their own masters, how can they know whether their actions are right or wrong? For if human beings devise their own moral law, nothing prevents some among them from promulgating a law that exclusively favors *them* while condemning the rest of humanity—for instance, a law that authorizes the lawmakers to kill other people. Imagine an individual deeply convinced of his superiority over his fellow men—many of the protagonists in older and more recent idealist novels harbor such a conviction and act accordingly. Since this individual is the only arbiter of his conduct, he might look around and determine who deserves to live and who does not. He could then decide to kill some of the undeserving people. This superior individual could, for example, target an old woman in his neighborhood who practices the shameful trade of usury, who therefore does not seem truly worthy to live. Who would have the right to judge this individual's pretensions, when great personalities can do whatever they see fit? And who would tell our character that he is not such a personality?

Let's say that our man, or rather our superman, after committing the murder as planned, manages to evade the police and the courts—institutions with no legitimacy in his eyes, since they are not founded on the only authority he recognizes: his own judgment. Let's also suppose that to prove to himself his superiority over the rest of humanity, he approaches the judicial investigators posing as an innocent bystander who witnessed the crime, and believes he has convinced them. Surely his impassibility when facing the investigators and the superhuman intelligence with which he foresees and avoids all the traps they set up for him offer sufficient proof of his right to impose his own law on others? The demonstration wouldn't be convincing, though, if the man in question were a seasoned scoundrel, for whom lies and crimes came naturally. Defending the greatness of villains as villains—as the Marquis de Sade had done at the end of the eighteenth century—would amount to perpetuating the old hierarchy of values that the experiment was meant to subvert. In order for Dostoevsky's superman to deserve the authority he claims, he must be free of malice and must kill only by virtue of an intellectual decision; he must not enjoy the act the way a hardened criminal might. Moreover, since he is supposed to possess the requisite moral strength to implement his plan, he must feel no remorse.

The student Raskolnikov, protagonist of *Crime and Punishment* (1866), meets the first requirement: his actions are usually generous, and when he decides to kill the old usurer Alyona Ivanovna, wickedness has nothing to do with it. He just wants to prove to himself that he is capable of exercising the freedom to act reserved for superior beings. It remains to be seen, though, whether he can resist remorse.

A series of factors related to the crowded conditions disturb Raskolnikov's plans. Lizaveta Ivanovna, the victim's sister, catches him in the act, and he has to murder her as well. Neighbors walk up the stairs, visitors try to get into the apartment, and Raskolnikov only just manages to avoid them. Later, during the judicial investigation, a housepainter named Nikolai, who happened to be in the vicinity of the crime scene, falsely confesses to the murder. Raskolnikov's decision to kill the old usurer thus involves the lives of others: the woman he must eliminate to escape the police, the man who is ready to sacrifice himself in his place.

In addition, the superior man who promulgates his own law has failed to predict what his state of mind will be after the crime:

Terror was gaining an increasing hold on him. . . . A dark, tormenting thought was rising up inside him—the thought that he was behaving like a madman. . . . He was in a kind of delirium.[9]

[9] Fyodor Dostoevsky, *Crime and Punishment*, trans. David McDuff (London: Penguin Books, 1991), pt. 1, chap. 7, pp. 98, 99, 103.

Back home and relatively safe, Raskolnikov remains for several days in "a state of fever, with delirium and semi-wakefulness" (pt. 2, chap. 3, p. 143). The unhealthy agitation goes on, as though his body and mind, unable to bear the tension, have let him down. But how can this man enact his own moral law when he cannot even control his physical and mental faculties? Their rebellion suggests that Raskolnikov's crime has deeply upset some preexisting equilibrium.

Beyond the immediate practical obstacles and his involuntary reactions, Raskolnikov's self-assurance is challenged by his family, by institutional justice, and by a few exemplary destinies he observes, which force him to reflect on his own actions. Raskolnikov's sister and mother have strong claims on the young man, not only because he owes them a large amount of money, but also because he is the only person who can protect his sister against unscrupulous suitors. The investigator Porfiry Petrovich shows formidable cunning and perception. Convinced of Raskolnikov's guilt but lacking evidence, he does not arrest the young man, thus depriving him of the peace and quiet he would have found in prison. For a long time Raskolnikov believes that his superior intelligence has defeated justice, while in fact his freedom is just a reprieve provided by the detective, who correctly foresees that sooner or later he will betray himself.

The Marmeladov family, Marmeladov-père and his daughter Sonya in particular, offer Raskolnikov two potential mirror images of his own moral character. The lamentable state of the father, whom he meets in a tavern at the very beginning of the novel, warns him against egocentrism. An incurable drunk, Marmeladov ruins his family to the extent that Sonya must sell her body to feed her mother and younger siblings. Sonya herself, by contrast, embodies the highest generosity.

> 'This very jug of vodka was purchased with her money,' Marmeladov enunciated. . . . 'Thirty copecks she gave me, with her own hands, the last money she had, I could see it for myself . . . She didn't say anything, just looked at me in silence . . . That's what it's like, not here upon earth, but up there . . . ' (pt. 1, chap. 2, p. 28)

Sonya's kindness does not belong to this world: her utter selflessness redeems her father's self-absorption.

From time to time a supernatural glimmer becomes visible, as though God and the devil were fighting backstage, as in a medieval morality play, over the protagonist's soul. On the day before the murder, Raskolnikov is returning home after a long walk, but instead of taking the shortest way, for no particular reason he crosses the Haymarket, where he hears that the usurer's sister, who lives with her, will be out at seven the next evening. This detail, learned by chance, determines the hour of the crime. Later in the day, Raskolnikov steps into a tavern, where he overhears a discussion that echoes his own thoughts. A student is deliberating on the ethics of killing the usurer Alyona Ivanovna, the very act Raskolnikov has been planning. The stranger lays out the utilitarian argument—one Dostoevsky deeply despised—which holds that it is permissible to sacrifice the life of a noxious individual in order to increase the happiness of the greatest number. Raskolnikov is extremely agitated. Why did he have to hear these people discussing precisely the ideas that had been spinning in his mind? Is there some kind of predestination involved in his decision? However one reads these passages—and the author deliberately makes them ambiguous—they clearly question Raskolnikov's claim to have more rights than other mortals. For either the devil himself has staged these episodes to lead him into temptation—which would make the legislative power Raskolnikov asserts a demonic one—or they are mere coincidences, in which case there is something rather ridiculous about his pretensions to moral greatness, given that his actions are so obviously dependent on chance. As for God, his presence is felt, as always in Dostoevsky, through that of a human being touched by grace—Sonya, who reads aloud to Raskolnikov, from the gospel according to John, the story of Lazarus's resurrection. Her copy of the New Testament was recently given to her by Lizaveta Ivanovna herself, as though the dead woman wanted to speak to her assassin about Christian forgiveness.

Trapped by unpredictable circumstances, by the strange behavior of his own mind and body, by the people around him, and by the supernatural struggle for his salvation, Raskolnikov gradually realizes that his place in the world and, still more, his freedom of action depend on a much larger order of things. Though his first victim may well have been an old, stupid, and destructive woman, once embarked on a criminal career, he cannot avoid sacrificing innocent, even admirable people like Lizaveta Ivanovna and Nikolai. The institutional power of justice forces the self-appointed superior man to live on permanent alert. His own anxiety compels him to recognize how limited his options now are. Far from clearing his way to complete freedom from social chains, the murder turns out to be an ordinary crime. Raskolnikov's choice is either to punish himself by committing suicide or to return to human society by confessing his guilt.

Divine grace, operating through Sonya, dissuades the young man from suicide and encourages him to denounce himself. In the last scene before the epilogue, Raskolnikov goes to the police, ready to confess his crime, but finds out that he is no longer a suspect. Relieved, he leaves the station. Not far from the gate he sees

> the pale, utterly rigid figure of Sonya, looking at him with wild, wild eyes. He came to a halt in front of her. There was an expression of pain and exhaustion on her face, something akin to despair. (pt. 6, chap. 8, p. 632)

This look, as Marmeladov noted at the beginning of the novel, belongs "not here upon earth, but up there . . ." Having escaped human justice, Raskolnikov surrenders to a superior force. "He stood there for a moment, smiled ironically, then turned back and began to ascend the stairs to the bureau again" (p. 632).

In *Crime and Punishment*, Dostoevsky examines the first, strictly individual step in the human struggle to achieve self-rule. Raskolnikov is aware that the planned murder is only a preparatory phase, whose success will qualify him to become a leader of like-minded people. In his system of thought, a violent act perpetrated without hesitation against an individual would confer on him the right to act violently against society as a whole. Raskolnikov fails this test. It is Stavrogin, the protagonist of *Devils* (1871–1872), who succeeds in passing it. As Stavrogin admits in a written confession entrusted to Bishop Tikhon, he began his career by raping a little girl and then letting her commit suicide when he could easily have saved her. At the request of the editor of the *Russian Messenger*, the journal that published the novel, Dostoevsky withdrew this chapter. The confession, however, is essential not only for understanding *Devils*, but also for grasping the novel's links with *Crime and Punishment*.

Having left the moral law behind, Stavrogin moves on to the next stage. With the help of his friend Pyotr Verkhovensky, he founds a secret society whose goal is to set up a new world of perfect freedom and equality for all. At a meeting of revolutionaries and nihilists, a man named Shigalyov presents his scientific social ideas. His system is quite puzzling, as he admits:

> I became lost in my own data and my conclusion contradicts the original premise from which I started. Beginning with the idea of unlimited freedom, I end with unlimited despotism. I must add, however, there can be no other solution to the social problem except mine.[10]

Dostoevsky makes fun of social utopias, but his main interest is less in their concrete features than in the moral character and conduct of those who aim to create them.

This conduct entails the rejection of existing links between human beings. In Verkhovensky's words:

> Our people aren't just those who slit throats and set fires, who use pistols in the classic manner and bite other people. . . . Listen, I've counted them all over: a teacher who laughs with his children at their God over their cradle is already

---

[10] Fyodor Dostoevsky, *Devils*, trans. Michael R. Katz (Oxford: Oxford World Classics, 1992), pt. 2, chap. 7, p. 426.

one of us. A lawyer who defends an educated murderer by arguing he's more cultured than his victims, and couldn't help murdering to acquire money, is one of us already. [Perhaps an allusion to *Crime and Punishment* . . .] Juries who acquit criminals right and left are with us. (pt. 2, chap. 8, p. 445)

Injustice and disorder are on Verkhovensky's side.

The partisans of the new society must ensure that their movement is highly disciplined. As conspirators, they cannot tolerate dissidence. When Shatov, a member of Verkhovensky's cell, rediscovers his devotion to Russia and its traditions, his boss decides to have the others execute him. Not only will the traitor's punishment serve as an example, but the collective guilt will guarantee the group's cohesion. In fact, however, far from establishing the cell's solidarity, Shatov's murder leads to its dissolution. Overcome by fear and remorse, the members abandon the fight, hide, and denounce each other.

Dostoevsky thus rejects both narrative idealism, which extols human greatness and independence, and anti-idealism, which finds human imperfection either amusing or dismal. Against the idealist tradition, Dostoevsky implies that its heroes' constancy and magnanimity are nothing but pipe dreams. Raskolnikov's fate shows how absurd it is to believe that exceptional beings can sanction their own actions. In *Devils*, Stavrogin's behavior confirms that the supposedly superior man is in fact a beast of prey. As though Dostoevsky wanted to avert any suspicion of idealism, the majority of his characters, including those with whom he sympathizes, are ill-mannered, sometimes unmistakably mean, often incapable of articulating their intentions clearly, and always whimsical and unreliable.

Literary critics have at times interpreted these characters' inconstancy and inability to express themselves as signs of their freedom. Mikhail Bakhtin in Russia and François Mauriac in France have even argued that Dostoevsky's characters act independently of the author's will. The characters do indeed astonish the reader with their cranky behavior and sudden changes of mind, the frequent discrepancies between their words and their real intentions. But far from indicating *freedom*, these features highlight the characters' *fallibility*. Raskolnikov goes to the police bureau to give himself up, changes his mind, leaves the building, sees Sonya in the street, changes his mind again, and goes back into the station. Does this suggest an excess of freedom? He behaves more like a man who does not know exactly what he is doing. Likewise, the verbal animation Dostoevsky's characters display, their way of digressing and rambling, is not at all a symptom of freedom, as Bakhtin argued, but rather the sign of an inner confusion that prevents them from knowing themselves and expressing their suffering in simple terms. The proof *a contrario* is the transparency of Prince Myshkin's language in *The Idiot* (1869). His clear conscience and serenity make his speech logical and simple.

The presence of a character like Myshkin also shows that, unlike anti-idealist writers, who see imperfection as the final truth of the human condition, Dostoevsky does believe in the possibility of genuine goodness, which he identifies, in accordance with Greek Orthodox Christianity, with restraint and self-immolation for the good of the others. Impossible to attain by mere human means, goodness belongs to those visibly touched by grace (Sonya in *Crime and Punishment*; Zosima in *The Brothers Karamazov*, 1880) or, as in Myshkin's case, blessed with a strange physiological disease. Occasionally, lost people like Raskolnikov or Shatov find the right path, but their conversion always takes place under the influence of the divinity or its representatives on earth: individual pure souls or the Russian people as a whole. And, perhaps as a reaction against the idealist habit of giving noble hearts full control over their thoughts and behavior, in Dostoevsky's novels characters who have been granted grace (Sonya, Myshkin, Shatov) are always humble and ill at ease, as though asking others' forgiveness for being chosen by God despite their imperfection. We have already met such characters, both inspiring and awkward, in Tolstoy's novels. In a world corrupted by sin, as Dostoevsky sees it, or by civilization, in Tolstoy's view, only a few artless, poorly adjusted beings can radiate beauty. They are self-effacing because they are innocent, and their difficulty in taking action (medical in Myshkin's case, psychological in Pierre Bezukhov's and Levin's) signals the gap that separates them from the surrounding world.

Far from attempting a synthesis between idealism and anti-idealism, Dostoevsky turns his back on both, replacing them with a formula that contrasts the most repugnant forms of human abjection with the most ethereal sainthood. Inspired by the French and English popular novel, this formula takes up Dickens's, Sue's, and Hugo's method of juxtaposing purity and filth, sanctity and crime. But while the characters in Dickens, Sue, and Hugo, whether good or evil, exhibit strong, remarkable qualities, Dostoevsky emphasizes confusion and distress, the inability either to embrace and conform to moral norms or to break loose from them. As a result, his novels are filled with profoundly unstable people, unable to formulate and carry out any coherent project, enslaved by momentary impulses, and tormented by their failure to follow society's rules. Their complexity is that of a piece of land taken over by weeds, where the good seed survives only by a miracle.

As important as Dostoevsky's rejection of human autonomy is his refusal to believe that people are decisively shaped by their milieu. Although he adopts the techniques of descriptive realism (to the extent that later, when André Breton in his 1924 *Surrealist Manifesto* wanted to show how terrible realism is, he chose a passage from *Crime and Punishment*), Dostoevsky does not subscribe to social and historical determinism. Most of his characters are equally indifferent to the usual moral norms and to social conventions. Those who follow such conventions, like Verkhovensky-père and the governor von Lembke in *Devils*, are assigned the role of buffoon. This disconnect between the individual person, his or her social role, and the norms of moral life certainly reflects the difficulties of nineteenth-century Russian society, where a western European model was being uncomfortably superimposed on older local traditions. But although the normative failures Dostoevsky portrays correspond to a specific sociological situation, their metaphysical implications are of much greater interest to him.

The only social category that appeals to Dostoevsky is the nation. But he makes it clear that Russianness is not something acquired simply by birth. Virtually all his characters are born in Russia, but few of them truly find their Russian destiny. Roots are not given to anyone: they are an end to be achieved. Morally reborn, Raskolnikov and Shatov discover a reality they have ignored completely: their own country. This secret Russia, a mystic land blessed by God, is located within the visible, distressing Russia, showing its unbelievable beauty only to those who, moved by grace, are able to see it.

Dostoevsky is one of the most formidable adversaries of the belief that human beings can discover the moral law and follow it freely. Left to themselves, he tells us, people are fallible, unstable, incapable of principled behavior. Only rarely does an otherworldly perfection adorn a small elect.

The Dreamy Soul on the Edge of Madness

The Spanish revolution of 1868 and the relatively liberal regime that followed encouraged a genuine renaissance of Spanish literature, including the novel. Writers had to face the genre's main challenge at the time: how to represent human excellence as a deeply personal feature while also portraying the social and historical context that makes it possible, or even necessary. The nineteenth-century Spanish novel's distinct physiognomy can be traced to the belated rise of social realism, the originality of Spain's narrative tradition, and the resilience of its religious belief.

In the 1830s and 1840s, the Spanish disciples of Walter Scott (Mariano José de Larra, Enrique Gil y Carrasco) had turned their attention to local manners and color, as did the *costumbrista* Ramón de Mesonero Romanos and the novelists interested in the specificities of regional life, like Cecilia Böhl de Faber and, in the next generation, Pedro Antonio de Alarcón and Juan Valera. Their production, which for a long time was quite limited, only partially satisfied the needs of the cultivated public, who avidly read the latest English, French, and sometimes Russian novels.

Spanish novelists in the second half of the nineteenth century were in touch with the work of their immediate contemporaries—the naturalist Goncourt brothers and Zola in particular—but they also read Balzac, Dickens, and the other earlier nineteenth-century writers. As a result, they felt free to create their own synthesis between a variety of idealist and anti-idealist positions. This is probably the reason why the novels of Emilia Pardo Bazán, Benito Pérez Galdós, and Leopoldo Alas (Clarín) display less pessimism and contempt for human beings than do those of French naturalists. Focusing on generosity and inner strength, they often sound closer to the work of Stifter, George Eliot, or Tolstoy.

There is a difference, however. Stifter, Eliot, and Tolstoy practice a moderate idealism, an idealism "with a human face," so to speak, which takes such reassuring forms as kindness in Stifter, secular morality in Eliot, and authenticity in Tolstoy. By contrast, the tender hearts in Spanish novels show a touch of madness. Fortunata Izquierdo's obstinacy and Maximiliano Rubín's all-consuming love in *Fortunata and Jacinta* (1887) by Pérez Galdós, the saintliness of his protagonist in *Nazarín*, and the tortured femininity of Ana Ozores in Alas's *La Regenta* (1884–1885)—all reveal true nobility sustained by a considerable supply of energy, but they also hint at psychological unbalance. Cervantes's perennial prestige is responsible for this blend of idealism and folly, which resurrects and modernizes *Don Quixote*. Without the example of the knight of La Mancha and the phantasms his mind projected, Pérez Galdós and Alas might not have imagined Maximiliano's monomania, Nazarín's angelic antics, or Ana Ozores's hysteria. Conversely, Maximiliano's lunacy, Fortunata's lonely resilience, and Ana Ozores's rebellious chastity threw a new light on Don Quixote, who retroactively acquired the aura of a lone, forlorn pilgrim on the road to the absolute.

The distance separating the slightly deranged characters from their society is also an old subject in Spanish fiction. In the first part of *Quixote* and in the picaresque tradition exemplified by *Lazarillo de Tormes*, Quevedo's *El Buscón*, and *Don Guzmán de Alfarache* by Mateo Alemán, the overwhelming gap between the main character and the surrounding world is taken for granted and never bridged. Similarly, in the nineteenth-century works, the lack of sensitivity to society's requirements—shown by Fortunata, Maximiliano, Nazarín, Tristana (in Pérez Galdós's story bearing her name), Ana Ozores, and, in Pardo Bazán's *The House of Ulloa* (1886), the priest Julián Alvarez and Don Pedro's unhappy wife,

Nucha Pardo—is in each case the result of the character's irreducible, incurable singularity.

In Stendhal, Balzac, and Dickens, the reader always gets the impression that the protagonists' misfortune could perhaps have been avoided if those around them had been less hostile to their aspirations. Balzac's Eugénie Grandet could have lived happily if only her father had been less avaricious, and a bit of discretion on the part of Mme de Rênal (in *The Red and the Black*) would have ensured Julien Sorel's social success. In *Great Expectations*, it is so clear that Pip would find happiness if Estella could be cured of her misanthropy, that Dickens had no difficulty in altering the first, pessimistic version of the denouement to give his novel a happy ending. For Spanish writers, this kind of resolution is inconceivable. For their characters, as for pícaros, even favorable circumstances lead eventually to failure. Maximiliano Rubín may marry the beautiful Fortunata, but she remains perpetually inaccessible to him; Fortunata sees her beloved Juanito Santa Cruz again, only to suffer still more at his hands; Ana Ozores discovers the pleasures of the body, but happiness will elude her; Nucha Pardo and Julián Alvarez are forever separated by the double sanctity of her marriage and his ecclesiastical vocation. Since these characters have an obscure sense that they will never reach an enduring reconciliation with the world, they accept their condition and, in a psychological move characteristic of those living in traditional societies, they often feel quite at ease in an ambience unsympathetic to their hopes. Thus the characters' misfortune—a tragic feature—is tempered by their complicity with the milieu that excludes or torments them.

One recognizes in this configuration an echo of the religious attitude that extols the poor, the humble, and the powerless precisely insofar as they accept their condition. The world rejects them, but since they have no alternative, they settle in and feel at home with their inferior status. Characters who in Balzac and Dickens—and even more so in the Goncourt brothers and Zola—would be deeply dissatisfied and perhaps plot a rebellion, show a unique mixture of resignation and pride in Pérez Galdós, Pardo Bazán, and Alas, content to accept hardship while still maintaining the most perfect self-assurance. Though she bows to the social superiority of her rival, Jacinta, Juanito Santa Cruz's legitimate wife, poor Fortunata clings to the one thing she can offer: thanks to her fertility, she can give her lover the descendants his marriage will never provide. But this advantage, far from making her proud, instead enhances her modesty and her desire to please Jacinta. Tristana, Nazarín, Nucha Pardo, and Ana Ozores all live out their misfortune with the same serenity.

The novels do not elaborate on the possible links between this haughty species of humility and the virtues preached by Christianity. But the external trappings of religion, and the figure of the priest in particular, are often present in the nineteenth-century Spanish novel, undoubtedly because the clergy played a major role in the Spanish society of the time, but perhaps also because they could trigger powerful idealist associations.

If in some cases the priest is as ignorant and gluttonous as any of his literary counterparts since the Middle Ages—e.g., Nicolás Rubín, Maximiliano's brother, in *Fortunata and Jacinta*—in others, his mission is to guide the noble characters toward salvation. In Pardo Bazán's *House of Ulloa*, Julián Alvarez, a well-intentioned young priest witnesses the Ulloa family's decay. As soon as he arrives in the village of Ulloa, he tries to mend the ways of the impulsive master of the house, Don Pedro, who openly lives with Sabel, the daughter of his steward, Primitivo. On Julián's advice, the young marquis goes to Santiago to look for a legitimate wife. He chooses Nucha, the least attractive and best behaved of his cousins. After the marriage, he returns to the village, where, under Primitivo's evil influence, he returns to his former mistress, Sabel. Depressed and ill, Nucha tries to escape from the village but fails. The young priest, her only support, faces the hostility and morbid suspicions of the villagers. He has no power other than to make his flock aware of this world's imperfection, and in the end he must leave Ulloa.

In *Nazarín* (1895), Pérez Galdós takes up this theme, focusing on a saintly character indifferent to worldly satisfactions. Nazarín, a poor, half-crazy priest, refuses all possessions, gives everything he receives to the needy, and turns the other cheek when he is hit. For a while, he manages to keep the forces of evil at bay. His innocence disarms the hard-hearted Don Pedro de Belmonte, a wealthy landowner addicted to material pleasures, who cannot help admiring the priest for his poverty and detachment. A modern disciple of Christ, as his name suggests, Nazarín soon suffers a similar fate: he is hunted down and sent to prison by narrow-minded persecutors. In the final scene, the imprisoned priest gets ready to become a martyr. Feverish, he hallucinates that Christ himself is soothing him by saying: "My son, you are still alive. You are in my blessed hospital, suffering for me . . . Rest now, you deserve it. You did something for me. Be happy." [11]

No less strikingly, in Alas's *La Regenta* the priest character keeps his links with the ideal, but in reverse: Canon Fermín De Pas embodies moral perversity. His corruption has nothing to do with the gluttony

[11] Benito Pérez Galdós, *Nazarín*, trans. Jo Labanyi (Oxford: Oxford World Classics, 1993), p. 190.

and ignorance usually targeted by anticlericalism. Fermín's fall is that of a genuinely superior being, stifled by the prison of celibacy. Not unlike Ambrosio, the protagonist of Lewis's *The Monk*, or Claude Frollo, the maleficent priest in Hugo's *Notre-Dame de Paris*, Fermín falls desperately in love with one of his flock, the beautiful Ana Ozores, whom he attempts to seduce through religious teaching. As her confessor, he can keep a close watch on her thoughts and desires, and as long as her quiet life with a much older husband leaves her sexually unsatisfied, Fermín is keen to keep his passion under the veil of religious friendship. Since virtue consists in the soul's inner balance, he argues that asceticism is only one of the ways to reach it: music, the arts, contemplating nature, or reading philosophical and historical books can all elevate the soul, bringing it closer to sainthood. "Ah! and then," the canon suggests, "when one reached higher regions, and was sure of oneself . . . many entertainments which had previously been fraught with peril were found to be edifying." "The person who achieves a certain degree of strength," he concludes, "finds that the presence of evil uplifts him, in a sense, because of the contrast which it provides."[12]

Instead of congratulating himself on his hypocrisy, Fermín is tortured by remorse—all the more so since his tactic for seducing the beautiful Ana leads nowhere. Flattered by the distinguished prelate's friendship, she is careful not to confess her soft spot for the handsome Alvaro Mesía, who eventually becomes her lover. Having used up all his treasures of theological subtlety to no avail, Fermín discovers her affair with Mesía and, in his anger, denounces them to her peaceable husband, inciting him to defend his honor. The good man is killed in the duel with Mesía, who sneaks away, and the dishonored widow is reduced to poverty. In the final scene, Ana returns to Fermín—God's emissary—hoping to earn heaven's forgiveness and find her faith again. But the canon, choking with hatred, barely refrains from strangling her. His effort to sublimate his love has failed, and the quest for an impossible ideal has turned into a demonic passion.

Among these novels, only *La Regenta* has a touch of bitterness, but even Alas does not remotely share the French naturalists' scorn for the world. An irony both harsh and compassionate, a calm acceptance of human wretchedness as well as virtue, an absence of resentment—these are features of virtually all nineteenth-century Spanish realism. The compromise between idealism and skepticism allowed Pardo Bazán, Pérez Galdós, and Alas to mix distance with empathy and treat their characters with as much lucidity as tenderness. At once sublime and ludicrous, these

---

[12] Leopoldo Alas, *La Regenta*, trans. John Rutherford (London: Penguin Books, 1984), vol. 1, chap. 9, p. 189.

people subscribe to chimerical ideals with a passion worthy of respect, but equally doomed to failure. The defeat of the noblest dreams is portrayed as a general law of human life: the protagonists know in advance that they will fall short of their ideals; they hold to them in the face of inevitable disappointment.

Fate, Inner Strength, Inner Torment

Equally constant in the midst of sorrow are the characters in *The Return of the Native* (1878), although for quite different reasons. Thomas Hardy is often considered a representative of English naturalism, but his work, just like that of his contemporaries Eça de Queirós in Portugal and Bolesław Prus in Poland, goes far beyond the social and genetic determinism professed by naturalism's founders. Naturalism specializes in showing how heredity and social injustice inexorably grind and crush even the best-intentioned characters from the inside, as it were, whereas Hardy, Queirós, and Prus portray strong, independent individuals who could achieve success and happiness were it not for *fate*—an archaic fate that rules over events as brutally as it does in ancient Greek myth and tragedy.

Hardy's novel, one of his most interesting, takes place on the isolated, sparsely populated Egdon Heath, where a few characters dream of happiness and struggle to achieve it, only to be thwarted in the end. They are all definite types, and none evolves or changes in the course of the action. Generous Clym Yeobright was a successful jeweler in Paris but came back to his birthplace to devote himself to educating the poor. Eustacia Vye, the beautiful, willful young woman, loathes the heath and wants to lead a glamorous life. Mrs. Yeobright, Clym's mother, is a typically old-fashioned, intransigent parent. Damon Wildeve, the local innkeeper, serves as the fickle, corrupt man. Thomasin Yeobright, Mrs. Yeobright's niece, is the gentle, innocent girl. Diggory Venn, a peddler who sells red paint for marking sheep, plays the role of sincere young man, always ready to help.

Eustacia Vye, the young femme fatale, has a premarital affair with the innkeeper, Wildeve, but when the good-natured Clym returns to Egdon, she falls in love with him and his Parisian past. Clym and Eustacia marry against Mrs. Yeobright's advice, and Wildeve marries Thomasin. The two marriages are not happy. Eustacia is disenchanted when she realizes Clym will never go back to Paris. Wildeve inherits a large amount of money and begins to court Eustacia again. Soon tragedy strikes. The first victim is Clym's mother: she knocks at her son's door, but, as fate would have it, Wildeve is inside with Eustacia, so there is no answer; brokenhearted,

Mrs. Yeobright walks back home across the wild heath, and, worn out by the heat and snakebites, she dies. Eustacia is next: one cloudy night, on her way to run off with Wildeve, she falls into a pond and drowns. Wildeve also dies in his attempt to save her. Clym is there too, but he survives and becomes a preacher, while the kind peddler, Diggory Venn, ends up happily married to Thomasin.

The plot's plausibility is limited, and what with the archaic symbolism of the heath and the farmers' pagan feasts, it requires a reader eager to be convinced. Yet the novel is unequaled in its portrayal of unusually strong and self-aware characters who nonetheless very rarely achieve their aims. The protagonists, Clym, Eustacia, and Wildeve, are fully conscious of their desires and impulses, as are the less central characters. They consider the implications and possible consequences of each step they take, and they act decisively, convinced that they can elbow their way through life.

For example, when still early in the novel Wildeve tells Eustacia that Thomasin, his intended, is to marry someone else, and suggests they elope, she realizes that she is not interested in him anymore:

> Eustacia watched his shadowy form till it had disappeared. She placed her hand to her forehead and breathed heavily; and then her rich, romantic lips parted under that homely impulse—a yawn. . . . Her lover was no longer to her an exciting man whom many women strove for, and herself could only retain by striving with them. He was a superfluity.[13]

Her feelings are not noble, but they are hers, and by accepting them, she soon finds her way to Clym. Later, after realizing that Clym is not the man of her dreams either, Eustacia ponders her situation:

> her state was so hopeless that she could play with it. To have lost is less disturbing than to wonder if we may possibly have won: and Eustacia could now, like other people at such a stage, take a standing-point outside herself, observe herself as a disinterested spectator, and think what a sport for Heaven this woman Eustacia was. (bk. 5, chap. 4, p. 327)

No illusion is allowed to cloud this mixture of despair and lucidity. A moment later, Wildeve signals his presence by dropping a stone in the nearby pond, and she goes to meet him. Wildeve asks her forgiveness for having married Thomasin and again asks her to elope with him, letting her know

---

[13] Thomas Hardy, *The Return of the Native*, ed. Simon Gatrell (Oxford: Oxford World Classics, 2005), bk. 1, chap. 11, p. 100.

that he is now rich. Calm, self-possessed, she answers that if one evening she sends a signal at eight o'clock sharp, it means she has decided to meet him at midnight. Fate has its own designs, however—they will both drown on that very night.

ıııııııııııııııııııııı

The characters in Eça de Queirós's *The Maias* (1888) are just as self-aware and in control of their actions, but much less suspect. The novel, the crowning achievement of nineteenth-century Portuguese literature, both emulates the naturalist observation of social life and goes far beyond it. The main character, Carlos da Maia, a doctor descended from the old aristocracy, indirectly attacks Zola (labeling him realist) by declaring in conversation with his elegant friends in Lisbon that

> the most insupportable thing about realism was its great scientific airs, its pretentious aesthetics deduced from an alien philosophy, and the invocation of Claude Bernard, experimentalism, positivism, Stuart Mill and Darwin, when it was simply a matter of describing a washer-woman sleeping with a carpenter![14]

Characters, he immediately adds, "can only be depicted through action." The action here occurs in a clearly defined social and historical environment: the Maias are a declining family living through Portugal's difficult nineteenth-century economic and political transitions. But individual passions and choices are equally important. The liberal, freethinking Anglophile Afonso de Maia has a son, Pedro, who is a devout Catholic, like his mother. Pedro develops a violent attraction to the seductive Miss Monforte, daughter of an adventurer and former slave trader. Against his father's advice, Pedro courts and marries her, but she soon elopes with a young Italian prince, taking her newborn daughter with her. In despair, Pedro commits suicide. His son Carlos, raised by Afonso, wants to be useful to society and becomes a doctor.

This drama is just the prologue of the novel, narrated in a lively, confident tone. Once Carlos becomes the center of the story, its tempo slows down. An attentive reader of Flaubert's *Sentimental Education* and Alexandre Dumas-fils's sentimental novel *The Lady of the Camellias* (1848), Eça de Queirós depicts Lisbon's restless, frivolous high life and imagines generous hearts infinitely nobler than the world around them. When Carlos makes a house call to treat Rosa, the daughter of a wealthy Brazilian couple, he meets her mother, the beautiful Maria Eduarda. In the

---

[14] Eça de Queirós, *The Maias*, trans. Patricia McGowan Pinheíro and Ann Stevens (London: Penguin, 1998), bk. 1, chap. 6, p. 146.

absence of her husband, Mr. Castro Gomes, Carlos and Maria Eduarda fall in love—a celestial love, profound and pure. But their liaison becomes known, and when Mr. Castro Gomes hears of it, he seeks Carlos out to tell him that Maria Eduarda is not in fact his wife, but a concubine whose real name is Mrs. MacGren.

In a fury, Carlos needs to see her once more, to "drag out the secret of that infamous farce from the depths of her turbid soul" (bk. 2, chap. 4, p. 432). When they do speak, Maria Eduarda tells him about her terrible past: her father was an Austrian she never met, her mother an elegant, shady Portuguese woman living in Paris. Maria Eduarda spent her school years in a religious community at Tours, and wished to enter a convent, but her mother tried to corrupt her instead. In order to escape, she agreed to a liaison with a young Irishman that should have led to marriage as soon as both turned twenty-one, but he was killed as a volunteer in the French army during the Franco-Prussian War of 1870. Then little Rosa was born, and Castro Gomes was the only alternative to destitution. But before Carlos, she had never truly loved any other man.

The duet reaches peaks worthy of Verdi or Puccini: "Even if I could forgive you, how could I ever believe you again?" Carlos asks. "Everything was a lie, your marriage was a lie, your name was a lie, your whole life was a lie" (p. 442). She answers in a sublime tone:

> What about me? Why should I believe in this great passion you have sworn that you have? What was it you loved in me after all? Go on, tell me! Was it the wife of another man, or my name, or the titillating thrill of adultery perhaps, or my fashionable clothes? Or was it myself, my body, my soul and my love for you? I am the same woman, look at me! These arms are the same, this breast is the same! (p. 442)

Falling to her knees, she swears on the soul of her daughter that she will love him, adore him madly, frantically, till she dies. Carlos wants to reach out to her but the memory of her lies makes him step back. Out of the ensuing silence, Maria speaks again, in a trembling voice: "You're right, everything is finished! You don't believe me, so everything's finished! You'd better go. . . . Everything's over for me" (p. 443). Carlos turns to look at her. A burst of compassion overcomes him: "Obscuring all her weaknesses he saw only her beauty, her grief, her supremely loving soul" (p. 443). He bends down and asks her to marry him.

In Eugène Sue's *The Mysteries of Paris*, Fleur-de-Marie, who has remained pure of heart throughout her forced prostitution, refuses to marry the young nobleman who proposes to her. Her past, she cries out, makes her forever unworthy of the sacred names of wife and mother. Maria Eduarda, however, can accept Carlos's hand, not only because *The*

Maias is so far from being a hyperidealist popular novel, but also because, thanks to her liaison with Castro Gomes, she has never sunk into the lower depths of society. What's more, she is already a mother, and her beloved child is illegitimate only because of the father's heroic death.

If *The Maias* ended here, it would have achieved a beautiful synthesis between an ideal and reality, and between passionate love and moral generosity. But the story continues, destroying the protagonists' plans. Fate punishes transgressions, taking a hidden course worthy of Greek tragedy. By chance, an old family friend who knew Maria Eduarda's mother well learns of the intended marriage, and in order to prevent the *tragedy*—the word he uses—he makes sure Carlos finds out that his future bride is none other than his own sister. Her mother, Pedro da Maia's adulterous wife, took her along when she left her husband. After the death of the Italian prince she ran off with, she moved to Paris, and later told Maria Eduarda that her father was an imaginary Austrian.

In the end, the most sincere and generous love is dirtied, debased. The mother's fault has destroyed her children. Heirs to the Maias' fortune, the heartbroken brother and sister leave Lisbon on separate paths. Persecuted by fate, they are nonetheless innocent. Their shock and pain is not tinged with remorse: the immorality of their actions is not *theirs*.

||||||||||||||||||||||||||||||

Bolesław Prus's *The Doll* (1890) also resonates with the period's pessimism. Like earlier nineteenth-century social realism, it contemplates the way in which social position inflects human passions and decisions—but these passions also have an inexplicable side. At the very beginning of the novel, the protagonist, Stanisław Wokulski, a strong, generous tradesman, falls desperately in love with the young aristocrat Izabela, who cannot get over her narcissism and her contempt for the middle class. As Prus sarcastically explains:

> From her cradle, Izabela had lived in a beautiful world that was not only superhuman but even supernatural. For she slept in feathers, dressed in silks and satins, sat on carved and polished ebony or rosewood, drank from crystal, ate from silver and porcelain as costly as gold.[15]

The inhabitants of this world, selected by birth and wealth, lead a life of elegant manners, permanent vacation, visits, concerts, theater performances, conversations in drawing rooms, and late dinners. They sometimes take in ordinary mortals, but usually they keep their distance from

---

[15] Bolesław Prus, *The Doll*, trans. David Welsh (New York: New York Review of Books Classics, 2011), chap. 5, p. 34.

the outside world. In her dreams, Izabela makes love to Greek gods. In real life, though her family cannot provide her with a decent dowry, she despises Wokulski, who in spite of his wealth and kindness is just a hyperactive middle-class nobody.

Rather than obsessively focusing on a single aim in life, as a Balzac character would do, the inexhaustibly energetic Wokulski heads in all directions, allowing Prus to depict a vast array of social milieus and characters, all of them lively and garrulous. Wokulski is just the most remarkable amongst a crowd of unusual people, but in his country such individual energy, the fuel of nineteenth-century society, does not help. An admirer of England and France, Wokulski is depressed by Polish society's inertia. When all his dreams have failed—his often irrational, imprudent, vain dreams—he commits suicide. In Prus's world, as in those of Thomas Hardy and Eça de Queirós, ideals cannot take root. Here, however, fate does not strike from above; it takes the form of an archaic, unjust, and malevolent society that surrounds and defeats the protagonist.

MATURITY?

At the end of the nineteenth century, the novel appeared to have reached full maturity. In its various forms, it could portray complex human beings whose development and actions did not merely illustrate a preestablished set of norms and values. Writers knew how to connect these characters, their thoughts, and their deeds to a plausible social and historical environment. They reflected on the various ways in which love and couple formation succeeds or fails. And most of them used clear, comprehensible language, meant to reach a large group of educated readers. These achievements—social realism, complex characters, nuanced reflections on love, and accessibility—were in no danger of forcing writers into a uniform mold. Victor Hugo, Alessandro Manzoni, Dickens, and the popular novelists defended an idealized view of humanity, while Stendhal, Thackeray, and Anthony Trollope ironically exposed human imperfection. The moral optimism of George Eliot and Tolstoy, Flaubert's mixture of contempt and indulgence, the Goncourts' and Zola's dismal view of human nature, Dostoevsky's rejection of autonomy, Fontane's serenity, Thomas Hardy's earnestness, the enlightened despair of Eça de Queirós, Benito Pérez Galdós, and Bolesław Prus—they were all flourishing within the same literary framework.

And yet . . .

PART FOUR

The Art of Detachment

CHAPTER 12

Loners in a Strange World

ΙΙΙΙΙΙΙΙΙΙΙΙΙΙΙΙΙΙΙΙΙΙΙΙΙΙΙΙΙΙΙΙΙΙΙΙΙΙΙΙΙΙΙΙΙΙΙΙΙΙΙΙΙΙΙΙΙΙΙΙΙΙΙΙΙΙΙΙΙΙΙΙΙ

. . . and yet beneath this sociable landscape, a tectonic fault had been growing for a while. Until the 1850s in France and England, and until a bit later elsewhere, the best, most revered novelists were eager to be read and appreciated by the largest possible public. After that point, however, writing popular fiction became an increasingly specialized activity, while in some circles, art and literature inspired a new kind of worship.

Greater social mobility and the embrace of democratic ideals favored this split, as did the spread of literacy through mass education, and the lower cost of books and newspapers brought about by industrial development. Alexis de Tocqueville had argued as early as 1840 that when more and more people were able to buy and read more and more books, they would naturally be drawn to the most exciting, captivating works and would pay little attention to formal refinement:

> Authors will aim at rapidity of execution more than at perfection of detail. . . . literary performances will bear marks of an untutored and rude vigor of thought, frequently of great variety and singular fecundity. The object of authors will be to astonish rather than to please, and to stir the passions more than to charm the taste.[1]

In an age of widespread literacy, Tocqueville thought, literature would become one business among others, artistic merit would no longer be a requirement for success, and a few great authors would be surrounded

---

[1] Alexis de Tocqueville, *Democracy in America*, trans. Henry Reeve, Francis Bowen, and Phillips Bradley (New York: Vintage, 1945), vol. 2, chap. 13, pp. 62–63.

by a multitude of idea-mongers. The genuine artists would write only for the small public capable of appreciating their genius:

> Here and there, indeed, writers will doubtless occur who will choose a dif-
> ferent track and who, if they are gifted with superior abilities, will succeed
> in finding readers in spite of their defects or their better qualities; but these
> exceptions will be rare. (p. 63)

These lines point to a situation that already prevailed in Romantic poetry, particularly in Germany, but as far as the novel was concerned, they were prescient.

THE WORSHIP OF ART, THE END OF HISTORY

In *Heinrich von Ofterdingen* (1802), Novalis depicted a Romantic ge-nius who soars far above his fellow creatures. The third chapter tells of a prosperous kingdom whose aging king, father of a beautiful princess, has no male heir. Walking in the forest, the princess comes across a small, lonely estate where she meets a young poet. The two fall in love at first sight, and after a while the princess bears a child. They return to the royal court, where the young man sings a song about the sufferings and hero-ism of poets. The king's eagle lays a golden crown on the poet's head, and the king takes the young couple in his arms and accepts their child. From then on, the country's existence takes the form of a splendid feast—poetry has transfigured everyday life.

It was only during the second half of the nineteenth century, however, that the cult of poetry was generalized to include art and literature as a whole. By then, the conception of history as progress toward secular salvation had been widely accepted. As we saw earlier, Hegel, Auguste Comte, and Marx each argued that history had arrived at its happy end-ing or was getting close to it, either by leading the human spirit to its ultimate self-understanding (Hegel), ensuring the triumph of science (Comte), or preparing the imminent proletarian revolution (Marx). For all three thinkers, religion was a thing of the past, and for Hegel art too had lost its power to lead, while in Comte's view philosophy had to be re-placed by positive knowledge. They assumed that historical development had reached—or would soon reach—a threshold at which only one kind of pursuit would be relevant: philosophy for Hegel, science for Comte, and political struggle for Marx. Art and literature were considered obso-lete (Hegel) or at least subordinate (Marx).

Arthur Schopenhauer, by contrast, saw human history as nothing but a cruel, senseless manifestation of blind Will, incessantly generating desire, conflict, anguish, and unreason. In this schema, outstanding souls cannot but find society unbearable; they feel like political prisoners condemned to work in the galleys with common criminals, and they have no choice except isolation. They can overcome the rule of Will, however, transcending desire and conflict through aesthetic reflection, moral compassion, and, at the highest level, denial of the will to live. As a form of contemplative detachment, art puts people in touch with the realm of ideas and gives them a hint of a higher, nobler existence, brightened by compassion. Art is thus expected to show the way toward a secular salvation profoundly different from the Hegelian flowering of the human spirit, Comte's triumph of science, or Marx's revolutionary redemption. Far from promising collective happiness or saving the whole of humanity, art, like an ascetic religion, brings consolation to only a chosen few. Art does not rule or transform the world—as poetry aspired to do in Novalis's story—rather, it frees the great artists and their admirers from the world's bondage.

Seeing themselves as exceptional souls, aesthetes naturally looked down on commercially successful literature, as well as on the traditions of social realism, complex characterization, nuanced exploration of feelings, and accessibility. The highbrow writers who set the most exacting standards for the novel in the late nineteenth century and the first half of the twentieth—those, in other words, who created modernism—were convinced that their task was to produce astonishingly original, demanding works. They claimed to be the first to discover the genuine criteria for superior art, which included perpetual innovation. Instead of keeping fiction subject to reality, these writers promoted a new sense of artistic autonomy. Instead of being reader-friendly, they expected the public to devote an ever-increasing amount of attention and patience to their groundbreaking prose. Tocqueville's prediction that popular authors would aim to "astonish rather than to please" was just as true, perhaps even truer, of more serious writers.

As if alluding to Schopenhauer's world of blind Will and suffering, modernist novels often take place in a pervasive atmosphere of emptiness and sorrow. The characters do not entirely know who they are or why they act the way they do. Focusing on their fragile psyches, the all-powerful writer leads readers through an intricate stylistic labyrinth whose gloomy incoherence, biting irony, or uncanny intellectual sophistication emphasizes its distance from real life. The links between characters and their society grow weak or disappear, and the figure of the loner—an educated loner of good social standing who generally cannot find satisfaction—increasingly holds center stage.

DISCONSOLATE LONERS

Oversensitive individuals who fail to integrate into society, and outsiders who despise conventions and moral laws, have long played a significant role in novels. Unruly outsiders were usually of low social status—medieval tricksters, sixteenth- to eighteenth-century pícaros or pícaras, and outcasts like the creature in Mary Shelley's *Frankenstein*, Balzac's Vautrin, or Heathcliff in Emily Brontë's *Wuthering Heights*—but some of them belonged to more privileged groups and yet chose to adopt a rebellious stance, as did Lovelace in Richardson's *Clarissa*, Valmont in Laclos's *Liaisons dangereuses*, and gothic evildoers like Ambrosio in Lewis's *The Monk*. The nineteenth-century dandies—Henri de Marsay in Balzac's *Human Comedy*, Pechorin in Lermontov's *A Hero of Our Time*—were of this type. Sensitive loners, by contrast, were superior beings who, failing to find their true soul mate and place in the community, ended up in solitude, resignation, deliberate withdrawal from society, or death. The well-bred, unhappy women in elegiac stories by Boccaccio and Guilleragues, Goethe's vulnerable Werther, Hölderlin's lofty Hyperion, Chateaubriand's René, and Mme de Staël's Corinne were all doomed to the pains of isolation.

In the second half of the nineteenth century, the novel brought forth another, more ordinary kind of solitary being. The average person's inability to settle lastingly in the world was explored in Flaubert's *Sentimental Education*, Fontane's *Cécile* and *Effi Briest*, and Hardy's *Tess of the d'Urbervilles* (1891). In such works, solitude and disappointment are not necessarily seen as inevitable. Happier outcomes still seem possible: Flaubert's Frédéric Moreau could have found contentment, if not with Mme Arnoux then at least with his friendly mistress, Rosanette; Effi could have carried on as Baron von Innstetten's sociable wife; and Tess could have been spared her terrible fate. True, the French naturalists imagined an irreversible social exclusion, but in the Goncourts' *Germinie Lacerteux* and Zola's *L'Assommoir*, the female characters end up forlorn because an unjust society prevents them from resisting corruption. Since the Goncourts and Zola imply that a society organized on fairer lines would have spared these characters, they do not present the individual's inability to adjust to the world as the ultimate truth of our condition.

In the last third of the nineteenth century, though, a wave of pessimistic novels made precisely this contention, reviving the old elegiac, disconsolate loneliness and enshrining it as a fundamental truth. In Iginio Ugo Tarchetti's *Fosca* (1869), Jens Peter Jacobsen's *Niels Lyhne* (1880), Joaquim Maria Machado de Assis's *Dom Casmurro* (1899), and Marcellus Emants's *A Posthumous Confession* (1894), the main characters find themselves irremediably excluded. Their sad fate is not determined, as in naturalist works, by social background, heredity, or illness. Although such factors put considerable strain on them, these people still enjoy a certain freedom of action. This freedom, however, not only fails to break down the barriers between the protagonists and their world, but in the end, as it did in Goethe, Hölderlin, Chateaubriand, and Mme de Staël, it intensifies their distress.

Fosca (translated into English as *Passion*) is a short novel about a young Italian officer who, like many fictional men of the period, finds happiness in a relationship with a beautiful and willing married woman. Military obligations take Giorgio away from his beloved Clara to an unpleasant small town, where he meets his colonel's niece, Fosca, a lonely, strangely unattractive woman undergoing medical treatment for severe attacks of hysteria. Fosca does not hide her passion for Giorgio, who predictably rebuffs her. Her doctor, worried that Giorgio's rejection might aggravate her nervous condition and even kill her, begs the young man to see her regularly for a while. Giorgio agrees, and the doctor, whose apartment is connected to Fosca's, lets him in for secret visits. Fosca becomes more and more insistent, and when Giorgio, exasperated, tries to leave town, she follows, telling him she is determined to hold on to him whether he likes it or not:

> It is I who loved you, who love you, who want to love you. . . . I want you to believe it, I shall compel you to believe it. . . . I don't care that you don't love me; you can even hate me, it is all the same. . . . I want to force you to remember me.[2]

She soon declares her passion in front of her uncle, the colonel, and he, convinced that Giorgio has dishonored her, challenges the young man to a duel. Just then, Giorgio receives a farewell letter from Clara, who has decided to become a virtuous wife. On the eve of the duel, Giorgio, in spite of his revulsion, spends the night with Fosca. The colonel is hurt in the fight, though not mortally; Fosca dies shortly afterward, and Giorgio, racked by nervous depression, returns to his native village.

The story deals with naturalist themes of sickness and degeneration, but the reader's attention is mainly directed to the young, healthy, well-behaved protagonist. There is no sense of inevitable doom here: Giorgio loses his grip on life, but it is never quite clear why. He is fairly down-to-earth in his aspirations—a military career, a benign affair with Clara—and he is an altruist, who does not hesitate to spend time with the ailing Fosca. When fate strikes, it does not hit him directly: Clara withdraws, but she has never really been his; Fosca dies, but her fate is hardly unexpected; the colonel is wounded but survives. Nevertheless, by the end of the story, the world has shown Giorgio its true, nightmarish face, and he resorts to solitude.

---

[2] I. U. Tarchetti, *Passion*, trans. Lawrence Venuti (San Francisco: Mercury House, 1994), p. 152.

Jens Peter Jacobsen's *Niels Lyhne* also stays away from naturalist clichés. A calm Nordic light bathes this Danish bildungsroman, whose main character slowly discovers the power of love and death, becomes an atheist, and, having experienced the most profound loneliness, leaves the world without complaining or giving in. The son of a romantic woman and her pragmatic husband, Niels inherits his father's sense of reality and his mother's love for poetry: he even becomes a poet, although without much success. As a teenager he falls in love with Edele, his young aunt from Copenhagen who has moved to healthy Lønborggaard to treat her lung condition. When Edele gets sicker and dies, Niels, who has been praying fervently for her survival, understands that there is no God to alleviate human suffering. He later moves to Copenhagen, writes poetry, and has a platonic affair with an older woman, Mrs. Boye, apparently not picking up on her hints about physical love.

One Christmas Eve, he discusses religion with Dr. Hjerrild, who is known for his nonconformist views. When Niels criticizes Christianity, Hjerrild describes how hard it is to be a heretic in a world ruled by opinion:

> Think what such a man's life would be like, if he is to do his utmost. Unable to speak without boos and hisses foaming up in the footsteps of his speech. To have all his words distorted, besmirched, twisted out of joint, twined into cunning snares, thrown at his feet, and then before he has even gathered them up out of the dirt and untangled them from one another, suddenly to discover that the whole world is deaf. And then to start all over again from another point, with the same results, over and over.[3]

The young man's bitter answer calls to mind Ludwig Feuerbach's rejection of religion; Niels says: "There is no God, and the human being is His prophet."

Back in Lønborggaard, Niels tastes love's pleasures with his cousin Erik's wife, Fennimore. But when Erik, a failed artist who has become a drunk, dies in an accident, Fennimore is convinced God is sending her a message, and she breaks up with Niels. He soon marries the young, pious Gerda, who loves him dearly: she is even willing to abandon her faith to please him. But both she and their child die, once again in spite of Niels's desperate prayers—the prayers of an atheist this time. Desolate, Niels enlists as a volunteer in the Danish-German War. During a battle he is shot in the chest. Dr. Hjerrild, visiting Niels on his deathbed, advises him

---

[3] Jens Peter Jacobsen, *Niels Lyhne*, trans. Tiina Nunnally (London: Penguin Classics, 2006), p. 105.

to call a priest. But Niels remains firm: his suffering cannot be assuaged by what he considers a lie. He dies the difficult death.

Just as disturbing as the fundamental aloneness Niels accepts as his lot is the belated discovery made by Bentinho, protagonist and narrator of Machado de Assis's *Dom Casmurro*, that his whole life—love, family, fatherhood—has been nothing but a series of deceptions. He married below his station; Capitu, his childhood friend and beloved wife, has been manipulating him all along. As their son Ezequiel grows up, he increasingly resembles the couple's close friend Escobar. Devastated by jealousy, Bentinho separates from his wife but still carries her image in his heart. A weak man in love, an enigmatic young woman, a double betrayal—Bentinho narrates it all in a calm, slightly ironic tone.

Edging closer to nightmare, Marcellus Emants's *A Posthumous Confession* is the first-person narrative of a man who cannot relate at all to anyone around him and accuses the world of pushing him aside. While still a teenager, talking to the first young woman he desires, he is already aware of his isolation:

> I made no attempt to fathom her, but immersed myself exclusively in the emotions aroused in my heart by the sight of her, by her touch, her words, her kisses. *I enjoyed myself.*[4]

Unable to choose a profession, make friends, or even cultivate acquaintances, he marries Anna, a young, inexperienced woman who soon realizes he is abnormal, and will no longer allow him any physical intimacy. He wants to divorce her, but she refuses: a true anti–Emma Bovary, she is eager to lead a life of self-denial. Deeply humiliated by her indifference—and by a brief platonic relationship she has with a neighbor—the narrator befriends a courtesan, who makes increasing financial demands on him. Supporting the courtesan becomes less and less affordable; thinking he may be able to marry her instead, he poisons his wife. He carries out the murder so intelligently as to escape suspicion:

> For once I enjoyed the illusion of having revenged myself on normal humanity, of having had a chance to triumph over the society that had always confined me and denied me what was mine. (p. 190)

Will he be able to stifle his remorse, forget Anna's innocence, and woo the courtesan? The story ends without an answer.

---

[4] Marcellus Emants, *A Posthumous Confession*, trans. J. M. Coetzee (New York: New York Review of Boks Classics, 1986), p. 21.

CONVERTS AND IMMORALISTS

The echoes of Schopenhauer's pessimism are clearly perceptible in these novels. Tarchetti's and Jacobsen's evoke a cluster of themes—maladjustment, renunciation, compassion—that can also be found in Flaubert to some extent, as well as in Fontane, Hardy, Pérez Galdós, Eça de Queirós, Machado de Assis, and even, infinitesimally, in Emants. Schopenhauer's idea of salvation through art was even more influential than his pessimism, especially once Friedrich Nietzsche, in the 1870s and 1880s, envisaged a new, more energetic version of the cult of art. For him, artistic endeavor is not remotely about the denial of the Will: it is the highest form of human activity, a joyous affirmation of life, particularly enticing at a time when, according to him, God is dead and the slave morality imposed by Christianity will soon disappear.

Not that every form of late nineteenth-century aestheticism would bear the mark of Nietzsche's amoral enthusiasm. One of the most articulate aesthetes, the French novelist Joris-Karl Huysmans, began his career as a disciple of naturalism, but soon broke with Zola and his followers. Durtal, the protagonist of his novel *The Damned* (*Là-bas*, 1891), pays tribute to the naturalists' matter-of-fact attitude, but is repelled by their obsession with physiology, their tendency to reduce the mystery of the soul to the diseases of the body. Instead of portraying human beings as wholly defined by their biology and social context, literature should imagine individuals who succeed in detaching themselves from the world around them.

The main, in fact the only character in Huysmans's *Against the Grain* (*À rebours*, 1884) rejects the social world and turns to art as the path to redemption. Des Esseintes is an aesthete who withdraws from society, shutting all the doors and windows of his country house and living alone, surrounded by lit candles, rare books, and expensive artworks. Nothing happens in the novel—Des Esseintes's goal is precisely to avoid participating in the world of events. Art alone, however, cannot provide long-term sustenance, and in the end Des Esseintes returns to Paris. Yet his experiment proved to Huysmans's readers, including Oscar Wilde, Paul Bourget, the poets Stéphane Mallarmé and Paul Valéry, and the painter Whistler, that one could imagine a way of life whose sole foundation and aim is art.

For Huysmans, rejection of society is the first step on the path of religion, as it was for Baudelaire and their mutual friend Jules-Amédée Barbey d'Aurevilly. After *The Damned*, which blends the story of a famous medieval child murderer, Gilles de Rais, with a description of underground Satan-worship in late nineteenth-century Paris, Huysmans portrayed a gradual conversion to faith in *En Route* (1895), and eventually, in *The Cathedral* (*La Cathédrale*, 1898), a full acceptance of the religious outlook, albeit with a strong aestheticist bent.

But devotion to art does not always lead in a saintly direction. It may also serve a Nietzschean celebration of the body freed from the shackles of morality. Aesthetes may turn against the prevailing hypocrisy and embrace the realm of the senses. The worship of beauty, in such cases, is "aesthetic" in the original sense of the word, which refers to sensuous perception, and remains by definition indifferent to moral requirements. Oscar Wilde's *The Picture of Dorian Gray* (1890) tells the story of a handsome young man whose search for pleasure leads him from debauchery to lies and murder. This kind of life would be sure to leave its mark on Dorian's face, were it not for a hidden portrait of him, which bears the traces of his decay. Dorian appears attractive only because his true physiognomy has been magically transferred to a work of art: the picture projects its beauty onto the character, while absorbing his growing moral corrosion.

Sensual aestheticism found a resolute defender in André Gide. *The Fruits of the Earth* (*Les Nourritures Terrestres*, 1897), written in an exhortative tone akin to that of Nietzsche's *Thus Spake Zarathustra* (1883–1885), values passionate experiences over moral judgment and advocates the cult of the self. Gide illustrates these ideas in *The Immoralist* (1902). Raised to become a scholar, Michel, the protagonist and narrator, discovers the charms of the senses. With his beautiful, adoring wife, he travels to Algeria to recover from a lung disease. Thanks to the sunny climate, his wife's devotion, and some clandestine encounters with local young men, Michel is cured. The couple returns to France, where the artificiality of social life disgusts him, all the more so since his friend Ménalque—based on Oscar Wilde—encourages him to seek his own unique form of happiness. After giving birth to a child, Michel's wife falls ill. They go back to North Africa, where he spends his time with handsome teenagers while her condition worsens. He does try to take care of her, but she senses his disdain. His doctrine, she tells him, leaves out the weak. Michel agrees: the weak should be left out. True to his own desires, fashioning himself, as he sees it, into a superior being, the protagonist brushes aside all obstacles.

Loners Turn into Artists

Some devotees of beauty decide to live for art and art alone. Huysmans's Des Esseintes is one of them, but his approach is rather naive—the mere consumption of expensive artifacts. Art requires a deeper commitment: the artistic vocation, which played an important role in fiction from the early nineteenth century onward—in works by E.T.A. Hoffmann,

Balzac, Gérard de Nerval, Gottfried Keller, and Zola—emerges in Proust's *Remembrance of Things Past* (1913–1927) as the protagonist's route to redemption. In Gide, the emphasis on sensuality and egotism makes detailed psychological analysis and social observation unnecessary: once the character discovers sensual pleasure, inner struggles and the social order melt away. *Remembrance of Things Past*, by contrast, portrays the complications of the human psyche and its painful interactions with others by expanding its descriptions, scenes, first-person self-examinations, and philosophical speculations on a scale never attempted before.

Swann, an elegant connoisseur, and Marcel, the middle-class young man who beguilingly narrates the story, are both victims of inexplicable passions. In the novel, falling for people as bland and devious as Odette, a demimondaine Swann desperately pursues, or Marcel's love object, Albertine, is a mysterious mishap, an illness impossible to diagnose, similar in many ways to Anselmo's condition in Cervantes's *An Ill-Advised Curiosity*, or the Princess of Clèves's ardor for M. de Nemours in Mme de Lafayette's novel. In *Manon Lescaut*, Prévost hinted at how distressing this kind of infatuation can be, but he justified Des Grieux's fixation on Manon to some extent by endowing her with a few praiseworthy features that might have prevailed in a more prosperous or more solitary environment. In Proust, desire has nothing to do with the beloved's actual qualities: it is aroused exclusively by her inaccessibility; her real personality and intentions remain indiscernible. We understand others only in the absence of desire, the novel seems to say.

Moreover, because Proust's lovers do not know themselves, they cannot measure the cunning and tenacity of their own obsessions. Once in a stable romantic relationship, Swann (in the section "Swann in Love") and Marcel (in *The Captive*) both imagine that their peaceful state is a sign that their love has eased or even disappeared. Yet the slightest doubt about the other person's loyalty, the smallest twinge of jealousy is enough for the passion to reignite with astonishing violence. The lover's desertion suddenly feels like the worst thing that could happen: the mere possibility of it rekindles a desire that has no other raison d'être. On the very day when Marcel has decided that he is strong enough to break up with Albertine, indeed, that he is now indifferent to her, he learns that she has left him, and in an instant is plunged into despair; stunned by the reversal in his feelings, he nonetheless starts frantically trying to get her back. The resulting sense of vertigo recurs over and over in the long introspective passages of the *Remembrance*.

As for social life, Proust, in line with the French moralist tradition (fully supported on this issue by Schopenhauer), thinks it is ruled by vainglory. The desire to succeed blinds us, puts us at the mercy of those we want to impress, and prevents us from understanding their attitudes and motivations. Like Balzac's or Flaubert's, Proust's descriptions of those who bustle about in the social world do not aim simply to teach a moral lesson. Instead, he lingers patiently on the physiognomy and manners of the members of various classes—the Guermantes, old aristocracy; the Verdurins, upper-middle-class patrons of the arts; the narrator's grandfather, a provincial bourgeois; Françoise, a servant—and also examines people whose place in society is less stable, such as the fashionable writer Bergotte; Bloch, a Jew trying to assimilate; and gay men like Charlus and Jupien. He meticulously paints their language, their gestures, the subtle causal web that governs their desires and actions, and fixes them, at least to some extent, within their social niche. It is as though the extended passages delving into the narrator's vulnerable psyche require a staunchly plausible social context to back them up.

These characters cannot, however, be fully identified with their social origin and milieu, because they never entirely manage to settle, in either their native environment or one of their choosing. Just as Proust's lovers are torn between the feeling that their desire has run its course and the wild impulse to control their love objects, his snobs, like Legrandin, for instance, vacillate between pretending not to care about high society and scrambling to be accepted into it. The Verdurins, meanwhile, ambitious founders of an avant-garde artistic salon, snobs and antisnobs at once, do whatever is necessary to help the friends they invite to their dinners, so long as these friends (nicknamed "the faithful") swear not to go to other people's parties. And just as, in order to decode the relations between the *Remembrance*'s lovers, you need to answer the question "Which one of them cannot live without the other?" the key to understanding Proust's *beau monde* is to ask "Who moves in what circles?"— precisely because no one feels secure in society or, more generally, at home in the world.

Remembrance of Things Past is truly of its time, not so much because it depicts the pitfalls of life in the highest social circles—a theme Balzac handled so brilliantly—and the tortures of loveless jealousy, though Proust was one of the great experts on that subject, but because it explores the irresolvable conflict between the sensitive individual and the rest of the world, which causes pain that cannot be salved. But only a few characters—Marcel's mother, his grandmother, and, barely noticeably, the composer Vinteuil—live by Schopenhauer's moral precepts. Their inexhaustible kindness protects them, if not from others' wickedness, at least from the torment of misdirected love or thwarted snobbery. Yet because these good people, whose grace and discretion rival those of Stifter's and Fontane's characters, are without desire or ambition, they cannot be said, in Proust's world, to have lived a full life.

The story is told by the older Marcel, who contemplates his younger self's inexperience and missteps from afar. The underlying question in his narrative is Schopenhauer's: how can we avoid the suffering that inevitably accompanies desire, rivalry, and conflict? The answer includes two elements present in *The World as Will and Idea*: the denial of the will to live and the worship of art. But, taking his cues from Henri Bergson's reflections on memory, Proust infuses these answers with a new energy.

Very early in this huge text, the young Marcel eats a tea cake, a madeleine, whose taste brings back a flood of memories. Filled with wonder, he realizes that memory stores traces of life's savor, to be rediscovered only much later. The true flavor of existence cannot be experienced here and now, in the quick of life, since the present is always jammed with futile desires and the suffering they cause. Life's true essence is sensed later, from afar, through involuntary recollection: the madeleine Marcel dips in a cup of tea, as he used to at his aunt Léonie's house, stirs up the echoes of early happiness, a happiness he could not possibly have felt as a child, caught in a turmoil of cravings and frustrations. Thus the denial of the will to live here and now does not entail a rejection of the world as such. This world *is* a paradise, but one that can be grasped only in the recollection of things past. In and of itself, however, the involuntary rediscovery of lost happiness cannot grant lasting relief from solitude. The end of the novel tell us, almost echoing Nietzsche's ecstatic view, that true deliverance is brought by art—not as a refuge from life, but as the only true access to its plenitude. Literature is life, finally discovered and clarified; Marcel understands that writing is both his true calling and his personal salvation.

EXHAUSTED FEELINGS, EXUBERANT LANGUAGE

Ulysses (1922) by James Joyce paints a darker picture of human loneliness than Proust's and expresses it in more exuberant language. Joyce's characters feel just as alien to the world, but the difference is that in *Ulysses*, suffering is caused not so much by misguided passion as by passion's extinction, by a kind of moral impotence that overtakes action and thought. Stymied by regrets, remorse, and hesitation, feeling spurts of desire that lead nowhere, incapable of pursuing definite ends, the characters wander through Dublin without understanding what prevents them from taking action. The story told over more than seven hundred pages amounts to a small number of events that take place during the same day, as though the plot is of only minor import, the work's real aim being to convey lived experience in its blinding immediacy.

The two protagonists, Leopold Bloom and Stephen Dedalus, are each haunted by the loss of a loved one several years before—Dedalus's mother and Bloom's son. Dedalus cannot forget how grievously he offended his dying mother, whose dearest wish was for him to recover his faith in God. As for Bloom, ever since the death of his child he has been unable to have conjugal relations with his wife, Molly. He suspects she is unfaithful and plans to find out whether her lover is visiting her at home. But because he lacks the nerve to catch them in the act, Bloom rambles around the city, its offices, parks, and bars. On his way, he meets Dedalus and ends up carrying the younger man home, blind drunk after a binge in a tavern. Returning too late to discover and punish the adultery, Bloom joins his sleeping wife in bed. Molly's long monologue as she lies next to him serves as an epilogue.

Joyce's prose combines the many aspects of external reality captured by human perception with the images, ideas, and half-thoughts that make up the stream of consciousness. Richardson's *Pamela* had already put these two facets of experience together by alternating scrupulous descriptions of the setting with those of the main character's thoughts and feelings. To this venerable technique, Joyce adds the lively precision of the naturalists, as well as a Jamesian notation of his characters' states of mind. Joyce's astounding innovation consists in including a vast array of extraneous details. From Richardson to the naturalists, novelists had always used perceptual and psychological minutiae to keep the story's events and their meaning present in the readers' minds and help them understand its atmosphere, the milieu, the characters, and the moral thesis. In *Ulysses*, by contrast, the extraordinary discursive proliferation is mostly independent of plot and character.

The abundance of inessential details is particularly striking in the representation of the characters' stream of consciousness. Rather than merely reporting the characters' inner deliberations in an abstract moral vocabulary, as writers had done for so long, or evoking their tacit interactions, as Henry James did, Joyce offers his readers a kaleidoscope of ideas, remembrances, commonplaces, and fragments of sentences that cross their minds:

> Bloom looked, unblessed to go. Got up to kill: on eighteen bob a week. Fellows shell out the dibs. Want to keep your weathereye open. Those girls, those lovely. By the sad sea waves. Chorusgirl's romance. Letters read out for breach of promise. From Chickabiddy's own Mumpsypum. Laughter in court. Henry. I never signed it. The lovely name you.[5]

---

[5] James Joyce, *Ulysses*, ed. Hans Walter Gabler (New York: Vintage, 1986), chap. 11, p. 234.

Does this passage, which continues for many pages, truly represent the spontaneous movement of thought? More likely, these linguistic fireworks, closer to poetry than prose, aim to elicit ill-defined, unfamiliar, breathtaking emotions.

In this translucent, multifarious text, states of mind are refracted into myriad pieces, not unlike the impressionists' brushstrokes, spots of color whose individual impact on the overall effect, real as it is, remains almost imperceptible. According to *Ulysses*, the human mind, overflowing with images and unexpected associations, is afflicted by a strange inability to concentrate or decide, a problem that may be caused by this very jumble of ideas and imagery. As a consequence, the more carefully readers try to follow the flow of lyrical and imagistic impressions, the more plausible they find the characters' paralysis.

This paralysis never subsides. In Joyce's novel, art, which in Proust was presumed to free people from the world of everyday suffering, brings pain to light without abolishing it. Art does not influence the characters' fate but places a twofold emphasis on its meaninglessness. First, the parodic references to Homer's *Odyssey* lend a modicum of sense to the characters' disordered thoughts and behavior. Bloom represents a cowardly, indecisive Ulysses who never leaves his Ithaca, Molly an unfaithful Penelope, Dedalus a Telemachus abandoned by the gods. The silent force of the myth orients their apparently chaotic movements, but crucially, since the characters themselves do not possess this key, the secret meaning of their tribulations escapes them. Only the author and astute readers understand that derision has replaced epic grandeur, that Ulysses's successful return to his kingdom is mirrored here by Bloom's and Dedalus's humiliating failure to make peace with their losses. Second, Joyce's stylistic verve, instead of helping make the story comprehensible, uses it for its own purposes. The novel deliberately challenges readers' expectations, relentlessly surprising them and forcing them to appreciate Joyce's virtuosity. Formal artistic splendor is the true goal of *Ulysses*.

Joyce thus innovates by representing the characters' confused inner life in minute detail, by freeing style from the obligation to serve narrative content, and by building his novel on a mythic framework that remains virtually invisible. Does this mean that Joyce's answer to the old question raised by novels, "Are we at home in the world?" is less important than his formal inventions? Joyce is certainly more famous for his verbal dexterity than for his social observation or the depth of his psychology. Yet paradoxically, patient readers will discover that the dizzying style does suggest an answer to fiction's familiar question, revealing a gloomy world whose inhabitants must accept its ways without ever understanding them.

Disorienting Proximity

The novelists after *Ulysses* who continued to focus on formal innovation and, like Joyce, found various ways of immersing readers in their characters' experience took two different paths: some, including Italo Svevo, Virginia Woolf, William Faulkner, Samuel Beckett, and Nathalie Sarraute, chose to depict human isolation, while others, like Ford Madox Ford, Alfred Döblin, Richard Wright, and John Dos Passos, envisaged or at least hoped for a possible reconciliation between the individual and the world.

Historical factors were decisive. We saw earlier how the late eighteenth- and early nineteenth-century European wars inspired Kleist and Walter Scott to bring narrative prose closer to the epic tradition. World War I played an equally important part in the development of modernism, but in contrast with the nineteenth-century reflections on greatness, this time war was felt to reveal the extent of human weakness, irrelevance, and folly. In Walter Benjamin's perceptive terms:

> never has experience been contradicted more thoroughly than strategic experience by tactical warfare, economic experience by inflation, bodily experience by mechanical warfare, moral experience by those in power. A generation that had gone to school on a horse-drawn streetcar now stood under the open sky in a countryside in which nothing remained unchanged but the clouds, and beneath these clouds, in a field of force of destructive torrents and explosions, was the tiny, fragile human body.[6]

By demonstrating how drastically unstable things were, war validated both Schopenhauer's pessimism and Marx's revolutionary message, thus encouraging modernist writers to reject "polite," deluded, self-destructive society. In a disorienting world, disorienting literary techniques became, at least in theory, the best way for the novel to generate new insights.

In *Zeno's Conscience* (1923) by Italo Svevo, the irremediably lonely protagonist examines his capricious, compulsive behavior through the lens of Freudian psychoanalysis. The bitterly humorous story jumps from one topic to the next, never becoming wholly coherent or reliable. In Virginia Woolf's *Mrs Dalloway* (1925) and *To the Lighthouse* (1927), individuals from the same family, who spend their lives together, behave as though in fact they were moving in entirely different orbits. Woolf's specialty is the successive third-person narration of various characters' thoughts: her technique, less shocking than the exclamations, metaphors,

---

[6] "The Storyteller" (1936), in Walter Benjamin, *Illuminations: Essays and Reflections*, ed. Hannah Arendt, trans. Harry Zohn (New York: Schocken Books, 1969), p. 84.

and incomplete sentences flying around in the heads of Joyce's characters, suggests that each person is a prisoner of his or her perceptions, managing to grasp—very intensely—only a small section of the shared world. Within this section, other people, even those one might think important, like spouses, friends, or children, actually occupy a marginal position and are noticed only with a kind of surprise, slightly colored by repulsion. The secret questions that seem to lie behind the thoughts of even Woolf's most generous and praiseworthy characters (Mrs. Ramsay, for instance, in *To the Lighthouse*) are "Why do other people exist?" and "Why are their lives mixed up with mine?" Only through complex, silent maneuvers do these people avoid the obstacles placed in their path by the presence of others.

The protagonists' solitude is even more severe in the novels of William Faulkner. What goes on can be understood only indirectly, through inner monologues full of pained lamentations and the murmurs of unappeased desires. Neurotic, psychotic, handicapped individuals populate this world, their infirmities and flaws indicating the human inability to cross interpersonal borders. In *The Sound and the Fury* (1929) the thread is almost impossible to follow on first reading. Only by returning to the text or consulting commentaries can the reader figure out exactly how the four poetic monologues making up the novel converge. Hazily, links emerge between the young Quentin Compson, the beautiful Caddy whom he incestuously loves, the rest of the family, and the mentally retarded Benjy, kept alive by the black servants' kindness. Virtually nothing in the interminable dialogues Benjy uncomprehendingly overhears, almost nothing in Quentin's divagations or Jason's ratiocinations helps the story move forward—the reader may well wonder whether the concept of "helping the story move forward" retains any meaning in Faulkner's foggy, torrid world. Moreover, as in *Ulysses*, the speech, thoughts, and memories presented, rather than rendering the story intelligible, form a mass of raw narrative matter from which a smart reader might contrive to piece the book's argument together.

One thus needs to differentiate between *fully crafted* novels with neatly constructed plots, and *rough, unprocessed* works, like *Ulysses* and *The Sound and Fury*, which expose the reader to vast quantities of disorienting material. To a certain extent, the second approach continues the late nineteenth-century effort to emphasize pure observation, eliminating abstract reflections and explicit moral judgments. Since real human lives are not interlaced with authorial commentary, many novels of that period described the characters' immediate experience without remarking on it. But the work of Joyce, Woolf, and Faulkner radicalizes this technique: not only does the author's voice fall silent, but the author as the story's inventor and architect fades away.

These trends—pure observation over authorial comment and rough narration over coherent plot—were inherited and developed by two branches of the modernist novel. One of them became popular in the mid-twentieth century thanks to a generation of American writers whose best-known representative is Ernest Hemingway. Prosaic, direct, even brutal, his novels, in particular *A Farewell to Arms* (1929) and *For Whom the Bell Tolls* (1940), take up modernism's naturalist heritage. By contrast, Hermann Broch's *The Death of Virgil* (1945), Samuel Beckett's unforgettable *Molloy* (1951) as well as his entire oeuvre—perhaps the most faithful continuation of the Schopenhauerian tradition—and the *nouveau roman*, as exemplified by Nathalie Sarraute, Claude Simon, Marguerite Duras, and Michel Butor, build on the lyrical potential of rough, seemingly unfiltered narration. Sarraute in particular excels in representing marginal states of mind, involuntary impulses, and linguistic automatisms; in such works as *Tropisms* (1939), even as she renders everyday life almost unrecognizable, she evokes the humble poetry inherent in it.

There is a more optimistic strain of high modernism. In Ford Madox Ford's *Some Do Not . . .* (1924), from the cycle of war novels *Parade's End* (1924–1928), the episodes do not observe chronology, the viewpoint constantly shifts, and the narrative teems with striking but superfluous details. Yet the conflict, the characters, and their motivations are perfectly coherent and historically plausible. Moreover, while the novel depicts Edwardian high society as deeply corrupt, the protagonist, Christopher Tietjens, stands out as a model of magnanimity and self-restraint. Constantly persecuted by jealous, malevolent rivals, he remains silent, impassive. He does not resent his unfaithful, manipulative wife, who seduced him while pregnant by another man, nor his best friend, who breaks with him after using his work to win a knighthood. The knowledge that the world is a terrible place does not deter Tietjens from acting in accordance with his ideals. Although, once they form a society, people become experts in "oppressions, inaccuracies, gossip, backbiting, lying, corruptions and vileness,"[7] as the title reminds us, *some do not*. Furthermore, Christopher feels the most sublime kind of romantic love—passionate, complete, and pure—for the young Valentine Wannop, a virtuous suffragette who devotes all her energies to enabling her mother, a talented novelist of modest means, to keep writing. For a long time, Christopher does not even realize he is in love, but in the book's final pages, as he prepares to go to war, probably to die, he asks Valentine to be his lover. She agrees— how could she not?—but in the end they remain chaste. (Only in *Last Post*, the concluding part of the cycle, do the two finally get together.)

[7] Ford Madox Ford, *Parade's End*, with an introduction by Malcolm Bradbury (London: Everyman's Library, 1992), p. 84.

Behind the disorienting narrative, there is a love story as uplifting as one of Jane Austen's. Modernist technique here turns out to be the multicolored wrapping of a neatly crafted story.

Although critics rule out a direct influence, Alfred Döblin's *Berlin Alexanderplatz* (1929) is similar in many ways to Joyce's *Ulysses*, in its use of vivid images, slang, bits of everyday speech, pop-song lyrics, newspaper headlines, and advertisements. However, even as he confronts the reader with what looks like a mass of raw material, the author pointedly retains his rhetorical power and interpretive responsibility. At the very beginning of the book, he explicitly announces its argument in a half-solemn, half-comical tone somewhere between a medieval morality play and a variety show. The main character, Franz Biberkopf, a lower-class man who struggles to survive in the jungle of the modern city, had associated with criminals and ended up in prison for his apparent involvement in the murder of his girlfriend. The novel opens with his return to Berlin, where he now intends to go straight. After trying to keep a stall, he takes up with his old friends again and becomes a pimp for a good-hearted prostitute, Mieze. She gets killed during a clash between gangsters. Deeply depressed, Franz is confined to a mental hospital where, on the verge of dying, he beholds the forces of good and evil fighting for his soul. The sight gives him courage. He leaves the hospital and volunteers as a witness in the trial of Mieze's murderer. The author, whose voice alternates with Franz's, takes care to draw the right moral conclusions and celebrate human solidarity.

Like other modernist writers, Döblin pays considerable attention to his characters' inner life, uses a mythic foundation for his story, opens up his style to ordinary language, and gives it a poetic dimension. But he never shies away from the task of constructing a clear plotline. His rapid changes of register, far from making the story hard to follow, help the reader empathize with Franz's despair or hope at every step.

Intellectual Ingenuity

Rather than trying to immerse the reader in the characters' immediate experience, other modernist writers incorporated philosophical speculation in the very texture of their fiction, as though to defy Hegel's prediction that art, no longer of use, would be replaced by philosophy. They were convinced that novels must soar above the realm of sensory perception and provide the most sophisticated intellectual approach to life. Proust himself loaded his *Remembrance* with theoretical passages, sometimes almost literally borrowed from Schopenhauer. His contemporary Thomas Mann, who in many ways remained close to the tradition of Flaubert,

Dostoevsky, and Fontane, skillfully integrated essayistic sections into his well-crafted stories.

In *The Magic Mountain* (1924), Hans Castorp, a healthy young man representative of the early twentieth-century north German upper middle class, meets the elegant patients at a TB sanatorium in Davos, Switzerland—an allegory of refined, ailing modern Europe. Castorp is there to visit his brother, one of the patients, but he stays, attracted by the excellent food, the doctors' pseudoscience, the brilliant, pointless conversations between the liberal Settembrini and the authoritarian Naphta, and the troubling beauty of the Russian adventuress Clawdia Chauchat. Castorp's decision to join the hospital's polished milieu is a mistake. The atmosphere inevitably generates solitude: each patient faces death alone, th conversations are dialogues of the deaf, and the gorgeous Mrs. Chauch remains forever elusive. The novel implies—ironically, ambivalentl that it would have been better for Castorp to stay in his native city, v in his wealthy family's business, and enjoy the dependable satisfactic philistinism. He ends up going to face the horrors of World War I.

Doctor Faustus (1947) continues the critique of twentieth-cent ropean civilization with a nuanced reflection on aestheticism. It a musician who, in order to devote himself to his art, cuts all ot tional ties. Adrian Leverkühn, an avant-garde composer, signs a the devil that offers him musical glory in exchange for the mus rifice of any claims to human affection. Is this agreement a d Will, leading to salvation through art? It's hard to believe: pursuit of musical success uncannily resembles the manifesta Will. In Goethe's *Faust*, the main character, who sells his s for an instant of happiness, does find that happiness wl he devotes himself to the common good. By contrast, M severs all links with the community, living only for his a fastidiously described by his friend and biographer, Ze cerebral, dissonant constructions, indifferent to the n human ear. Mann's irony comes through in Zeitbl attitude toward his friend, whom he considers the rary composer, and in the adulation Leverkühn ge of novelties, ready to endure incomprehensible a they are supposedly devised by a genius. Leverkü he has created an immortal oeuvre—his punishn never really touch anyone. The worship of art f concludes, is more likely to lead to damnation

The blending of narrative prose and abs termed the "novel-essay." Balzac, who believ all human pursuits, including philosophica

in *Louis Lambert* (1832), the biography of a young philosopher whose passion for ideas leads to madness. In modernist novel-essays, abstract thought becomes a target for observation, as is the case in Settembrini and Naphta's long political debates in *The Magic Mountain* or in Zeitblom's diatribes about Germany's sins in *Doctor Faustus*. These political or artistic tirades, however, should not always be taken at face value. Just as, in Balzac's and George Eliot's fiction, the description of the setting and social context help situate the novel's world, Mann's essayistic passages aim to convey the intellectual resources of a certain character, milieu, or period. As a result, the long sections dedicated to politics, theology, and music in *Doctor Faustus* make better sense when considered as part of the world of high culture portrayed—and viewed with irony—in the novel. Hence Zeitblom's endless praise for Leverkühn's avant-garde music is both moving and unreliable: clearly, selling his soul has in no way guaranteed the composer an enduring artistic triumph.

Another example of a novel-essay portraying a loner's fragile links with the community is Robert Musil's unfinished *The Man without Qualities* (1930–1942), which once again reflects—indirectly, ironically—on the destructive effects of World War I. *The Man without Qualities* contrasts the quest of the main character, Ulrich, for the meaning of life with the collective efforts made by the Viennese elite, on the very brink of the war, to define the future of the Austro-Hungarian Empire. A group of highly placed civil servants and their spouses have set up a "Parallel Action" movement, preparing for the seventy-fifth anniversary of Emperor Franz Joseph's coronation, in December 1918—by which time the empire will in fact have ceased to exist. They look for an idea to rally the empire's various nationalities and social groups, and even reach beyond its borders to the whole of Europe. Count Leinsdorf, the project's instigator; Diotima, the beautiful wife of Tuzzi, the secretary of state; Arnheim, a Prussian Jewish industrial tycoon and polymath; General Stumm von Bordwehr, the incarnation of common sense; and Ulrich himself—they all converse endlessly about the meaning of modern life, the choices opened by the gradual secularization of the world, and the difficulty of finding a unifying, inspiring goal.

Ulrich is an atypical creature, but despite his contempt for the usual human qualities, he remains among his fellow men for a while. Financially secure, he can afford to take leave from his scientific work and join the Parallel Action in order to bolster his social position. But during a popular demonstration against the group, Ulrich realizes he has no love for society or for human company in general. He has this revelation when, through the windows of the Leinsdorf Palace, he sees a vast crowd caught in its natural, communitarian emotion. Aware that the multitude he is watching is largely engaged in a kind of theatrical performance,

Ulrich undergoes a singular transformation. He realizes he cannot take part in this life anymore but can't rebel against it either.

> Then, his sense of the room behind him contracted and turned inside out, passing through him or flowing past him as if turned to water, making for a strange spatial inversion. . . . Is it really possible, he wondered, to leave one's own space for some hidden other space? He felt as though chance had led him through a secret door.[8]

Just as in Proust the madeleine opens up a new dimension in time, Ulrich's discovery of a "second space" shows him that he does not belong among other people. The Parallel Action's quest for a common goal fails, destroyed by the weakness of the elites and the brutality of the crowds. Ulrich begins his own individual quest. Cut off from the world, he will find peace in his love for his sister Agathe. It is difficult to work out exactly how Musil intended to conclude the novel, but it seems reasonably clear that the complex, sensitive Ulrich needs Agathe's companionship.

The Man without Qualities has no real plot: its two thousand pages of text are almost entirely devoted to intellectual conversations between the characters, third-person accounts of Ulrich and Agathe's musings, and, from time to time, the author's own digressions. The book reads less like a novel than a collection of reflections and essays that readers could open at random with considerable intellectual pleasure, the way they can with La Rochefoucauld's maxims or Nietzsche's philosophical fragments. Like Joyce's *Ulysses* and Faulkner's *The Sound and the Fury,* Musil's novel challenges the usual rules of the genre, though in the opposite direction. Whereas Joyce and Faulkner eschew neat, fully crafted plots in favor of rough, concrete presentations of the characters' perceptions and thoughts, in Musil the action fades away through an excess of intellectual digressions. Readers of Joyce and Faulkner feel invited to witness a stream of sensation and reverie that leaves little room for external events; Musil's novel, with its countless meaningful discourses, has an equivalent effect.

But why would these great writers neglect the art of telling stories? Why, instead of presenting a strong conflict, developing it along credible lines, and resolving it persuasively, would they choose either to examine the chaotic workings of ordinary minds or to produce reams of brilliant intellectual reflections?

The answer to these questions may have something to do with the two ways of writing fiction described earlier: on the one hand, *ideographic* narratives present moral ideals and norms through exemplary characters

---

[8] Robert Musil, *The Man without Qualities,* trans. Sophie Wilkins (New York: Knopf, 1995), vol. 1, chap. 120, p. 689.

who either *fully* embody or *completely* reject them. On the other hand, stories sensitive to *singularity* delineate striking, complicated cases and invite readers to draw their own conclusions. Ideographic works like Heliodorus's *Ethiopian Story*, which promotes the highest virtues, and *The Life of Guzmán de Alfarache* by Mateo Alemán, which skewers the worst human faults, tend to accumulate long sequences of episodes, each making the same point about the qualities exemplified by the characters. As a consequence, the action advances slowly and its main line is often obscured by the multiplicity of incidents. The second type of narrative, for instance the novella, concentrates on a single event or a short, coherent, sequence meant to take readers to the heart of the matter and help them find, by induction, the lesson therein. From the eighteenth century onward, sharply defined plots prevailed over long sequences of episodes in more ambitious literature, while the latter technique became a distinctive feature of the popular novel.

Many modernist authors, however, rejected the requirement for a neat, tightly focused plot. Both the wealth of rough psychological notations in Joyce and Faulkner and Musil's refined intellectualism were intended as entirely new experiments in fiction. Yet when you consider these innovative techniques in light of the long-term conflict between ideographic plots half-buried in a profusion of episodes, and plots that hone in on a single, dramatic point, it turns out that the modernist authors, perhaps without fully realizing it, were reviving the earlier model. The modernist works cited above do not concentrate on *specific conflicts*, as did older novellas and many eighteenth- and nineteenth-century novels—they use great quantities of rough-hewn narrative matter or of sophisticated digressions for a relentless depiction of the breakdown of connections between the individual and the world.

THE INEXPLICABLE WORLD

This breakdown is also the subject of Franz Kafka's fiction, but Kafka respects, or rather appears to respect, some of the usual constraints of well-structured narratives: plausible characters and setting, clearly defined subject matter, informative dialogue, and an accessible style, equally far removed from the disorienting, unfiltered stream of consciousness and from smooth intellectual speculation. Kafka places the most prosaic, ordinary characters in profoundly disconcerting situations: in *The Trial* (published posthumously in 1925) the protagonist is summoned to appear in a secret court for unspecified reasons; in *The Castle* (1926), a land surveyor is hired to perform a geodetic task but is unable to make contact with the shadowy authorities employing him. A series of depressing episodes, tinged with dark humor, gradually convince the protagonist that his bizarre, outrageous situation is simply inescapable. He struggles to understand what is going on, but always fails. In the end, he realizes that all his ties to the world have been severed. The breakdown is not caused, as in Joyce and Musil, by the individual's idiosyncrasies, for Kafka's protagonist is always an average, unexceptional person: it happens because behind the world's apparent normality lurks a frightening, though partly comical nightmare.

In both novels, the opening scene recalls the best traditions of the nineteenth century. The reader soon realizes, however, that instead of a unified plot, the story consists of a sequence of similar episodes that demonstrate, over and over, the dissolution of the main character's links with normal life. *The Trial*'s protagonist is the target of a covert, incomprehensible threat; *The Castle*'s faces an equally incomprehensible indifference. Both the threat and the indifference are presented as a general, unavoidable feature of human existence, rather than the result of any specific incident.

Like picaresque stories, Kafka's novels portray the main character's persecution by an unreasonably hostile milieu, and as a result his protagonists, like the pícaros, feel entitled to live and act as they see fit. But while pícaros, always flexible and cunning, manage to survive, Kafka's characters are not up to the struggle. They seem convinced that sooner or later things will sort themselves out, that order and justice will prevail. They never do. Providence, as Kafka's short stories emphasize, is at an infinite remove ("An Imperial Message," 1919); not unlike the divinity spoken of in the medieval Jewish Kabbalah, it has long ago withdrawn from the world.

By virtue of a logic that the old idealist authors would easily have understood, Providence's disappearance brings about the demise of the moral law and undermines individuals' ability to grasp or affirm it. Thus, in "In the Penal Colony" (1919), the law, which bears no relation to the human conscience, is engraved by a machine into the flesh of the delinquents, without their ever being told what they have done wrong. Similarly, a parable told in *The Trial* holds that the Creator designs a specific law for each individual, with a gate leading to it, and yet the gate remains forever closed to the person in question.

These stories call to mind the medieval and Renaissance theme of "the world upside down." In the old texts, error and irregularity is portrayed as an exception, whereas in Kafka, the gruesome law and the absent Providence embody the actual truth of the world. Kafka's protagonists gradually find out that normality is an illusion, and that the world is ruled by an unfathomable logic which, curiously enough, all the other characters know about but avoid discussing, as though it were an embarrassing family secret.

This layer of strangeness barely hidden beneath the everyday—a layer the Romanian Jewish writer Max Blecher called the *immediate unreality*—was the main object of study for surrealist writers, particularly for André Breton. His autobiographical *Nadja* (1928, new version in 1963) describes a liaison with a mentally ill woman, whose lyrical innocence exposes the hidden marvels of daily life. For Breton, art, inspiration, and here insanity liberate the mind from the confines of the commonplace. While earlier aestheticism turned its back on ordinary life to seek salvation through art, for Breton the very banality of existence can open the way to poetic revelation.

A similar attitude had already been illustrated in Luigi Pirandello's influential *The Late Mattia Pascal* (1904), whose recurrent theme is the fragility of the walls between reality and fiction, and the kind of metaphysical superiority enjoyed by the fictional. In Pirandello's world, fiction is preferable to reality not because aesthetic insight allows access to the essence of life (as Proust suggested), but rather because fiction can create an ideal world, free of the imperfection and lies that rule empirical reality. Bruno Schulz's *The Street of Crocodiles* (1934) and Mikhail Bulgakov's *The Master and Margarita* (1928–1940) attempt something similar: they transfigure the ordinary world, surrendering it to the powers of poetry and folklore. One strikingly original figure in this vein is S. Y. Agnon, whose novels and short stories are steeped in the Hasidic tradition.

Later, "magical realism" extended this approach, making use of Kafka's and surrealism's insights. Rejecting the idea that literature should be hemmed in by empirical plausibility, it sought instead to represent all kinds of poetic, mythic, and paranormal phenomena. Michel Tournier's *The Ogre* (1970), for instance, tells the story of a French garage mechanic, Abel Tiffauges, who is in touch with supernaturally powerful ogres. With their help, he mysteriously triggers World War II. Is Tiffauges a crazy person who imagines it all, or is the novel a fantastical tale in which such things really happen? Similarly, *On Mantuleasa Street* (1967) by Mircea Eliade mixes the fantasy world of older fairy tales with twentieth-century historical events. In *The Tin Drum* (1959), Günter Grass, with dark humor, conjures a fanciful allegory of recent German history.

Authors who delight in disorienting readers and blurring their sense of reality have been nicknamed "postmodern," a term that stresses their independence from the high modernist work of Joyce, Woolf, and Faulkner. Some postmodern writers inherit from Kafka and surrealism an interest in the unreality concealed behind everyday routine; they also hold on to the modernist technique of presenting mental activity in its "rough" form. Vladimir Nabokov's *Lolita* (1955) might perhaps be considered an early instance of this trend. In Thomas Pynchon's *Gravity's Rainbow* (1973), for instance, people must confront an unreliable world shot through with strong currents of irrationality. Salman Rushdie's *Satanic Verses* (1988) belongs to the same family and, rather as Ismail Kadare (*Doruntine*, 1980) does, adds a wealth of elements drawn from myth and folklore. The return to fiction's oral origins is also a distinctive feature of Toni Morrison's novels, particularly *Song of Solomon* (1977) and *Beloved* (1987). Her writing to some extent recalls Faulkner's poetic prose to mind, but Morrison, leaving his modernist austerity far behind, gives African American sufferings a mythic dimension.

In Latin America, magical realism and postmodernism more generally gave new life to the older techniques. Gabriel García Márquez's *Love in the Time of Cholera* (1985) grafts a picaresque plot onto a sublime love story straight out of early idealist and nineteenth-century popular novels. Told with humor and tenderness, both plotlines are completely implausible. Florentino Ariza is in love with the beautiful Fermina Daza, but unfortunately her family marries her to Doctor Juvenal Urbino—Ariza's passion survives undimmed. After many years of happy marriage, Doctor Urbino finally dies, and Ariza is united with Fermina on the threshold of death. But this shows only one aspect of Ariza's personality: in all the time he spends waiting for Fermina, he keeps up an impressive career in business and an equally successful one as a lady-killer. Precisely because of his devotion to Fermina, Ariza feels free to seduce any woman he wants, as long as he does not truly love her. No woman resists, and each of his innumerable conquests enhances his virility. *Love in the Time of Cholera* reads like a popular novel, yet its human warmth, the quaint elegance of its style, and the paradoxical plot make it unforgettable.

Other postmodern authors invented dizzying fictional worlds, playing with logic, history, and cosmology. Following the example of Jorge Luis Borges (whose short story "The Aleph," 1945, is the earliest model of this approach), Italo Calvino (*If on a Winter's Night a Traveler*, 1979) and Umberto Eco (*The Name of the Rose*, 1980, and *Foucault's Pendulum*, 1988) envisage alternative universes in which the stable convictions of common sense vanish, replaced by never-ending labyrinths of imagination. The irresistibly funny *Aunt Julia and the Scriptwriter* (1977) by Mario Varga Llosa offers an intricate mixture of real-life adventures and wild products of popular fiction. *Life: A User's Manual* (1978) by Georges Perec, subtitled *novels* in the plural, presents a Parisian rental building unit by unit, describing their contents and the lives of their inhabitants in great detail. The whole text is built on the contrast between the hyperrealist depiction of the objects in each apartment and the implausible fate of the people who live or have lived there. Human beings float in the unreal space of popular fiction—serials, comic books, film noir—while material objects silently testify to a concrete truth.

The Difficulty of Self-Reliance; Pluralism

While continuing the high modernist search for originality, postmodernist writers abandoned their predecessors' conviction of art's revelatory power, that its worshippers can access the single, ultimate meaning of the world. Celebrating playfulness, irony, paradox, and perplexity, postmodern writers reminded the "few great artists" (to use Tocqueville's expression) that the novel offers its practitioners a multiplicity of choices.

The tendency to reject turn-of-the-century pessimism and its remedy, the religion of art, is particularly visible in the American novelists who highlighted individual independence instead. Ralph Waldo Emerson's essay on self-reliance, published in 1841, preached trust in oneself and one's path in life, the avoidance of ambivalence, firm acceptance of one's place in the world, nonconformism, indifference to social disapproval, and a strong, all-consuming sense of one's uniqueness. Solitude here is by no means the romantic choice of rebels or weaklings. Self-reliance creates wider spaces between people, but they do not become "individuals-outside-the-world." On the contrary, the self-reliant person fully inhabits the world, even when pursuing a strange, obsessive mission, like Herman Melville's Captain Ahab in *Moby Dick, or the Whale* (1851), or neglecting usual duties, like his protagonist in "Bartleby the Scrivener" (1853). This tradition powerfully shaped the work of realist writers like Edith Wharton, Frank Norris, Theodore Dreiser, Willa Cather, and Sinclair Lewis. Dreiser's *An American Tragedy* (1925), for instance, portrays a pedestrian form of self-reliance, defined by success within a materialistic society and the enjoyment of its trifling pleasures, rather than any higher ideals.

Published the same year as Dreiser's novel, *The Great Gatsby* by F. Scott Fitzgerald centers on a more complex character, an American loner-dreamer, self-reliant and yet astoundingly immature. The clear, straightforward plot, free of high modernism's intricacy, unfolds in Long Island and New York in the early 1920s, among reckless, noisy young people who live in magnificent villas, drive expensive cars, and don't care much about each other. The narrator, Nick Carraway, back home from World War I, lives next to Gatsby's mansion, where luxurious parties are held for whoever happens to be around. When Gatsby was young and penniless, he had a passionate love affair with Nick's distant cousin Daisy, before she married the wealthy Tom Buchanan. Now quite rich, Gatsby tries to win her back, but Tom lets her know that he made his money by illicit means. One day, Daisy is driving Gatsby's yellow Rolls and hits Myrtle Wilson, her husband's mistress. Myrtle dies instantly. To protect

Daisy, Gatsby keeps quiet, but Tom Buchanan tells Myrtle's husband that it was Gatsby at the wheel. Mr. Wilson takes revenge, shooting Gatsby and then himself. Virtually none of Gatsby's friends, business associates, or party guests attends his funeral.

"They were careless people, Tom and Daisy—" Nick concludes, "they smashed up things and creatures and then retreated back into their money or their vast carelessness or whatever it was that kept them together, and let other people clean up the mess they made."[9] Gatsby, however, had "something gorgeous about him, some heightened sensitivity to the promises of life, . . . an extraordinary gift for hope, a romantic readiness such as I never found in any other person" (chap. 1, p. 8). And like the lyrics of a pop song, the last line laments: "So we beat on, boats against the current, borne ceaselessly into the past" (p. 159).

Equally sharp and cogent, *The Heart Is a Lonely Hunter* by Carson McCullers and Richard Wright's *Native Son*, both published in 1940, sensitively explore poverty, gender inequality, and racial prejudice during the period after World War I. Both novels project an intense empathy with their characters, who are engulfed by loneliness, broken dreams, insanity, and violence, without ever being totally humiliated or destroyed.

||||||||||||||||||||||||||||

As these American novels show, the cult of art and high modernism did not prevent other artistic approaches from flourishing. Yet I feel reluctant to impose a definitive pattern on the novel's myriad trends, debates, and achievements over the last fifty to seventy years. The next few pages should therefore be taken as no more than a brief, provisional view of an extraordinarily productive period. I leave the task of drawing a better, more detailed picture of recent political and cultural exploits to the specialists in late twentieth-century literature.

One does not need to be a specialist, however, to notice that thanks to the tectonic fault mentioned earlier, the popular novel prospered immensely during this period. Tocqueville was right to note that in democratic times literature tends to become one trade among others; he was wrong, however, to despise this trade, whose energy and seductive force can be dazzling. Born in the nineteenth century as serials in the press, popular novels relied on three main subjects from the idealist tradition: adventure, justice, and love. Since aesthetes turned away from this material, popular literature had a splendid opportunity to take over. Novels about dispensers of justice—and their counterparts, innocent fugitives—such as

---

[9] F. Scott Fitzgerald, *The Great Gatsby* (New York: Charles Scribner's Sons, 1953), end of chap. 9, p. 158.

Sue's *The Mysteries of Paris* and Pierre Alexis Ponson du Terrail's *Rocambole* were of the same family as Balzac's *History of the Thirteen* and Hugo's *Les Misérables*, and they enjoyed a lasting success. Mystery novels about detectives solving crimes, by Wilkie Collins, Arthur Conan Doyle, Maurice Leblanc, Agatha Christie, Dorothy Sayers, Raymond Chandler, and Georges Simenon (to mention just a few), developed a similar theme, as did western stories about the exploits of lonely cowboys. Spy novels by Ian Fleming, John le Carré, Ken Follett, and Robert Ludlum should perhaps be included among the tales of dispensers of justice, since they portray brilliant, courageous individuals who defend their country against equally intelligent, vicious enemies. Adventure novels usually take place in distant countries or even, in the case of science fiction, far in the future or in outer space. Robert Louis Stevenson's *Treasure Island* (1883) and *The Strange Case of Dr Jekyll and Mr Hyde* (1886) are still widely read, Karl May is famous in Central Europe for his *Winnetou* (1893), and Edgar Rice Burroughs's *Tarzan of the Apes* (1914) was followed by a long series of novels and films: they flooded the literary market with highly effective stories of villains and heroes. From Jules Verne and H. G. Wells to Stanisław Lem and Philip K. Dick, science fiction transports its readers into a fantasy world where the protagonists, unbending in their resolve, overcome ever more surprising obstacles. As for love, popular romance is the literary subgenre that sells best all over the world. Nor should one forget literature for children and teenagers, exemplified by the immensely successful works of Lewis Carroll, Mark Twain, the Countess of Ségur, Frances Hodgson Burnett, L. Frank Baum, Beatrix Potter, Laura Ingalls Wilder, Erich Kästner, C. S. Lewis, J.R.R. Tolkien, and Roald Dahl.

|||||||||||||||||||||||||||||

Among the "highbrow" writers, in addition to modernists and postmodernists, several groups stand out: the specialists in the human psyche, many of whom learned their trade from Dostoevsky but also deeply respected Flaubert; the heirs to the comic and skeptical traditions; the neo-Romantics; and the social realists.

The experts in inner life formed a vast international community that included Joseph Conrad (*Heart of Darkness*, 1899), Graham Greene, and Iris Murdoch (*The Black Prince*, 1973) in the United Kingdom; Heinrich Böll in Germany; John Updike (*Rabbit, Run*, 1960) and Walker Percy in the United States; and, in France, François Mauriac (*Thérèse Desqueyroux*, 1928), Georges Bernanos (*Diary of a Country Priest*, 1936), and the existentialists Jean-Paul Sartre and Albert Camus. These authors share the conviction that we are imperfect moral beings, and that, despite superficial historical and geographic variations, our imperfection always has similar features. People now are not very different from their ancestors, but the world in which they live does not offer them the means to take charge of their own enigmatic psyches. The weakening of religious belief, assumed to be a defining feature of the modern age, is deplored by religiously oriented novelists and extolled by secular existentialists. Graham Greene's *The Power and the Glory* (1940) depicts a priest who lacks the strength to keep his faith. In Sartre's *Nausea* (1938) and Camus's *The Fall* (1956), the main characters are shattered by the discovery of their own finitude; Pascual Duarte, in Camilo José Cela's *The Family of Pascual Duarte* (1942) lives—and kills—outside accepted morality; Kochan struggles with his latent homosexuality in Yukio Mishima's *Confessions of a Mask* (1949); and in Walker Percy's *The Second Coming* (1980), the protagonist pursues an idiosyncratic quest for God that ends with his falling in love with a young handicapped woman. The prolific Alberto Moravia (*Time of Indifference*, 1929), whose novels were adapted for the screen by the best directors, belongs to the same tradition, as does Cesare Pavese (*The Moon and the Bonfires*, 1950), a connoisseur of loneliness.

Politically, most of these writers rejected totalitarianism and racism in their various forms. In *And Where Were You, Adam?* (1951) and *Group Portrait with Lady* (1971), Heinrich Böll uses Germany before 1933, and those Germans who subsequently opposed the National Socialist regime, to exemplify a steadfast morality. Imre Kertész's *Fatelessness* (1975) is an understated, profoundly moving evocation of the Shoah. More recently, J. M. Coetzee's *Disgrace* (1999) focuses on the moral dilemmas that burdened South Africa at the end of the twentieth century.

The heirs to the comic and skeptical tradition, proud of their kinship with picaresque novels as well as with Fielding, Diderot, Stendhal, and Thackeray, make fun of the "irresponsible self" (to use James Wood's apt term) caught in a difficult, unpredictable environment. In France, Louis-Ferdinand Céline's *Journey to the End of the Night* (1932) revives the carefree pícaro figure, who moves around in a world that has lost its bearings. Raymond Queneau (*Zazie in the Metro*, 1959) is of the same line, as is Philippe Sollers, whose *Women* (1983) inherits Céline's energy and bitter humor. In a gentler style, and with a certain irony, Pierre Michon (*Small Lives*, 1984) deplores the fate of insignificant people. Mixing elegy, pornography, and satire, *Elementary Particles* (1998) by Michel Houellebecq indicts consumer society and the loneliness it engenders. Central Europe has proved particularly fertile ground for such writers—including Jaroslav Hašek, the Czech author of the unforgettable *Good Soldier Svejk* (1921–1923), and Milan Kundera, whose *Life*

Is Elsewhere (1973), *The Book of Laughter and Forgetting* (1979), and *The Unbearable Lightness of Being* (1984) show how bureaucratic dictatorships and the lives of the narcissistic populace mirror one another in their futility. The tradition continues, in an increasingly bitter tone, in Bohumil Hrabal's *I Served the King of England* (1971) and Thomas Bernhard's *Wittgenstein's Nephew* (1982)—the title alludes to Diderot's sarcastic *Rameau's Nephew*. This is probably where Evelyn Waugh (*A Handful of Dust*, 1934) belongs, as well as, more recently, Julian Barnes (*Flaubert's Parrot*, 1984) and Ian McEwan (*Black Dogs*, 1992) with their precise ironies. In American literature, where darker tones have often predominated, John Dos Passos (*1919*, 1932) was one of the earliest ironists, followed by Philip Roth (*Portnoy's Complaint*, 1969), Don DeLillo's *White Noise* (1985), and, more recently, by David Foster Wallace, whose cult novel *Infinite Jest* (1996) sarcastically portrays a dystopian future.

The works of those novelists who have affinities with Romanticism display a preoccupation with historical and personal grandeur. Marguerite Yourcenar's *Memoirs of Hadrian* (1951) portrays the great emperor under whom Rome and its possessions—perhaps all humanity, if we trust Edward Gibbon's judgment—were at their peak. *The Ides of March* (1948) by Thornton Wilder offers contemporary statesmen the example of Julius Caesar and his reform of Rome at the end of the Civil Wars. *Il Gattopardo* (published posthumously in 1958) by Giuseppe Tomasi di Lampedusa meditates on the glory and decay of the old Sicilian aristocracy during the nineteenth-century fight for the unification of Italy. In Ernst Jünger's *Eumeswill* (1977), the cruelty and cunning of political tyrants cannot crush individual resistance and freedom.

Reflecting on Romantic love, A. S. Byatt's *Possession: A Romance* (1990) contrasts a secret, passionate Victorian affair with a cooler, safer, late twentieth-century relationship. Byatt makes the two stories equally attractive—the older one has its otherworldly tragedy; the more recent is so friendly and relaxed—and equally deficient, for the Victorian affair ends sadly, while the contemporary love story remains essentially banal. Published around the same time, Penelope Fitzgerald's *The Blue Flower* (1995), a biographical novel about Novalis, expresses deep, convincing doubts about Romanticism.

Devoted to analyzing individuals and their relation to society, the literary progeny of Balzac, George Eliot, and Tolstoy prospered throughout the twentieth century and continue to thrive. In the United Kingdom, they included John Galsworthy (*The Forsyte Saga*, 1906–1921), Arnold Bennett (*The Old Wives' Tale*, 1908), and E. M. Forster (*A Passage to India*, 1924) in the first half of the century, and Doris Lessing (*The Golden*

Notebook, 1962) later; in the United States, Henry Roth (*Call It Sleep*, 1934), John Steinbeck (*The Grapes of Wrath*, 1939), Robert Penn Warren (*All the King's Men*, 1946), and Saul Bellow (*Herzog*, 1964); in France, Roger Martin du Gard (*Jean Barois*, 1913), Jules Romains (*Men of Good Will*, 1932–1946), and Irène Némirovsky (*Suite française*, posthumously published in 2004); Gabrielle Roy (*The Tin Flute*—*Bonheur d'occasion*, 1945) in Québec; Hans Fallada (*Alone in Berlin*, 1947) in Germany; Joseph Roth (*The Radetzky March*, 1932) in Austria; Sándor Márai, a Hungarian writer who spent the second half of his life in exile (*Embers*, 1942); and, in Russia, Boris Pasternak (*Doctor Zhivago*, 1957), as well as Alexander Solzhenitsyn (*The First Circle*, 1968) and Vasily Grossman (*Life and Fate*, posthumously published in 1980) who wrote haunting tales about Stalinism and the Gulag. All of them felt that what they had to convey required a simple, direct, transparent style.

Equally important is the novel's global expansion after the end of the colonial empires, an expansion that brought crucial political issues to the forefront. Thus the beginnings of colonial power in Africa are vividly portrayed from the point of view of the colonized in Chinua Achebe's *Things Fall Apart* (1958). In *Two Thousand Seasons* (1973), Ayi Kwei Armah reflects on African slavery, as does V. S. Naipaul, from a different angle, in *A Bend in the River* (1979). Naguib Mahfouz's *Cairo Trilogy* (1956–1957) is a panorama of Egyptian life, both traditional and modernized, from the end of World War I to the end of World War II. A. B. Yehoshua's *Mr. Mani* (1990) tells the complicated, sometimes scandalous story of six generations of Jewish settlers in Palestine, before and after the establishment of the State of Israel. The fate of exiled Palestinians is Elias Khoury's subject in *The Gate of the Sun* (1998), a novel that adds a powerful political dimension to postmodernism. *Wives and Concubines* (1990) by Su Tong is part of a harvest of novels about the wretched lives of women in patriarchal early twentieth-century China. In *Clear Light of Day* (1980), Anita Desai depicts a young woman's coming of age in an Indian city in the foothills of the Himalayas. The Francophone novel has been equally dynamic, as evidenced by the works of Émile Ollivier (*Mère-Solitude*, 1983), Tahar Ben Jelloun (*The Sand Child*, 1985), and Amin Maalouf (*Leo Africanus*, 1986).

Like their American and European colleagues, these writers are sensitive to themes of isolation, yet their strong investment in social and political struggles protects them against the temptations of egocentrism. Gatsby in Fitzgerald's novel, the young von Trotta in *The Radetzky March* by Joseph Roth, Mick Kelly in Carson McCullers's *The Heart Is a Lonely Hunter*, Bigger Thomas in Richard Wright's *Native Son*, the two male protagonists in *Embers* by Sándor Márai, Florentine Lacasse in *The*

Tin Flute by Gabrielle Roy, the tenants of the building in which Hans Fallada sets *Alone in Berlin*, Okonkwo at the end of Achebe's *Things Fall Apart*, and Songlian in Su Tong's *Wives and Concubines*—they are all lonely. Yet they never reject the world of common experience, nor do they become trapped in a prison of their own impressions and reflections. It is hard to find a stable reconciliation between the individual and society in these novels; they nevertheless sustain the hope that we are not solitary beings.

Envoi

||||||||||||||||||||||||||||||||||||||||||||||||||||||||||||||||

I will conclude this long journey with a comment on the *division of literary labor* between novelists who innovate, those who implement recent innovations, and those who write the best, most enduring books.

The translation of Heliodorus's *Ethiopian Story* into several languages around 1550 offered writers a reliable model of idealist narrative, a model followed by scores of sixteenth- and seventeenth-century novelists; Richardson's *Pamela* (1740) blended several previous subgenres, including the idealist novel, the picaresque, the pastoral, and the novella; *Waverley* (1814) by Walter Scott reflected on the social and historical roots of individual greatness; Joris-Karl Huysmans's *Against the Grain* (1884) was an early manifesto for the cult of art that eventually led to the rise of high modernism. Notably, though they are commendable achievements, none of these novels can match *Don Quixote*, *Tom Jones*, *Middlemarch*, or *Remembrance of Things Past*. A literary work's historical importance does not coincide with its artistic strength.

Hence I distinguish between, on the one hand, adventurous minds ready to explore new avenues—the anonymous author of *Lazarillo de Tormes*, Richardson, Walter Scott, and Huysmans (and with equal courage but less success, Marivaux and Maria Edgeworth)—and, on the other hand, the writers of works that outlive their competitors, like Cervantes, Austen, George Eliot, Dostoevsky, or Proust. The *history* of the novel depends less on these geniuses than on initiatives and interactions involving a multitude of writers. Precisely because it relies on individual innovation and social exchange, this history might have been different. And for the same reason, its advance, while often subject to contingent factors, was never entirely arbitrary: individual writers made choices that triggered controversies, bringing real artistic problems to light that the innovators who followed aimed to solve. History is neither anonymous, nor inevitable, nor arbitrary: its actors have a human face, they make genuine choices, and there are strong reasons behind those choices.

I therefore doubt that the spirit of an epoch (its *Zeitgeist*, or *episteme*) impersonally determines all art produced during that time. Men and women who live at a given moment have many common concerns; their tastes and interests converge; their disagreements are frequently about the same issues; and the works of art they make and appreciate often share a set of family resemblances. Friedrich Schlegel, Chateaubriand, Mme de Staël, Heinrich von Kleist, and Benjamin Constant were contemporaries; some of them knew each other, their lives were disrupted by revolutions and wars, and these events influenced their writings in various ways. Should one conclude that all their books bear the *same* historical marks? That *René*, *Michael Kohlhaas*, *Corinne*, *Lucinde*, and *Adolphe* are all, and to the same extent, "Romantic" works? They may well be, but the word "Romantic," rather than designating a unified historical force that gave birth to these works, describes the cultural atmosphere that arose under their influence. The term points to a *final result* rather than an invisible guiding principle that made all these writings possible.

The division of literary labor and the rivalries it causes make it difficult to find a single main current in the history of the novel. And yet it is hard to resist the temptation to subject a long history to a single concept. The great critic Erich Auerbach, for instance, argued in his *Mimesis: The Representation of Reality in Western Literature*[1] that from Homer to Virginia Woolf, literature gradually advanced toward an ever closer observation of life in all its minute details and historical implications, in other words, toward realism. Cervantes was better at this job than earlier chivalric writers, Prévost and Laclos outdid Cervantes, Balzac advanced a bit further, the Goncourt brothers soon surpassed him, and Proust and Woolf each achieved a new breakthrough.

Auerbach's thesis identifies an important tendency in the history of the novel, which did indeed, over the centuries, consider all aspects of human life more and more seriously. Situations that were assumed, as late as the eighteenth century, to be by definition comic or sordid—the love life of a female servant, for example—acquired a dramatic, even a tragic dimension in Richardson's *Pamela* and in the Goncourt brothers' *Germinie Lacerteux*, where they were described in a dignified style full of specific detail. To nuance this thesis, however, one needs to pay attention to the *polemical principle* that shaped the history of the novel.

In accordance with this principle, rival tendencies—serious and comic, idealist and derogatory—coexist over the long term, fighting against each other and influencing one another. When, occasionally, one of them gets the upper hand, the opposite tendency is soon reborn, this time armed with the previous winner's most effective weapons. Consider the

[1] Trans. Willard R. Trask (1946; Princeton, NJ: Princeton University Press, 1953).

propensity to take every aspect of human life seriously. To understand how it worked, one must take into consideration not only the abundance of descriptive details, but also the artistic goals these details served. In *Pamela*, such details lend plausibility to the sensitive protagonist, and to the novel's idealism more generally. In *Germinie Lacerteux*, however, the details illustrate the biological and social determinism that governs life, thus helping to discredit idealism. Borrowed across the polemical aisle, stylistic devices can serve profoundly different ends.

Sometimes writers do adopt a common artistic method, which then inevitably bursts out into a variety of approaches. In the second half of the nineteenth century, many writers, from Flaubert to Thomas Hardy, shared an attention to the real world in all its disappointing cruelty. Within this realist-naturalist community, however, a closer look reveals a wide range of choices, including Flaubert's ironic contempt for bourgeois mediocrity, Theodor Fontane's generous pessimism, Eça de Queirós's mixture of splendor and tragedy, Tolstoy's emphasis on authenticity, and Hardy's praise for inner strength.

It is nevertheless difficult to avoid all historical generalizations, and my own version of the history of the novel relies (prudently, I hope) on a small number of conceptual tools, including the opposition between the individual and the world as a whole, and the double edge of moral norms and ideals—often self-evident, yet difficult to follow. I am by no means arguing, however, that these concepts *engendered* the history of the novel all by themselves; rather, I suggest that we can choose to trace the way in which *these* concepts rather than others oriented, inflected, intensified, or moderated various movements in the course of the genre's evolution.

We have seen how complex the history of the novel is, how many strands, each with its own trajectory, are intertwined within it. Nonetheless, a few overall tendencies are apparent: not just the historical transition from specialized subgenres in the early modern period to the later creation of complex, unified versions of the novel, but also the slow, diversified, halting movement from souls to hearts to psyches as the center of novelists' attention. The lives of the novel have one thing common: the bid to make the ideal visible within a world of transitory, fragile, imperfect human interactions.

Reading List

⁞⁞

The reader will find here easily available editions of the stories I discuss in some detail. Since they were selected for the sake of this book's overall argument, the following list should not be mistaken for a repertory of the best novels ever written.

CHAPTER 1
STRONG SOULS, DEGREES OF PERFECTION

Heliodorus. *An Ethiopian Story*. Translated by J. R. Morgan. In *Collected Ancient Greek Novels*, edited by B. P. Reardon. Berkeley: University of California Press, 1989.

Chretien de Troyes. *Yvain*. In *Arthurian Romances*, introduced and translated by William W. Kibler (Carleton W. Carroll translation of *Erec and Enide*). London: Penguin Books, 1991.

Wolfram von Eschenbach. *Parzival* and *Titurel*. Introduced by Richard Barber. Translated by Cyril Edwards. Oxford: Oxford World Classics, 2006.

Gottfried von Strassburg. *Tristan*. Introduced and translated by A. T. Hatto. London: Penguin Books, 2004.

The Quest of the Holy Grail. Introduced and translated by P. M. Matarasso. Harmondsworth: Penguin Books, 1969.

The Nibelungenlied. Translated by A. T. Hatto. Harmondsworth: Penguin Books, 1969.

The Mabinogion. Introduced and translated by Jeffrey Gantz. Harmondsworth: Penguin Books, 1976.

Martorell, Joannot, and Martí Joan de Galba. *Tirant lo Blanc*. With a foreword and translated by David H. Rosenthal. New York: Schocken, 1984.

Amadis of Gaul. Translated by Edwin B. Place and Herbert C. Behm. 2 vols. Lexington: University Press of Kentucky, 1974–1975.

CHAPTER 2
HELPLESS SOULS, TRICKSTERS, AND RASCALS

Petronius. *The Satyricon*. Introduced by Helen Morales. Translated by J. P. Sullivan. London: Penguin Books, 2011.

Apuleius. *The Golden Ass*. Introduced and translated by E. J. Kenney. London: Penguin Books, 1999.

Renard the Fox. Translated by Patricia Terry. Boston: Northeastern University Press, 1983. The publication of a more complete translation deserves to be considered.

Rabelais, François. *Gargantua and Pantagruel*. Introduced and translated by Michael A. Screech. London: Penguin Books, 2006.

Lazarillo de Tormes. In *Lazarillo de Tormes and The Swindler: Two Spanish Picaresque Novels*, introduced and translated by Michael Alpert. London: Penguin Books, 2003.

Quevedo, Francisco de. *The Swindler*. In *Lazarillo de Tormes and The Swindler: Two Spanish Picaresque Novels*, introduced and translated by Michael Alpert. London: Penguin Books, 2003.

Alemán, Mateo. *The Life of Guzmán de Alfarache* is unfortunately not available in English in a recent, reliable translation made directly from the original. It deserves a good publisher's attention.

Grimmelshausen, Hans Jakob Christian von. *Simplicissimus*. Translated by Mike Mitchell. Sawtry, UK: Dedalus, 1999.

Defoe, Daniel. *The Life and Misfortunes of the Famous Moll Flanders*. Edited and introduced by G. A. Starr. 1971. Oxford: Oxford World Classics, 2009.

Defoe, Daniel. *Roxana or the Fortunate Mistress*. Edited and introduced by David Blewett. London: Penguin Books, 1982.

CHAPTER 3
THE CENTER OF ACTION:
ELEGIAC STORIES AND NOVELLAS

Boccacio, Giovanni. *The Elegy of Lady Fiammetta*. Introduced by Mariangela Causa-Steindler. Translated by Mariangela Causa-Steindler and Thomas Mauch. Chicago: University of Chicago Press, 1990.

Guilleragues, Gabriel de la Vergne, vicomte de. *The Love Letters of a Portuguese Nun*. Translated by Guido Waldman. London: Harvill Press, 1996.

Boccaccio, Giovanni. *The Decameron*. Introduced and translated by H. G. McWilliam. London: Penguin Books, 2003.

Cinzio, Giraldo. See *Italian Renaissance Tales*. Introduced and translated by Janet Levarie Smarr. Rochester, MI: Solaris Press, 1983.

Bandello, Matteo. See *Italian Renaissance Tales*, Introduced and translated by Janet Levarie Smarr. Rochester, MI: Solaris Press, 1983. In addition to

Smarr's excellent selection, both Cinzio and Bandello's collections of stories deserve to be published in their entirety.

Cervantes Saavedra, Miguel de. *Exemplary Stories*. Translated by C. A. Jones. Harmondsworth: Penguin Books, 1972.

Cervantes Saavedra, Miguel de. *An Ill-Advised Curiosity*. In *Don Quixote de la Mancha*, translated by Charles Jarvis. Oxford: Oxford World Classics, 1998.

Zayas y Sotomayor, María de. *A Shameful Revenge and Other Stories*. Introduced and translated by John Sturrock. London: The Folio Society, 1963. It would be wonderful if more stories by María de Zayas were to become available in an equally elegant translation.

Saint-Réal, abbé de. *Don Carlos* has unfortunately been not available in English since its first translation in 1676. It deserves to be reissued, perhaps in a volume of seventeenth-century French prose that would also include Guilleragues's *Letters of a Portuguese Nun*.

Lafayette, Marie de. *The Princess of Clèves*. Introduced and translated by Robin Buss. London: Penguin Books, 1992.

CHAPTER 4
AN ISOLATED REALM, HESITANT LOVERS: THE PASTORAL

Longus. *Daphnis and Chloe*. Introduced and translated by Ronald McCail. Oxford: Oxford World Classics, 2002.

Boccaccio, Giovanni. *L'Ameto*. Translated by Judith Serafini-Sauli. New York: Garland, 1985.

Sannazaro, Jacopo. *Arcadia &, Piscatorial Eclogues*. Introduced and translated by Ralph Nash. Detroit: Wayne State University Press, 1966.

Montemayor, Jorge de. *Diana*. Introduced by Judith M. Kennedy. Sixteenth-century translation by Bartholomew Yong. Includes Gil Polo's *Enamoured Diana*. Oxford: Clarendon, 1968. Worth being considered by a classics series.

Cervantes Saavedra, Miguel de. *Galatea*. In vol. 2 of his *Complete Works*, edited by Jason Fitzmaurice-Kelly. Glasgow: Gowans & Gray, 1901–1903. Worth considering for a new edition.

Sidney, Sir Philip. *Old Arcadia*. Introduced and with notes by Katherine Duncan-Jones. Oxford: Oxford World Classics, 2008.

D'Urfé, Honoré. *Astrea: Part One*. Introduced and translated by Steven Rendall. Binghamton, NY: Medieval & Renaissance Texts & Studies, 1995.

CHAPTER 5
DON QUIXOTE AND THE HISTORY OF THE NOVEL

Cervantes Saavedra, Miguel de. *Don Quixote de la Mancha*. Translated by Charles Jarvis. Oxford: Oxford World Classics, 1998.

CHAPTER 6
THE NEW IDEALISM

Gomberville, Marin le Roy. *The History of Polexander*. Translated by William Browne. London: Thomas Walkley, 1648. Available online.

Richardson, Samuel. *Pamela or Virtue Rewarded*. Introduced by Margaret A. Doody. Edited by Peter Sabor. London: Penguin Books, 1987.

Richardson, Samuel. *Clarissa or the History of a Young Lady*. Introduced and with notes by Angus Ross. Harmondsworth: Penguin Books, 1985.

Rousseau, Jean-Jacques. *Julie, or the New Heloise*. Translated and with notes by Philip Stewart and Jean Vaché. Hanover, NH: University Press of New England. 1997.

CHAPTER 7
RESISTANCE TO NEW IDEALISM

Fielding, Henry. *Joseph Andrews*. Edited by Douglas Brooks-Davies. Revised with a new introduction by Thomas Keymer. Oxford: Oxford World Classics, 1999.

Fielding, Henry. *Tom Jones*. Introduced by Thomas Keymer. London: Penguin Books, 2005.

Sterne, Laurence. *The Life and Opinions of Tristram Shandy, Gentleman*. Edited by Ian Campbell Ross. Oxford: Oxford World Classics, 2009.

Diderot, Denis. *Jacques the Fatalist and His Master*. Translated by J. Robert Loy. New York: Norton, 1959.

Walpole, Horace. *The Castle of Otranto*. Introduced and with notes by Michael Gamer. London: Penguin Books, 2001.

Radcliffe, Ann. *The Mysteries of Udolpho*. Introduced by Bonamy Dobrée. With explanatory notes by Frederick Garber. Oxford: Oxford World Classics, 1980.

Lewis, Matthew. *The Monk*. Introduced and with notes by Emma McEvoy. Oxford: Oxford World Classics, 1980.

CHAPTER 8
LOVE: ROMANTIC AND IMPOSSIBLE

Burney, Frances. *Evelina*. Introduced and with notes by Vivien Jones. Oxford: Oxford World Classics, 2002.

Goldsmith, Oliver. *The Vicar of Wakefield*. Introduced and with notes by Robert L. Mack. Oxford: Oxford World Classics, 2006.

Goethe, Johann Wolfgang von. *The Sufferings of Young Werther*. Translated by Stanley Corngold. New York: Norton, 2012.

Hölderlin, Friedrich. *Hyperion*. Translated by Ross Benjamin. Brooklyn, NY: Archipelago Books, 2008.

Novalis. *Henry von Ofterdingen*. Translated by Palmer Hilty. New York: F. Ungar, 1964. Reissued by Waveland Press, 1990.

Schlegel, Friedrich. *Lucinde and the Fragments*. Introduced and translated by Peter Firchow. Minneapolis: University of Minnesota Press, 1971.

Goethe, Johann Wolfgang von. *Elective Affinities*. Introduced and translated by David Constantine. Oxford: Oxford World Classics, 2008.

Constant, Benjamin. *Adolphe*. Translated by Margaret Mauldon. Introduced and with notes by Patrick Coleman. Oxford: Oxford World Classics, 2001.

CHAPTER 9
NOVELS AND SOCIETY

HISTORICAL FICTION

Kleist, Heinrich von. *Michael Kohlhaas*. In Kleist, *The Marquise of O—, and Other Stories*, introduced and translated by David Luke and Nigel Reeves. Harmondsworth: Penguin Books, 1978.

Scott, Walter. *Waverley*. Introduced by Claire Lamont. Oxford: Oxford World Classics, 1986.

Scott, Walter. *Old Mortality*. Introduced and with notes by Jane Stevenson and Peter Davidson. Oxford: Oxford World Classics, 1993.

Scott, Walter. *The Heart of Midlothian*. Introduced by Tony Inglis. London: Penguin Books, 1994.

Manzoni, Alessandro. *The Betrothed*. Introduced and translated by Bruce Penman. Harmondsworth: Penguin Books, 1972.

Nievo, Ippolito. *The Castle of Fratta*. Translated by Lowett F. Edwards. London: Folio Society, 1954.

FARAWAY SOCIETIES

Cooper, James Fenimore. *The Last of the Mohicans: A Narrative of 1757*. Introduced and with a historical essay and notes by John McWilliams. Oxford: Oxford World Classics, 1990.

Lamartine, Alphonse de. *Graziella*. Translated by Ralph Wright. London: The Nonesuch Press, 1929.

Lermontov, Mikhail. *A Hero of Our Time*. Introduced and translated by Vladimir Nabokov and Dmitri Nabokov. Oxford: Oxford World Classics, 1984.

Tolstoy, Leo. *The Cossacks and Other Stories*. Introduced by Paul Foote. translated by David McDuff and Paul Foote. London: Penguin Books, 2006.

IDEAL CHARACTERS HERE AND NOW

Dickens, Charles. *Oliver Twist*. Introduced by Angus Wilson. Harmondsworth: Penguin Books, 1966.

Dickens, Charles. *Little Dorrit*. Introduced by Dennis Walder. Oxford: Oxford World Classics, 1982.

Brontë, Charlotte. *Jane Eyre*. Introduced and with notes by Sally Shuttleworth. Oxford: Oxford World Classics, 2000.

Sand, Georges. *The Devil's Pool*. Translated by Andrew Brown. London: Hesperus, 2005.

Brontë, Anne. *The Tenant of Wildfell Hall*. Edited by Herbert Rosengarten. Oxford: Oxford World Classics, 2008.

Balzac, Honoré de. *The Duchess of Langeais*. In Balzac, *History of the Thirteen*, introduced and translated by Herbert J. Hunt. Harmondsworth: Penguin Books, 1974.

Balzac, Honoré de. *The Black Sheep (La Rabouilleuse)*. Introduced and translated by Donald Adamson. Harmondsworth: Penguin Books, 1976.

Balzac, Honoré de. *The Country Doctor*. With a preface by George Saintsbury. Translated by Ellen Marriage. London: J. M. Dent; New York: Macmillan, 1895. Reprint, Charleston, SC: Bibliolife, 2007.

Balzac, Honoré de. *Lost Illusions*. Introduced and translated by Herbert J. Hunt. Harmondsworth: Penguin Books, 1971.

Shelley, Mary. *Frankenstein or The Modern Prometheus*. Introduced and with notes by Maurice Hindle. London: Penguin Books, 1992.

Sue, Eugène. *The Mysteries of Paris*. 6 vols. Free Kindle download.

Hugo, Victor. *Les Misérables*. Introduced and translated by Norman Denny. London: Penguin Books, 1982.

CHAPTER 10
FROM SENSITIVE HEARTS TO ENIGMATIC PSYCHES

Stendhal. *The Red and the Black*. Introduced and translated by Roger Gard. London: Penguin Books, 2002.

Stendhal. *The Charterhouse of Parma*. Introduced and translated by John Sturrock. London: Penguin Books, 2006.

Thackeray, William Makepeace. *The Memoirs of Barry Lyndon, Esq*. Introduced by J. P. Donleavy. Harmondsworth: Penguin Books, 1975.

Thackeray, William Makepeace. *Vanity Fair: A Novel without a Hero*. Introduced and with notes by John Carey. London: Penguin Books, 2004.

Austen, Jane. *Emma*. Edited by Steven M. Parrish. New York: Norton, 1972.

Austen, Jane. *Persuasion*. In Austen, *The Complete Novels*, introduced by Karen Joy Fowler. London: Penguin Books, 2006.

Flaubert, Gustave. *Madame Bovary: Provincial Manners*. Introduced by Malcolm Bowie. Translated by Margaret Mauldon. With notes by Mark Overstall. Oxford: Oxford World Classics, 2004.

Flaubert, Gustave. *Sentimental Education*. Translated by Robert Baldick. Revised with an introduction and notes by Geoffrey Wall. London: Penguin Books, 2004.

Goncourt, Edmond de and Jules de. *Germinie Lacerteux*. Introduced and translated (1922) by Ernest Boyd. New York: Mondial, 2007.

Zola, Émile. *L'Assommoir*. Introduced by Robert Lethbridge. Translated by Margaret Mauldon. Oxford: Oxford World Classics, 1995.

James, Henry. *Daisy Miller*. Introduced and with notes by David Lodge. London: Penguin Books, 2007.

James, Henry. *The Portrait of a Lady*. Introduced by Geoffrey Moore. With notes by Patricia Crick. London: Penguin Books, 2003.

James, Henry. *The Ambassadors*. Introduced by Harry Levin. Harmondsworth: Penguin Books, 1986.

CHAPTER 11
SYNTHESES, HIGH POINTS

Eliot, George. *Middlemarch*. Introduced by W. J. Harvey. Harmondsworth: Penguin Books, 1985.

Tolstoy, Leo. *War and Peace*. Translated by Anthony Briggs. With an afterword by Orlando Figes. London: Penguin Books, 2006.

Tolstoy, Leo. *Anna Karenina*. Translated by Richard Pevear and Larissa Volokhonsky. With a preface by John Bayley. London: Penguin Books, 2003.

Stifter, Adalbert. *The Bachelors*. Translated by David Bryer. London: Pushkin, 2008.

Stifter, Adalbert. *Brigitta*. Introduced and translated by Helen Watanabe-O'Kelly. London: Penguin Books, 1994.

Fontane, Theodore. *Effi Briest*. Introduced by Helen Chambers. Translated by Hugh Rorrison and Helen Chambers. London: Penguin Books, 1995.

Fontane, Theodore. *Cécile*. Translated by Stanley Radcliffe. London: Angel Books, 1992.

Dostoevsky, Fyodor. *Crime and Punishment*. Introduced and translated by David McDuff. London: Penguin Books, 1991.

Dostoevsky, Fyodor. *Devils*. Introduced and translated by Michael R. Katz. Oxford: Oxford World Classics, 1992.

Pardo Bazán, Emilia. *The House of Ulloa*. Introduced and translated by Paul O'Prey and Lucia Graves. London: Penguin Books, 1990.

Pérez Galdós, Benito. *Fortunata and Jacinta*. Introduced and translated by Agnes Moncy Gullión. London: Penguin Books, 1988.

Pérez Galdós, Benito. *Nazarin*. Introduced and translated by Jo Labanyi. Oxford: Oxford World Classics, 1993.

Alas, Leopoldo. *La Regenta*. Introduced and translated by John Rutherford. London: Penguin Books, 2005.

Hardy, Thomas. *The Return of the Native*. Introduced by Margaret R. Higonnet. Edited by Simon Gatrell. Oxford: Oxford World Classics, 2005.

Eça de Queirós, José Maria de. *The Maias*. Introduced by Nigel Griffin. Translated by Patricia McGowan Pinheiro and Ann Stevens. London: Penguin Books, 1998.

Prus, Bolesław. *The Doll*. Introduced by Stanislaw Baranczak. Translated by David Welsh. New York: New York Review of Books Classics, 2011.

CHAPTER 12
LONERS IN A STRANGE WORLD

Tarchetti, Iginio Ugo. *Passion*. Translated by Lawrence Venuti. San Francisco: Mercury House, 1994.

Jacobsen, Jens Peter. *Niels Lyhne*. Introduced by Eric O. Johannesson. Translated by Tiina Nunnally. London: Penguin Books, 2006.

Machado de Assis, Joaquim Maria. *Dom Casmurro*. Introduced and translated by John Gledson. Oxford: Oxford University Press. 1997

Emants, Marcellus. *A Posthumous Confession*. Introduced and translated by J. M. Coetzee. New York: New York Review of Books Classics, 1986.

Huysmans, Joris-Karl. *Against Nature*. Introduced by Nicholas White. Translated by Margaret Mauldon. Oxford: Oxford World Classics, 1998.

Wilde, Oscar. *The Picture of Dorian Gray*. Introduced by Joseph Bristow. Oxford: Oxford World Classics, 2006.

Gide, André. *The Immoralist*. Introduced by Alan Sheridan. Translated by David Watson. London: Penguin Books, 2000.

Proust, Marcel. *Remembrance of Things Past*. Translated by C. K. Scott Moncrieff and Terence Kilmartin. 3 vols. New York: Vintage Books, 1981.

Joyce, James. *Ulysses*. Edited by Hans Walter Gabler. With a preface by Richard Ellmann and an afterword by Michael Groden. New York: Random House, 1986.

Woolf, Virginia. *To the Lighthouse*. Introduced by David Bradshaw. Oxford: Oxford World Classics, 2006.

Faulkner, William. *The Sound and the Fury*. Introduced by Richard Hughes. New York: Vintage Books, 1995.

Ford, Madox Ford. *Some Do Not . . .* In Ford, *Parade's End*, introduced by Max Saunders. London: Penguin Books, 2002.

Döblin, Alfred. *Berlin Alexanderplatz*. Translated by Eugene Jolas. New York: Continuum, 2003.

Mann, Thomas. *The Magic Mountain*. Introduced by A. S. Byatt. Translated by
   John E. Woods. London: Knopf, Everyman's Library, 2005.

Mann, Thomas. *Doctor Faustus*. Translated by John E. Woods. New York:
   Vintage Books, 1999.

Musil, Robert. *The Man without Qualities*. Translated by Sophie Wilkins. 2
   vols. New York: Vintage International, 1996.

Kafka, Franz. *The Trial*. Translated by David Wyllie. New York: Tribeca Books,
   2011.

Kafka, Franz. *The Castle*. Introduced by Ritchie Robertson. Translated by
   Anthea Bell. Oxford: Oxford World Classics, 2009.

Fitzgerald, F. Scott. *The Great Gatsby*. New York: Scribner, reissued 2004.

||||||||||||||||||||||||||||||

The extraordinary wealth of twentieth-century literature goes far beyond these few works. Here is a series of chronological lists of most
authors and works cited in the various sections of the closing pages of
the book.

Disorienting Proximity

Italo Svevo, *Zeno's Conscience* (1923); Ernest Hemingway, *A Farewell to Arms*
   (1929) and *For Whom the Bell Tolls* (1940); Nathalie Sarraute, *Tropisms*
   (1939); Hermann Broch, *The Death of Virgil* (1945); Samuel Beckett, *Molloy*
   (1951).

The Inexplicable World

Luigi Pirandello, *The Late Mattia Pascal* (1904); André Breton, *Nadja* (1928);
   Bruno Schultz, *The Street of Crocodiles* (1934); Mikhail Bulgakov, *The Mas-
   ter and Margarita* (1928–1940); Vladimir Nabokov, *Lolita* (1955); Günter
   Grass, *The Tin Drum* (1959); Mircea Eliade, *On Mantuleasa Street* (1967);
   Michel Tournier, *The Ogre* (1970); Thomas Pynchon, *Gravity's Rainbow*
   (1973); Toni Morrison, *Song of Solomon* (1977) and *Beloved* (1987); Mario
   Varga Llosa, *Aunt Julia and the Scriptwriter* (1977); Georges Perec, *Life:
   A User's Manual* (1979); Italo Calvino, *If on a Winter's Night a Traveler*
   (1979); Umberto Eco, *The Name of the Rose* (1980) and *Foucault's Pendu-
   lum* (1988); Gabriel García Márquez, *Love in the Time of Cholera* (1985);
   Ismail Kadare, *Doruntine* (1980); Salman Rushdie, *Satanic Verses* (1988).

The Difficulty of Self-Reliance

Theodore Dreiser, *An American Tragedy* (1925); Carson McCullers, *The Heart
   Is a Lonely Hunter* (1940); Richard Wright, *Native Son* (1940).

PLURALISM

Joseph Conrad, *Heart of Darkness* (1899); François Mauriac, *Thérèse Desqueyroux* (1928); Alberto Moravia, *Time of Indifference* (1929); Georges Bernanos, *Diary of a Country Priest* (1936); Jean-Paul Sartre, *Nausea* (1938); Graham Greene, *The Power and the Glory* (1940); Camilo José Cela, *The Family of Pascual Duarte* (1942); Yukio Mishima, *Confessions of a Mask* (1949); Cesare Pavese, *The Moon and the Bonfires* (1950); Albert Camus, *The Fall* (1956); John Updike, *Rabbit, Run* (1960); Iris Murdoch, *The Black Prince* (1973); Walker Percy, *The Second Coming* (1980).

Heinrich Böll, *And Where Were You, Adam?* (1951) and *Group Portrait with Lady* (1971); Imre Kertész, *Fatelessness* (1975); J. M. Coetzee, *Disgrace* (1999).

Jaroslav Hašek, *Good Soldier Svejk* (1921–1923); John Dos Passos, *1919* (1932); Louis-Ferdinand Céline, *Journey to the End of the Night* (1932); Evelyn Waugh, *A Handful of Dust* (1934); Raymond Queneau, *Zazie in the Metro* (1959); Philip Roth, *Portnoy's Complaint* (1969); Bohumil Hrabal, *I Served the King of England* (1971); Milan Kundera, *Life Is Elsewhere* (1973), *The Book of Laughter and Forgetting* (1979), and *The Unbearable Lightness of Being* (1984); Thomas Bernhard, *Wittgenstein's Nephew* (1982); Philippe Sollers, *Women* (1983); Pierre Michon, *Small Lives* (1984); Julian Barnes, *Flaubert's Parrot* (1984); Don DeLillo, *White Noise* (1985); Ian McEwan, *Black Dogs* (1992); David Foster Wallace, *Infinite Jest* (1996); Michel Houellebecq, *Elementary Particles* (1998).

Thornton Wilder, *The Ides of March* (1948); Marguerite Yourcenar, *Memoirs of Hadrian* (1951); Giuseppe Tomasi di Lampedusa, *Il Gattopardo* (1958); Ernst Jünger, *Eumeswill* (1977).

A.S. Byatt, *Possession: A Romance* (1990); Penelope Fitzgerald, *The Blue Flower* (1995).

John Galsworthy, *The Forsyte Saga* (1906–1921); Arnold Bennett, *The Old Wives' Tale* (1908); Roger Martin du Gard, *Jean Barois* (1913); E. M. Forster, *A Passage to India* (1924); Joseph Roth, *The Radetzky March* (1932); Jules Romains, *Men of Good Will* (1932–1946); Henry Roth, *Call It Sleep* (1934); John Steinbeck, *The Grapes of Wrath* (1939); Irène Némirovsky, *Suite française* (posthumously published in 2004); Sándor Márai, *Embers* (1942); Gabrielle Roy, *The Tin Flute* (*Bonheur d'occasion*, 1945); Hans Fallada, *Alone in Berlin* (1947); Boris Pasternak, *Doctor Zhivago* (1957); Doris Lessing, *The Golden Notebook* (1962); Saul Bellow, *Herzog* (1964); Alexander Solzhenitsyn, *The First Circle* (1968); Vasily Grossman, *Life and Fate* (posthumously published in 1980).

Naguib Mahfouz, *Cairo Trilogy* (1956–1957); Chinua Achebe, *Things Fall Apart* (1958); Ayi Kwei Armah, *Two Thousand Seasons* (1973); V. S.

Naipaul, *A Bend in the River* (1979); Anita Desai, *Clear Light of Day* (1980); Émile Ollivier, *Mère-Solitude* (1983); Tahar Ben Jelloun, *The Sand Child* (1985); Amin Maalouf, *Leo Africanus* (1986); Elias Khoury, *The Gate of the Sun* (1998); Su Tong, *Wives and Concubines* (1990); A. B. Yehoshua, *Mr. Mani* (1990).

Debts

||||||||||||||||||||||||||||||||||||||||||||||||||||||||||||||||

Rather than providing a vast scholarly bibliography, I prefer to name here a few authors and books that inspired my work.

I am deeply indebted to several thinkers who brought the historical development of human consciousness back to the center of the intellectual conversation: Charles Taylor, *Sources of the Self: The Making of the Modern Identity* (Cambridge: Cambridge University Press, 1989); Louis Dumont, *Essays on Individualism: Modern Ideology in Anthropological Perspective* (Chicago: University of Chicago Press, 1986 [1983]); Marcel Gauchet, *The Disenchantment of the World: A Political History of Religion* (transl. by Oscar Burge, Princeton, NJ: Princeton University Press, 1997 [1985]). Robert Pippin and Terry Pinkard's course on Hegel's *Aesthetics* (University of Chicago, Winter 2001) helped me formulate the historicist theses of the present book, without ever fully shaking my old conviction that, to paraphrase Leopold Ranke, "the art and literature of every epoch is immediately close to my heart." Reinhart Koselleck, *Futures Past: On the Semantics of Historical Time* (transl. by Keith Tribe, Cambridge, MA: MIT Press, 1985 [1979]), and Constantin Fasolt, *The Limits of History* (Chicago: University of Chicago Press, 2004), warn against historical absolutism, while Vincent Descombes, *The Mind's Provision: A Critique of Cognitivism* (transl. by Stephen Adam Schwartz, Princeton, NJ: Princeton University Press, 2001 [1995]), provides a welcome philosophy of the objective spirit.

Regarding the links between literary history and the social, political, and cultural context, I followed the example of Franco Moretti's *The Way of the World: The* Bildungsroman *in European Culture* (London: Verso, 1987), Claude Bremond's chapters in Jamel Eddine Bencheikh, Claude Bremond, and André Miquel, *Mille et un contes de la nuit* (Paris: Gallimard, 1991), and David Quint, *Epic and Empire: Politics and Generic Form from Virgil to Milton* (Princeton, NJ: Princeton University Press, 1993). Conversely, Marc Fumaroli, *Héros et Orateurs: rhétorique et dramaturgie cornéliennes* (Geneva: Droz, 1990), taught me about the transhistorical powers of the imagination.

I owe a great deal to the philosophers who, in the last few decades, have explored the links between literature and moral reflection: Martha Nussbaum, *Love's Knowledge: Essays on Philosophy and Literature* (Oxford: Oxford University Press, 1990); Charles Larmore, *The Practices of the Self* (transl. by Sharon Bowman, Chicago: University of Chicago Press, 2010 [2004]); Alexander Nehamas, *Only a Promise of Happiness: The Place of Beauty in a World of Art* (Princeton, NJ: Princeton University Press, 2007); and Robert Pippin, *Henry James and Modern Moral Life* (Cambridge: Cambridge University Press, 2000). Equally illuminating was Hans Joas, *The Genesis of Values* (Chicago: University of Chicago Press, 2001 [1997]). I feel close to the work of literary scholars interested in this subject: Tzvetan Todorov, *Literature and Its Theorists: A Personal View of Twentieth-Century Criticism* (transl. by Catherine Porter, Ithaca, NY: Cornell University Press, 1987 [1984]); Wayne Booth, *The Company We Keep: An Ethics of Fiction* (Berkeley: University of California Press, 1988); Joseph Frank, *Dostoevsky: The Miraculous Years 1865–1871* (Princeton, NJ: Princeton University Press, 1995); Michael André Bernstein, *Foregone Conclusions: Against Apocalyptic History* (Berkeley: University of California Press, 1994); Gary Saul Morson, *Narrative and Freedom: The Shadows of Time* (New Haven, CT: Yale University Press, 1994); Caryl Emerson, *The First Hundred Years of Mikhail Bakhtin* (Princeton, NJ: Princeton University Press, 1997); and James Wood, *The Irresponsible Self: On Laughter and the Novel* (New York: Farrar, Straus and Giroux, 2004).

In the introduction to this book I explained how much I owe to Georg Lukács's *The Theory of the Novel: A Historico-Philosophical Essay on the Form of Great Epic Literature* (1916; Cambridge, MA: MIT Press, 1971). Equally important for me were Franco Moretti, ed., *The Novel*, 2 vols. (Princeton, NJ: Princeton University Press, 2006–2007); Margaret Anne Doody, *The True Story of the Novel* (New Brunswick, NJ: Rutgers University Press, 1996); and Didier Souiller, Armand Strubel, Wladimir Troubetzkoy, and Sophie Rabau, "L'aventure du roman," "L'ailleurs et l'inexploré," "La nouvelle," in Didier Souiller, with Wladimir Troubetzkoy, *Littérature comparée* (Paris: PUF, 1997), pp. 231–307. Steven Moore, *The Novel: An Alternative History. Beginnings to 1600* (New York: Continuum, 2010), confirmed my sense of the novel's worldwide presence.

Several scholars in the formalist tradition showed me how formal analysis can assist the understanding and interpretation of literary works: Wayne Booth, *The Rhetoric of Fiction* (Chicago: University of Chicago Press, 1961); Jonathan Culler, *Structuralist Poetics: Structuralism,*

Linguistics, and the Study of Literature (London: Routledge, 2002 [1975]); Dorrit Cohn, *Transparent Minds: Narrative Modes for Presenting Consciousness in Fiction* (Princeton, NJ: Princeton University Press, 1978); Gérard Genette, *Narrative Discourse: An Essay in Method* (transl, by Jane E. Lewin, Ithaca, NY: Cornell University Press, 1980 [1972]); Meir Sternberg, *The Poetics of Biblical Narrative: Ideological Literature and the Drama of Reading* (Bloomington: Indiana University Press, 1985); and Lubomír Doležel, *Heterocosmica: Fiction and Possible Worlds* (Baltimore, MD: Johns Hopkins University Press, 1998).

For the English novel, I dialogued with Ian Watt, *The Rise of the Novel: Studies in Defoe, Richardson and Fielding* (Berkeley: University of California Press, 1957); Paul Salzman, *English Prose Fiction 1558–1700: A Critical History* (Oxford: Clarendon, 1985); Michael McKeon, *The Origins of the English Novel, 1600–1740* (Baltimore, MD: Johns Hopkins University Press, 1987); J. Paul Hunter, *Before Novels: The Cultural Contexts of Eighteenth-Century English Fiction* (New York: Norton, 1990); and Jenny Mander, ed., *Remapping the Rise of the European Novel* (Oxford: Voltaire Foundation, 2007).

Among feminist critics who redirected scholarly attention toward idealism in the novel, several were particularly helpful: Naomi Schor, *George Sand and Idealism* (New York: Columbia University Press, 1993); Catherine Gallagher, *Nobody's Story: The Vanishing Acts of Women Writers in the Marketplace, 1670–1820* (Berkeley: University of California Press, 1994); and Margaret Cohen, *The Sentimental Education of the Novel* (Princeton, NJ: Princeton University Press, 1999).

Concerning fiction written before the eighteenth century, Pierre Hadot, *The Inner Citadel: The Meditations of Marcus Aurelius* (transl. by Michael Chase, Cambridge, MA: Harvard University Press, 1998 [1992]) and *Exercices spirituels et philosophie antique* (Paris: Albin Michel, 2002 [1987]), gave me the key to the meaning of ancient Greek novels. I am equally indebted to Niklas Holzberg, *The Ancient Novel: An Introduction* (transl. by Christine Jackson-Holzberg, London: Routledge, 1994 [1986]); Gareth Schmeling, ed., *The Novel in the Ancient World* (Leiden: E. J. Brill, 1996), in particular J. R. Morgan's "Heliodoros," pp. 417–456; and Laurence Plazenet, *L'ébahissement et la délectation: Réception comparée et poétique du roman grec en France et en Angleterre au XVIe et XVIIe siècles* (Paris: Champion, 1997).

For the Middle Ages, my guides were Michel Stanesco and Michel Zink, *Histoire européenne du roman medieval: esquisses et perspectives* (Paris: PUF, 1992); Maurice Keen, *Chivalry* (New Haven, CT: Yale University Press, 1984); Volker Mertens and Ulrich Müller, eds., *Epische Stoffe des Mittelalters* (Stuttgart: Kröner, 1984); and Kevin Brownlee and Marina Scordilis Brownlee, eds., *Romance: Generic Transformation from Chrétien de Troyes to Cervantes* (Hanover, NH: University Press of New England, 1985), which includes Cesare Segre's important paper "What Bakhtin Left Unsaid: The Case of the Medieval Romance," pp. 23–46. For courtly love: H. U. Gumbrecht, "The Transgression(s) of the First Troubadour," transl. by Michael Schultz, in *Stanford French Review* 14, nos. 1–2 (1990), pp. 117–142; and Sarah Kay, "Courts, Clerks, and Courtly Love," in *The Cambridge Companion to Medieval Romance*, ed. Roberta L. Krueger (Cambridge: Cambridge University Press, 2000).

On the ancient comic novel: P. G. Walsh, *The Roman Novel* (1970; London: Bristol Classical, 1995). For the picaresque: Alexander A. Parker, *Literature and the Delinquent: The Picaresque Novel in Spain and Europe 1599–1753* (Edinburgh: The University Press, 1967); Claudio Guillén, *The Anatomies of Roguery: The Origin and the Nature of Picaresque Literature* (1953; New York: Garland, 1987); Robert Alter, *Rogue's Progress: Studies in the Picaresque Novel* (Cambridge, MA: Harvard University Press, 1964); and M. Molho's "Introduction à la pensée picaresque," in *Romans picaresques espagnols* (Paris: Gallimard, Bibliothèque de la Pléiade, 1968), pp. xi–cxlii.

For elegiac stories: Lawrence Lipking, *Abandoned Women and Poetic Tradition* (Chicago: University of Chicago Press, 1988); Robert Hollander's *Boccaccio's Two Venuses* (New York: Columbia University Press, 1977); and Janet Levarie Smarr, *Boccaccio and Fiammetta: The Narrator as Lover* (Urbana: University of Illinois Press, 1986). On novellas: Robert J. Clements and Joseph Gibaldi, *The Anatomy of the Novella: The European Tale Collection from Boccaccio and Chaucer to Cervantes* (New York: New York University Press, 1977); Didier Souiller, *La nouvelle en Europe: De Boccace à Sade* (Paris: PUF, 2004); Guiomar Hautcoeur's *Parentés franco-espagnoles au XVIIe siècle: poétique de la nouvelle de Cervantès à Challe* (Paris: Champion, 2005); and Lakis Proguidis, *La Conquête du roman: de Papadiamantis à Boccace* (Paris: Belles-Lettres, 1997).

Françoise Lavocat, *Arcadies malheureuses: Aux origines du roman moderne* (Paris: Champion, 1998), and Mark Payne, *Theocritus and the Invention of Fiction* (Cambridge: Cambridge University Press, 2007), helped me decipher the complex issues of the pastoral. For the anthropological background of the pastoral, I followed Ernest Gellner, *Plough, Sword, and Book: The Structure of Human History* (Chicago: University of Chicago Press, 1988). The importance of *Persiles and Sigismunda* in Cervantes's oeuvre was emphasized long ago by Alban Forcione, *Cervantes, Aristotle, and the* Persiles (Princeton, NJ: Princeton University Press, 1970), and Martín de Riquer, "Cervantes y la caballeresca," in *Suma Cervantina*, ed. J. B. Avalle-Arce and E. C. Riley (London: Tamesis

Books, 1973), pp. 273–292. Félix Martínez-Bonati, *Don Quixote and the Poetics of the Novel* (transl. Dian Fox and the author, Ithaca, NY: Cornell University Press, 1992), casts doubt on the assumption that *Don Quixote* is a realist novel.

With regard to the novel's evolution since the eighteenth century, I constantly had in mind Milan Kundera's *The Art of the Novel* (transl. by Linda Asher, New York: Grove, 1988 [1986]). For the eighteenth-century novel, Alain Montandon, *Le Roman au XVIIIe siècle en Europe* (Paris: PUF, 1999), is the best, most reliable guide. Philip Stewart, *Imitation and Illusion in the French Memoir Novel 1700–1750: The Art of Make-Believe* (New Haven, CT: Yale University Press, 1969), was highly useful. For the Romantic theory of the novel, my guide was Marshall Brown, "The Theory of the Novel," in *The Cambridge History of Literary Criticism*, vol. 5, *Romanticism*, ed. Marshall Brown (Cambridge: Cambridge University Press, 2000), pp. 250–271, bibliography pp. 421–425. Continuing the tradition of Ian Watt and Michael McKeon, Ian Duncan, *Modern Romance and Transformations of the Novel: The Gothic, Scott, Dickens* (Cambridge: Cambridge University Press, 1992), and Katie Trumpener, *Bardic Nationalism: The Romantic Novel and the British Empire* (Princeton, NJ: Princeton University Press, 1997), introduced me to the cultural and political context of the nineteenth-century English novel. From Peter Brooks, *The Melodramatic Imagination: Balzac, Henry James, Melodrama, and the Mode of Excess* (New Haven, CT: Yale University Press, 1976), I learned that realism does not rule alone over the nineteenth-century novel. For the political stakes of the nineteenth-century French novel: Mona Ozouf, *Les Aveux du roman: le XIXe siècle entre Ancien Régime et Révolution* (Paris: Fayard, 2001). On the question of the couple in nineteenth-century novels, I benefited from Tony Tanner, *Adultery in the Novel: Contract and Transgression* (Baltimore, MD: Johns Hopkins University Press, 1979), and Nathalie Heinich, *États de femme: l'identité féminine dans la fiction occidentale* (Paris: Gallimard, 1996).

Matei Calinescu, *Five Faces of Modernity: Modernism, Avant-Garde, Decadence, Kitsch, Postmodernism* (Durham, NC: Duke University Press, 1987); Jean-Marie Schaeffer, *The Art of the Modern Age: Philosophy of Art from Kant to Heidegger* (transl. by Steven Rendall, Princeton, NJ: Princeton University Press, 2000 [1992]); Antoine Compagnon, *The Five Paradoxes of Modernity* (transl. by Franklin Philip, New York: Columbia University Press, 1994 [1990]); and Jacques Rancière, *Aesthetics and Its Discontents* (transl. by Steven Corcoran, Cambridge: Polity, 2009 [2004]), steered me through the labyrinth of modern aestheticism.

Index

||||||||||||||||||||||||||||||||||||||||||||||||||||||||||||||

319